Working with Fan ̲ ̲ ̲ of Children with Special Needs

FAMILY AND PROFESSIONAL PARTNERSHIPS AND ROLES

Nancy M. Sileo
University of Nevada Las Vegas

Mary Anne Prater
Brigham Young University

Boston Columbus Indianapolis New York San Francisco Upper Saddle River
Amsterdam Cape Town Dubai London Madrid Milan Munich Paris Montreal Toronto
Delhi Mexico City São Paulo Sydney Hong Kong Seoul Singapore Taipei Tokyo

Vice President and Editor in Chief: Jeffery W. Johnston
Executive Editor and Publisher: Stephen D. Dragin
Editorial Assistant: Jamie Bushell
Marketing Manager: Weslie Sellinger
Marketing Coordinator: Brian Mounts
Senior Managing Editor: Pamela D. Bennett
Project Manager: Sheryl Langner
Operations Supervisor: Central Publishing
Operations Specialist: Laura Messerly

Senior Art Director: Jayne Conte
Cover Designer: Suzanne Duda
Photo Coordinator: Lori Whitley
Cover Art: Fotolia
Full-Service Project Management: Niraj Bhatt, Aptara®, Inc.
Composition: Aptara®, Inc.
Printer/Binder: Courier/Stoughton
Cover Printer: Courier/Stoughton
Text Font: Garamond

Credits and acknowledgments borrowed from other sources and reproduced, with permission, in this textbook appear on appropriate page within text.

Every effort has been made to provide accurate and current Internet information in this book. However, the Internet and information posted on it are constantly changing, so it is inevitable that some of the Internet addresses listed in this textbook will change.

Photo Credits: Thinkstock, pp. 1, 107; Shutterstock, pp. 23, 202, 245; Krista Greco/Merrill, pp. 40; Lori Whitley/Merrill, pp. 59, 153; Anthony Magnacca/Merrill, pp. 91; Laura Bolesta/Merrill, pp. 131; George Dodson/PH College, pp. 173; Scott Cunningham/Merrill, pp. 224.

Library of Congress Cataloging-in-Publication Data

Sileo, Nancy M.
  Working with families of children with special needs : family and professional partnerships and roles / Nancy M. Sileo, Mary Anne Prater.
     p. cm.
  ISBN-13: 978-0-13-714740-3
  ISBN-10: 0-13-714740-6
  1. Special education—Parent participation—United States. 2. Special education teachers—Professional relationships—United States. 3. Children with disabilities—Education—United States. I. Prater, Mary Anne. II. Title.
  LC4031.S55 2012
  371.90973—dc22
                                                                                                    2010054548

10 9 8 7 6 5 4 3 2 1

www.pearsonhighered.com

ISBN-10:   0-13-714740-6
ISBN-13: 978-0-13-714740-3

PREFACE

Everyone belongs to a family—it doesn't matter if you are married, single, divorced, heterosexual or homosexual, have children/don't have children, have siblings/don't have siblings, have a disability/don't have a disability—each of us have people we consider to be part of our family. Families come in all shapes and sizes, and as we move further into the 21st century, new and different family configurations are emerging. Today, within the same classroom, you can find children from traditional two-parent households, gay or lesbian partnered households, single-parent households, or grandparent-led households.

The focus of this text is on families of children with special needs. We have designed the text to be used in preservice and professional development special education courses that focus on working with families of children with disabilities. The text provides a timely discussion of legal aspects of special education, as well as an emphasis on strategies and skills that can be employed when working with families of children with special needs.

The first chapter provides a thorough review of special education legislation, as it relates to and affects families of children with disabilities. In this chapter, we examine general education legislation, such as the No Child Left Behind (NCLB) Act, and its impact on children with special needs and their families. Civil rights legislation, such as the Americans with Disabilities Act, is discussed, as well as the application of FERPA (Family Education Rights and Privacy Act) to families of children with special needs.

In Chapters 2 and 3, we begin with a historical review of the treatment of individuals with disabilities and their families. A great deal of emphasis in these chapters is focused on the many roles and responsibilities of families of children with special needs. We discuss siblings of children with disabilities, including siblings as caretakers or interpreters of their siblings with disabilities.

Effective communication and collaboration with families of children with special needs is the focus of Chapter 3. In particular, we address collaborative practices and communicative skills that practitioners need when working with families. Chapter 4 then focuses on the application of those skills and discusses strategies that can be applied to ensure effective communication and collaboration with families and children with special needs. Finally, this chapter provides a timely discussion of the application and uses of technology such as email when working with families.

Changing family structures, diversity and cultural competence, and working with families from diverse backgrounds provide the framework for Chapters 5 and 6. Although no textbook will ever be exhaustive in its discussion of diversity in the United States, we provide a comprehensive overview and discussion of family role patterns, language communication, culture, and some traditionally held beliefs about disabilities for the major cultural groups living in the United States. In addition, we present barriers to working effectively with families from diverse backgrounds and provide strategies designed to help practitioners overcome these obstacles.

In Chapters 7 and 8, we focus on understanding the family's perspective of special education and provide tips on how to facilitate family involvement in the special education process. In addition, we address family involvement in the IEP process and provide approaches for not only family involvement, but student participation as well.

Ethics and ethical practice in the field of special education are often assumed but rarely discussed in terms of family involvement. In Chapter 9 we detail the ethics and ethical practices that need to be considered when working with families of children with special needs. Not only do we address the ethical codes and standards produced by national professional associations such as the Council for Exceptional Children (CEC), the National Education Association (NEA), and the National Association for the Education of Young Children (NAEYC), but we also provide a sound discussion of the concept of "doing no harm" when working with children with disabilities and their families.

In Chapters 10 and 11 of this text, special considerations when working with families of children with disabilities across the age span are discussed. The focus of Chapter 10 is on the different roles, responsibilities, and patterns that families undertake as their children with special needs move from birth into adulthood. A great deal of emphasis in this chapter is placed on the different challenges that families face as their child with special needs ages. In Chapter 11, we discuss issues related to postsecondary situations, including strategies that can be used with families as the students move out of the public school environment and onto their postsecondary lives.

The last chapter of this text focuses on "A Family's Voice." The family voice features were contributed by parents/family members of children with disabilities and provide readers with an inside look into how different families react to and cope with the special education system. This chapter contains six family voices and links discussion and application items to previous chapters in the text.

Each chapter of the text identifies resources designed to support family–professional involvement. In addition, all chapters provide scenarios and examples of how different strategies and skills can be applied when working with families of children with special needs. Each chapter also provides an overview of how chapter content link to CEC and Interstate New Teacher Assessment and Support Consortium (INTASC) professional practice standards.

ACKNOWLEDGMENTS

This book would not have been possible without the contributions of Betty Ashbaker, Nari Carter, Tina Dyches, Wendy Murawski, Tessie Rose, Jane Sileo, and Michelle Tannock. Each served as coauthor on one or more of the chapters. They contributed greatly to the content and scope of this book, and we give them our deepest thanks. Moreover, we would like to thank the families that contributed their voices to this text: Elizabeth and Michael Ferro, Lee Haney and Jennifer and Sarah Hanson, Karolyn King-Peery, Angela Quidileg, Ramon, and Claire Lynough Tredwell.

In addition, we would like to thank Steve Dragin, Jamie Bushell, and Sheryl Langner of Pearson for their support and guidance with this project. The merger of Allyn & Bacon and Merrill took place while we were writing this book, and Steve, Jamie, and Sheryl worked diligently to ensure that we made a smooth transition from one publisher and editor to another. We particularly wish to thank them for answering all our questions and providing timely input into the development of this text.

Further, we wish to thank the following reviewers who provided feedback on draft versions of the book. Their ideas and suggestions contributed greatly to the overall quality of the book. They are Stephen Denney, Ashland University; Barbara Fiechtl, Utah State University; Lee Ann Jung, University of Kentucky; Patricia S. Lynch, Texas A & M University; Lisa Vernon-Dotson, Duquesne University; and Alandra Weller-Clarke, Benedictine University.

This book is dedicated to our families—Nancy's daughter, Cassie A. Sileo, and her parents, Tom and Ann Sileo, and Mary Anne's parents, Herman and Barbara Prater.

NMS and MAP

BRIEF CONTENTS

CONTENTS

ABOUT THE AUTHORS

Nancy M. Sileo, EdD is a professor of early childhood special education (ECSE), Director of Teacher Education for the College of Education at the University of Nevada Las Vegas, and has worked in the field of ECSE for more than 20 years. Her current interests include early intervention, family involvement in special education, HIV/AIDS prevention education, and ethical issues in HIV/AIDS prevention education and special education teacher education. Dr. Sileo has been involved with special education teacher education for 12 years and currently serves as Director of Teacher Education in the College of Education at UNLV. In addition, she has been a member of the Council for Exceptional Children for over 19 years and is actively involved in the Teacher Education Division and the Division for Early Childhood. Dr. Sileo is author and coauthor of myriad publications related to HIV/AIDS prevention education and research, as well as numerous publications in the field of special education teacher education.

Mary Anne Prater, PhD is a professor and chair of the Department of Counseling Psychology and Special Education at Brigham Young University. Dr. Prater has been a teacher educator for over 20 years. Prior to being employed at BYU, she was a professor at the University of Hawaii at Manoa and Southern Illinois University at Carbondale. Her interests and expertise include special education teacher education, cultural and linguistic diversity issues in special education, instructional strategies for students with mild disabilities, and the portrayal of disabilities in children's literature. Dr. Prater has published over 80 articles and chapters and 5 books. She has been an active member of the Council for Exceptional Children (CEC) and various divisions of CEC, including the Teacher Education Division and the Division for Autism and Developmental Disabilities for over 25 years.

CHAPTER 1

Historical and Legal Foundations of Family Involvement in Special Education

OBJECTIVES

After reading this chapter you will

1. Discuss the historical and legal foundations for family involvement in special education.
2. Explain the key components of the Individuals with Disabilities Education Improvement Act (IDEA), and describe the influence IDEA has on family involvement in special education.
3. Describe how the No Child Left Behind Act influences families of children with special needs.
4. Understand the legal implications that the Family Educational Rights and Privacy Act has on the field of special education.
5. Discuss the influences of Section 504 of the Vocational Rehabilitation Act on families of children with special needs.
6. Describe the interrelationship between the Americans with Disabilities Act and special education.

INTRODUCTION

Today, federal laws have more effect on classroom teachers in the United States than at any other time in the history of education. In this chapter we identify important principles that teachers must know about collaborating with families of children with disabilities according to federal legislation, specifically the Individuals with Disabilities Education Improvement Act (IDEA) of 2004 and the No Child Left Behind Act (NCLB) of 2002 (National Center for Education Statistics [NCES], n.d.). Teachers should also know how other laws are important to children and parents, such as Section 504 of the Vocational Rehabilitation Act of 1973, the Americans with Disabilities (ADA) Act, and the Family Educational Rights and Privacy Act (FERPA, 1974). FERPA affects the way schools share information about students and gives parents the right to regulate who accesses the information. We discuss each of these laws in relation to family involvement in the educational process. Before doing so, we provide a historical overview of the laws and litigation leading up to these important legislative acts.

HISTORICAL OVERVIEW OF LAWS AND LITIGATION

The American Civil Rights Movement of the 1950s and 1960s brought about substantial legal, societal, and educational changes that were intended to eliminate racial discrimination. One of the most influential landmark cases was the Supreme Court ruling in the case of *Brown v. Board of Education of Topeka* (1954), which challenged the practice of segregating schools according to the race of the children. The U.S. Supreme Court declared that education must be made available to *all* children. The Supreme Court majority opinion stated,

> Today, education is perhaps the most important function of state and local governments. Compulsory school attendance laws and the great expenditure for education both demonstrate our recognition of the importance of education to our democratic society. It is required in the performance of our most basic responsibilities. . . . In these days, it is doubtful that any child may reasonably be expected to succeed in life if he is denied the opportunity of an education.

The *Brown* decision, with its effect of extending equality in public school education to children of color, began a period of intense concern and questioning among parents of children with disabilities. Why did the same principles of equal access to education not apply to their children as well? More than 1 million children with disabilities were excluded from attending public schools, often with reasons that were related to inconvenience, untrained teachers, or fears that other students would be adversely affected by associating with children with disabilities (Gibb & Dyches, 2007). This was of grave concern to parents. In fact, in 1970, U.S. schools educated only one in five children with disabilities, and many states had laws excluding certain students, including children who were deaf, were blind, had an emotional disturbance, or had mental retardation (U.S. Department of Education, n.d.).

One of the landmark court cases was the *Pennsylvania Association for Retarded Children v. Commonwealth of Pennsylvania* (PARC; 1972). The Association challenged a state law that denied public school education to certain children who were at the time considered unable to profit from public school attendance. Parents based their arguments on the 14th Amendment to the Constitution, which provides that "no state shall deny any person within its jurisdiction equal protection of the law" and affirms that no state "shall deprive any person of life, liberty, or property" without due process of law.

Fortunately, parents and advocates for children with disabilities were persistent in obtaining equal access to public education. Their efforts led to the passage of the Education for All Handicapped Children Act of 1975, Public Law (P.L.) 94-142, mandating that all children have the right to a free and appropriate education at public expense. Although it is difficult to imagine today, the passage of this law generated much debate, both in and out of the courtroom.

The concepts of equal protection and due process are fundamental in special education today. P.L. 94-142 included the basic principles established in such cases as *PARC*—namely, the rights of parents to be informed—and provided procedural safeguards throughout every step of the special education process from child find to evaluation and appropriate placement in the least restrictive environment. Table 1.1 summarizes major legislation and court rulings affecting special education.

TABLE 1.1 Legislation and Court Rulings Affecting Special Education		
Year	**Legislation or Court Case**	**Laws and Rulings**
1954	*Brown vs. Board of Education of Topeka, KS*	Ends educational segregation based on race/ethnicity.
1972	*Pennsylvania Association for the Retarded Children v. Commonwealth of Pennsylvania*	Requires schools to provide a free appropriate public education to students with mental retardation.
1973	Section 504 of the Rehabilitation Act of 1973	Protects qualified individuals, including students with disabilities, from discrimination based on their disabilities.
1975	Education for All Handicapped Children Act of 1975 (P.L. 94-142)	Guarantees a free and appropriate education to all students with disabilities 5–21 years of age.
1986	1986 Amendments to the Education for All Handicapped Children Act of 1975 (P.L. 99-457)	Extends P.L. 94-142 to mandate services to include children 3–5 years of age; provides for discretionary grants to extend services to infants and toddlers birth to 3 years of age.
1990	Americans with Disabilities Act (ADA; P.L. 101-336)	Comprehensive civil rights law for people with disabilities; prohibits discrimination against people with disabilities in employment, public services, public accommodations, and telecommunications.
1990	Individuals with Disabilities Education Act (IDEA; P.L. 101-476)	Mandates services for persons with disabilities birth to 21 years of age; focuses on person-first language.
1997	1997 Amendments to the Individuals with Disabilities Education Act (IDEA 1997; P.L. 105-17)	Strengthens academic expectations and accountability for students with disabilities; bridges the gap between what children with disabilities learn and the general education curriculum.
2002	No Child Left Behind Act (NCLB; P.L. 107-110)	Specifies academic progress and assessment for all students, including students with disabilities; requires teachers to be highly qualified.
2004	Individuals with Disabilities Education Improvement Act (IDEA 2004; P.L. 108-446)	Aligns IDEA with NCLB; requires teachers of students with disabilities to be highly qualified.

INDIVIDUALS WITH DISABILITIES EDUCATION IMPROVEMENT ACT OF 2004

The Education for All Handicapped Children's Act, or P.L. 94-142—originally passed in 1975—was amended in 1986 (P.L. 99-457) to include services for preschoolers with disabilities. It was again amended in 1990 (P.L. 101-476) and renamed the Individuals with Disabilities Education (IDEA) Act. This reauthorization kept intact the primary provisions of the original law, yet it extended services to infants and toddlers with developmental delays or disabilities and added new categories of identification for children with disabilities, such as autism and traumatic brain injury. The act was reauthorized in 1997 (P.L. 105-17) and again in 2004 (P.L. 108-446). This most recent reauthorization attempted to align the law with the No Child Left Behind (NCLB) Act and contains changes such as disciplinary measures, paperwork and meetings, procedures for evaluating students with specific learning disabilities, definitions of highly qualified special education teachers, and early intervention services, such as using evidence-based research and response to intervention procedures.

> The act indicates that the purpose of the IDEA 2004 is to Ensure that all children with disabilities have available to them a free appropriate public education that emphasizes special education and related services designed to meet their unique needs and prepare them for further education, employment and independent living . . . [and] to ensure that the rights of children with disabilities and parents of such children are protected. (Section 601 (d) (1) (A & B))

The 2004 reauthorization of IDEA provides the foundation for identifying children who have disabilities and, as a result of those disabilities, need special education services. Special education is defined as

> Specially designed instruction, at no cost to parents, to meet the unique needs of a student with a disability, including instruction conducted in the classroom, in the home, in hospitals and institutions, and in other settings; and instruction in physical education. (34 CFR §300.39)

To qualify for state-funded and state-defined educational services under IDEA, a student must meet three statutory requirements. The student must (a) be between the ages of three and 21, (b) have a specifically identified disability, and (c) need special education and related services.

Each state must ensure that students with disabilities have access to the following six provisions:

1. Procedural Safeguards of Parental Participation and Due Process
2. Child Find/Zero Reject
3. Appropriate Evaluation
4. Free Appropriate Public Education
5. Least Restrictive Environment
6. Individualized Education Program

These six principles have been foundational elements of special education since the original act was passed in 1975. Some of the requirements have been adapted in subsequent reauthorizations of IDEA, but the primary framework for providing special education services in the United States has remained the same. Each of these principles will be discussed in relation to parents and teachers working collaboratively for the benefit of students with disabilities. (See Chapter 11 for a discussion on services available to infants and toddlers from birth to 3 years of age.)

On a cool October morning, our daughter Rachel was in a terrible auto–pedestrian accident, which changed our lives forever after. Previously she had been a vivacious and verbal 2-year-old. Now a severe head trauma left her comatose and nonresponsive. Gradually she recognized stimuli, opened her eyes, and began to relearn and regain all the abilities and skills she had lost. She first learned to swallow and to hold her head up. She then learned to sit, feed herself, speak, and stand. The last abilities she worked to regain, and those that were most difficult for her, were motor skills, visual skills, and cognitive skills.

Procedural Safeguards: Parent Participation and Due Process

The first provision of IDEA (2004) recognizes that parents are essential partners in the education of their children. As such, parents are afforded legal rights to participate in all phases of their child's involvement in the special education process. When appropriate, students with disabilities also collaborate in the shared decision-making process.

Not only are parents guaranteed shared decision-making rights, but they are also protected through procedural due process. Both schools and parents are accountable. Schools are accountable for providing a free, appropriate public education to students with disabilities, and parents are accountable to their children (Turnbull & Cilley, 1999). In creating IDEA, the U.S. Congress anticipated that parents and school personnel may disagree over the evaluation, placement, and delivery of appropriate special education and related services for students with disabilities. Therefore, they included grievance procedures as part of the act.

The first step of the grievance process is mediation, which is a voluntary process available whenever the parent(s) or school district requests a hearing. Either party (the parents or the school) can file a complaint that alleges a recent violation of the law. The written complaint must conform to specific guidelines and be sent to the state director of special education. Each state must provide parents and schools with model forms to assist in this process. After the complaint is filed, a qualified and impartial mediator conducts a mediation hearing where both parties meet at a convenient time and place. When disputes are resolved through mediation, both parties sign a legally binding agreement that their conversations remain confidential and may not be used as evidence in later due process hearings or civil lawsuits.

Preferably, disputes should be resolved through the mediation process; however, if both parties are unable to agree, then schools should provide an explanation of the procedure for a due process hearing. An impartial and qualified hearing officer conducts the due process hearing. This is a formal meeting where legal counsel presents evidence and confronts and cross-examines witnesses. Parents are afforded the right to have their child present, keep the hearing open to the public, and obtain a record of the hearing at no cost to them. The primary purpose of the hearing is to determine whether the child with a disability was provided a free, appropriate public education and whether the parents had sufficient opportunity to participate in the decision-making process regarding their child's education. Either party may appeal the final decision. If an appeal is filed, the State Department of Education conducts an impartial review. If the dispute remains unresolved, the next level of grievance is through civil action, where any party aggrieved by the previous hearings or reviews may initiate a civil suit.

Written notice of due process procedures and procedural safeguards must be provided to parents in their native languages, unless use of this language is clearly not feasible. These documents must also be written in an easily understandable style. Procedural safeguards help guard against past practices of placing students in programs—or removing them from programs—without the knowledge or involvement of parents. When schools and parents work collaboratively, disagreements can be resolved without involving the legal system. School personnel must understand their rights and responsibilities as well as the rights and responsibilities of the parents of the children they serve.

In Rachel's mom's words: Educators provided me with the Procedural Safeguards booklet each year at Rachel's IEP meetings, but I don't think the policies were ever really explained to me. This left me at a definite disadvantage in understanding what recourse I had to obtain further occupational and physical therapy.

Child Find/Zero Reject

The second provision of IDEA includes Child Find and Zero Reject. *Child Find* means that public school personnel must locate, identify, and evaluate children who are suspected of having a disability, including those who attend public schools, private schools, and home schools. Generally, Child Find activities are directed by school district personnel and typically consist of distributing informational pamphlets, airing regular public service announcements over the radio or television, and displaying exhibits at health and community fairs.

Zero Reject means that no children who have been identified as having a disability and thereby require special education services (regardless of the severity of the disability) will be denied a free, appropriate education. In the past, many students with disabilities received inferior educational opportunities compared to those of their nondisabled peers. They were often excluded from accessing the general curriculum and from being educated in environments that were least restrictive to their educational progress. Prior to the passage of IDEA, some teachers who felt that a student could not succeed with the class curriculum merely sent the child away or told the parents not to bring their child to school. By developing school policies that prohibited students with disabilities from participating in general education classes, a child who was not toilet trained or who exhibited disruptive behavior, for example, could be excluded from attending the school.

A great deal of progress has been made since the passage of P.L. 94-142 in 1975, but educators still struggle to provide an appropriate education to all students. Each state that receives federal special education funding is required to create and implement policies and procedures to ensure that children with disabilities are identified, located, evaluated, and if eligible, receive special education or related services. These Child Find requirements are inclusive of all children, birth to 21 years of age, who are suspected of having a disability.

Although the Child Find requirements of the law permit referrals from any source that has reason to believe the child may be eligible for special education services, the primary responsibility to initiate the evaluation procedures rests on the parents and the school. (See Chapter 11 for a discussion on the Child Find requirements for infants and toddlers from birth to 3 years of age.) However, parents who enroll their children in private or home schools have the right to not participate in the state or district's child find activities. In such cases, the public agency is not required to consider the child for services.

Parents are often highly involved in the Child Find process. If they recognize that their child is not developing at a typical rate or course, they have the right to contact the school or early intervention provider to request an evaluation. Generally, this initial Child Find activity includes a screening process to determine whether the child should be referred for a full eligibility evaluation.

However, most disabilities are identified when a student does not achieve as expected in school. In this case, the classroom teacher usually recognizes that the student is not progressing as he or she should. Before requesting an evaluation, the teacher must provide evidence that the student has received scientifically based instruction to address his or her individual needs. The teacher must also provide data about the effects of the interventions on the student's achievement. Once it has been determined that classroom interventions have not met the student's needs, the child is referred for an eligibility evaluation for special education services.

A major change in the most recent authorization of IDEA is the inclusion of response to intervention to identify students with learning disabilities. Regulations state that districts must allow a process for identifying students with learning disabilities that is based on the student's response to scientific, research-based interventions, thus the name, response to intervention (RTI). RTI is a responsibility of general education with support from special education.

The RTI process does not replace the need for a comprehensive evaluation. A variety of data-gathering tools and strategies must still be used. The results from the RTI process form one component of the information reviewed as part of the comprehensive evaluation procedure. The evaluation must also include a variety of assessment tools and strategies and cannot rely on any single procedure as the sole criterion for determining eligibility for special education and related services.

Using RTI procedures, teachers provide increasingly intense instruction and interventions to students who have difficulty learning. By monitoring student progress at each intervention level, data can be used to determine whether the student needs additional instruction or intervention in general education or should be referred for special education services.

If the interventions are unsuccessful at meeting the student's needs, the teacher can initiate a referral to determine if the student has a disability. This referral is submitted to a school team (sometimes called the teacher assistance team or the special education referral team), along with work samples, assessment data, behavior reports, and other descriptions of student progress in the general curriculum. If the referral is forwarded for an individual evaluation, school personnel must obtain written parental permission to conduct the evaluation. This prereferral and referral process requires the collaboration of all individuals involved in the child's education (i.e., school personnel, parents or guardians, and the student, if appropriate).

Rachel's pediatrician referred her to a special education preschool according to the state's Child Find guidelines. The medical diagnosis of traumatic brain injury made eligibility decisions easy. She definitely was delayed according to their assessments, and the reason was apparent.

Appropriate Evaluation

The third provision of IDEA is appropriate evaluation. Appropriate evaluation means that schools must conduct valid evaluations to determine three things: (a) if the student has a disability, (b) if the disability inhibits progress in the general curriculum, and (c) if special education is needed to meet the student's individual needs (Gibbs & Dyches, 2007). This evaluation must use a variety of assessment tools and strategies to gather relevant functional, developmental, and academic information. No single measure or assessment may be used to determine if a student has a disability. The evaluation must use technically sound instruments to assess cognitive, behavioral, physical, and/or developmental factors. In addition, professionals must select and administer these instruments with care to avoid racial or cultural discrimination (Gibb & Dyches, 2007).

Caution must be taken to ensure that only those students with disabilities are identified and served so that students who do not have disabilities are not misidentified. Historically, there have been two problems in the evaluation and identification process: (a) overidentification of students from diverse racial/cultural backgrounds and (b) underidentification of those same students. The latter has occurred for several reasons. First, assessment tools used to identify disabilities have not been reliable enough to differentiate between issues of language or culture and issues of disability. Second, assessments must be given in the student's native language, and many of the assessment tools used to identify disabilities have not been translated and standardized in multiple languages for multiple populations. (See Chapters 5 and 6 for a comprehensive discussion of disability and diversity.)

Evaluation for eligibility is only conducted on receipt of parental consent. Schools must provide written notice to the parents regarding the proposed evaluation, an explanation of why the evaluation should be conducted, a description of each evaluation procedure and assessment, a statement of the parents' legal protections, sources for parents to contact to obtain assistance, and a description of other options considered by the individualized education program (IEP) team and why those options were rejected. This notice must be provided in the native language or communication mode of the parents, unless it is not reasonably feasible to do so.

Although teachers regularly use assessment to determine specific instructional strategies for curriculum implementation, such assessment is not considered to be an appropriate evaluation for special education eligibility. Rather, a comprehensive evaluation must be completed by a team of qualified professionals, including assessments in all areas related to the suspected disability, such as health, vision, hearing, social and emotional status, intelligence, academic performance, communication skills, and motor abilities, as appropriate. The assessments must be conducted in the student's native language or mode of communication (such as sign language), and the tests must be valid for the specific purpose for which they are used. The classroom teacher plays an important role in the identification and accurate evaluation of children with disabilities because the teacher sees the student in a variety of settings, such as in the classroom hallways, in the lunchroom, and on the playground, as well as boarding or exiting the bus.

Input from parents is also important to the process. Parents watch how their child performs in extracurricular activities, and they know how well the child problem-solves and gets along with others. Parents may be asked to complete questionnaires regarding their child's behavior, social-emotional skills, functional skills, or other skills. Parents may also be interviewed by school professionals and can bring previous assessment data for the team to consider.

Evaluations for eligibility are to be conducted within 60 days of receiving parental consent. On completion of this evaluation, the team determines whether the student qualifies for special education and/or related services, or no services. Students who qualify are those who have documented developmental delays (ages 3–9) or who are classified with one of 13 disabilities (autism; deaf-blindness; hearing impairment; deafness; mental retardation; multiple disabilities; orthopedic impairment; other health impairment; serious emotional disturbance; specific learning disabilities; speech or language impairment; traumatic brain injury; visual impairment/blindness) and who by reason of their disability require special education.

Once a student has been classified as having a disability that requires special education services, the education and evaluation team reevaluate the child for eligibility every 3 years, unless the parents and school agree that reevaluation is not necessary. Parents and teachers have the right to request an annual reevaluation if they have reason to believe it is warranted. Parent consent must be received prior to any changes in the student's education program, and schools should provide a statement about parents' procedural safeguards annually.

Parents are entitled to obtain an independent educational evaluation of their child if they disagree with the evaluations provided by the school. The school or the local education agency incurs the cost of this evaluation. However, the school is entitled to file a due process complaint if they have evidence to claim that the original evaluation is appropriate. If the hearing officer determines the school's evaluation is appropriate, parents may still obtain an independent evaluation, but it is not provided at public expense.

When Rachel was released from the hospital, two neurologists, several ophthalmologists, a pediatrician, and our family doctor followed her. The pediatrician provided documentation to the schools for special education eligibility. It was determined by the doctors that this child was previously developing quite normally, but now had significant needs based on the severe brain injury.

Free Appropriate Public Education

To meet the fourth provision of IDEA, each state must assure that all 3- to 21-year-old students with disabilities have access to a free appropriate public education (FAPE). "This is defined as special education and related services that

- are provided at public expense, under public supervision, and without charge;
- meet the standards of the state educational agency;

- include appropriate preschool, elementary school, or secondary school education; and
- are provided consistent with each student's individualized education program." (Gibb & Dyches, 2007, p. 1).

A free public education means that students with disabilities have a right to an education at no additional cost to their parents even though the students may require additional curricular instruction, classroom accommodations, special transportation, and/or assistive equipment.

An appropriate education means that eligible students receive special education, defined in the act as specially designed instruction necessary to meet the unique needs of a student with a disability. Special education includes instruction conducted in various environments and can also include physical education, speech–language pathology services, other related services, travel training, and vocational education. These services are provided to address the particular needs of the student resulting from the disability and should ensure access to the general education curriculum.

Part of FAPE is the assurance that parents have access to their student's educational records. All student documentation kept by the school must be made available, on request, to the parents of the student. By law, parents are allowed to view their child's educational records. Furthermore, schools must have written permission from the parent or eligible student to release any information from a student's education record to others.

My daughter Rachel had a teacher who visited each week from the Parent Infant Program developed by the Schools for the Deaf and Blind. Her teacher, Cindy, and I formulated goals for Rachel together based on input from the ophthalmologist and the school. I remember doing activities to increase her visual tracking and eye muscle movement and decrease her eyestrain and fatigue. I took her to physical and occupational therapy 2–3 times weekly. Therapists worked with Rachel to increase her muscle strength, coordination, and balance. Each month we discussed progress and concerns and set goals for Rachel. Although she made continuous and remarkable progress, her skills were still significantly delayed according to her age.

When she left the special needs preschool, Rachel attended kindergarten in our neighborhood school. This was what we had hoped for, and it was appropriate for her because she participated in general, grade-level education for all subjects except math. She was instructed at her skill level in the classroom and in a resource class. Her IEP contained goals to help her with some academics, vision, and physical skills such as balance and writing.

As time went on, she was placed with very good teachers in general education classes. Rachel learned grade-level curriculum with her peers except for math, which she learned in a resource setting. She did much better with a small group and more specialized instruction. She was a good student who sang in programs, participated in the science fairs, and loved to read, but she did not have many friends. She needed social skills training, but none was available. A vision specialist consulted with Rachel's teachers and helped with difficult tasks like map reading and copying from the board. The following year the school district told us that she no longer qualified for physical and occupational therapy, but I know she did not have the age-appropriate skills she needed. When I pressed for these services, they said that the therapists' schedules were full with other students who had greater needs than Rachel. I wish that I had known at that time how to assert myself and be a better advocate for Rachel's legal rights.

Least Restrictive Environment

The fifth provision of IDEA is least restrictive environment. One of the original purposes of IDEA was to ensure that students with disabilities were educated in the same schools as other students. IDEA states that students with disabilities must be educated with their nondisabled peers in the least restrictive environment (LRE) to the maximum extent appropriate. This provision extends beyond public schools to private institutions and other care facilities. Special classes, separate schooling, or other removal of students with disabilities from the general education environment should occur only when satisfactory education cannot be achieved, even with the provision of appropriate supplementary aids and services, regardless of the nature and severity of the student's disability.

IDEA does not identify the LRE for each student; this is the responsibility of each IEP team. However, the act assumes that the general classroom is the most appropriate placement for most students with disabilities unless the IEP team decides that the general education class is not the LRE for a particular student. For some students, the LRE will be the general classroom with supplementary aides and services provided. For others, it may be a pullout program for part of the day, where special education services are provided in a separate setting. Still others may benefit most from a separate classroom within the school. Some students may need to be educated in separate schools. Whatever the individual needs, the IEP team must determine the environment that will provide an appropriate education and allow students with disabilities to be involved with students without disabilities to the maximum extent appropriate.

Rachel has certainly had a better educational experience because of her participation in special education. Dedicated teachers and professionals have worked to equip her with skills she needs to succeed in life. I appreciate their help with developing her talents and gifts and not only focusing on her difficulties. In addition to earning a regular diploma, Rachel was able to sing as a soloist in choir and was a member of choirs honored with all-state recognition. She performed significant parts in the school musicals. She has learned to swim, ski, dance, ride a bike, and even drive. She took honors sections of some English classes. And she did quite well learning French. She has since traveled to France and used her skills to translate for her family. She was awarded a partial scholarship to the local university where she currently is taking classes to become a teacher.

Individualized Education Program

The last provision of IDEA is the individualized education program (IEP). Every child who qualifies to receive special education services must have an IEP. The IEP is a legal document with two essential roles. First, it is the individualized component of special education planning, defining what an *appropriate* education means for the individual student. The IEP describes a student's special education program for 1 year, including goals for improvement and the manner in which the school will help the student achieve these goals. The emphasis is on the student making progress in the general curriculum and participating in extracurricular activities of an appropriate nature and extent. Students with disabilities are not to be isolated and separated from their peers but are to take part in school as other students do.

1. Statement of the student's present levels of academic achievement and functional performance.
2. Statement of measurable annual goals, including academic and functional goals.
3. Description of how the student's progress toward meeting the annual goals will be measured and when periodic reports on the student's progress will be provided.
4. Statement of the special education, related services, and supplementary aids and services to be provided, to help the student attain the annual goals and participate and progress in the general education curriculum and participate in extracurricular and other nonacademic activities.
5. Explanation of the extent, if any, to which the student will not participate with nondisabled students in the general education class and in extracurricular and other nonacademic activities.
6. Statement of any individual appropriate accommodations that are necessary to measure the academic achievement and functional performance of the student on state and districtwide assessments.
7. The projected date for the beginning of the IEP and the anticipated frequency, location, and duration of the services and modifications.
8. For students at least 16 years old, individualized transition plans, which include postsecondary goals and transition services needed to assist the student in reaching those goals.

FIGURE 1.1   Major Components of an Individualized Education Program (IEP)

Second, the IEP serves as a communication tool between parents and teachers regarding the student's educational growth and achievement. When both parents and teachers know the goals for student improvement, they have common reference points for discussion and decisions. The recent reauthorization of the act clearly emphasizes the need for both general- and special education teachers to collaborate in the provision of appropriate education to all students, regardless of the students' abilities or disabilities. Additional IEP requirements are mandated for students who need alternate assessment, including a statement of why the student cannot participate in the regular assessment and which alternate assessment has been selected. Benchmarks or short-term objectives are also required for each annual goal (Gibb & Dyches, 2007). Figure 1.1 identifies the major components of an IEP.

THE IEP TEAM.   The IEP is developed by a collaborative team, including the parents of the student with a disability, general education teacher(s), special education teacher(s), related service providers (if appropriate), local education agency representative (usually a school administrator like the principal), an individual who can interpret evaluation results, other individuals who have specialized expertise or knowledge, and if appropriate, the student.

Each member of the IEP team contributes unique and essential information. Parents may be intimidated by the IEP process or may feel less qualified than the professionals on the team. However, parents know their children better than anyone else. Parental input must be sought and valued throughout the IEP process. Because general education teachers know the curriculum and how students can access the general curriculum, they also act as full participants in developing the IEP. All service providers responsible for the implementation of the student's IEP will be informed of their specific responsibilities. (See Chapters 7 and 8 for an extended discussion of parent and student involvement in the IEP process.)

The IEP team considers the student's present levels of educational achievement and functional performance and develops a plan for improvement during the school year. The plan begins with identifying goals and objectives designed to help the student succeed in school. Based on these goals, the team then decides what special education and related services are required to help the student achieve the goals and objectives. The IEP team also must determine how progress will be measured and how parents will be informed of progress toward accomplishing the IEP goals. The IEP team must meet at least annually to update the IEP.

For students who are age 16 or older, the IEP must address transition planning. This means the parents, the student (if appropriate), and the rest of the IEP team collaborate to decide what the student needs to prepare for the transition from school to adult life. At age 16, transition planning includes any community agencies and work experiences that will be part of the student's school day.

IEP MEETING.   Parents' right to participate in their child's education is at the heart of IDEA. School districts are required to take steps to ensure that one or both of the child's parents are present or have an opportunity to attend each IEP meeting. Therefore, school personnel must give parents enough advance notice and schedule IEP meetings at a mutually agreeable time and place. The meetings usually take place at the school, but this is not required.

Notices to parents must include the purpose of the meeting, the time and location of the meeting, and who will be in attendance. There are also provisions in IDEA for participation of other individuals who have knowledge or special expertise about the student. For example, other people may include representatives from the early intervention system or social service agencies. Also, for students who turn 16 (or younger, if determined appropriate by the team), the notice must inform parents that a purpose of the meeting will be to consider the postsecondary goals and transition services, and that the student will be invited to attend the meeting. The notice must identify any other agency that will be invited to send a representative to the meeting.

If neither parent can be present at the IEP meeting, the school district or school personnel may use other methods to ensure parental participation such as a telephone, a computer, or videoconferencing. School personnel may proceed with the meeting when the parents cannot attend only if the school has a record of efforts made to arrange the meeting at a mutually agreeable time and place. These records may include detailed records of telephone calls made or attempted and the results of those calls, copies of correspondence sent to the parents and any responses, and detailed records of visits made to the parents' home or place of employment and the results of those visits. School personnel are also obligated to provide the parents with interpreters or other services necessary to ensure that they fully understand the IEP process, and the parents must be given a free copy of their child's IEP. (For more information about the IEP meeting, see Chapters 7 and 8.)

IEP DEVELOPMENT.   When an IEP is developed, the team considers the student's strengths, the parents' concerns for improving their child's education, and the student's academic, developmental, and functional needs. Additional factors such as native language, behavior, and communication needs may be considered if they apply. For example, if the student has limited English proficiency, the IEP team must consider the child's language needs in relation to the IEP. Other special factors must also be considered. First, in the case of a child whose behavior impedes his or her learning or that of others, the IEP team must consider the use of positive behavioral interventions and supports and other strategies to address the behavior. Second, when a child is blind or visually impaired, the IEP team must provide for instruction in Braille and the use of Braille unless the team determines from the child's reading and writing skills, needs, and appropriate reading and writing media that instruction in Braille or the use of Braille is not appropriate for the child. Third, the team must consider the child's language and communication needs, opportunities for communications with peers and professional personnel, the child's mode of language and communication, academic level, and full range of needs. This should also include consideration of opportunities for direct instruction in the child's language and communication mode. And fourth, the team must consider whether the child needs assistive technology devices and services.

EXTENDED SCHOOL YEAR SERVICES.   Some students with disabilities have significant regression in their knowledge and skills when they are not receiving services, such as during the summer months when they are not in school. If these conditions exist, extended school year (ESY) services may be provided. The IEP team must ensure that ESY services are available to students as necessary to enable them to receive a free, appropriate public education. However, ESY services are required only if the IEP team determines that the services are necessary for the provision of FAPE for a specific student. Determination must be made on an individual basis.

INDIVIDUALIZED FAMILY SERVICE PLANS.   Special education is provided for infants and toddlers birth to age 3 who have been diagnosed with disabilities or developmental delays, but such interventions are based on an individualized family service plan (IFSP) instead of an IEP. The IFSP focuses not only on the child, but also on the concerns, needs, and resources of the family. The IFSP facilitates the child's transition to preschool or other services or discontinues special education services that are no longer needed. If a toddler transitioning to preschool needs an IEP, then the IEP team must consider the child and family's IFSP when they develop the IEP. Alternatively, some states allow children beyond age 3 to receive services based on an IFSP rather than an IEP. In these cases, special services must be included, such as school readiness, preliteracy, language, and numeracy skills (U.S. Department of Education, n.d.; CFR 34 §300.323). Chapter 11 provides a more detailed discussion of IFSPs.

INDIVIDUAL TRANSITION PLANS.   IDEA 2004 requires transition planning prior to the age of 16. The term *transition services* means a coordinated set of activities for students with disabilities that (a) are designed within a results-oriented process; (b) are based on the individual student's strengths, taking into account the student's preferences and interests; and (c) includes instruction, related services, community experiences, the development of employment and other postschool adult-living objectives, and when appropriate, acquisition of daily living skills and functional vocational evaluation. Chapter 11 provides a more detailed discussion of individualized transition plans (ITPs).

It should be noted that the word *coordinated* was the first reference to a systematic approach to transition, and it means both the linkage between each of the component activities encompassing the transition activities that comprise transition services and the interrelationship between the various agencies that are involved in the provision of services to a student. Because the transition process relies on the involvement of many individuals and many service providers, coordination is essential.

Adults with disabilities are not eligible for special education services after their 22nd birthday; therefore, these individuals do not have IEPs. Families, the community, or other government agencies provide services beginning with age 22. Unfortunately, there is no guarantee that services will be available for all adults who need them. Availability of services for adults with disabilities varies greatly across the United States.

In IEP meetings the teachers would tell me things I already knew about Rachel's progress according to my observation. I feel like her teachers in elementary school enjoyed Rachel, and they tried to be positive about her disability and skills. But it is always difficult to hear that your child is performing below grade level, and your child has not passed assessments, and your child's social skills are poor, etc. Rachel was particularly sensitive to this information and also reacted emotionally, so I chose not to have her attend IEP meetings in elementary school. In middle school and high school she did participate and had opinions about most things and even suggested goals.

In secondary schools it was more difficult for teachers to understand Rachel's needs because they typically taught her for only one period for one, or maybe two, semesters. At this point it was easy for her to fall between the cracks. However, she did continue through high school to receive services from the district vision specialist. They developed a positive and lasting friendship. This provider became a good advocate for Rachel and communicated with the general education teachers.

NO CHILD LEFT BEHIND ACT

The No Child Left Behind (NCLB) Act of 2002 has been described as making the most dramatic U.S. legislative impact on general education in the last 30 to 40 years (Bloomfield & Cooper, 2003). NCLB focuses on education for all students, including those with disabilities. The act includes five major principles: (a) increased accountability for states, local school districts, and schools for student achievement; (b) increased parental choices for their child's school placement; (c) more flexibility for school districts in use of federal funds; (d) strong emphasis on using scientifically based instructional methods; and (e) each teacher and paraeducator must be highly qualified. Each of these is further described in Table 1.2.

Right to Educational Achievement

The major focus of NCLB is positive achievement outcomes for all students, including those with disabilities. The act indicates that all students have rights to educational achievement and access to the general education curriculum in the general education environment. Under NCLB, states establish goals for the performance of students with disabilities that are consistent with the goals for all students. Schools (and ultimately, teachers) are held responsible for the achievement of all students—including students with disabilities. With only a limited percentage exempt, students with disabilities must be included in state- and districtwide assessment programs. Students with disabilities must receive appropriate accommodations and alternate assessments where necessary to evaluate the progress toward these goals.

IDEA emphasizes that special education teachers must be "appropriately and adequately prepared" and encourages the use of research-based practices in instruction to

TABLE 1.2 Key Principles of No Child Left Behind (NCLB)	
Principle	**What It Means for Parents and Students**
Accountability to demonstrate that students are meeting outcomes	High-stakes tests have been developed to measure the academic progress of all students. *Adequate yearly progress* is the term used to refer to whether or not students are making academic progress, and it is used as a measure to hold schools responsible.
Increased parental choice	Parents have been given more ability to control their child's school placement if the child's current placement is not meeting his or her specific academic needs. Vouchers for private schools and enrollment in public charter schools offer parents more options.
School district flexibility and local control	State educational agencies, communities, local education agencies, and schools have more flexibility in the use of federal funds.
Scientifically based teaching methods	Emphasis is placed on the use of evidence-based teaching methods/practices and the integration of professional wisdom in making decisions about how to deliver instruction and assess student progress.
Highly qualified teachers and paraprofessionals	Higher standards have been set for teachers and paraprofessionals so that the most qualified professionals are being brought into the educational system. These professionals are trained in the latest research-based methods, which have been shown to demonstrate, at minimum, adequate outcomes for students.

boost student achievement. NCLB also directly affects the professional preparation and employment of school personnel. Through NCLB, the U.S. Congress directed that teachers and paraprofessionals must meet certain standards to be considered *highly qualified.*

Under NCLB, schools must demonstrate adequate yearly progress (AYP). AYP is based on student achievement on standardized assessments. Schools that fail to demonstrate AYP are likely to have federal funding rescinded. The goals of NCLB state (a) all students will reach high standards, attaining at least proficiency in reading and mathematics (by 2014); (b) all students will be able to read by the end of the third grade (by 2014); (c) all limited English proficient (LEP) students will be proficient in English; (d) all students will be taught by highly qualified teachers (by 2006); (e) all students will be educated in learning environments that are safe and drug free; and (f) all students will graduate from high school.

Applications for Parents

Parents' rights are protected under NCLB to ensure that children have access to quality education provided by highly qualified teachers. Parents have the right to know (a) the quality of education that their child is receiving; (b) the teachers' and paraprofessionals' qualifications; (c) when their child has a substitute teacher (if an unqualified person has taught for four consecutive weeks the district must notify parents); (d) the quality of schools and districts, including detailed report cards on schools and districts, which includes student achievement data and qualifications of teachers; and (e) whether their child's school has been identified as needing improvement, corrective action, or restructuring, along with options available to parents, including the right to transfer schools or receive supplemental educational services in the community.

FAMILY EDUCATIONAL RIGHTS AND PRIVACY ACT

In 1974 the U.S. Congress passed the Family Educational Rights and Privacy Act (FERPA), a federal privacy law that gives parents certain rights with respect to their children's education records, such as report cards, disciplinary records, educational transcripts, contact information, and class schedules. FERPA applies to all agencies and institutions that receive federal funds, including elementary and secondary schools, colleges, and universities. The purposes of FERPA are threefold. The first purpose is to ensure that parents have access to their children's educational records. The second is to protect the privacy rights of parents and children by limiting access to these records without parental consent. The third purpose is to provide for the amendment and destruction of records.

Prior to the passage of FERPA, there were many abuses with regard to student records. For example, school personnel kept K–12 public school records, and parents were denied access. Many schools developed extensive records on each student, including such things as identification of a child as *mentally retarded* and reasons for the child being transferred to a class for students with mental retardation, but parents were never told about the child being identified as having special needs, nor were they told the child was moved to a special education classroom or given access to the information in the student's file. According to one study (Divorky, 1973) the records were usually open to government inspectors, employers, and other nonschool personnel but not to parents. Another study from the 1960s found that the Federal Bureau of Investigation (FBI) and the Central Intelligence Agency (CIA) had complete access to student files in more than 60% of school districts in the United States, whereas parents had access in only about 15% of the school districts (Stone, 1975). FERPA changed these practices.

Access to Records

The law's careful description of access rights has two purposes: (a) it defines who has access to a student's personally identifiable information, and (b) it informs schools and parents that this information is *confidential*, meaning that unauthorized people do not have access to it. For schools this generally means that the school district may presume that a parent has the authority to inspect and review records relating to their child unless the school district has been legally advised that the parent does not have such authority. For IEP team members, strict confidentiality is required regarding students served by special education. Team members may not disclose confidential information to others, spoken or written, in or out of school (Ashbaker & Minney, 2007).

This law also gave adults who are students (for example, college students) the right to seek access to their school records. University students have the right to inspect and review their institutional records. They also have the right to challenge the content of their school records through a hearing, as well as the right of privacy for their student records.

Limiting Access to Records

Simply stated, schools must have written permission from the parent or eligible student to release any information from the student's education record. However, FERPA allows schools to disclose some records, without consent, to the following parties or under the following conditions:

- School officials with legitimate educational interest
- Other schools to which a student is transferring
- Specified officials for audit or evaluation purposes
- Appropriate parties in connection with financial aid to a student
- Organizations conducting certain studies for or on behalf of the school
- Accrediting organizations
- To comply with a judicial order or lawfully issued subpoena
- Appropriate officials in cases of health and safety emergencies
- State and local authorities, within a juvenile justice system, pursuant to specific state law

Schools may disclose, without parental consent, *directory* information that is not considered harmful or an invasion of privacy. This information can include a student's name, address, telephone number, e-mail address, date and place of birth, honors and awards, and dates of attendance. However, schools must tell parents and eligible students about the directory information, and they must allow parents and eligible students a reasonable amount of time to request that the school not disclose directory information about them. Furthermore, schools must notify parents and eligible students annually of their rights under FERPA. The actual means of notification (e.g., special letter, inclusion in a PTA bulletin, student handbook, or newspaper article) is left to the discretion of each school.

FERPA permits school officials to disclose education records, including disciplinary records and special education, to another school or postsecondary institution in which the student seeks enrollment. However, schools should not release other health or mental health records related to the student that are not included under FERPA.

Amending and Destroying Records

Parents or eligible students may request a school amend or destroy records that they believe to be incorrect or misleading. If the school decides not to amend or destroy the record, the parent then has the right to a formal hearing. Following the hearing, if the school still does not amend or destroy the record, the parent has the right to insert a personal comment in the record declaring his or her perception about the contested information.

Age of Majority

Parents serve as the guardians of their children until they reach the age of majority. These rights transfer to the student when he or she reaches the age of 18 or attends a school beyond the high school level. However, parents have the right to inspect their child's educational records while the child remains in high school or if the child attends a postsecondary institution prior to turning 18. In these cases, both the parent and the child have the right to examine or request records be amended or destroyed.

IDEA and FERPA

IDEA uses the FERPA definition of *education records* and requires schools to maintain a publicly visible record of access on which authorized people must record their name, position, date, and reason for accessing these confidential materials. Parents may request copies of a student's IEP and other confidential information, as defined by FERPA.

The right to inspect and review education records under IDEA includes (a) the right to a response from the school district to reasonable requests for explanations and interpretations of the records; (b) the right to request that the school district provide copies of records containing the information, and (c) the right to have a representative of the parent inspect and review the child's records. However, if permission is granted to a third party, the school must keep a record of who reviewed the record, why it was needed, and when it was released. Parents also have the right to restrict access to their child's school records by third parties.

Confidentiality of the IEP and special education student records is regulated by both the IDEA and FERPA. The provisions in IDEA incorporate FERPA's confidentiality requirements but then go beyond FERPA by specifying additional requirements that apply only to the records of children with disabilities. For example, parents of children with disabilities must have the opportunity to inspect all education records associated with the special services their children receive. In particular, they must have access to state or local records pertaining to the identification, evaluation, and education placement of their child and services their child receives.

SECTION 504 OF THE VOCATIONAL REHABILITATION ACT OF 1973

The Vocational Rehabilitation Act is a broad civil rights law that protects individuals with disabilities from discrimination in programs and activities that receive federal financial assistance. Section 504 of this law requires state and local government agencies to carry the responsibility of ensuring that accommodations and/or services are provided for people with disabilities, offering protection to individuals under a broader concept of impairment—rather than disability. It is important to note that Section 504 covers all individuals, whereas IDEA focuses exclusively on students from birth through age 21.

Under Section 504, a person is considered to have a disability if he or she has a physical or mental impairment that substantially limits a major life activity, or has a history of a disability, or is regarded by others as having a disability. Major life activities include functions such as learning, thinking, seeing, hearing, walking, breathing, caring for oneself, performing manual tasks, sitting, standing, and lifting.

Section 504 prohibits discrimination against *all persons* with disabilities, including school-age children, regardless of whether they require special educational services. This law applies to any business or agency (such as school districts) with more than 15 employees. Because most school districts have more than 15 employees, most will appoint someone to serve as the Section 504 coordinator who works to ensure that the requirements of the Section are met. Section 504 also applies to programs and activities that receive funds from the U.S. Department of Education. Recipients of these funds include public school districts, institutions of higher education, and other state and local education agencies.

As this law applies to both employees and students, the Section 504 coordinator may work with individual students, their parents, and teachers to adapt the learning environment in ways that will accommodate the environmental or learning needs of the student. General educators are typically responsible for meeting the student's learning needs in the general education classroom based on recommendations made in the student's 504 plan.

504 Plans

A *504 plan* refers to Section 504 of the Rehabilitation Act. These plans may also be used to fulfill the Americans with Disabilities Act requirements that specify that no one with a disability can be excluded from participating in federally funded programs or activities, including elementary, secondary, or postsecondary schooling. A 504 plan is developed in a manner similar to an IEP; a team approach is used. Members of the team should include those who are knowledgeable about (a) the student (including family members), (b) the evaluation data, and (c) appropriate modifications and accommodations. They review the student's needs and decide if specialized services are necessary for the student to access education to perform at the same level as peers. They then select modifications and/or accommodations, which may include such things as wheelchair ramps, a tape recorder or keyboard, materials written in Braille, a set of textbooks to use at home, blood sugar monitoring, or a peanut-free lunch environment.

Section 504 requires a school district to provide FAPE to each qualified student with a disability who is in the school district's jurisdiction, regardless of the nature or severity of the disability. This regulation is very similar to IDEA. Under Section 504, FAPE consists of the provision of general or special education and related aids and services designed to meet the student's individual needs. The Office for Civil Rights enforces Section 504.

THE AMERICANS WITH DISABILITIES ACT

Section 504 of the Rehabilitation Act served as a springboard for the Americans with Disabilities Act of 1990 (ADA). Like Section 504, ADA is a civil rights law. The act does not list specific disabilities covered but uses the definition of disability as found in Section 504. ADA protects people with significant, long-term conditions rather than those with minor, short-term conditions.

ADA also provides a clear and comprehensive national mandate for elimination of discrimination against individuals with disabilities. It applies to private-sector employment, public services, public transportation, and telecommunications. It requires that employers do not discriminate solely on the basis of a person having a disability. If the person with a disability can perform the activities required for the job as well as a nondisabled person, then the employer may not eliminate the person who has a disability as a candidate for employment without making reasonable accommodations. The effects of ADA are visible in most communities, for example, sidewalk cutouts, telecommunication devices in malls and airports, Braille on automated teller machines, and sign-language translators at public meetings. Any one of the ADA protections may apply in a school setting to either students or employees.

Summary

- The U.S. Congress has passed several laws to ensure persons with disabilities have and retain their rights to a public education.
- These laws include the Individuals with Disabilities Education Act, the No Child Left Behind Act, Section 504 of the Rehabilitation Act, and the Americans with Disabilities Act.
- These laws identify and protect the rights of parents and their children.
- All teachers are well advised to know the principles of these laws and to follow them.

- Key to these laws are the provisions that (a) school personnel must include parents in the decisions that will affect their children, (b) student information be kept confidential, and (c) all personally identifiable information must be protected and kept confidential at the parent's request.
- These laws support the protection of parents' rights and those of their children.

Linking Standards to Chapter Content

After reading this chapter, you should be able to link basic knowledge and skills described in the CEC Standards and INTASC Principles with information provided in this text. Table 1.3, Linking CEC Standards and INTASC Principles to Major Chapter Topics, gives examples of how they can be applied to each major section of the chapter.

TABLE 1.3 Linking CEC Standards and INTASC Principles to Major Chapter Topics

Major Chapter Headings	CEC Knowledge and Skill Core Standard and Associated Subcategories	INTASC Core Principle and Associated Special Education Subcategories
Historical Overview of Laws and Litigation	1: Foundations	1: Subject Matter
Individuals with Disabilities Education Improvement Act of 2004	ICC1K1 Models, theories, and philosophies that form the basis for special education practice.	1.13 Special education teachers know major trends and issues that define the history of special education and understand how current legislation and recommended practice fit within the contact of this history.
No Child Left Behind Act	ICC1K4 Rights and responsibilities of students, parents, teachers, and other professionals, and schools related to exceptional learning needs.	1.11 Special education teachers have knowledge of the requirements and responsibilities involved in developing, implementing, and evaluating individualized education programs (IEPs), individualized family service plans (IFSPs), and individualized accommodation plans (IAPs) for students with disabilities.

(continued)

TABLE 1.3 *(continued)*		
Major Chapter Headings	**CEC Knowledge and Skill Core Standard and Associated Subcategories**	**INTASC Core Principle and Associated Special Education Subcategories**
Family Educational Rights and Privacy Act	ICC1K5 Issues in definition and identification of individuals with exceptional learning needs, including those from culturally and linguistically diverse backgrounds.	3: Diverse Learners
Section 504 of the Vocational Rehabilitation Act of 1973	ICC1K6 Issues, assurances and due process rights related to assessment, eligibility, and placement within a continuum of services.	3.03 All teachers understand that a disability can be perceived differently across families, communities, and cultures based on differing values and belief systems.
Americans with Disabilities Act	ICC1K7 Family systems and the role of families in the educational process.	3.04 All teachers understand and are sensitive to cultural, ethnic, gender, and linguistic differences that may be confused with or misinterpreted as manifestations of a disability.

Sources: Council for Exceptional Children (2005); Interstate New Teacher Assessment and Support Consortium INTASC Special Education Subcommittee (2001).

Web Resources

INTERNET WEB SITES AND SUPPORT

www.ada.gov/—Provides information and technical assistance on the Americans with Disabilities Act.

http://www.adata.org/Static/Home.aspx—The Disability and Business Technical Assistance Center (DBTAC) is a national network of ADA centers that provide services for up-to-date information, referrals, resources, and training on the Americans with Disabilities Act (ADA).

www.access-board.gov/Network Error (tcp_error) it says—The Access Board is an independent federal agency devoted to accessibility for people with disabilities.

http://www.gsa.gov/portal/content/101096—Provides information on Section 508 and requires that federal agencies' electronic and information technology is accessible to people with disabilities.

http://www2.ed.gov/about/offices/list/osers/osep/index.html—Home page for the Office of Special Education and Rehabilitative Services (OSERS).

http://www2.ed.gov/policy/gen/guid/fpco/ferpa/index.html—Home page for the Family Educational Rights and Privacy Act (FERPA).

http://idea.ed.gov/—Home page for the Individuals with Disabilities Education Act (IDEA).

www.adi.org/parentguide.html—The Academic Development Institute provides parents guidance to help their children succeed in school.

www.ed.gov/parents/needs/speced/iepguide/index.html—Provides a guide to the components and process of an individualized education program.

Parent Resource Centers: The Office of Special Education and Rehabilitative Services funds centers designated for information and training for parents of children with disabilities, including community parent resource centers. These are often located in local schools or community centers. Visit your local school district website for a center near you.

CHAPTER 2

Historical and Current Perspectives of Family Involvement

OBJECTIVES

After reading this chapter you will

1. Outline major historical efforts that promoted families' involvement in their children's education.

2. Describe current perspectives and models of parental involvement.

3. Define parent involvement mechanisms and barriers to school involvement.

4. Describe profiles of families unique to those with children with special needs.

INTRODUCTION

Families play a crucial role in the education of students with special needs by working in partnership with teachers and other service personnel to support and enhance their child's educational experience. Families have effected change in local, national, and international policies. In fact, the most significant changes in special education practice have come about through family advocacy. Families are fundamental not only in understanding the history of special education, but also in creating quality programs for children in classrooms.

However, just as no universal family composition exists, there is no absolute in determining the roles families will hold. For some families, communication and participation in the schools involves parents, siblings, and/or extended family such as grandparents. For others, a single member of the family will take responsibility for working with teachers and other school personnel. Some families will express interest in working extensively in the school; others will desire minimal involvement. As all families differ, so does who and how they will participate in the student's educational experience.

Within this chapter we discuss the historical treatment of individuals with disabilities and the history of family involvement in education. We then present current perspectives of family involvement and provide profiles of families of children with special needs.

Kyle was the firstborn child for his parents and the first grandchild for both sets of grandparents. At birth, he presented in a breech position with the umbilical cord wrapped around his neck. The cord cut off circulation, and Kyle was without oxygen until delivered by emergency cesarean section.

Typically hospitals conduct an Apgar evaluation (Appearance, Pulse, Grimace, Activity, Respiration; Apgar, 1953) with newborn infants. The Apgar is conducted immediately after the infant is born, again 5 minutes after birth, and again at 10 minutes after birth, if warranted. Apgar scores reflect the general health of the baby and range from 1 to 10, with scores between 7 and 10 considered normal. A 5-minute Apgar is conducted if the initial Apgar falls outside the normal range; a 10-minute Apgar is conducted if both the initial and 5-minute Apgar evaluations fall outside the normal range.

An initial Apgar for Kyle at birth was very low but within normal ranges during the second scoring. However, although the medical team and family members hoped the second Apgar would be more representative of Kyle's prognosis, they realized within a few months that this was not to be the case. An unfortunate experience at birth resulted in Kyle's lifelong cognitive disability that would manifest in language, comprehension, motor, and social delays. Throughout the course of Kyle's childhood, he and his family, including a younger sister, would navigate the complex world of service delivery both in schools and in the community.

HISTORICAL PERSPECTIVE

Historical Treatment of Individuals with Disabilities

Family involvement in education is a relatively modern practice. Laws that protect students' and families' rights have evolved over time as schools moved from community-centered institutions to state and federally funded entities. Historically, families exerted some control over schools in their communities. For example, they had a say in the development of local curriculum and influenced who was hired or fired. As modern public school systems developed, parents were less directly involved in school governance. Elected school boards, local administrators, and state officials determined curriculum and school policy. Although public school systems were established to educate children, throughout the 20th century, many children, including children with disabilities, were excluded from public schools or did not receive access to the same services as other children. The civil rights movements of the 1950s and 1960s highlighted the need to protect children's rights to education. As civil rights laws were passed to end discriminatory practices, the federal government also mandated parent involvement in education to ensure that children's advocates had a say in their education.

Examining various historical attitudes and practices provides an overview of the treatment of individuals with disabilities in educational systems and explains why family involvement is necessary. Fortunately, school systems have moved from excluding individuals with disabilities in education to including them, and school practices have become more collaborative.

PHILOSOPHICAL INFLUENCES. Educational theory finds its roots in the 17th and 18th centuries. During these centuries children were viewed as miniature adults, and they worked to contribute to the survival of the family. Children commonly worked in textile mills, mines, and factories. Often children were paid low wages and worked long hours to earn enough money to contribute to their family's economic survival. Although work was viewed as necessary for a better life, education began to gain prominence as a method for training young children. Philosophers such as John Locke (1632–1704) put forward the idea that education was a means to instill religiously based ideology and self-discipline in children (Crain, 2011). Locke argued that the depth and breadth of one's knowledge (both moral and practical) was the product of education and experience. He believed that children developed intellectual and social skills by practicing, and the role of parents or good tutors was to fashion children aright, to keep them from evil, and to encourage appropriate behavior early in their lives (Aldrich, n.d.).

Thus, early ideas about education were based on preconceived notions of what children were and ought to be. Opportunities for education were available for typically developing children whose families were financially stable and able to survive without child labor. During the 18th century, philosophers challenged the idea that children were miniature adults in need of training. Jean-Jacques Rousseau (1712–1778) argued that children should be allowed to develop without interference from adults. For Rousseau, the purpose of education was to support the innate nature and growth of children.

During Rousseau's time, such ideas were revolutionary. For the first time, education was viewed as a means to promote human happiness and facilitate children's natural development at school and at home. The idea that child development should be considered in educational practice influenced education during Rousseau's time and provided a foundation for the work of Jean Piaget, Maria Montessori, John Dewey, and Lev Vygotsky.

By the 19th century, education had gained a foothold as a rite of passage for normally developing children. Public and private schools gained prominence, and the practice of separating children with disabilities was established. Children and adults with disabilities were placed in state-controlled institutions because they were viewed as potentially dangerous to the general population. The practice of isolating individuals with disabilities continued well into the 20th century. As a result, institutions became overcrowded, and professionals began to question the appropriateness of this practice. During the 1960s, the U.S. President's Panel on Mental Retardation (1962) identified concerns with institutional overcrowding, quality of care, funding, programming, administration, and the attitudes of the staff toward the patients as problems. Concern for the care of persons with disabilities resulted in reforms directed at deinstitutionalizing individuals and including them in general society (Smith, 2010).

ADVOCACY.   Although inclusion in the general populace held advantages, inclusion required additional supports and protections for individuals with disabilities. Parents began to advocate for support for their children through organizations such as the National Association for Retarded Children (ARC, 2008), who lobbied for funding for programs at local and national levels. The personal interest of families in improving supports and programs for their children with special needs proved to be a powerful force for reform in special education. A national example of the influence of families was the Kennedy family. President John F. Kennedy was a powerful proponent of the rights of individuals with special needs. He worked to improve the lives of those, like his sister Rosemary, who had intellectual disabilities. Kennedy formed the U.S. President's Panel on Mental Retardation and mandated that the panel examine ways to improve the quality of life for persons with disabilities (Murdick, Gartin, & Crabtree, 2007). The panel's work led to new legislations and influenced reform in disability law over the next two decades.

Although Kennedy's focus on the rights of those with disabilities served as a catalyst for educational reform, his family's advocacy for individuals with disabilities achieved national and international prominence through the Special Olympics. Eunice Kennedy Shriver founded the Special Olympics in 1968 to highlight the abilities and value of those with disabilities. Because of her experience with her sister, Eunice recognized the need to focus on the abilities of individuals with disabilities (Murdick et al., 2007). Special Olympics has grown into an internationally respected organization serving 2.5 million individuals with intellectual disabilities in more than 180 countries. Although the Kennedy family had more political power and financial support than most families, their momentous influence demonstrates the monumental changes that families can bring about.

LEGAL PROTECTION.   By 1971 advocacy groups had exerted influence at national and international levels. The United Nations General Assembly issued a declaration calling for countries to ensure individuals rights of persons with disabilities. Nationally, U.S. Supreme Court rulings paved the way for Congress to pass special education laws. As discussed in Chapter 1 and seen in Table 1.1, several significant laws and court rulings influenced the field of special education. Table 2.1 summarizes those laws and court rulings.

Education is constantly being reformed as society changes, laws are enacted, and technology improves. Just as today's classrooms are very different from those of previous generations, future classrooms will be different from today. Education in the last century has moved toward respecting the rights and capabilities of all students and preparing them to make contributions to society. Table 2.1 summarizes society's changing perceptions of educating individuals with disabilities.

History of Family Involvement in Education

FAMILIES AND SCHOOLS.   Family involvement in education changed as school systems evolved from private institutions to public institutions. During the 18th and 19th centuries

			Children with	Social
Time Period	**Influential Ideas**	**Impact of Ideas**	**Disabilities**	**Implications**
17th and 18th centuries	Children could be trained.	The purpose of education was to instill religious beliefs and teach children self-discipline.	There were no provisions for children with special needs.	Children worked to support their families. If families had the means, children attended school.
18th century	Children's development should not be ignored.	Children developed without interference from adults.	This position supported the innate nature and growth of children.	Families began to consider their children's needs.
19th century	Education was a means for greater public good.	Public and private schools grew in prominence.	Children with disabilities were trained in separate institutions.	Society isolated individuals with disabilities.
Early 20th century	Education was a rite of passage for typically developing children. Child labor laws restricted child labor in factories.	Education became an expectation, and more children enrolled in public schools.	Children with disabilities were institutionalized and were not educated in public schools.	Individuals with disabilities were perceived as a danger to the general population.
1960s	Society had a responsibility to protect and care for individuals with disabilities.	Changes in the treatment of individuals were necessary. Living conditions and quality care were problems.	Children with disabilities were included in public schools. The government supported special education programs.	Groups lobbied for services and support for individuals with disabilities.
1970s	Individuals with disabilities had rights that were legally protected.	Children with disabilities had the right to public education within general public school classrooms.	Schools were required by law to provide children with disabilities the same educational opportunities that were afforded their nondisabled peers.	Federal laws required educators to involve parents in special education processes.

TABLE 2.1 Summary of Historical Treatment of Individuals with Disabilities

many schools in the United States were private schools. Because most schools were private institutions, communities and parents exerted considerable control over school decisions. Churches, families, and communities generally supported the same agenda for student learning, and parents were directly involved in making school decisions such as hiring and firing teachers, developing school curriculum, and creating the school calendar (Anafara, 2008).

By the end of the 19th century and into the 20th century, different structures in school and family relations developed. Child labor laws were enacted to end the exploitation of children, and public schools grew in number and prominence as children moved from the workforce into schools. As the number of public schools increased in the nation, family and school relationships changed. Schools began to distance themselves from parents, and teachers believed they had specialized knowledge that parents did not have and that parents were not qualified to determine curriculum or instruction. By the 1950s, teachers typically held the view that they were the educators, and parents should support their efforts (Anafara, 2008).

LAWS.   The expectation for parent involvement changed during the 1960s when the U.S. Congress passed the Elementary and Secondary Education Act of 1965 (ESEA, 1965, reauthorized as the No Child Left Behind [NCLB] Act in 2002). This federal law mandated parent involvement in schools and was the first legislative act that linked parent involvement to education. Title 1 of NCLB required parents to serve on school advisory boards and to participate in classroom activities. NCLB also stated that schools that receive Title 1 funds should develop school–parent compacts that outline how parents and school staff share responsibility for student academic achievement.

Families hold more extensive rights within the educational environment today than at any previous time in history. However, this focus on the rights of parents to be active consumers of their child's education is not a uniquely American experience. In Canada, for example, families are protected through the School Act that guards their rights and the rights of their children. Parents, under the stipulations of the School Act (section 7(1) and (2)), are entitled to be informed of a student's attendance, behavior, and progress in school and to receive, on request, annual reports respecting general effectiveness of educational programs in the school district. For children in care, Canadian school boards are required to ensure that the guardian is receiving relevant information from the school.

CURRENT PERSPECTIVES OF FAMILY INVOLVEMENT

Government support of parent involvement in education is based on research that indicates parents can have a positive effect on their children's academic lives. For example, parent involvement is associated with improvements in students' achievement, attendance, sense of well-being, readiness to complete homework, grades, and behavior. When parents are involved with school, students perform better academically, learn effective work habits, acquire prosocial behaviors, have higher self-esteem, and have positive perceptions of attending college and acquiring higher education (Harvard Family Research Project, 2007).

Overlapping Spheres of Influence

The benefits of parent involvement in education are optimized when parents and schools work together. Although most academic learning takes place at school, home and school should not be perceived as separate spheres of influence. Otherwise, educators and parents are more likely to project responsibility for children's education to someone else (i.e., "It's the teacher's job to educate my child," or "Parents need to do their job so that we can do ours"; Epstein, 1995). On the other hand, when home and school are perceived to be overlapping spheres of influence (i.e., "I communicate with the teacher so that I know how to help at home"), teachers and parents both support learning (see

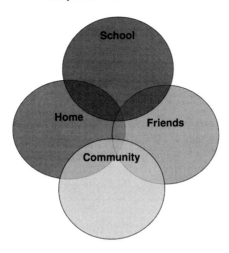

FIGURE 2.1   Overlapping spheres of influence

Figure 2.1). Overlapping spheres of influence support the idea that what happens at home can have an effect or influence on school performance. Although school and home provide different contexts for learning, parents and educators in both settings can support student achievement. The "Ten Truths of Parent Involvement" (Figure 2.2) is a list of assumptions of overlapping spheres of influence.

1. All parents have hopes and goals for their children. They differ in how they support their children's efforts to achieve those goals.
2. The home is one of several spheres that simultaneously influence a child. The school must work with other spheres for the child's benefit, not push them apart.
3. The parent is the central contributor to a child's education. Schools can either co-opt that role or recognize the potential of the parent.
4. Parent involvement must be a legitimate element of education that deserves equal emphasis with elements such as program improvement and evaluation.
5. Parent involvement is a process, not a program of activities that requires ongoing energy and effort.
6. Parent involvement requires vision, policy, and framework. A consensus of understanding is important.
7. Parents' interaction with their own children is the cornerstone of parent involvement. A program must recognize the value, diversity, and difficulty of this role.
8. Most barriers to parent involvement are found within school practices. They are not found within parents.
9. Any parent can be "hard to reach." Parents must be identified and approached individually; they are not defined by gender, ethnicity, family situation, education, or income.
10. Successful parent involvement nurtures relationships and partnerships. It strengthens bonds between home and school, parent and educator, parent and school, and school and community.

FIGURE 2.2   Ten truths of parent involvement   *Source:* Adapted from: Carter & Consortium for Appropriate Dispute Resolution in Special Education [CADRE] (2003).

One of the first models of involvement that reflected the overlapping spheres of influence concept was the school impact model (Gordon, 1977). The school impact model was defined as teachers learning from parents and parents learning from teachers (reciprocal relationships between teachers and parents). The model suggested that teachers develop new attitudes toward parents and acquire communication skills for working with parents (Berger, 1991). Epstein (1995) developed a model of parent involvement that described different types of parent involvement. Types of parent involvement are parenting, communicating, volunteering, learning at home, decision making, and collaborating with the community. Table 2.2 summarizes Epstein's model and lists school practices that support parent involvement.

Model of Parental Involvement

Parents can become involved with their child's education in many ways, and schools can greatly support that involvement. However, parent involvement is not solely dependent on school factors. Parents' motivational beliefs, perceptions of invitations for involvement from others, and their perceived life context all influence forms of involvement (Walker, Wilkins, Dallaire, Sandler, & Hoover-Dempsey, 2005; see Figure 2.3). In the Hoover-Dempsey and Sandler model, parent involvement is defined as school-based behaviors (e.g., volunteering in school classrooms and attending school events such as parent–teacher conferences) and home-based behaviors (e.g., helping with homework, reading with a child, and engaging in academic discussions).

The Hoover-Dempsey and Sandler model illustrates the following ideas.

- ***Parents' beliefs about their ability to support education influence their level of involvement.*** When parents have high self-efficacy (they believe they can help their child academically), they are more likely to support academics at home and at school. On the other hand, if parents do not believe that they can help their child, they are less likely to engage in academic behavior at home (e.g., reading with their children) or to volunteer at school.
- ***Parents construct roles for themselves based on their beliefs about their ability to become involved in their child's academic lives.*** When parents' self-efficacy is high, parents may assume the role of teacher at home and not only support education at home, but also teach their child skills necessary for academic success. If parents' self-efficacy is low, they may assume the role of bystander and defer to teachers when making decisions about their child's education.
- ***Parents' perceptions of invitations for involvement affect their level of involvement.*** Invitations for involvement come from schools, teachers, or the child. Schools and teachers may actively recruit parent volunteers and thus encourage parent involvement. Children may ask for their parents' help with an assignment or for the parents to read to them. When parents perceive that their child, a teacher, or the school wants them to help, it is easier to support academic activities and become involved with a child's education.
- ***Circumstances of parents' lives will influence school involvement.*** Parents' assessments of their situations will influence school involvement. For example, if a two-parent family is financially secure enough for one parent to stay at home, this parent may perceive that he or she has the time and energy to fully engage in academic involvement of their child. If, on the other hand, the same parent has a chronic illness or perceives that he or she lacks the necessary skills, academic involvement may be limited.

TABLE 2.2	Framework of Six Types of Involvement	

Type of Involvement	Description	Sample Practices
Parenting	Help families establish home environments that support children. Assist families with parenting and provide opportunities for parents to inform school personnel about family background, culture, and goals for children.	• Provide access to parenting information. • Make home visits. • Suggest home conditions that support learning such as scheduling time for students to do homework or providing a place for students to work. • Offer opportunities for parents and children to learn together. • Organize family support groups.
Communicating	Develop two-way communication systems between school and home.	• Send home weekly or monthly folders so that parents can review work. • Provide families with clear information on school policies and programs. • Communicate via newsletters. • Use a variety of technology tools to communicate with families. • Translate written information into families' native languages. • Host informal meetings with the school principal.
Volunteering	Provide opportunities for family members to volunteer at school.	• Invite parents to volunteer in classrooms. • Provide volunteer information packets. • Match volunteers with meaningful activities. • Help volunteers feel welcome at school. • Express appreciation to volunteers.
Learning at Home	Involve parents with their children's academic learning. Design homework activities that enable students to discuss academic learning with family members.	• Provide parents with information on homework policies. • Create a homework schedule so that parents know when their child should be completing work at home. • Send home calendars and include activities students and families can do at home. • Provide guidance on developmentally appropriate practices at home. • Provide guidance on how parents can help children with homework.
Decision Making	Include parents as participants in making school decisions. Comply with legal requirements for involving parents in IEP processes.	• Provide parents with information about school councils. • Involve parents in behavioral assessments. • Seek parent input when making educational decisions.
Collaborating with the Community	Coordinate resources and services for families, students, and the school community.	• Make information about community health, recreation, and social support available to families. • Arrange for families and students to provide service for community organizations. • Involve diverse parent and community members in school planning.

Sources: Anafara, 2008; Carter & CADRE, 2003

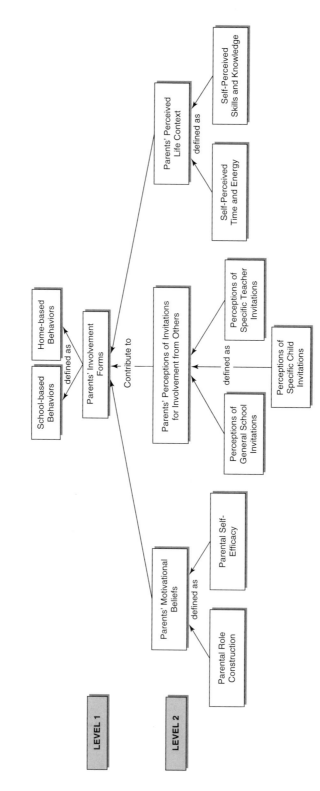

FIGURE 2.3 Hoover-Dempsey and Sandler Model of Parent Involvement *Source:* Figure 2.3 Levels 1 and 2 of Hoover-Dempsey and Sandler's theoretical model of parental involvement process (Walker, Wilkins, Dallaire, Sandler, & Hoover-Dempsey, 2005, p. 88) Copyright granted © 2005 University of Chicago Press.

Schools and teachers can invite parent involvement when they are "family friendly." Check to see if a school in your neighborhood is a family-friendly school.

- Does the school have welcome packets for new families?
- Are school information packets translated into languages spoken by students' families?
- Is a map of the school available in the school office?
- Does the school staff attend to parents' needs when parents visit the school, or are parents kept waiting while the secretary answers phones or attends to other business?
- Are there parking spots for visitors?
- Do administrators and teachers take time to answer parents' questions?
- Do administrators and teachers schedule meetings when it is convenient for parents to attend?
- Do teachers invite parents to volunteer in classes?
- Do parents serve on school site councils or advisory boards?

FIGURE 2.4   Parent-friendly schools

Parent Involvement Mechanisms

When parents perceive that they have the resources (i.e., time, energy, and knowledge) to become involve in their child's education, they support education in different ways, namely through modeling, reinforcement, and direct instruction (Hoover-Dempsey & Sandler, 1995). Each of these mechanisms reflects different forms of involvement and influences children's education.

- *Modeling.* **Parents model school-related behaviors that help their children learn to value education.** When parents ask their children about their school day, attend a school basketball game, or volunteer at a school fair, parents communicate through their behavior that school-related activities are important. As children observe their parents supporting the school community, they learn to value school activities.
- *Reinforcement.* **Parents' reinforcement of academic behavior motivates their children to expend effort to learn.** The importance of school and schoolwork is emphasized at home when parents reinforce academic behavior. Parents reinforce learning by praising their children for completing schoolwork, giving their children attention, and rewarding school success. Reinforcement helps maintain behaviors that contribute to school success.
- *Direct instruction.* **Parents' instruction at home helps students advance academically.** Sometimes children need help with academic work to acquire the skills necessary for school success. Parents often provide closed-end instruction, which is directly teaching specific skills such as correct spelling or math facts, or parents provide open-ended instruction that involves asking children questions about their schoolwork or discussing academic issues with children. Whether parents provide direct, closed-end instruction, or open-ended instruction, parental involvement is likely to yield enabling and enhancing effects on children's learning (Hoover-Dempsey & Sandler, 1995).

Barriers to School Involvement

Parent involvement in education depends on school personnel and parents having the perspective that schools and homes are overlapping spheres of influence and on both parties expending effort to support education. However, parents and teachers may encounter problems developing supporting relationships. Teacher attitudes may create barriers for parent involvement. For example, if a teacher believes that parents who do not attend school functions do not care about education, that parents from diverse cultures don't know how to support learning at home, or that parents are responsible for finding out what is happening at school, it is unlikely that such a teacher would extend invitations to families to collaborate. Family members may believe that there is little they can do to support education, and they may be reluctant to interact with teachers. Family and school barriers to family involvement include the following:

- School environments may not support parent–family involvement. Teachers may not allow parents to volunteer in classrooms, and schools may not solicit parent input on school policies.
- School practices may not accommodate diverse family needs. Schools may not provide information about the school in languages spoken in the community, or teachers might be reluctant to plan meetings that accommodate families' schedules.
- Parents may not be aware that they are expected to be involved in their child's education. Without an invitation from teachers to volunteer in classes, parents may not know that their help is expected and welcomed.
- Parents may believe that the teacher has special authority and they should not question that authority. This may be particularly true for parents from cultures other than the majority culture of the community.
- Parents may feel uncomfortable if there are few or no teachers representing their culture group.
- Parents may feel their family status is demeaned if their children are used as interpreters.
- Parents may not be aware that they have power concerning decision making about their child's education. Unless explicitly informed, parents may not know their rights regarding their child's education (Carter & CADRE, 2003).

Although it may be challenging to work with families, their support brings a profusion of resources for teachers seeking avenues to enhance children's education. Each teacher should strive to clearly understand the home and community of children, while also encouraging families to become active participants in the classroom.

PROFILES OF FAMILIES OF CHILDREN WITH SPECIAL NEEDS

In encouraging and supporting family involvement in education, educators should understand that families of children with disabilities face different challenges than other families. When children become disabled or are born with disabilities, the family unit is generally affected in some fashion by the child's disability. The experience of raising a child with disabilities can be both positive and negative for families. Family coping depends on parents' attitudes, skills, coping mechanisms, and support systems. Whether families cope well or not, parents of children with disabilities will have different experiences and stresses than families that do not include individuals with disabilities. Specifically, a child's condition might affect family finances and contribute to financial stress, parents and the child might contend with social stigmatization, and depending on the level of care a child requires, parents may experience emotional difficulty and stress caring for their child.

Financial Stress

Parents often have extra expenses when they have a child with disabilities, and meeting a child's needs may contribute to financial stress. All children need to be fed and clothed, and periodically most children have minor medical problems. In families of children with disabilities, children often have chronic medical conditions that require ongoing treatment. A family might incur large medical bills caring for a child with cancer or cystic fibrosis. Even if a family has adequate medical insurance, deductibles and copayments for office visits, medications, surgeries, hospitalizations, and therapy may strain family budgets. Often, a child will require services or devices that are not covered by insurance. If family resources are limited, addressing the child's needs may be stressful.

Social Stigmatization

Another source of potential stress is social stigmatization. As discussed previously, individuals with disabilities have historically been shunned by society. Although much progress has been made in accepting individuals with disabilities as members of society, individuals and their families are still stigmatized. Some family members may be unaffected by social stigmatization, and others may find it distressing.

The visibility of a child's disability, the perceptions of others about whether the disability can be controlled or not, and whether a child is perceived as being dangerous influences stigmatization of the child's condition (Deaux, Reid, Mizrahi, & Ethier, 1995). A child who is in a wheelchair will most likely be perceived differently than a child who has a reading disability. It is unlikely that others would assume that the child in the wheelchair could control the condition or would be a danger, given the child's limited mobility. However, teachers or other adults might perceive that the child with a reading disability can control the condition. Although most would not consider children with learning disabilities as being dangerous, children who have emotional and behavioral disorders might be perceived as being threatening.

The perceptions of others can create social stress for parents. Parents may feel stress when they think that they are stigmatized by their child's condition, or when they perceive that their child is stigmatized.
Josephine, who had a son with autism, dreaded going into stores with her son. When Alex was young, he frequently became overstimulated by store environments—running through aisles and grabbing objects from shelves. When Josephine tried to control Alex, he would become overwhelmed and throw tantrums (he would yell and scream that he didn't want to put the objects back and didn't want his mother to touch him). It was exhausting and stressful for Josephine to not only deal with Alex's behavior, but also to realize that others were stigmatizing them. When Alex misbehaved, Josephine didn't know if Alex's disability was apparent to others. She assumed that people in the stores who would stare at them thought that he (and she) could control his behavior, and sometimes—by the looks on strangers' faces—she perceived that some people thought Alex was dangerous. Consequently, whenever Josephine could avoid going in stores with Alex, she avoided stores. It was just too hard to be in public with Alex (personal communication, 2005).

FIGURE 2.5 A mother's voice—social stigmatization

Emotional Difficulty and Stress

Not all parents who have children with disabilities develop emotional problems or experience difficulty dealing with the perceptions of others. Although many parents cope well with the demands of having a child with disabilities, parents of children with disabilities may experience more stress related to their child's condition than parents of children who do not have disabilities (Downing, 2008). Greater amounts of stress may be due to child-

TABLE 2.3 Family Response to Disability	
Disabling Condition	**Family Response**
Developmental Disabilities	Parents of children with developmental disabilities may be at risk for depression. However, studies have indicated that over time, long-term adjustment to disability improves.
Attention-Deficit Hyperactivity Disorder	Mothers with children with more severe behavior symptoms may become more critical, commanding, and less responsive to their children. When their children are given medication, mothers' behavior toward their children may improve as their children's behavior improves. ADHD is highly inheritable, and parents may also have the condition.
Autism	Children's behavior problems may cause considerable stress for parents. Risk factors for poor coping include the following: ambiguity of diagnosis, severity of the condition, behavioral problems, and duration of condition. Autism is a spectrum disorder, and children are differentially affected.
Deafness	Deafness affects families in different ways. The child's impaired communication may be a source of frustration for parents who are not deaf. Typically, children with deafness are not diagnosed quickly, which contributes to increased stress, anxiety, and family conflict. Some view the deaf community as a cultural group with its own identity, rituals, and communication patterns. Within the deaf community, there is growing acceptance of deafness as a cultural phenomenon, as opposed to a disabling condition.
Chronic Illness	Approximately 10–25% of children become chronically ill. Chronic illnesses range in severity and degree of impairment (e.g., cystic fibrosis, cancer, arthritis, asthma, and diabetes). Parents may experience, negative, positive, or no effects from caring for children who have chronic illnesses. Because children's illnesses vary in severity and outcomes (the child's death in some cases), parents will encounter different challenges dealing with chronic illnesses.
Physical Impairments	The nature and severity of a child's physical impairment may determine family emotional response. Parents will have different challenges to adjust to if a child has a quadriplegic condition compared to muscular dystrophy, which is degenerative and requires continual adjustment as the disease progresses.
Blindness	Many children with blindness have normal cognitive abilities. Blindness may be less devastating to the child and the family than other types of disabilities.

Source: Seligman & Darling, 2007

care responsibilities associated with the child's condition. In raising a child with ADHD, a parent might expend considerable energy managing the child's impulsive behavior and helping the child acquire organizational skills, which may exhaust an already busy parent. A parent's stress and emotional response is often related to the magnitude of the child's needs and condition. Table 2.3 summarizes research on parents' responses to different disabling conditions.

Although family response to disability has been documented, it is impossible to predict how a family will cope with a child's condition. Emotional coping is influenced by (a) caregiver demands, (b) the child's temperament, (c) the severity of the child's behavior problems, (d) the child's social responsiveness, and (e) the level of support parents receive in the home and from others (Seligman & Darling, 2007).

As a family confronts unfamiliar circumstances, it may be the community, including the school and teachers, who can strengthen the family through the provision of resources and support. Although it would be difficult for any individual who does not have a member of the family with special needs to fully comprehend and understand the impact of a child's disability on a family, teachers and other members of the community support team should remain cognizant of the tremendous impact they can have in the family's sense of purpose, identity, and triumph in managing a child's special needs.

Summary

- Historically parents have been granted opportunities for participation in their child's education based on philosophical influences, advocacy, and legal protection.
- Although a relatively recent practice, today parents play a crucial role in the education of their children.
- Students are affected by overlapping spheres of influence, which include home, school, friends, and community.
- Epstein identified six types of parent involvement to be: parenting, communicating, volunteering, learning at home, decision making, and collaborating with the community.
- Parent participation is influenced by their beliefs about their abilities, perceptions of invitations for involvement, and life circumstances.

- Parents help their children improve academically by modeling school-related behaviors, reinforcing academic behavior, and directly teaching skills.
- Barriers exist that prevent parents from participating, such as cultural mismatch between family and school personnel and parents misunderstanding their role in partnership with the school.
- Parents of children with disabilities are often affected by financial stress, social stigmatization, and psychological stress, which may influence their ability to participate in their child's education.

Linking Standards to Chapter Content

After reading this chapter, you should be able to link basic knowledge and skills described in the CEC Standards and INTASC Principles with information provided in this text. Table 2.4, Linking CEC Standards and INTASC Principles to Major Chapter Topics, gives examples of how they can be applied to each major section of the chapter.

TABLE 2.4	Linking CEC Standards and INTASC Principles to Major Chapter Topics	
Major Chapter Headings	**CEC Knowledge and Skill Core Standard and Associated Subcategories**	**INTASC Core Principle and Associated Special Education Subcategories**
Historical Perspective	1: Foundations ICC1K8 Historical points of view and contribution of culturally diverse groups. 2: Development and Characteristics of Learners ICC2K4 Family systems and the role of families in supporting development.	1: Subject Matter 1.13 Special education teachers know major trends and issues that define the history of special education and understand how current legislation and recommended practice fit within the contact of this history. 2: Learning Concepts 2.07 Special education teachers seek to understand the current and evolving development and learning of individual students from a life span perspective 3: Learning Styles and Differences 3.07 Special education teachers share the values and beliefs underlying special education services for individuals with disabilities in the United States with students, families, and community members and seek to understand ways in which these are compatible or in conflict with those of the family and community.
Current Perspectives of Family Involvement	1: Foundations ICC1K7 Family systems and the role of families in the educational process. 2: Development and Characteristics of Learners ICC2K4 Family systems and the role of families in supporting development. 9: Professional and Ethical Practice ICC9S12 Engage in professional activities that benefit individuals with exceptional learning needs, their families, and one's colleagues.	1: Subject Matter 1.11 Special education teachers have knowledge of the requirements and responsibilities involved in developing, implementing, and evaluating individualized education programs (IEPs), individualized family service plans (IFSPs), and individual accommodation plans (IAPs) for students with disabilities. 10.10 Special education teachers understand the impact that having a child with a disability may have on family roles and functioning at different points in the life cycle of a family.

Sources: Council for Exceptional Children (2005); Interstate New Teacher Assessment and Support Consortium INTASC Special Education Subcommittee (2001)

Web Resources

INTERNET SUPPORT—ORGANIZATIONS

http://www.familysupportamerica.org/—Family Support America provides a wide range of information and support for families.

http://www.parentsasteachers.org/—Parents as Teachers provides information and support for parents on child development knowledge.

CHAPTER 3

Family Members' Roles and Characteristics

CHAPTER OUTLINE

OBJECTIVES

After reading this chapter you will

1. Describe the roles parents play in terms of advocacy, learning, and teaching.

2. Identify similarities and differences between fathers and mothers as caregivers.

3. Describe issues related to isolated parents, extended family, and nontraditional families.

4. Describe concerns of siblings and outline ways in which teachers can assist them.

INTRODUCTION

Although the traditional image of a family composed of a father, mother, siblings, and extended members such as grandparents is still prominent within societal images, the reality for many children with and without special needs is very different. Within society today, family configurations represent broad scopes of arrangements. For example, children may live with parents and siblings, reside with a single parent, split time between two homes (if their parents are divorced), be assigned to foster care, live in poverty, or grow up in homes of guardians.

Within this chapter we discuss the roles and characteristics of family members. First, we begin with the roles parents play (e.g., advocates, learners, teachers), followed by a discussion of the characteristics and concerns of siblings. We then address issues related to extended families and nontraditional families, such as teen parents, foster families, or gay or lesbian families.

ROLES OF PARENTS

Parents as Advocates

Regardless of family configuration, parents relate uniquely with their children and have a tremendous responsibility to care for their children. Home is where parents nurture their children. While parents attend to their children's material needs and do their best to ensure their child's physical safety, much time and energy is expended attending to children's development and social and emotional needs. Parents' strong emotional commitment to meeting their children's needs often becomes the impetus for parent advocacy.

Just as the Kennedy family advocated support for individuals with mental retardation (see Chapter 2), parents may adopt roles as advocates to ensure that their child's needs are met. Most parents are satisfied with school performance. However, if parents perceive that their child's needs are not being met, they may view advocacy as not only a necessity, but also their moral obligation in providing care for their child (Wang, Mannan, Poston, Turnbull, & Summers, 2004).

In its simplest form, advocacy occurs any time a person speaks or acts on behalf of themselves or others (Alper, Schloss, & Schloss, 1995). Advocacy can be informal and flexible (e.g., parents converse with teachers and discuss their child's need), or formal and structured (e.g., formal IEP meetings, court proceedings, or due process hearings). Different forms of advocacy are social support advocacy, interpersonal advocacy, and legal advocacy.

SOCIAL SUPPORT ADVOCACY.   The most informal type of advocacy is social support advocacy. It occurs without reference to specific individuals. An example of social support advocacy is campaigning for a school board member who supports services for students with disabilities. Social support advocates often work as much to improve attitudes as to improve services. Unfortunately, social support advocacy is often insufficient for addressing the needs of individual students and would probably not be used if parents need to address specific concerns.

INTERPERSONAL ADVOCACY.   Interpersonal advocacy involves members interacting directly with school personnel or other professionals—talking face-to-face. Parents most often engage in interpersonal advocacy, and it can occur during parent–teacher meetings and IEP meetings (Alper et al., 1995). When parents perceive that teachers or other school professionals are not adequately addressing specific problems, they may schedule parent–teacher conferences, call IEP meetings, or meet with the school principal to discuss problems.

As a teacher, your ability to communicate with parents and develop relationships with them will have a significant influence on outcomes when problems are discussed. Following are some important points:

- Take time to develop positive relationships with parents. When meetings are scheduled, be prepared and establish rapport with parents.
- Help family members clarify concerns and define the nature of their child's needs.
- Strive to understand the problem the parents present, and consider all solutions discussed at meetings.
- As alternative solutions are considered, strive to reach consensus regarding priorities. Evaluate all acceptable alternatives with the parents.
- If necessary, request assistance and support from individuals who could help resolve problems. For example, the cafeteria worker could ensure that a child has a safe place to sit in a school cafeteria, or the yard supervisor could protect a child from being bullied.
- During meetings, listen empathetically and be responsive to parents' concerns. (Alper et al., 1995; Dunst, Trivette, & Deal, 1988)

When teachers are responsive to parents' concerns, both parties can usually resolve problems. In the event that parents perceive teachers, administrators, or other service providers are not responsive to their concerns, parents may initiate legal advocacy. Legal advocacy begins when interpersonal advocacy fails.

LEGAL ADVOCACY. Parents can initiate legal processes at any point when they are unable to reach agreements with school personnel. Legal proceedings provide parents a way to address perceived violations of their or their child's rights. Parent advocates most frequently address school violations that are associated with the following rights (Alper et al., 1995):

- Review of educational records
- Prior notice of assessment
- Removal of inaccurate records
- Notice of changes in educational programs
- Comprehensive evaluations
- Reevaluations every 3 years or when warranted
- Independent evaluations when district evaluations are questioned
- Education in least restrictive environments
- Support services in inclusive settings
- Participation with nondisabled peers in nonacademic activities

Family members have a right to request an impartial due process hearing if they believe their rights have been violated. During hearings, family members and school personnel present their positions before an impartial hearing office or panel. The judgment of the hearing office is binding unless the family or school appeals the ruling to a state hearing. Both parents and schools are entitled to appeal state rulings in court systems.

Although parents may perceive that advocacy is necessary to ensure their child's needs are met, advocacy can be both beneficial and detrimental to families. If parents perceive that their advocacy efforts enhance coping and solve problems (e.g., they acquire more information, gain accesses to services that they or their child needs, cooperate with professionals, and feel empowered), they are more likely to engage in advocacy on behalf of their child (Wang et al., 2004). On the other hand, advocacy has its costs. Advocacy typically involves adversarial struggles, which can cause stress and anxiety for parents. Parents may think that they are "coming up against brick walls" when they try use advocacy in school systems, or "that professionals react negatively" (Nashshen, 2000, p. 45). In a research study, a parent stated the following: "You need to go back and fight so your child has a fair shot at this education just as much as every other student in the building" (Hess, Molina, & Kozleski, 2006, p. 152).

Teachers should strive to understand the parents' perspectives. Most often, parents' motivations are good, and they are doing their best to nurture and care for their child. How teachers respond to parents' advocacy matters. When parents viewed professionals as cooperative partners in their advocacy efforts, their advocacy was related to decreased stress and increased quality of life. On the other hand, when professionals reacted negatively to advocacy, parent advocacy resulted in increased stress (Nachshen, 2000). The reaction of professionals is critical to parents' perceptions of the relationship of advocacy and stress or improved quality of life. Cooperative partnerships are preferred relationships. Instead of perceiving parent advocacy as a threat, parent advocacy can be perceived as beneficial for children and schools. Parents' efforts can benefit not only their children, but other children as well (see Parent's Voice, Figure 3.2). Table 3.1 provides a list of suggestions for educators to use in facilitating parent advocacy.

TABLE 3.1	Tips for Facilitating Parent Advocacy

Take action to support parent advocacy
- Become an agent of change within your school system.
- Speak up for the interests of students and their families.
- Ask families about the roles they would like to assume in their child's education.

Take action to improve the quality of the child's education
- Provide families with information during all phases of interventions and service delivery processes.
- Provide supports to promote students' access to general education curriculum.
- Work with families to achieve IEP goals.
- Provide families with information about their child's educational program.
- Focus on improving your skills for effectively instructing students with disabilities.

Take action to improve partnerships
- Listen to families without being judgmental.
- Protect families' privacy.
- Express differences of opinion in ways that do not promote conflict with family members.
- Treat family members as equal partners in decision-making processes.

Source: Adapted from Wang, Mannan, Poston, Turnbull, & Summers (2004, p. 153). Copyright granted © 2004 Research & Practice for Persons with Severe Disabilities; TASH.

Parents as Learners

Parenting involves on-the-job learning. As an infant grows into a toddler, preschooler, young child, and adolescent, parents learn about themselves and their children and often redefine their roles. Parents are presented with new concerns and challenges with each new stage of development and must continually adapt their skills and understanding of the child. Gestwicki (1987) identified implications for working with parents that include the following:

- Parents need additional support from teachers as they develop parenting skills to match the changing needs of their developing children.
- Positive feedback and recognition of parents' parenting skills helps parents develop a positive sense of themselves as parents and enhances self-efficacy.
- Teachers need to treat parents as individuals as well as parents and to be prepared to work with parents of many different ages and stages of personal identity. (p. 33)

Some schools create family centers that provide information and services that support parents. Family support centers may be small (e.g., occupying a corner of a school library) or large (e.g., occupying several rooms or housed in separate buildings). Regardless of the size or type of center, the purpose of family support centers is to provide a place where parents can go for training and support and to access resources and services they need. At some family support centers, parents may borrow books, videos, educational games, and software. Through parent support centers, schools can also sponsor classes and support groups for parents. Parents benefit when schools provide them information about community services and how to access resources they may need in caring for their child. Such information can help parents develop better parenting skills and can foster supportive school relationships.

Teachers can also offer support to parents of children with special needs by researching and communicating with local parenting groups in collaboration with the family. For example, a parent of a child who is both deaf and blind may need access to information and services. A search of the Internet quickly reveals resources that can serve as a support system for the parents, such as DB-LINK (http://nationaldb.org/), a national consortium on deaf-blindness sponsored by the U.S. Department of Education, Office of Special Education Programs. The consortium offers information on local parent training and state resources.

Parents as Teachers

Given that parents hold extensive knowledge not only about their children, but also about the culture in which they were raised, parents can be excellent resources for teachers when developing individual education programs and educational goals. Teachers need to recognize the "teacher" within the parents, who can provide insight in the planning, development, and implementation of educational programs. A connection between the home and school increases the effectiveness of education.

Parents can be instrumental in helping children develop positive attitudes about schoolwork, and you can help parents and extended family members gain knowledge about supporting education at home. As the classroom teacher, you can describe to parents the content that is covered at school and suggest ways that they can help with homework. More than other children, children with disabilities will need support at home when completing homework. You can help parents understand how to best support their children at home. Table 3.2 provides a list of homework tips for parents.

TABLE 3.2 Tips for Parents	
Parent Tip	**What to Do**
Make sure the child has a quiet place for completing homework.	Turn off the TV when your child is completing homework, and minimize environmental distractions (i.e., people coming and going).
Provide the materials the child needs to complete homework.	Have paper, pencils, the computer, and other materials available when your child begins homework.
Help the child learn to manage time.	Establish routines for completing schoolwork. Manage your child's schedule so that the child has time to complete homework before bedtime and before the child is fatigued. Help the child plan how to complete large projects.
Be positive about homework and help the child understand how homework is relevant to his or her life.	Discuss the importance of home-learning with your child. As your child completes work ask, "Why do you need to do this?" Help the child make connections between schoolwork and real life.
When the child does homework, do your own homework.	When your child is doing homework, show the child that adults learn at home as well. If the child is reading, read one of your books. If the child is completing math problems, you can pay bills or balance a checkbook.
When your child asks for help, provide guidance, not answers.	Giving your child answers may hinder the child from learning. Instead, help your child find answers by teaching him or her how to find information in books or on the Internet.
Stay informed about your child's school assignments.	Ask the teacher about homework expectations and policies. If your school uses Internet programs for reporting students' progress, log onto your child's account to be informed about completed and turned-in assignments.
Encourage your child to make and keep a homework checklist.	Children with disabilities often have difficulty with organization. Create a homework checklist that helps the child determine how long an assignment will take, how to prioritize assignments, materials needed to complete work, and a schedule for work completion.
Before beginning homework, encourage the child to decide which assignments are easy and which ones are hard.	Learn about your child. If it is easier for your child to complete simple assignments first, then have your child identify assignments that he or she can complete without assistance and do those first. However, if your child fatigues easily, it may make more sense for the child to complete more difficult assignments first and to save easier assignments for later.
Provide support to help a child get started with a task.	Children with disabilities often encounter problems beginning tasks. Clarify directions, or monitor your child as he or she completes the first problem of an assignment. Praise the child for focusing attention and for beginning to work.
Watch for signs of frustration and failure.	Encourage your child to take short breaks. If your child is consistently frustrated with homework, discuss your concerns with the child's teachers.
Reward progress in homework.	Consistently reward your child for working hard and for completing homework. Rewards can be simple such as going to the park or praising the child for good work.

Sources: Cooper & Gersten (2002); All Kinds of Minds (2006).

1. Read to your child.
2. Have your child read aloud to you every night.
3. Monitor your child's reading so that the child does not practice making mistakes.
4. When your child makes a mistake, point out the word and help the child read it correctly.
5. After a child has corrected an error, have the child go back and reread the entire sentence to make sure the child comprehends the sentence.
6. As your child reads, point out spelling and sound patterns such as cat, pat, and hat.
7. Have your child retell what happens in a paragraph, page, or chapter.
8. To check understanding, pause occasionally and ask your child questions about the characters or events in the story.
9. Before reading a story, or as the child is reading, encourage your child to make predictions about what will happen next.
10. After reading a story, have your child summarize the story.

FIGURE 3.1 Ten ways to support reading in your home

In addition to helping with homework, parents can also support reading development. Most children with learning disabilities and other mild disabilities will experience difficulty learning to read. Although parents are not expected to become reading teachers at home, you can provide suggestions for ways they can help their child become a better reader. Figure 3.1 is an example of reading suggestions you can give to parents (Cooper & Gersten, 2002).

In encouraging parents to support learning at home, you should evaluate your own behavior to ensure that you are supporting families. When students need textbook information to complete assignments, make sure that textbooks are sent home. Parents cannot assist their children when they do not have access to needed information. If specialized materials are needed for completing an assignment, provide the materials. Do not expect parents to purchase or locate materials. Make certain that assistive technology devices used at school are available for home use. Effective strategies used at school should be communicated to parents so that they can implement them at home. At the beginning of the school year, establish routines for bringing homework home and returning it to school, and inform parents about homework routines so that they can help monitor their child's performance (Office of Special Education Programs, 2001).

Greenwood Elementary was undergoing systematic seismic upgrades while classes were in progress. Mrs. Juarez, the parent of a student with attention-deficit disorder and asthma, noticed the impact of noise and dust in the classrooms. Mrs. Juarez was concerned about the effect the construction had on her child's ability to effectively learn and shared her thoughts with the school administration. Although the principal politely recognized her position, the principal did not respond to her concerns. Not satisfied, and feeling somewhat dismissed by the administration, Mrs. Juarez contacted the school board and was invited to present her concerns at the next school board meeting. Mrs. Juarez' presentation alerted the school board to the problem and also clarified the nature of the problem. The school board made a decision to conduct an environmental review of the conditions in the school.

As a result of the review, the school board established a new policy on construction of schools. Essentially, schools in the district were required to complete internal construction projects when school was not in session. A significant shift in policy resulted from a concern from a parent who was willing to be an advocate for her child.

FIGURE 3.2 Parent's voice—Advocacy for children

PARENT AND FAMILY CHARACTERISTICS

Fathers

When we refer to "parents," we don't tend to differentiate between mothers and fathers. Yet, mothers and fathers often assume different roles parenting their children, and they may respond in different ways to a child's disability. When initially informed of a child's disability, fathers may respond less emotionally than mothers. Fathers may focus on long-term concerns, and mothers may focus on their concerns about childcare. As fathers learn of their child's disability and adjust to the child's condition, many fathers adapt well. They accommodate the child and grow from their experience. Fathers' positive adaptation is important in a family. A father's reaction to a child's disability may be related to how other family members accept or reject a child with disabilities, and the father's reaction may also set the tone for family members in the home (Seligman & Darling, 2007).

Fathers can provide emotional and physical support for all family members, or if they experience difficulty accepting a child's condition, they may contribute to family stress. If a father has difficulty adjusting to a child's disability, the father may decrease family involvement and adopt avoidance behaviors. When fathers withdraw, not only is the child affected, but also the entire family suffers. A mother's burdens may increase as the mother is forced to cope with the demands of caring for the child and for other children in the family. Children in the family may lose opportunities to develop relationships with their father. For example, of his father, one child stated the following, "Already busy, [dad] became a workaholic. He left the house at six or six-thirty in the morning to prepare for his clients, and returned at seven-thirty at night with his briefcase full" (Greenspan & Wieder, 2003, p. 368).

Fathers may withdraw for a number of reasons. It may be difficult for fathers to express their feelings about their child's condition. In many cultures, fathers are not socialized to express feelings, and fathers may suppress their emotions. In one study, Lillie (1993) reported that fathers withdrew in part because of (a) their inability to cope with children with disabilities, and (b) female domination of service delivery systems. In schools, teachers should welcome fathers and encourage their involvement at school and in their child's academic development. The following list provides suggestions for involving fathers at school.

1. Greet fathers as they drop off or pick up their child.
2. Invite fathers as well as mothers to participate in class activities such as field trips.
3. Ask fathers for their suggestions on ways they can become involved at school.
4. Keep noncustodial fathers informed of a child's progress.
5. During meetings, be sure to solicit both the father's and mother's opinion when discussing a child's education program.
6. When asked, provide fathers and mothers with at-home suggestions for enhancing their child's development.

Mothers

Mothers tend to assume different roles than fathers. Generally, mothers assume more of the day-to-day care responsibilities than fathers (Pelchat, Lefebvre, & Perrault, 2003). By assuming more responsibilities for caring for a child with disabilities, the mother's workload may increase. A mother who is already busy working and caring for her family has more work if she assumes most of the responsibility for meeting the child's needs.

Mothers may assume that role for a number of reasons. If a couple adopts traditional roles (i.e., the father works outside the home and the mother cares for children, or both parents work and the mother works and cares for children), then the mother would perceive that caring for the child and meeting the child's needs was her responsibility. Mothers may also believe that fathers are not as capable of providing adequate care for the child and that they are more qualified. Fathers might confirm that belief if they are reluctant to become "fatherly" and actively engage in childcare responsibilities (Pelchat et al., 2003).

When a mother has a child with disabilities who has significant needs, the roles the mother assumes may create stress. One of the author's colleagues, who is enrolled in a doctorate program and has a toddler with hearing impairments, shared that every time his son's speech therapist comes to their home, the therapist leaves a list of "to do's" for the mother. Although the mother wants to help her son, she feels stressed by the added responsibility of incorporating speech therapy into family routines. Although the mother feels a bit overwhelmed, she believes that helping her son learn to speak is more her responsibility than her husband's.

Mothers' behavior and their relationships with their children tend to receive more scrutiny than fathers'. Historically, it has not been uncommon for mothers to be identified as the cause of a child's problems. Until the 1960s, it was not unusual for "refrigerator mothers" to be blamed for their children's autistic behavior (Ryan & Runswick-Cole, 2008). Professionals, school personnel, and the general public tend to scrutinize mothers and make them the subject of surveillance more than fathers. As an educator, you will interact with mothers of children with disabilities. As you interact with them, consider the following:

- What assumptions are you making about the mother of the child? Do you assume that the mother is supportive of the child, a neutral influence in the child's life, or a contributor to the child's problems?
- What are your expectations for the mother? Are your expectations reasonable, considering the mother's other responsibilities?
- Do you alleviate stress for the mother, or do interactions with you generate stress in the mother's life?
- How can you work with the mother to support the child's education?

Isolated Parents

Parents of children with disabilities may have needs for connecting with others and feeling part of communities. Parents of children with special needs often encounter unforeseen restrictions, which may lead to social isolation. For example, rather than simply calling on a neighborhood teenager to care for their child for an evening, parents may need to hire a specialized caregiver, which limits the frequency with which the parents interact with other adults. In other situations, a child's inappropriate behavior, such as public tantrums, may limit family activities in public places (e.g., zoos, stores, parks) and restrict opportunities for social interactions in communities. In addition, parents feel alienated from school systems when school personnel are not responsive to a child's needs, or when their culture is different than the culture of the majority of school personnel.

- ***Parents may perceive that their experience raising a child with disabilities isolates them because others may not relate to their experience.*** Woodgate, Ateah, and Secco (2008) interviewed parents of children with autism. In their study, parents reported feeling isolated because they perceived that society did not understand their child (see Parents' Voice, Figure 3.2). Parents even felt disconnected from family members who seemed to lack understanding of the parents' experience or who failed to provide support and assistance when needed.

• ***Parents may isolate themselves when their child behaves inappropriately.*** Depending on a child's disabling condition and the severity of the condition, a child my exhibit inappropriate behaviors at home and in public. A child may exhibit aberrant, hyperactive, or impulsive behavior at home, but the situation may become worse when the child is in a setting other than home. As a result, parents may avoid taking their child places where the child is likely to exhibit inappropriate behaviors. In one study, 29% of children with severe learning disabilities showed aggression toward others, and 27% presented self-injurious behaviors. Children with learning disabilities may experience difficulty sleeping, which is correlated with higher incidence of daytime behavior problems in children (Benderix, Nordstöm, & Sivberg, 2007; Woodgate et al., 2008; Woolfson, 2004).

• ***Parents may feel alienated at their child's school.*** When parents and teachers have discrepant views of a child, differences in their perspectives may create home–school conflicts. Parents often feel frustrated when they perceive that school personnel do not understand their child, or when teachers consistently describe the child from a deficit-model perspective (i.e., emphasizing the child's limitations; Lake & Billingsley, 2000). If parents perceive that school personnel have a limited understanding of their child's condition and the child's overall needs, their feelings of isolation may be intensified.

• ***Immigrant families or families whose primary language is not English often experience a sense of isolation in the community, whether or not a child has special needs.*** Immigrants and English language learners are often living with isolation as they adapt to a new language and establish understanding of the new culture. The added dimensions of navigating the world of special needs can be an overwhelming experience. Teachers can actively support and respond to immigrant families and those who are learning English by creating opportunities to communicate with and understand all families. In an effort to be culturally responsive to family needs, teachers should seek opportunities to connect with families on both a formal and informal basis.

Recruiting classroom volunteers is one way to involve families in the school community and is an avenue for addressing parents' isolation. Involving family members as volunteers is discussed in Chapter 7. In addition to recruiting parents as volunteers,

---

- The school is stigmatizing my son. The resource person said I should not expect other kids in Grade 1 to buddy with [my son who has autism]. They are saying, "Why would another kid want to play with your kid?"
- We have no life; we only have a program [referring to the applied behavior analysis program].
- Maybe my husband would not like me using this word, but really, the total brutality of how parents are treated [by childcare agencies]. You are really made to feel like an outsider in your child's life (Woodgate et al., 2008, pp. 1078–1079).

FIGURE 3.3 Parents' comments

communicating with families on an ongoing basis is essential for maintaining relationships and helping parents feel connected to the school community. Making home visits is one way to communicate with families and to demonstrate concern and caring. When teachers visit students in their homes, home visits allow teachers to understand their students better. During a home visit, a teacher might notice that a child is sensitive and adept at caring for animals—something the teacher would not observe at school. Visits in a student's home may also be more comfortable for parents if there are cultural barriers or if the parents have had negative experiences in schools.

Although there are many benefits of home visits, there are disadvantages as well. It may be difficult to schedule home visit, and the visits may be time consuming for a busy educator. Some families may regard home visits as intrusive, and families in poverty may be embarrassed to have teachers visit their homes (Carter & CARDE, 2003). In some cases, it may not be safe for teachers to make night visits or to visit families alone. It may, therefore, be necessary for teachers to visit families in teams and to take precautions to ensure their personal safety. In all situations, teachers should be sensitive to a family's needs and the feelings of family members.

Extended Family

According to Bronfenbrenner's ecological perspective, children live within a complex ecosystem composed of many layers of influence, including the extended family (Bronfenbrenner, 1979). The role of the teacher is to effectively incorporate the layers of influence on the child into a cohesive unit of support. When teachers limit their involvement with the family to just one parent, they also limit their understanding of the family and, therefore, limit the comprehensiveness of their approach to education. More often than not, other family members are involved in the care of children with disabilities. Teachers' efforts to involve and work with extended family members can enhance a child's education.

More than other extended family members, grandparents probably provide the most support to families who have children with disabilities. In a study of 120 mothers of children with profound and intellectual disabilities, 45% of grandparents provided help with childcare, 40% gave advice and encouragement, 16% helped with household chores, and 15% provided financial assistance (Heller, Hsieh, & Rowitz, 2000). In another study, Green (2001) described how grandparent involvement affected parents of children with disabilities. Based on survey and interview data, Green reported the following:

1. Grandparents help parents access more sources of support. For example, grandparents may help parents find a tutor for a child with reading disabilities.
2. Grandparents help parents have more positive feelings about their child's condition. Their involvement in the child's life communicates hope.
3. Grandparents can generally do more than asked. However, they believe that parents won't ask for their help because of their age and needs.
4. Grandparent involvement helps normalize parent's perceptions of their parenting. When grandparents engage in typical grandparent activities (e.g., taking grandchildren to the zoo), the grandparents' example helps parents have more normalized views of parenting their child with disabilities.

Given that grandparents can enhance family functioning and coping, you should welcome them in your classroom. Children with disabilities might be especially proud to have Grandma or Grandpa come to their class or accompany them on a field trip.

Although grandparents can offer significant support for parents who have children with disabilities, they can also exacerbate family stress if parental relationships with grandparents are strained. Sometimes grandparents experience guilt related to a child's disability, or they may be in denial about a child's condition, which creates more stress for parents. You should be sensitive to the dynamics of family relationships and how extended family members respond to disability.

More than likely, you will have opportunities to interact with grandparents. As social structures change, more grandparents are assuming custodial responsibility for grandchildren, and many provide childcare for working parents. Grandparents' situations may be different than that of parents, and they may need different types of support from teachers.

- ***Grandparents who raise children with disabilities may not have anticipated parental roles later in life.*** Generally, grandparents look forward to the time when intense parenting ends, and they may experience difficulty adjusting to altered expectations (Kornhaber, 2002). Grandparents may need emotional support and encouragement.
- ***Grandparents may appear naïve in their perceptions and expectations of school processes.*** If a grandparent did not have a child with disabilities, the grandparent may not understand special education laws or processes. Ensure that grandparents understand special education processes and procedures.
- ***Grandparents may not have the same resources to help a child academically that parent might have.*** Grandparents might also have fewer resources in terms of time and energy to help with a child's education. Consequently, grandparents may rely more on teachers to meet a child's educational needs than would parents.

Nontraditional Families

According to the United Nations, "families assume diverse forms and functions from one country to another, and within each national society" (United Nations, 1994). Recognition of the diversity of families at the international level reflects a growing understanding that families encompass a variety of forms with a multiplicity of members. Nontraditional families commonly seen today include teen and single parents. In addition, teachers may find foster, multigenerational, and gay or lesbian families as part of the classroom community. The varied configuration of families within the United States was recognized by the Children's Defense Fund (2004) to include

- 60% of mothers of preschoolers who work outside the home
- 33% of children who find themselves living in poverty before they reach adulthood; 20% of children who are born in poverty
- 25% of children who are in single-parent households
- 20% of children who are immigrants or the child of an immigrant
- 12.5% of new mothers who are teenagers

With such diverse individualization within parenting roles, the family may be the most adaptable human institution. At the same time, given such diverse forms of family composition, teachers need to be prepared for as wide a range of family composition as possible. Teachers should be prepared to develop relationships with differing forms of families who bring a unique identity.

SINGLE OR TEEN PARENTS.   When developing relationships with teen or single parents, teachers need to maintain an open perspective of their ability to provide a healthy and supportive home. Particularly in the case of teen parents, assumptions are made in relation to the skills and maturity of these individuals. With single parents, assumptions about the gender of the parent or levels of isolation or poverty may surface. However, just as children represent a variety of temperaments and skill levels, so too will parents. These parents might find themselves struggling with issues of poverty and a sense of isolation from peers and family. Equally, they might also hold strong social ties, enjoy the support of family, and have a keen dedication to adapting to the role.

FOSTER FAMILIES.   Adaptation to new roles is particularly evident in foster families. Children entering foster families encompass a range of abilities and disabilities embedded with often traumatic personal histories. Clausen, Landsverk, Ganger, Chadwick, and Litrownik (1998) reported that approximately 75% of school-aged foster children have behavioral or emotional disorders. Placement of children in foster homes not only increases the level of trauma children are experiencing, but also thrusts foster parents into existing interventions that they must understand in a short time frame as they adapt to home-based strategies.

The families in which foster children are placed experience variations in terms of duration of custody and legal responsibilities. As a result, foster parents may not be fully included in collaborative processes with the intervention team due to legal restrictions placed on their authority. Consequently, teachers need to ensure that the role of these parents is clearly articulated prior to altering or implementing strategies for the child. Unfortunately, legal restrictions combined with the role of the custodial parent can result in foster families being dismissed or only involved at a superficial level, thus in effect becoming an invisible population in educational processes.

GAY OR LESBIAN FAMILIES.   One category of parents that has traditionally been an invisible minority is gay or lesbian populations. As with other family compositions, these families are not standardized in their history or personal experiences. Children within gay or lesbian families represent compositions found in every family, yet discrimination and social impediments restrain many parents from sharing their personal experiences. Considering that 6 to 12 million children have families with a gay or lesbian parent (Lamme & Lamme, 2003), teachers need to guarantee that classrooms and special needs support systems are not biased in approach.

Teachers can work to actively ensure that all parents and children are respected and valued, regardless of personal diversities. Welcoming children's families, photos, and stories from home and employing antibiased practices in the classroom not only supports inclusion for children with special needs but also supports acceptance of their families. More discussion about diverse families appears in Chapters 5 and 6.

SIBLINGS

Indisputably, a child's disability has a significant impact on parents, as well as on typically developing siblings. Unfortunately, children exist in a world "in which adults determine child needs through extensive surveillance and empirical study," which "gives authority to the adult/expert while eliminating the child as an agent in his/her own life" (Cannella, 1998, p. 160). Teachers need to consider the authentic experience of all children, particularly that of siblings of children with disabilities, who will probably need support and encouragement. Teachers can support the growth and development of siblings by providing appropriate information, acknowledging their feelings, and providing supportive attention.

Working with Siblings

PROVIDE INFORMATION.   Parents have the responsibility of informing their children about a sibling's condition. However, some parents may experience difficulty accepting a child's condition and may not provide their children with information to help them understand their sibling. When parents are unable to or do not provide information for their children, the siblings may seek information on their own. Children may ask you questions that they would not ask their parents.

Although teachers should not be intrusive in family relationships, providing information helps siblings cope with a brother's or sister's condition. Protecting siblings and withholding information from them can be more taxing for children than they have a clear understanding of a brother's or sister's disability. Children's reasoning skills develop as they mature, and without information, young children may develop misconceptions about disability. For example, young children are egocentric and think that things happen because of them. They may erroneously conclude that because they thought or did something "bad" (such as hit the family cat), a sibling was born with a disability. Or, a child might think that he or she can "catch" intellectual disabilities in the same way that the child can catch a cold (Siegel & Silverstein, 2001). Age-appropriate information can reduce a child's anxiety and self-blame.

You can help all students in your classroom learn about disabling conditions. Children's literature is a great resource for teaching children about different type of disabilities. Using children's literature to teach about disabilities allows children to discuss and deal with sensitive issues in ways that are nonthreatening (Prater & Dyches, 2008).

ACKNOWLEDGE FEELINGS.   As children learn about a sibling's condition, information may help them deal with conflicted feelings. It is normal for children to bond with siblings. In fact, sibling relationships are often the most enduring relationships in an individual's life. However, relationships can be complex, especially when a child's sibling has a disability. The child may feel protective of the sibling and may even provide care for a disabled sibling. On the other hand, the child may be embarrassed by the sibling or even be teased and bullied because the child's sibling has a disability. Although parents may wish to spare siblings from any embarrassment associated with a sibling with a disability, most children go through stages when they are easily embarrassed, and these experiences may be unavoidable. If siblings express feelings about a brother or sister, their feelings should be acknowledged without judgment.

GIVE ATTENTION.   Sibling relationships ebb and flow, and it is not uncommon for siblings to vie for their parents' attention. When a child has a sibling with a disability, parents may devote more time and attention to caring for the child with the disability than they devote to other children in the family. A sibling may feel somewhat neglected in the process. Teachers and caregivers should be sensitive to a child's need for attention and affirmation. Teachers can support a sibling's developing sense of self (separate from the

When her sibling with developmental disabilities began attending her preschool, Audrey began acting out. Before her sibling, David, attended school with her, Audrey was well adjusted and happy at school. After David joined her class, Audrey exhibited signs of anger and jealousy. Audrey's parents consulted a therapist, and the family therapist recommended that Audrey's teachers listen respectfully to her feelings when she expressed anger, jealousy, or resentment. The therapist emphasized the importance of providing positive attention when Audrey exhibited appropriate behaviors, such as cooperating with others or being helpful in class, and suggested that the teachers take advantage of opportunities to appreciate Audrey's traits and interests. The therapist also thought it would be appropriate for the teachers to help Audrey understand that although her world included her brother, she had her own identity and place in the classroom (Brodkin, 2006).

FIGURE 3.4 A sibling's experience

role of sibling to a child with a disability) by providing supportive attention and connecting with the child's interests.

Sibling Concerns

Siblings of children with special needs warrant special consideration by teachers. Although little research has been conducted, some research suggests that, as with parents, siblings may be susceptible to anxiety and depression. Teachers and families can offer support through understanding the unique experience of these children and recognizing the roles in which they find themselves.

SIBLING CARETAKERS. Siblings are often put in the caretaker role and may feel responsible for not only the safety, but also the socialization of their sister or brother with special needs. This can become a problem if a child is too immature to assume such responsibility. Although Audrey (see Figure 3.4) was expected to look out for her sibling at school, the child was too young to assume that role. Siblings should not become overburdened with caring and socialization responsibilities. Siblings need opportunities to connect with friends and to engage in independent interests and activities so that they have opportunities to develop normally and become emotionally healthy.

For many siblings, there is an understanding that eventual responsibility for the care of their brother or sister will rest with them. As parents age, siblings often assume the role of primary caregiver, and they usually oversee medical services and provide social support. The care for their sibling can become a lifelong responsibility to which childhood experiences become an introduction. Facilitating sibling achievement of healthy independence serves to guide future roles.

SIBLING INTERPRETERS. Siblings from culturally and linguistically diverse families may assume the role of interpreter for their family. A child from an immigrant family may be the only means by which the parents or other family members can effectively communicate with teachers. The sibling may attend school planning meetings or medical consultations to translate conversations for his parents. Concomitantly, the sibling may develop a unique connection with his or her brother or sister. A sibling may develop the ability to decipher her brother's or sister's need and then assume the role of communicator for a brother or sister. Although it may be necessary for a sibling to assist family members in understanding the child with the disability or in communicating for the family, that is a tremendous responsibility for a young child and may burden the child emotionally. Educators should not expect children to assume the role of interpreter at school and should take responsibility to arrange for translators to attend meetings and to translate classroom information into a family's native language.

IDENTIFYING SIBLING DIFFICULTY.   Issues with sibling well-being are obvious concerns for parents and teachers. However, as with the process of assessing disabilities, it can be difficult for adults to accurately identify functioning issues for siblings. Adults need to take into account all facets of a sibling's experience when considering why a display of depression or stress, for example, might be exhibited. Not all symptoms or indicators reflect siblings' relationships or experiences with their brothers or sisters who have disabilities.

Figure 3.5 outlines a sibling loop that adults can utilize in exploring points of concern and in identifying situations that might be a source of difficulty. The steps involved include

1. Observing the sibling and noting changes in behavior (changed moods, altered sleeping habits, and negative attitudes toward school or family).
2. Gathering information at school and at home.
3. Interpreting information within the context of the child's community. For example, if a child recently had a falling out with a good friend, the difficulty with the friend could explain mood changes or a negative attitude toward school.
4. Developing appropriate interventions for behavior concerns.

Typically, children will move through periods of malaise or uncertainty as they seek their own identity. With the added dimension of disability in the family, teachers and families should be cognizant of additional pressures for siblings and make every effort to support their optimal growth and development.

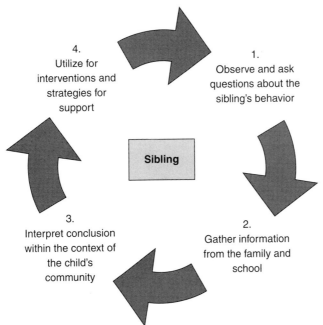

FIGURE 3.5   Sibling loop of intervention

Summary

- Parents assume many roles including that of learner, teacher, and advocate as they care for children with disabilities.
- Educators can support parents by responding to their concerns and by providing information and services that address families' needs.
- Fathers and mothers may respond differently to their child's condition, and educators should be sensitive to parents' responsibilities when interacting with parents.
- Educators can expect to work with grandparents and other guardians of children with disabilities.

- One cannot make assumptions about family dynamics based on family configuration; traditional and nontraditional families need support from educators.
- Siblings of children with disabilities may need information and attention from educators.
- Educators should be sensitive to the needs of siblings and not expect then to take on roles they are not developmentally able to assume.

Linking Standards to Chapter Content

After reading this chapter, you should be able to link basic knowledge and skills described in the CEC Standards and INTASC Principles with information provided in this text. Table 3.3, Linking CEC Standatds and INTACS Principles to Major Chapter Topics, gives examples of how they can be applied to each major section of the chapter.

TABLE 3.3	Linking CEC Standards and INTASC Principles to Major Chapter Topics	
Major Chapter Headings	CEC Knowledge and Skill Core Standard and Associated Subcategories	INTASC Core Principle and Associated Special Education Subcategories
Roles of Parents	1: Foundations ICC1K7 Family systems and the role of families in the educational process. 2: Development and Characteristics of Learners ICC2K4 Family systems and the role of families in supporting development. 9: Professional and Ethical Practice ICC9S12 Engage in professional activities that benefit individuals with exceptional learning needs, their families, and one's colleagues.	1: Subject Matter 1.11 Special education teachers have knowledge of the requirements and responsibilities involved in developing, implementing, and evaluating individualized education programs (IEPs), individualized family service plans (IFSPs), and individual accommodation plans (IAPs) for students with disabilities. 10.10 Special education teachers understand the impact that having a child with a disability may have on family roles and functioning at different points in the life cycle of a family.

(continued)

TABLE 3.3 (continued)		
Major Chapter Headings	**CEC Knowledge and Skill Core Standard and Associated Subcategories**	**INTASC Core Principle and Associated Special Education Subcategories**
Parents as Advocates Parents as Teachers Siblings Extended Family Nontraditional Families	3: Individual Learning Differences ICC3K4 Cultural perspectives influencing the relationships among families, schools, and communities as related to instruction. 8: Assessment GC8K3 Types and importance of information concerning individuals with disabilities available from families and public agencies. 10: Collaboration ICC10S3 Foster respectful and beneficial relationships between families and professionals. ICC10K2 Roles of individuals with exceptional learning needs, families, and school and community personnel in planning of an individualized program.	3: Learning Styles and Differences 3.03 All teachers understand that a disability can be perceived differently across families, communities, and cultures based on differing values and belief systems. 3.09 Special education teachers actively ask questions, seek information from others, and take actions to guard against inappropriate assessment and identification of students whose cultural, ethnic, gender, and linguistic differences may be confused with manifestations of a disability. 9.00 Reflective Practitioner 9.04 All teachers reflect on the potential interaction between a student's cultural experiences and their disability. 10 Collaboration and Relationships 10.04 All teachers accept families as full partners in planning appropriate instruction and services for students with disabilities and provide meaningful opportunities for them to participate as partners in their children's instructional programs and in the life of the school. 10.08 Special education teachers include, promote, and facilitate family members as partners on parent–professional, interdisciplinary, and interagency teams. 10.09 Special education teachers collaborate with families and with school and community personnel to include students with disabilities in a range of instructional environments in the school and community.

Sources: Council for Exceptional Children (2005); Interstate New Teacher Assessment and Support Consortium INTASC Special Education Subcommittee (May 2001).

Web Resources

INTERNET SUPPORT—ORGANIZATIONS

http://www.childrennow.org/index.php/—Children Now is a national organization focused on public policy.

http://www.childrensdefense.org/—The Children's Defense Fund focuses on the needs of children living in poverty, minority children, and children with disabilities.

http://www.childtrends.org/—Child Trends provides fact sheets and reports on early childhood topics, including poverty, working with families, and parenting topic areas.

http://www.familysupportamerica.org/—Family Support America provides a wide range of information and supports for families.

BOOKS FOR SIBLINGS

Koplow, L., & Velasquez, E. (1991). *Tanya and the Tobo man: A story for children entering therapy.* Washington, DC: Magination Press.

Maguire, A. (1995). *We're all special.* Santa Monica, CA: Protunus.

Meyer, D. J. (Ed.). (1997). *Views from our shoes: Growing up with a brother or sister with special needs.* Bethesda, MD: Woodbine House.

Pulver, R., & Wolf, E. (1999). *Way to go Alex!* Norton Grove, IL: Albert Whitman

Thompson, M. (1992). *My brother Matthew.* Bethesda, MD: Woodbine House.

TEACHER RESOURCES

PRINT RESOURCES FOR FAMILIES

Barrera, R. M. (2001). Bringing home to school. *Scholastic Early Childhood Today, 16*(3), 44–50.

Berger, E. H. (2004). *Parents as partners in education: Families and schools working together* (6th ed.). Upper Saddle River, NJ: Merrill/Pearson Education.

Burke, P. (2004). *Brothers and sisters of children with disabilities.* London: Jessica Kingsley.

Dunst, C., Trivette, C., & Deal, A. (1988). *Enabling and empowering families: Principles and guidelines for practice.* Cambridge, MA: Brookline.

Turnbull, A., Turnbull, R., Erwin, E., & Soodak, L. (2006). *Families, professionals, and exceptionality: Positive outcomes through partnerships and trust.* Upper Saddle River, NJ: Merrill/Pearson Education.

CHAPTER 4

Communicating and Collaborating with Families

OBJECTIVES

After reading this chapter you will

1. Describe the purposes and benefits of collaboration.
2. Explain the role of parity, common goals, trust and respect, styles of communication, and cultural influences on collaboration.
3. Discuss barriers of communication and collaboration and strategies for avoiding these barriers.
4. Describe ways to demonstrate collaborative attitudes.
5. Demonstrate understanding of active listening skills and appropriate nonverbal communication.
6. Discuss effective verbal language skills in context of collaborating with families.
7. Discuss ways to reduce miscommunication with family members.
8. Explain the steps of problem solving and negotiating.
9. Describe the different conflict management styles.

INTRODUCTION

Mr. and Mrs. Juarez adopted 6-month-old David as their first child. They were thrilled to become parents. The Juarezes loved their son and wanted the best for him. When David started school, he experienced considerable difficulty acquiring basic academic skills such as learning letter names and sounds. It was hard for him to write, and he was frequently distracted in class. David's kindergarten teacher suspected he had a disability and referred him for assessment. Although Mr. and Mrs. Juarez gave their consent for testing, they knew very little about special education services. When the IEP team meeting was held, and the assessment team recommended that David be placed in a special school, Mr. and Mrs. Juarez didn't know what to do. They didn't know what their options were, and they didn't understand why David couldn't be educated at their neighborhood school. They asked if they could visit the school before making a decision. They were told that they couldn't because of confidentiality issues and that the placement was appropriate for David. The special education teacher indicated that the sooner David was placed in the special school, the better. His development was significantly delayed, and he needed the services the school offered. By the end of the meeting, David's parents felt overwhelmed. Although they had noticed that David had difficulty learning how to do new things, they hadn't considered that he had disabilities. They thought that he just needed more time and practice to learn new skills. The diagnosis of developmental delay was surprising to them, as was the recommendation to place David in a special school. They thought that they should trust the teachers, but they needed time to understand the situation and to evaluate their options. Mr. and Mrs. Juarez wanted to make the decision about David's placement with the teachers—not have the teachers make decisions and inform them of what they had already decided (Personal communication, 2007).

Effective communication and collaboration are critical skills for special educators. Mr. and Mrs. Juarez would not have been so overwhelmed and confused if the school personnel had helped them feel more a part of the decisions for their son, David, and communicated better the purpose of the meeting and the options for David. Within this chapter we identify the factors that are necessary for true collaboration and productive communication to occur between school personnel and family members. The overall goal is to achieve collective empowerment for all parties involved. We begin with a brief overview, followed by a discussion of specific collaborative and communication skills.

OVERVIEW OF COMMUNICATING AND COLLABORATING WITH FAMILIES

The role of families of children with special needs as it relates to communicating and collaborating with school professionals has changed in the past few decades. Even as late as the 1950s and 1960s, families who had a child with a disability were themselves referred by professionals for counseling and psychotherapy. The underlying theory was that if the child was not typical, the parents would also have issues that only more professionals could solve (Turnbull, Turbiville, & Turnbull, 2000). During this time, professionals had power over parents. That is, professionals' decisions about children were absolute. Parents' input was generally not solicited nor considered. This attitude continued through the 1970s, as the psychotherapy model transitioned to more of an emphasis on parent training and involvement. This occurred concurrently with the many changes in the educational opportunities offered for individuals with disabilities through the Education of All Handicapped Children Act of 1975 (Downing, 2008; Turnbull et al., 2000). Again, however, professionals continued to have the upper hand, maintaining a position of power (or the *power position*) when working with families of students with special needs, as they *trained* parents on what to do with their own children.

In the 1980s, families increasingly influenced the way students with disabilities were provided services in the school and the community, and the concept of *family-centered approaches* became more prevalent (Dunst, 2002). As family-centered practice became more popular, the power between professionals and parents shifted from one of a *power-over* situation to one of a partnership, in which both parents and professionals have some power to decide the issues to be addressed and the resources to be provided (Turnbull et al., 2000). The new focus on families emphasized the need to recognize family choice, family strengths, and family resources.

Collaboration and communication increased and improved during the 1990s and moved the family–professional partnership more toward one of "collective empowerment." *Collective empowerment* may be described as a model that "assumes power-through family-professional partnerships" (Turnbull et al., 2000). A key element of this approach includes opportunities for families and professionals to participate in equal decision-making processes. The relationship between families and professionals is equal, not subordinate or hierarchical.

Over time, parents of children with disabilities have played many roles. For example, they have been viewed as the cause of their child's disability, organization members, service developers, recipients of professionals' decisions, teachers, political advocates, and educational decision makers (Turnbull, Turnbull, Erwin, & Soodak, 2006). With the movement toward collective empowerment, a new role of *partner* was added to the list of roles. However, such a role requires collaboration and communication with families.

Many school professionals, especially those who have been teaching a long time, may find it difficult to embrace the paradigm shift required to move from a *power-over* relationship to the *power-through* situation necessary for a real partnership (Osher & Osher, 2002). Likewise, many other communicative, collaborative, and cultural factors can influence the success of this endeavor from both families' and professionals' perspectives (Harry, 2008). Traditional special education programs in the past that have lacked meaningful parent participation have not been successful (Correa, Jones, Thomas, & Morsink, 2005). Therefore, many professionals support increased teacher preparation in the areas of teamwork, collaboration, and communication between families and professionals.

Regardless of the individuals involved, for effective collaboration and communication to occur, all participants must understand the key terms and minimize their use of jargon. Even when individuals are speaking the same language, misunderstandings may occur if words are misinterpreted (Walther-Thomas, Korinek, McLaughlin, & Williams, 2000). Therefore, we define two important terms that will be used throughout this chapter.

- *Collaboration.* "Interpersonal collaboration is a style for direct interaction between at least two coequal parties voluntarily engaged in shared decision making as they work toward a common goal" (Friend & Cook, 2009, p. 5). The focus of this chapter will be on the collaboration between families and school professionals, to include the benefits, barriers, and strategies involved.

- ***Communication.*** Communication is "the act of transmitting, giving, or exchanging information, or the art of expressing ideas" (Dettmer, Dyck, & Thurston, 1999, p. 6). Typically a sender transmits a message to a receiver. Communication is critical to the success of collaboration, and as such, we devote a large part of this chapter to examining communication skills, barriers, and needs.

Purpose of Communication

People communicate on a regular basis for a variety of needs that include physical needs (e.g., hunger), identity needs (e.g., to know who we are in comparison to others), social needs (e.g., to relate to others), and practical needs (e.g., to achieve a desired goal or give information to others; Adler, Rosenfeld, & Proctor, 2009). In the context of educators and families communicating, the more specific purposes may include sharing information, identifying and achieving educational goals, making requests, and problem solving (Minnesota Parent Center [MPC], 2000a). Because children with disabilities often have special issues that affect both home and school, the need for more frequent and more in-depth communication between both parties increases. Without strong communication, there can be no true collaboration.

Purpose and Benefits of Collaboration

MUTUAL SUPPORT.   The positive interaction between families and school personnel can result in numerous benefits to all three parties: the families, the educators, and the students themselves. The more parents share in decision making with teachers, work to create and achieve common goals, and communicate regularly with school professionals, the more research has found that those parents actively and confidently support schools and school professionals (MPC, 2000a). In addition, as parents' opinions are sought and valued by school professionals, parents in turn begin to value the opinions of school personnel to a greater degree (Walther-Thomas et al., 2000). Families who collaborate with educators report being more willing and able to enforce rules at home and to have a more positive attitude about their children attending postsecondary education (MPC, 2000a).

SHARED KNOWLEDGE.   School professionals also benefit from increased collaboration with parents. Teachers often need to be reminded that although they have contact with a child 5 days a week for the school year, most parents, families, and guardians are with the child daily for 18 or more years. Walther-Thomas and colleagues (2000) wrote, "[S]chools that are truly family-centered recognize that families are the constant in students' lives while educational systems and personnel are continually changing" (p. 76). Thus, the benefits of collaborating with parents include learning information about a child's past or current abilities that can positively influence the classroom. This information can aid teachers in creating appropriate instructional, behavioral, and social activities for the child. Learning more about a family's personal goals, cultural influences, and areas of strength can also help educators when working with a child with a disability (Harry, 2008; Murawski & Spencer, in press).

SUPPORTED STUDENT LEARNING.   Most important, students benefit when parents and teachers collaborate. When educators and providers work together, students have been found to have increased homework completion, improved academic performance (Turnbull et al., 2006; Walther-Thomas et al., 2000), and reduced absenteeism and disciplinary problems

Javier recently moved to the United States from Mexico. He lives with his parents and four other siblings and has a strong support system and extended family in the area. He is determined to be the first child in the family to attend college. If Javier told the teacher his goal, she could use the information when communicating with his parents. Then, both the teacher and Javier's parents could work together to help Javier develop a plan to achieve his goals.

FIGURE 4.1   A Case Study

(Walther-Thomas et al., 2000). Family members who communicate regularly and demonstrate that they value that communication are modeling effective communication skills for their children. As positive behavior support strategies are used consistently at home and school, students' positive behaviors increase. With the support of home–school collaboration, even friendships among children can improve (Downing, 2008; Turnbull et al., 2006).

COLLABORATIVE PRACTICES

Collaboration and Communication with Families

Family life is complex. Like ripples in a pond, what happens in one aspect of a child's life is certain to have an impact on many other areas, including the educational arena (Poston et al., 2003). As discussed in Chapter 2, home and school can be perceived as overlapping spheres of influence, and school professionals must be aware of changes and occurrences in a youngster's life. To do this requires ongoing communication and collaboration with the child's family. Effective communication hinges on an openness and willingness to communicate, and teachers' and parents' attitudes and beliefs about children's education affect collaborative endeavors. Effective communication and collaboration do not just happen. Effective collaboration requires parity, trust, and respect, as well as the use of appropriate styles of communication. Teachers and parents also need skills to negotiate differing agendas and cultural differences when working together to plan and support education. A discussion of each of these elements follows.

PARITY.   Parity, or equality, is a key aspect of developing a collaborative culture. If participants in an interaction do not feel that they are on equal footing with one another, they tend not to participate as actively or to value the interaction as highly (Friend & Cook, 2009). Family members and school personnel both need to have an equal say in decision making and an equal feeling of power in their ability to influence outcomes of children and families if they want to be able to collaborate effectively (Friend & Cook, 2009; Jackson & Turnbull, 2004).

Developing relationships with families and communicating parity takes time and effort. Parents and teachers have different perspectives. The following summarizes benefits and challenges in achieving parity in parent–teacher relationships.

Parents' Perspectives
- Parents respect teachers' opinions and value interactions when they have close relationships with teachers.
- Parents value teachers who become confidants and friends that they can turn to after school hours.

Teachers' Perspectives

- Teachers recognize the value of close relationships with families. However, it can be emotionally draining for teachers to establish close relationships with parents of all their students.
- Attending to a family's at-home needs can be overwhelming for teachers (Nelson, Summers, & Turnbull, 2004).

Thus, although parity is a goal to strive for, parents and teachers may both need to adjust expectations when working together.

COMMON GOALS.   Having shared values and common goals makes collaboration easier for parents and teachers. With shared goals, parents and teachers realize that they are working together for the common good of the child (Snell & Janney, 2005). Too often in the past, individuals at the school level have assumed the role of *expert,* telling parents about their children rather than asking them or talking to them about the child. "The fact that professionals are typically in a position of power in relation to the families they serve is a built-in barrier to learning from those families" (Harry, 2008, p. 384). Taking time during meetings to articulate and discuss common goals de-emphasizes the teacher's role as an expert and creates opportunity for parents to provide input and participate in planning and implementing their child's education.

TRUST AND RESPECT.   Communicating respect is important because individuals who do not trust and respect one another are not likely to engage in open collaboration. Both parties should seek to earn respect and demonstrate trust. Parents of children with disabilities have often had negative experiences with schools, sometimes resorting to fighting to get services to which they believe their children are entitled (Blue-Banning, Summers, Frankland, Nelson, & Beegle, 2004). When school professionals come to meetings armed with voluminous reports, completed recommendations, and descriptions of the child's failure, family members can become discouraged and question the value of their input in the process. Many parents report feeling devalued and disrespected by service providers and, therefore, less willing to engage in collaborative efforts (Zionts, Zionts, Harrison, & Bellinger, 2003). Educators need to demonstrate through their actions that they value and respect families' input (Blue-Banning et al., 2004; Jackson & Turnbull, 2004; Wang, Mannan, Poston, Turnbull, & Summers, 2004). Jackson and Turnbull stated that trust is "demonstrated through a sense of assurance about the reliability and dependability of the character, ability, strength, and truth of other members of the partnership" (2004, p. 167). For effective collaboration to occur, all members of the interaction need to be able to trust and respect one another (Blue-Banning et al., 2004; Snell & Janney, 2005).

When you interact with parents, you can create an atmosphere of trust by welcoming parents and attending to parents' needs and concerns during meetings.

- ***Greet parents and help them to feel welcome and comfortable at school.*** When parents enter your classroom or arrive for meetings, smile and make eye contact with them. At meetings, sit next to parents instead of sitting across from them. Offer them materials for note-taking. Provide them with copies of all reports. When appropriate, meet parents at the school office and escort them to your classroom. Time spent walking to your classroom is an opportunity to establish rapport with parents.

- ***Keep commitments.*** If you make appointments with parents, keep your commitments. Arrive on time to meetings, and come prepared with materials or information necessary to conduct and participate in meetings.
- ***Be honest with parents.*** To establish trust, you should be honest with parents. When parents ask questions, be truthful and honest. At the same time, be sensitive to parents' feelings and concerns and present information in kind, respectful ways. If parents ask about their child's future, share your professional opinion, but do so in a respectful and gentle manner.
- ***Respect family priorities.*** Teachers need to demonstrate respect for family priorities (Wang et al., 2004). Some parents may not attend school meetings because of financial, cultural, emotional, physical, or work barriers. Educators, who jump to the conclusion that these parents do not care about their children, or about education in general, may bring those assumptions with them into their communications with the parents (Harry, Rueda, & Kalyanpur, 1999). If parents do not perceive that educators respect their priorities, they may not be motivated to address involvement barriers.

STYLES OF COMMUNICATION.   The style of communication can also greatly affect the collaboration between school professionals and family members. In fact, professionals can be totally unaware of how their communication style acts as a barrier, rather than a facilitator for communication with family members (Harry, 2008). Although there are a variety of ways to identify styles of communication, Friend and Cook (2009) promote the categorization system first conceptualized by Schmuck and Runkel (1994), in which they identified communication as *unilateral, directive,* or *transactional.* Educators need to familiarize themselves with the various styles of communication prior to identifying which style is most appropriate for the specific communication and collaboration desired at that moment (Figure 4.2).

- ***Unilateral communication.*** A unilateral communication style is a one-way exchange, such as an announcement, phone message, e-mail, or letter home. Although unilateral communication may be efficient, it may also be limited in its ability to establish a collaborative culture (Adler et al., 2009). For many non-English-speaking parents of students with special needs, the least desirable mode of communication for exchanging important information is generally phone calls (Park & Turnbull, 2001; Song & Murawski, 2005). The unilateral approach would be most appropriate for quick information that can be disseminated easily via letters, memos, posters, or e-mails (e.g., The school dance will be on February 13 from 5 to 9 p.m. in the auditorium. Tickets are $5 each.).

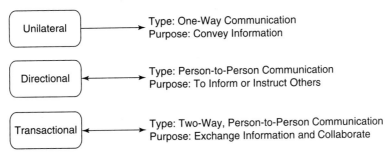

FIGURE 4.2   Styles of Communication

- *Directive communication.* Directive communication involves person-to-person contact and usually resembles consultation more than collaboration. Typically, school personnel are the *experts* or *consultants,* whereas the family member or student is seen as the *novice* or *consultee.* This approach is somewhat *interactive* in nature (Adler et al., 2009) because it involves more than one individual; however, it does not demonstrate the parity evident when two equal parties confer collaboratively. The directive approach is most appropriate when individuals are sharing information about which they are considered *expert* (e.g., a lecture, a teacher describing a unit students are doing in class, a mother explaining her son's interests and chores at home).

- *Transactional communication.* Professionals and families demonstrate the transactional approach when they are willing to listen to and communicate with one another. During meetings or interactions, all parties have input, and all input is equally valued. The open environment enables all participants to feel comfortable, valued, respected, and interested in sharing, as well as listening to what the other party has to say. However, not every interaction needs to be one that is transactional in nature. There are times when the other approaches are more appropriate and time efficient. The style of communication should reflect the purpose for communicating with parents.

CULTURAL INFLUENCES. Cultural factors are a major influence on collaboration and communication between families and schools. In Chapters 5 and 6, we address the major issues in this area; however, it is still important to mention some of the predominant cultural issues that influence home–school collaboration. School professionals need to develop competency in cross-cultural communication; this does not mean simply learning to speak a different language. In fact, the attitudes and beliefs one has about cultural differences often create more barriers to cross-cultural communication than the language itself (MPC, 2000a). Because cultural beliefs and expectations influence the priorities and concerns of families, school professionals must be aware of, sensitive to, and understanding of these varying priorities and concerns. Schools need to provide family members with an environment that is respectful of their culture and their children, and teachers should recognize the difficulties cultural differences can create for parents and children (DeLaTorre, Rubalcava, & Cabello, 2004; Harry, 2008).

Although culture can influence collaborative efforts in many ways, a major influence is the value families place on collaboration and how they believe it should manifest itself. For example, some families may value frequent input from other family members or friends, resulting in children turning more to their peers for support, especially in large classes where the teacher cannot give each child specific attention (MPC, 2000b). On the other hand, despite this value of a collaborative environment, those same parents may not be as quick to collaborate with school officials. Although professionals expect parents to advocate for their child, such advocacy may be against the parents' cultural values (Wang et al., 2004). A family may believe that it is disrespectful to question authority figures, such as a teacher. Thus, they may choose to attend meetings but never volunteer requests, questions, or comments (e.g., Park & Turnbull, 2004; Song & Murawski, 2005). Understanding cultural differences can help educators understand how to work with and help children in a manner that is respectful of the student and his or her family.

Janica's mom, Melisa, works two jobs to support her three children. Because of her work schedule, she rarely has time to attend school events or meetings. Back-to-School night is coming up, and Melisa's children beg her to attend so that she can meet their teachers. Melisa is scheduled to work the night of the event and doesn't feel that she can miss a night's work—so she doesn't go. Janica and her siblings are disappointed. They assume that they are the only students in their classes who didn't go to Back-to School night. Although Melisa felt bad, she wasn't sure that her involvement was valued, or that she could contribute much to her children's education.

You can support parents like Melisa by sending home information or by scheduling meetings when they can attend. Although you may firmly believe that Melisa should attend meetings and support school activities, respecting her priorities communicates sensitivity to her life and circumstances (Friend & Cook, 2009; Wang et. al., 2004).

FIGURE 4.3 A case study

Barriers to Communicating and Collaborating

A person's experiences, interests, cultural background, education, age, and gender, among other variables, influence an individual's *frame of reference* (Friend & Cook, 2009). Because families and school personnel often have different frames of reference when coming together to discuss students, conflicts are bound to arise. Using strong communication skills (both verbal and nonverbal) can help mitigate and avoid some of those issues but being aware of the common barriers that occur when communicating is also helpful. Pugach and Johnson (2002) described actions that create barriers to quality communication. These behaviors often engender miscommunication and become barriers for collaboration.

1. ***Avoid giving unsolicited advice or providing quick fixes to problems.*** Educators are prepared to be problem solvers and are often rightly expected to be the *experts* in educational issues. Teachers may feel that they will be judged as incompetent if they are unable to quickly *solve* an educational issue. This can lead to hasty, and at times ineffective or even undesired, advice. However, advice is more effective if it is sought after, rather than given when it is unsolicited (Friend & Cook, 2009).

2. ***Avoid minimizing feelings through false reassurances, clichés, and so forth.*** School professionals who minimize issues and broadly state that things will work out, without truly paying attention to the parents' concerns, will be viewed as dismissive and uninterested. Quickly dismissing a parents' concern may result in the parent not sharing other important issues in the future. Using clichés is also inappropriate. "Cliches diminish the feelings of the person with whom you are interacting. . . . In virtually no situation is a cliché an appropriate response" (Pugach & Johnson, 2002, p. 99). In addition to demonstrating a lack of true understanding, a cliché can also result in stereotyping and can make others uncomfortable.

3. ***Ask appropriate questions and actively listen.*** Question asking is a skill critical for effective communication. *Misdirected questions* hinder effective communication. Educators who ask too many questions, irrelevant questions, unfocused questions, or the wrong types of questions (e.g., closed vs. open) are likely to find that communication is choppy and unproductive. Practicing good question-asking skills can result in improved family interactions (Figure 4.4).

Mrs. Davies meets with you and expresses concern that her son Jung Su is not organized and frequently misplaces homework and assignments.

Don't Give Advice

"You should buy new binders and teach Jung Su how to be organized."

Do Say

"How can I help at school?" or, "I'm glad you brought that up, I've been concerned Jung Su's organizational skills as well."

* * * * * * * * * * * * * * * * * * * *

When discussing Mikah's reading problems with his parents, the father says, "I had difficulty learning to read when I was a child."

Don't Use Clichés

"The apple doesn't fall far from the tree, does it?"

Do Say

"Based on your experience, what are your concerns for Mikah?" or, "How did you feel about reading?"

* * * * * * * * * * * * * * * * * * * *

Mr. and Mrs. Kuja meet with you and express their worry about their son's temper tantrums. You have observed mild behavior problems in your classroom.

Don't Falsely Assure

"He's still young, that's probably normal. I'm sure he'll grow out of it."

Do Say

"I'd like to know more about what happens at home," or, "Please describe your concerns."

* * * * * * * * * * * * * * * * * * * *

Mr. and Mrs. Kiernan are at an IEP meeting and share that they are more concerned with their son Patrick's social interactions and peer relationships than with the academic side of school.

Don't Dismiss Feelings

"That's something you can address outside of school. My job is to focus on academic learning."

Do Say

"Do you have suggestions for how we can support Patrick's social development at school?" or, "I can understand how that would be a concern for you."

* * * * * * * * * * * * * * * * * * * *

During a parent–teacher conference, you learn that Justin's parents have recently separated.

Don't Ask Inappropriate Questions

"Do you think you're going to divorce soon?" or, "Was infidelity involved?"

Do Say

"Do you have suggestions for how I can support Justin at school?" or, "Do you have concerns for Justin?"

FIGURE 4.4   Examples of communication do's and don'ts.

4. ***Schedule meetings when you can focus your attention.*** Unfocused interactions can negatively affect collaboration and communication. If parents notice that you are distracted and trying to do other work while meeting with them, they will rightfully question your commitment to being collaborative. If you do not have time to discuss important issues with parents or have work to complete at the time of interaction with

parents, share these barriers to time and attention with them. If they catch you at a bad time and it's not an emergency, schedule a specific time to meet with them later.

5. ***Minimize interruptions.*** One of the most frustrating barriers to good communication is constant *interruption*. Interruptions can be external (e.g., phones ringing, people opening the door during meetings) or internal (e.g., team members interrupting each other with comments). The key to addressing both types of interruptions is to be proactive. For example, schedule meetings in places less likely to have interruptions. Place signs on the door stating *Meeting in Progress* and *Do Not Disturb*. Ask all participating team members to put their phone ringers on vibrate, and make certain that other school professionals know that you are not to be interrupted during this time. Do not send text messages during meetings.

Other barriers to effective collaboration relate to individuals' differing agendas or goals. Friend and Cook (2009) define collaboration as "a style for direct interaction between at least two coequal parties voluntarily engaged in shared decision making *as they work toward a common goal* [italics added]" (p. 5). If both parties do not take the time to ensure that they

TABLE 4.1 Collaborative Approaches: Examples of Do's and Don'ts		
Approach	**Do say**	**Don't say**
Describe, don't evaluate	"Johnny has been tardy four times this week."	"Why aren't you able to bring Johnny to school on time?"
Collaborate, don't control	"Let's discuss placement options for Javier. To make a decision, I think it would be helpful if we all discussed pros and cons of the placement options."	"Javier needs to be in a special school. Sign your consent right here."
Be honest, not strategic	"In order to provide the continued support that Sheree needs, I'd like to work with her in the inclusive classroom with other students who are receiving speech and language services."	"I don't think Sheree needs as much individual speech and language therapy with me."
Express empathy, not disinterest	"It sounds like you are worried about how to help your grandson cope with his parents' divorce."	"Well, divorce is hard on kids."
Communicate parity, not superiority	"I have had some classes in behavior management if you'd like to talk about strategies to use at home and school with Jeremy."	"You really shouldn't spank your son. Haven't you ever heard of positive behavior support?"
Use provisional language, avoid definitive statements	"In my opinion, Jiyun will struggle with the academics of a general education class. Can we talk about the level of support Jiyun needs in school?"	"Jiyun will never succeed in a general education class."

are actually interested in the same goal, the result is often wasted time and growing frustration. Although educators and family members enter a conversation with the common goal of *meeting the child's best interests,* this may mean different things to the different participants based on their own frames of reference (e.g., Harry, 2006). Be cognizant of individuals' agendas, and during meetings take time to understand parents' perspectives and agendas.

Collaborative Attitudes

The attitude with which two parties come together affects the success of the collaborative efforts. Gibb (1961) identified behaviors that can support positive collaborative cultures. They continue to be validated by more recent research and literature. An adapted version of these behaviors follows:

- *Use descriptive messages, rather than evaluative ones.* It is easier for others to accept statements that appear to merely describe a situation, as opposed to statements that contain value judgments. Value statements reflect judgments of what should be or should exist (i.e., a child should not be tardy) and are usually expressed in terms of something being "good" or "bad."
- *Use a collaborative message, rather than a controlling one.* Demonstrating to the other person that you are willing to be part of the solution, as opposed to telling them what to do, will more effectively establish a collaborative culture.
- *Use an honest approach, rather than a strategic one.* Forthrightness provides a clear understanding of a child's situation and does not obscure real issues. To create the trust and respect necessary for a strong collaborative climate, an honest approach is best.
- *Use an empathetic approach, rather than a neutral or casual one.* Collaborative climates require participants to understand one another. If one individual feels dismissed, irrelevant, or that the other party is indifferent to his or her concerns, then that person will not feel supported. Both parties need to be sensitive and empathetic to each other's needs.
- *Use an equal approach, rather than a superior one.* Teachers are *experts* in educational practices; parents are *experts* on their children. When working together to create a collaborative culture, both parties need to use statements that demonstrate their feelings of parity, not superiority.
- *Use a provisional approach, rather than a certain, definitive approach.* For a climate to remain positive, open, and communicative, all participants need to demonstrate that they are amenable to one another's ideas. An individual who seems to have a need to be right all the time may unconsciously close efforts at communication. Your communication should reflect your professional judgment but should also identify your statements as opinions, not facts, and should reflect an openness to others' ideas. Do not present opinions as facts, and avoid definitive statements such as *always* and *never.* Use language that informs parents that you are expressing your opinion, such as, "In my opinion, I think that Jeremy would benefit from ..." Ask parents what they think, or invite them to share their perspectives and opinions.

As a final note related to collaborative and communicative climates, remember that each family is different and has its own preferences—even family members within the same family may have differences. A particular Asian family, for example, may wait for invitations to participate in meetings or may only respond to communication rather than initiating it (Song &

TABLE 4.2	Intended Communications	
Type of nonverbal communication	**Communication**	**Purpose for nonverbal communication**
Face, eyes, and touch	A teacher smiles, looks at the parent, and extends her hand to shake theparent's hand.	To communicate friendliness and a desire to collaborate with the parents.
Touch	A mother tells a teacher that her spouse is seriously ill. The teacher touches the mother's arm.	To express sympathy and concern.
Touch and voice	A student is misbehaving, and the teacher holds the student's hand and uses a firm voice to tell the student to stop the behavior.	To communicate displeasure and disapproval.
Dress	A teacher's class is going to a field trip to the beach to study tide pools. The teacher wears jeans and a sweat jacket to school.	To participate in an activity with students.
Dress	A teacher arrives at an IEP meeting dressed in slacks, a button-up shirt, and a jacket.	To project a professional attitude toward work and collaboration.
Silence	During a meeting, a teacher asks parents if they have any comments. The teacher waits for the parents to respond.	To allow parents to contribute to meetings.

Murawski, 2005), but this does not mean that all Asian families will have the same preferences. Furthermore, even within that same family, the father may prefer to communicate via e-mail, the mother may want to communicate face-to-face, and the grandparents may wish to use an interpreter. Some families view frequent communication as necessary for collaboration, whereas other families may have time, work, and other pressures that make regular communication difficult. Thus, some families may be perfectly content with less frequent, yet still completely collaborative and positive, communication. In all situations, educators must identify the needs, goals, and preferences of each family with whom they wish to collaborate. Just as educators are familiar with the need to adapt to children's learning styles, we should be willing to adapt and be flexible to the communicative preferences of family members. "How do you learn about a family's preferences for communication? Simply ask" (Turnbull et al., 2006, p. 197).

COMMUNICATION SKILLS

Communication is such an integral part of our lives that most of us don't consider how we communicate, and we don't pay attention to skills we use when we communicate. As a professional, you should evaluate your skills and identify areas in need of improvement to work effectively with parents and families of students with disabilities. Figure 4.5 summarizes purposes for communicating and facets of effective communication.

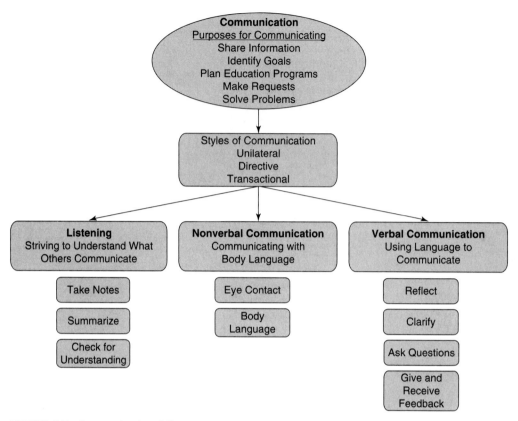

FIGURE 4.5 Communication skills

To ensure that communication is accurate and unambiguous, educators must also master foundations of good communication, including both verbal and nonverbal language (Pugach & Johnson, 2002). The skills involved in strong intra- and interpersonal communication include (a) creating a collaborative climate, (b) listening, (c) using nonverbal communication, including silence, and (d) using a variety of verbal language skills effectively (e.g., reflecting, clarifying, asking questions, giving and receiving feedback). In this section, we discuss active listening, nonverbal communication, and verbal communication.

Active Listening

Active listening is an important skill for any special educator. For individuals to feel their input is valued, they need to know that others are truly listening to them (Murawski & Spencer, in press). Active listening requires work and may not come easily, but there are techniques educators can use to improve these skills. First, school professionals need to consider the *location* of the interaction. A busy hallway right before class starts is not a good place for a quality conversation between teacher and parent. In situations like these, the teacher should ask the parent if they can reschedule the conversation at a time and place in which active listening can take place. The environment should be a quiet one, when the teacher is not feeling rushed, and when he or she can take notes on the conversation and respond appropriately to parents' concerns.

Mr. and Mrs. Weber scheduled a meeting with their son's third-grade teacher, Ms. Cox. When they arrived at Ms. Cox's classroom, she had Jared's folder on a table and was prepared for the meeting. When the special education teacher joined the meeting, Ms. Cox closed the classroom door and focused her attention on the parents. Ms. Cox began the meeting by greeting the parents and asking them to describe their concerns. The Webers told Ms. Cox and Mr. Jimeniz (the special education teacher) that they had noticed that Jared had difficulty comprehending stories. They related that when they read with him at home and asked him questions about stories they read, he had difficulty answering simple questions. The Webers were worried that Jared would fall farther behind in school if the problem wasn't addressed. Mr. Jimeniz acknowledged the parents' concerns. He said that although Jared was making good progress in basic reading skills, comprehension was still a problem. Ms. Cox agreed with Mr. Jimeniz' observations and asked the Webers if they had suggestions for addressing the problem. Mrs. Weber shared that when she read with Jared and previewed stories (looked at pictures and talked about the pictures before reading), Jared seemed to understand stories better. Mr. Jimeniz said that he had been teaching Jared comprehension strategies and thought his reading group would benefit as well. The Webers appreciated the teachers' willingness to help Jared and said that they would spend 30 minutes a day reading with him.

FIGURE 4.6   A case study

- ***Take notes to aid in active listening.*** Because teachers are bombarded with information daily about the students with whom they work, information can be lost or forgotten if it is not written down. In addition, in this day and age of documentation, educators will find it helpful to refer back to their notes to ensure accuracy, reduce chances of miscommunication, and summarize the information back to parents to demonstrate that they were listening.
- ***Summarize, paraphrase, clarify, and check for understanding when conversing with parents.*** These techniques will be discussed in more detail in the section on verbal language. We include them here because they are critical strategies for attentive listening. When teachers reiterate the main points of the conversation to family members, it shows that they were listening, and it helps to ensure that both parties share an understanding of the conversation. Wait until the other party has completed their thought and then restate, "What I'm hearing you say is . . ." This allows the provider to agree or disagree with the restatement (Figure 4.7).

Barriers to active listening include trying to conduct too many conversations at one time or trying to address too many issues simultaneously. Informal conversations that occur in the hallway or when educators are not fully focused can also lead to poor listening and poor content retention. Meetings that are scheduled too close to the teacher's class or other commitments result in educators glancing at the clock or appearing distracted,

You may find the use of *mnemonics* and other memory devices helpful in connecting information given in a conversation with information you already may have. For example, if parents come to a meeting and share numerous events that have clearly affected them emotionally, you may mentally number each event when listening. Then, to demonstrate that you were paying attention, you can respond by saying, "Wow. I can see how this month has been a real struggle for you and Gavin; I can't imagine how I would react if I had to deal with those four different issues. I really appreciate you sharing these with me so I can better understand why Gavin has been having such a hard time focusing and doing his work this month."

FIGURE 4.7   Teacher tip for communicating with parents

both of which are nonverbal messages to parents that the teacher is not actively attending to the interaction. Finally, all parties need to understand the purpose for the communication and the rationale for their involvement (Murawski & Spencer, in press); otherwise, a major barrier to listening will arise—a feeling from one or more of the participants that this doesn't relate to me, so I don't need to pay attention.

Nonverbal Communication

Facial expressions and body language can communicate desire and willingness to understand another person's perspective. Nonverbal communication has a greater impact on communication than use of language. In fact, up to 90% of the content of a message is conveyed through vocal inflections and nonverbal behaviors (Thomas et al., 2001). Nonverbal signals are strong indicators of good—or poor—communication skills (Snell & Janney, 2000).

   Researchers have well established that behavior has a communicative value (Albin, Dunlap, & Lucyshyn, 2002; O'Neill, Horner, Albin, Storey, & Sprague, 1997). Nonverbal communication can be demonstrated through more than just eye contact and paralanguage (e.g., minimal encouragers). Types of nonverbal communication involve (a) face and eyes, (b) body movement, (c) touch, (d) voice, (e) proximity and territoriality, (f) time, (g) physical attractiveness, (h) clothing, and (i) environment (Adler et al., 2009). Most educators are aware that facial expressions, eyes, and body movements communicate feelings and attitudes. Tone of voice, the use of silence, dress, and environmental factors also communicate information, attitudes, and feelings to others. The use of silence, in particular, is an effective nonverbal tool. Silence enables all parties to reflect and consider the information that has been shared. It also provides an opportunity for all persons to participate, especially those who have been quiet up until this point. Educators need to work to resist the urge to fill all gaps in conversation or moments of silence with more words. Often, parents who have been reluctant or too shy to ask questions or seek clarification will seize these opportunities to do so.

   For all types of nonverbal interactions, intended and unintended messages are conveyed to others. Table 4.3 illustrates what can be purposefully and inadvertently communicated through nonverbal communication.

   Nonverbal behaviors can have an enormous effect on the success of collaborative interactions. During interactions, pay attention to your nonverbal behavior and the nonverbal behavior of parents (Adler et al., 2009). In evaluating parents' nonverbal behavior, you should be aware of stereotypical interpretations that may be inaccurate. For example, although crossed arms may be seen as a signal that a teacher or parent is closed off and less willing to communicate, it may also mean that the individual is cold or simply is comfortable with crossed arms. Eye contact is highly valued in mainstream American society, and individuals who cannot maintain eye contact are characterized as shifty, uncomfortable, shy, or disinterested. However, individuals may be from cultures that believe that direct eye contact is disrespectful and that they are showing their respect and absolute interest in conversations by averting their eyes. In addition, some family members may themselves have disabilities that affect various social skills. Even nonverbal minimal encouragers, such as a nod or eyebrow raise, that are designed to indicate listening and interest may vary in their use. Tannen (1990) demonstrated that the use of minimal encouragers often varies by gender; females tend to use them liberally to encourage continued conversation and show interest, whereas males often state

TABLE 4.3	Unintended Communications	
Type of nonverbal communication	**Communication**	**Unintended Message**
Silence	At a meeting a teacher asks for comments, but quickly ends the meeting when no one speaks up immediately.	The teacher does not value the contributions of others.
Dress	A teacher wears a T-shirt and faded jeans to a meeting with parents.	The teacher is not concerned about her professional image.
Environment	A teacher asks parents to sit at a table in the back of her classroom. The table is covered with papers. The teacher has to move papers to make room for the parents.	The teacher is disorganized and doesn't value the parents' opinion.
Proximity	At an IEP meeting, a teacher moves her chair to sit right next to a mother. The teacher's chair touches the mother's chair.	The teacher does not understand professional boundaries.

that they believe they are showing more active listening by not interrupting at all. As in each of these cases, strive to understand students' parents so that misunderstandings are minimized.

Verbal Language

Educators constantly use language to communicate with others. Although some miscommunications are probably unavoidable, you can utilize techniques that will help reduce the frequency of miscommunications. Reflecting, clarifying and checking for understanding, and summarizing are ways to enhance the quality of verbal interactions. In addition, how questions are asked, the feedback provided to others, and the use of leading strategies can facilitate or hinder future communications.

REFLECTING.   When reflecting, teachers rephrase or restate (also known as *paraphrasing*) what the speaker has said, including any affective or emotional aspects of the statements made. In reflecting what others say, do not add information or opinions or provide feedback. The purpose of reflecting is to demonstrate to the speaker that you are employing active listening and that you understand what has been said. Reflecting can help the speaker clarify meaning, assist the receiver to ensure that he understands the critical intent of the message, and allow both parties to check that they have the same interpretation of the conversation. When understanding has been achieved, individuals can have more in-depth discussions of issues.

Reflecting should not, however, feel like a parroting of the speaker's words, the result of which may be that the speaker becomes annoyed by a sense of psychobabble or pseudo-listening. For example, consider the following interaction.

Mrs. Smith states, "I'm very concerned with how my son Darien is doing in your class."
     The teacher reflects, "You're very concerned with how Darien is doing in my class."
     Mrs. Smith continues, "Yes. I think he can do better." The teacher repeats, "You think he can do better."
     At which point, Mrs. Smith may respond, "That's what I just said!"
     The teacher could have reflected, "You're frustrated that Darien is not doing as well as he could in my class."

The aforementioned example demonstrates how reflection often involves capturing the affective component of the statement (Friend & Cook, 2009) or what is being implied (e.g., the parent is most concerned about his performance in class). Stating the implied is a helpful communication skill but must be used with care to avoid making excessive assumptions; communicators should have a solid rapport prior to engaging in this technique (Pugach & Johnson, 2002).

CLARIFYING.   Unlike reflecting, which is mainly restating ideas or verbalizing what has been implied, clarifying involves checking for understanding. As previously discussed, there are numerous opportunities for miscommunication among educators and family members based on cultural factors, frame of reference, differing goals or agendas, and so forth. Thus, teachers should frequently check for understanding. School professionals should be open to admitting that they do not understand information or that they did not get all the information because their attention was elsewhere for a moment. Given that one misunderstanding may lead to many more, immediately ask for clarification when you do not understand something that has been said. A benefit of using clarifying statements is that parents may recognize that asking for clarification is a welcome communicative device (see Figure 4.8).

SUMMARIZING.   Summarizing statements or interactions is a great way to clarify what someone has said and discussed. Summarizing typically takes place after a substantial part of the interaction has taken place. Two main reasons exist for summarizing an interaction. First, it provides all parties involved an opportunity to hear the key points. They can then agree or disagree on what was said. If there is disagreement, then revision can take place by

---

Read the following statements, and identify which statements parents would and would not understand. How would you check for understanding and clarify meaning for the parents?

1. "I'm concerned that Javier may have an SLD. And if he does, we'd like to hold an IEP meeting to determine if this class is really his LRE. I'll try to schedule it for next week when the LEA will be in town and can attend the meeting. As long as we're going to assess Javier, I'll have the SLP assess him for language difficulties, that way we're covering everything and should have all the information we need for qualification."
2. "We've tested Eldon's reading ability and he scored fairly low in his ability to hear sounds in words. In scoring low in sound awareness, it's not that Eldon doesn't hear sounds and has a hearing problem; he hears sounds but has difficulty separating different sounds in words. He might think that cat is one sound unit instead of three separate sounds blended together."
3. Rosa scored at the 17th percentile for math reasoning. Her grade equivalent reading scores were 1.2 and 1.9, so I think reading is more of a concern at this point.

FIGURE 4.8 Clarifying understanding

clarifying. Second, summarizing makes public the actions that all individuals need to take, thus avoiding misunderstanding about agreements or next steps (Pugach & Johnson, 2002).

ASKING QUESTIONS.   The manner in which questions are asked during an interaction between school professionals and parents can greatly improve or impede the conversation. Sincere questions are designed to clarify; learn about others' thoughts, feelings, and wants; encourage elaboration; and gather more facts and details. Insincere questions are "disguised attempts to send a message, not receive one" (Adler et al., 2009 p. 121). Using insincere questions, the question asker may try to trap the speaker, make a statement, cover a hidden agenda, seek a *correct* answer, or utilize questions that are based on unchecked assumptions. For example, when discussing placement options for Michelle, an insincere question would be, "So, are we all in agreement that Michelle should be placed in a self-contained classroom?" when in fact, placement has not previously been discussed. For effective communication, individuals need to practice asking sincere questions. A variety of types of questions can be used to elicit information and demonstrate a sincere interest to improve understanding, rather than a masked intent to advise or criticize. Familiarize yourself with the variety of types of questions and practice using each type effectively (see Table 4.4).

GIVING AND RECEIVING FEEDBACK.   Continuous feedback is required in any interaction, as it indicates whether the sender's message has been received or not and, even if it was

TABLE 4.4   Types of Questions

Types of Questions	Definition	Example	Benefits and/or limitations
Closed Questions	With closed questions, limited responses are available. Closed questions include yes/no questions, multiple-choice questions, and questions that require specific answers.	• "Are you satisfied with Christien's progress in math?" • "Would you like him to be in prealgebra, algebra I, or geometry next year?"	Closed questions focus discussions and can be useful when making decisions.
Open Questions	There are no boundaries for answering open questions. Responses will vary from individual to individual.	• "What goals do you have for Christien in math next year?" • "How do you think he has been doing academically?"	Open questions tend to invite more perspectives, support divergent thinking, and encourage more open communication between participants.
Direct Questions	Direct questions are made by a speaker to a specific individual or group of people and are in interrogative form. The questions should be clear and straightforward, avoiding vague language, jargon, or assumptions.	• "What do you think is happening differently in Annalia's math and English classes that is resulting in such varied behavior from her?" • "Does Nicholas have any friends at home?"	Direct questions are straightforward and invite discussion and the exchange of information and ideas.

(continued)

TABLE 4.4   *(continued)*

Types of Questions	Definition	Example	Benefits and/or limitations
Indirect Questions	Indirect questions are phrased in the form of a statement and are typically broad questions that invite a variety of responses.	• "I wonder why Annalia behaves well in math and not in English?" • "It would be interesting to know if Nicholas has more friends when he's not at school than when he is here."	Indirect questions may put family members at ease. They are less formal and may not seem as imposing or threatening. However, indirect questions may lead to misunderstandings, and individuals may not answer if they do not perceive that they are expected to answer.
Single Questions	A single question is one question asked at a time. A teacher or parent asks a question and then waits for a response.	• "Is Joshua required to complete chores at home?" • "Does Angelica bring home her work folder?"	When single questions are asked, the respondent knows what to answer and can focus the response.
Multiple Questions	Multiple questions are numerous questions asked in succession. A person asking the questions does not allow time in between the questions for the respondent to answer.	• "Does Joshua have any chores at home? What type of chores? • Does he seem to do better at morning or evening chores or is he the same at both?"	When multiple questions are asked in succession, a parent or other professional may be unable to process effectively or choose how to answer appropriately. She may choose to answer part of the question, possibly leading to misunderstandings.

Sources: DeBoer (1995); Friend & Cook (2009); Gamble & Gamble (2009); Snell & Janney (2000).

received, whether or not it was received accurately (Pugach & Johnson, 2002). Feedback can be verbal (e.g., "Sure, I can get you a copy of that book I was mentioning") or non-verbal (e.g., a frown, questioning look, or smile). The following is a list of guidelines for providing feedback (Friend & Cook, 2009).

1. *Feedback should be* **descriptive,** *rather than evaluative in nature.* By avoiding judgments, recipients of the feedback are more likely to be open to receiving the information. For example, instead of saying, "You don't help Laquita with her homework enough," a teacher might say, "Laquita has only turned in her homework once a week for the last three weeks."

2. *Feedback should be* **specific,** *rather than general.* The preceding example regarding Laquita demonstrates specificity in the second statement. The teacher has given the parent specific detail regarding how often she has turned in her homework. Now the parent and the educator can look for solutions to this specific problem.

3. *Feedback should be* **directed toward behavior or a situation** *that the individual can change.* Telling a parent who works three jobs that her son might improve his behavior if she were to come and sit in the class a few times a week may frustrate a parent and demonstrate a lack of consideration for her situation. On the other hand, simply saying, "I am open to your input or assistance if you have suggestions," or "How would you like us to collaborate on this issue?" opens the conversation up to possibilities.

4. *Feedback should also be* **concise.** Too many details, extraneous information, irrelevant comments, or redundant observations can impede, rather than clarify, the feedback provided.

5. *Feedback needs to be* **checked to ensure clear communication.** The use of paraphrasing or questions can help ensure that feedback was received as it was intended.

Verbal feedback should be solicited, rather than imposed. In other words, when family members ask for feedback, they are more likely to be receptive to what you say, than if you provide information or feedback that they have not sought. Feedback can be given indirectly (e.g., through notes, messages, or a third party), but this is not recommended. To be most effective and to minimize potential misunderstandings, feedback should be given verbally and in a timely manner. For example, a comment given to a family member in a crowded grocery store on a Friday night, days after an event occurred, would be received differently than if the same comment had been delivered in an appropriate setting the same day the event occurred (Friend & Cook, 2009).

Sometimes feedback is not provided in an effective manner or received as intended. Two indications that misunderstandings have occurred are silence and aggressiveness (Patterson, Grenny, McMillan, & Switzler, 2002). During interactions, if you notice that parents stop talking and become nonresponsive or that they argue with you and become verbally aggressive, miscommunications have probably occurred. A simple technique to clarify meaning is to state what you intended to communicate (e.g., "I wanted to communicate that I am concerned about your child's social skills."), and to contrast that with what you did not mean to inadvertently communicate (e.g., "I did not mean to communicate that I am criticizing your parenting.").

USING LEADING STRATEGIES.   Leading strategies are valuable strategies for individuals who need to facilitate efficient and effective interactions between multiple parties (see Table 4.5). Although the strategies described in Table 4.5 can be very effective in encouraging parties to listen, share, and even to avoid or work through disagreements or difficult moments, the effectiveness of these strategies depends on listening to and trusting one another (DeBoer, 1995).

Reducing Miscommunication

One of the easiest ways to avoid miscommunication is to ask parents how they prefer to communicate. Teachers should avoid phone calls as the primary mode of exchanging important information with parents for whom English is a second language (Park & Turnbull, 2001; Song & Murawski, 2005). However, some parents prefer phone calls to written notes, and others prefer a combination of both approaches. Teachers should identify which families need interpreters or translated materials. For communications that are especially important, school officials should initiate follow-up calls, send letters, or speak face-to-face to check understanding.

TABLE 4.5	Leading Strategies and Examples
Leading Strategy	**Examples**
Explanations: Explanations involves paraphrasing, reflecting, and clarifying to ensure that all parties are in agreement.	"We have been discussing using a token economy with Sarah Grace. Token economies can take many forms. Let's review how it would look at school and how it would look at home."
Encouragement. Encouraging statements are statements that keep the conversation going by validating and supporting behaviors of others.	"As a single parent, it must be difficult dealing with Raudel's aggressiveness at home without any additional support. It's clear that you have been very consistent in your interactions with him. I'm impressed with how much progress he's made."
Assurances. Positive statements and assurances help build confidence.	"I'm excited about the different ideas we've shared. I know that many of them will be effective in working with Liang."
Suggestions. Offering suggestions provides individuals a chance to share ideas without assuming the role of an expert.	"I was thinking that Maria may respond to a peer buddy at school; what do you think?"
Agreement and Disagreement Statements. Agreement and disagreement statements need to be clear, unemotional, and phrased as "I" statements.	"I love the idea of using computer time to motivate Chad!" Or, I like the idea of giving Juli Anna one On-one-time, but I don't see when that can be done without taking away from the other students or having her miss critical academic time."
Spontaneous Humor. Humor used appropriately can defuse tension and help to create rapport. Always consider the context of interactions and individuals' cultures and sensitivities' when using humor.	"You'd think with all of this paperwork that educators have stock in lumber companies."

Good communication does not always mean that parents and school professionals will agree. Understanding is not equivalent to agreement. Misconceptions about communication are common. Adler et al. (2009) identified the following three major areas of communicative myths and misperceptions.

1. *Myth: More communication is always better.* In reality, too much talking can lead to difficulties and be unproductive. In fact, if the communication is all negative, more of it will only result in more negative results. Silence is a key tool in good communication, as it can allow the other members of the interaction to process what has been said and allow them to think about their response.
2. *Myth: Open communication will solve all problems.* Despite accepted wisdom, complete honesty is not always the best policy. Sometimes, it is better not to share honest opinions than to express them. For example, members of an IEP team meeting might be asked to share their beliefs regarding a child's abilities. If an educator honestly states that he does not think the child will obtain a typical school diploma, and the parent disagrees with that educator's assessment of the child's abilities, conflicts may arise. Instead, the educator might describe the child's current abilities, rather than sharing opinions of the child's future.

3. *Myth: Communication is a natural ability.* Most people can communicate without formal communication training. However, most individuals are also communicating at a level far below their potential (Adler et al., 2009). It seems important, therefore, for school professionals to receive instruction in communication skills. If educators want to glean the benefits of communicating and collaborating with families, they need to be adequately prepared in those skills; school administrators who assume that teachers all have an innate ability to do so will inevitably be disappointed.

School personnel can take a variety of actions to demonstrate to families a sincere desire to collaborate. Parents want professionals who are available and accessible beyond specific hours and locations of jobs (Nelson et al., 2004). They want professionals who are willing to take on responsibilities that may appear beyond the strict definition of their job tasks, and they want professionals who act like a friend or part of the family in relating to them or their child (Hughes-Lynch, 2010; Nelson et al., 2004). Although not all these may be possible all the time, school personnel can take steps to be more accessible, responsive, and friendly.

Ultimately, parents want communication that has quantity and quality (Blue-Banning et al., 2004). Many parents prefer to keep the lines of communication open with educators but want their time and boundaries to be respected. The same holds true for educators (Nelson et al., 2004). Although both parties respect the need for ongoing collaboration, each also wants to avoid unnecessary and unproductive meetings, wasteful and time-consuming paperwork, and ambiguous or confusing communications. Schools need to ensure that parents have access to relevant information on their child, and they need to use positive communication strategies for sharing information and evaluations (Turnbull et al., 2006).

Problem Solving

When working with children with special needs, problems are bound to arise. What differentiates a collaborative home–school relationship from an indifferent, nonexistent, or hostile one is the manner in which all parties approach the problem-solving process. Educators who wish to have a productive, nonemotional and effective problem-solving session are wise to familiarize themselves with one of the many approaches available in education and related fields. Employing a structure, such as the five-step process can help all parties stay focused on the problem at hand, rather than resorting to emotion and frustration. All participants in the problem-solving session need to be aware of the steps and structure of the process, so that there is increased buy-in and equal participation by all. Various authors espouse approaches with different steps in the problem-solving process, but many agree on the following five steps as the most important.

1. *Identify the problem.* The first step requires that school professionals and parents agree on the problem. Too often, meetings are called, and it is assumed that everyone knows the reason for the meeting. Unfortunately, this can result in frequent miscommunication and misunderstandings—ultimately harming the communication and problem-solving process, rather than helping it.

2. *Generate potential solutions.* After agreeing on the problem, the team should generate potential solutions. If all participants feel equally valued and believe their input is encouraged, they will contribute more solutions to address the problem.

An IEP meeting is called to discuss Denzel, a fourth grader who has increasingly been fighting other boys and is concurrently failing his classes. At this meeting, the teacher is focused on the fighting and wants to determine why Denzel's behavior has changed recently. She thinks that if the aggressive behavior is addressed, his academic grades will improve. Denzel's parents, however, are not interested in talking about why Denzel might be fighting others; his father is a former boxer and feels that fighting is part of a young boy's rite of passage and that Denzel will grow out of it soon enough. Denzel hasn't had any incidents in the classroom itself. All fighting has occurred at recess, lunch, or after school, so the parents are confused about why the teacher is involved at all. In the meantime, though, they are concerned about Denzel's grades. They have impressed on him that grades are critical, and Denzel's dad states, "That boy knows we don't tolerate bad grades. He gets a whuppin' if he brings home less than a B." The first thing these parents and school officials need to do is agree on the problem that they are meeting to resolve. Is it Denzel's fighting or his grades? Or is it something else? By going through the problem-solving process and discussing their differing views on the problem, they can come to consensus. In this case, both parties agree that they want Denzel to improve his grades, even though they may continue to disagree about how much the fighting was affecting that area of his life.

FIGURE 4.9   A case study

The following bullet points provide some rules for brainstorming that can be extremely beneficial in helping teachers and parents generate solutions for multifaceted problems.
- Accept all ideas.
- Do not eliminate ideas that do not seem feasible.
- Present ideas as "rapid-fire" as possible.
- Generate as many ideas as possible.
- Invite all members of the group to suggest solutions.
- Write down suggestions as presented—do not reword ideas.
- Do not cut off brainstorming prematurely.

3. ***Evaluate the potential solutions.***   After brainstorming potential solutions, participants should determine which ones are feasible. Family members and educators should have equal input into which solutions are reasonable and which are not. Some suggestions may work for teachers but be too much work or time consuming for parents—and vice versa. Other suggestions may be cost prohibitive; all participants need to be willing to be open and honest about the drawbacks they see for each possible solution. At the same time, they need to be open-minded about the possibilities of different options in addressing the problem. Before the end of the meeting, participants need to agree on one or more solutions to the problem.

4. ***Implement the selected solutions.***   Once solutions have been selected and before they are implemented, parents and teachers need to discuss exactly what they will be doing, how they will be doing it, and for how long (Figure 4.10). This step is particularly critical if both the school and the home are involved in the intervention. If, for example, Emma Leigh's parents agree to reinforce her every time she comes home with a signed progress report, the teacher will need to ensure that she signs the report regularly and doesn't run out of time or forget to do it.

5. ***Evaluate the results of the solution.***   After implementation, school officials and family members meet again to discuss the outcomes of the solution and determine whether success was attained. Participants discuss why and how the intervention was or was not successful. This affords both parties an opportunity to build on the

Step 1: Identify the problem. Be specific and clearly describe the problem to be solved.

_____

_____

Step 2: Generate potential solutions. Brainstorm solutions, and list all ideas presented.

_____   _____   _____

_____   _____   _____

Step 3: Evaluate the proposed solutions. Determine which solutions are feasible to implement, and address the needs and interests of all parties involved. List the best solutions.

_____

_____

From the list of solutions, select a solution or solutions that will be implemented.

_____

Step 4: Implement the solution. Determine when and how the solution will be implemented.

_____

_____

Step 5: Plan to evaluate the results. Schedule a follow-up meeting, and discuss and describe how the effectiveness of the solution will be evaluated.

Next meeting: _____

Criteria for evaluating the solution:

_____

Notes:

FIGURE 4.10   Problem-solving process form

success for the future or to examine why the intervention was not effective and what changes need to occur. In either case, it is critical that both family members and educators come back together to assess the progress of the intervention. A common mistake is that team members do not meet again, which can result in later frustrations, ongoing miscommunications, and continuing issues for the child.

Resolving Conflict Constructively

Even when educators and parents effectively work together to plan a child's education or to address problems, conflicts can occur. Any time individuals with different goals or frames of reference come together, such as parents and educators, there is the potential for conflict. Conflict in education is unavoidable and is neither good nor bad. Judgments about conflict determine whether conflict is perceived as having positive or negative outcomes (Knackendoffel, 2005: Murawski & Spencer, in press). In special education, conflicts generally center on the design of educational programs, service delivery, and relationships between professionals and parents (Hughes-Lynch, 2010). Disagreements can arise in many areas such as assessing students to determine eligibility for special education services. Parents and educators may not agree with assessment results or on determinations of eligibility. Making placement decisions and decisions about the type and extent of services students receive can also be areas of disagreement (Hughes-Lynch, 2010). Schools are constrained by budgets, and parents may desire services the school is not prepared to provide. In addition, educators may not deliver services specified in students'

IEPs. Finally, conflicts can arise when trust is violated, communication breaks down, and cultural barriers are not addressed in parent and teacher relationships (Feinburg, Beyer, & Moses, 2002).

To resolve conflict constructively, the conflict must be identified and understood (Morse & Ivey, 1996; Snell & Janney, 2005). Not all conflict needs to be addressed head-on. Some conflict is best resolved through ignoring, particularly conflict that occurs infrequently or is unusual (e.g., a team member acting unusual because of having a stressful day). Other conflict can be handled through indirect confrontation through modeling the desired behaviors or via direct confrontation by applying the problem-solving process steps. Conflict management is a special example of the problem-solving process. The steps of the process, when shared with all the participating parties, help those in conflict remove the emotionality and focus on achieving consensus and resolution. When using the problem-solving process to resolve conflicts, utilizing effective communication skills such as identifying frame of reference, asking questions, and employing active listening facilitates problem resolution.

NEGOTIATING.   Listening and understanding the perspectives of others is critical for negotiating solutions to problems. Although you may not consider yourself a negotiator, you probably engage in informal negotiations every day and don't even realize that you are negotiating solutions to problems. When conflicts arise, negotiation strategies need to be more conscious and deliberate (Knackendoffel, 2005). The following four principles of negotiation can be used when addressing conflicts.

1. *Preserve relationships.* Separate the person from the problem, and strive to understand the other person's concerns.
2. *Focus on interests, not on opposing positions.* The following questions can be asked to identify interests.
   a. Why does an individual want what he or she wants?
   b. What does the individual dislike about your position?
   c. What are common goals or shared interests (e.g., Do both parties want the child to excel academically?)?
   d. Are the individual's interests centered on basic human needs such as security, sense of belonging, control over one's life, or recognition?
3. *Discuss options for mutual gain (emphasize "win–win" solutions).* The problem-solving process involves brainstorming and generating solutions to problems. When resolving conflicts, strive to identify options that are mutually satisfactory (Davidson & Wood, 2004). Refrain from judging ideas before solutions are agreed on.
4. *Use objective criteria for evaluating decisions.* For example, cost or feasibility may be the criterion for making decisions and resolving issues (Knackendoffel, 2005).

CONFLICT MANAGEMENT STYLES.   As individuals encounter problems and enter negotiations to solve them, they generally utilize different conflict management styles. Although a variety of conflict management styles exist (e.g., Cornille, Pestle, & Vanwy, 1999; Rudawsky & Lundgren, 1999; Thomas & Kilmann, 1974), successful educators know that styles can change. In fact, it is wise to recognize that different styles may be needed based on the situation, the people involved, and the desired goals. Therefore, you should become familiar with the advantages and disadvantages of different styles for specific situations (Adler et al., 2009). Styles of conflict management most commonly

Mr. and Mrs. Alonzo's daughter, Rosa, has learning disabilities. For the past 2 years she has qualified for special education services in math and has received remedial instruction in the special education classroom. Rosa's achievement in math has improved to the point that she no longer qualifies for special education services. Although Mr. and Mrs. Alonzo are pleased with Rosa's progress in math, they are concerned that she will fall behind again if she does not have support at school. When her parents meet with the IEP team, they request that Rosa continue to receive math instruction in the resource class. They do not have the means to hire private tutors for Rosa, and they expect the school to provide the instructional support Rosa needs. The special education teacher has a full case load and does not believe that she should continue to provide services for Rosa. Rosa's general education teacher has 30 students in her class, and although she is willing to provide some individualized instruction for Rosa, she doubts that she can provide all the support Rosa will need to continue to progress in math.

Thought questions:

What might threaten relationships in this situation?
What are the parents' interests, and what are the teachers' interests?
What common goals do the teachers and parents have regarding Rosa's education?
What "win-win" options would reflect the interests of the parents and the teachers?
What criteria could be used to evaluate potential solutions?

FIGURE 4.11   Case study problem

used are competitive, avoidance, accommodating, compromising, and collaborating (Friend & Cook, 2009; Knackendoffel, 2005; Ragin et al., 2000). A description of each style follows.

- *Competitive style.* Competitive individuals try to overpower other people. They focus on winning and are not as concerned about relationships. Competitive styles may be appropriate in some situations (e.g., when ethical issues are at stake), but in most cases, competitive styles are not conducive to forming collaborative relationships.
- *Avoidance style.* Individuals who are not comfortable with conflict may avoid confrontations and often appear apathetic or indifferent to the concerns of others. Avoiders may refuse to discuss problems. Avoidance may be appropriate when situations are emotionally charged or when there is not enough time for discussing issues. However, when issues are not discussed, problems can worsen if left unaddressed.
- *Accommodating style.* An accommodating individual tends to defer to others. For teachers, it may be easier in some situations to accommodate the concerns of others than to assert one's own position. Accommodating may be appropriate when issues are relatively unimportant (e.g., a teacher agrees to let a coteacher teach the main part of a lesson). However, if an individual frequently accommodates others, the individual may feel resentment if his or her interests are not met.
- *Compromising style.* Compromising involves negotiating and occurs when both parties give up something (e.g., a teacher may agree to a higher case load if the principal agrees to increase the number of paraprofessionals assigned to the teacher's class). Compromising may be appropriate when there are time constraints for making decisions and resolving problems. With compromising, individuals may agree on solutions in the short term; however, in the long term, individuals may be dissatisfied with compromises, and conflicts may surface again in the future.

• ***Collaborating style.*** Collaborating involves cooperating with others to develop new solutions to problems that meet the goals and objectives of all parties. Although collaboration is the preferred style for working with parents and other professionals, collaboration is often time consuming and may not be appropriate for all situations.

In the past, schools were isolated arenas in which teachers had the final say in the education of children. Doors were closed, and questions were discouraged. In today's more open society, interaction between educators and families is encouraged and, in some instances, even mandated. As has been stated, conflict is bound to arise when individuals with different backgrounds, expectations, interests, and skills interact. The strategies discussed in this section can help you resolve conflicts. Researchers have documented that conflict that is resolved constructively, is managed effectively, and is functional in nature can result in improved outcomes. Such outcomes include developing stronger interpersonal communication, improving clarity of purpose, generating new ideas and decision making, stimulating thinking, and increasing trust (Snell & Janney, 2000; Turnbull et al., 2006). Developing effective conflict resolution skills takes time. In addition to studying and implementing the strategies described in this section in your practice, take advantage of training offered in your school district and plan to expend time and effort to continually refine your communication and collaboration skills.

Summary

- The role of families in communicating and collaborating with schools has evolved over time. Today families and schools work more together than in previous times.
- Collaboration is a style of interaction that involves parity, communication, and mutual goals.
- Benefits of collaboration include mutual support, shared knowledge, and supported student learning.
- Important elements of collaboration include parity, common goals, trust and respect, styles of communication, and cultural influences.
- School personnel can avoid barriers to collaboration by engaging in specific behaviors.

- The attitude with which individuals come together affects the success of the collaborative efforts.
- Educators should master foundations of good communication, including active listening, nonverbal communication, and verbal language.
- When problem solving, educators should avoid emotional responses and rely on a step-by-step process.
- Conflict in education is unavoidable and neither good nor bad. Conflict can be resolved through the application of specific skills.

Linking Standards to Chapter Content

After reading this chapter, you should be able to link basic knowledge and skills described in the CEC Standards and INTASC Principles with information provided in this text. Table 4.6, Linking CEC Standards and INTASC Principles to Major Chapter topics, gives examples of how they can be applied to each major section of the chapter.

TABLE 4.6   Linking CEC Standards and INTASC Principles to Major Chapter Topics

Major Chapter Headings	CEC Knowledge and Skill Core Standard and Associated Subcategories	INTASC Core Principle and Associated Special Education Subcategories
Overview of Communicating and Collaborating with Families	1: Foundations ICC1K4: Rights and responsibilities of students, parents, teachers, and other professionals and schools related to exceptional learning needs ICC1K7: Family systems and the role of families in the educational process ICC1K8: Historical points of view and contribution of culturally diverse groups	1: Subject Matter 1.01 Special education teachers have a solid understanding of the major concepts, assumptions, issues, and processes of inquiry in the subject matter that they teach. 1.04 All teachers have knowledge of the major principles and parameters of federal disabilities legislation
Barriers to Effective Collaboration and Communication	3: Individual Learning Differences ICC3K3: Variations in beliefs, traditions, and values across and within cultures and their effects on relationships among individuals with exceptional learning needs, family, and schooling. 6: Communication ICC6K3: Ways of behaving and communicating among cultures that can lead to misinterpretation and misunderstanding 10: Collaboration ICC10K3: Concerns of families of individuals with exceptional learning needs and strategies to help address these concerns ICC10K4: Culturally responsive factors that promote effective communication and collaboration with individuals with exceptional learning needs, families, school personnel, and community members ICC10S3: Foster respectful and beneficial relationships between families and professionals	3.03 All teachers understand that a disability can be perceived differently across families, communities, and cultures based on differing values and belief systems. 3.04 All teachers understand and are sensitive to cultural, ethnic, gender, . and linguistic differences that may be confused with or misinterpreted as manifestations of a disability 3.06 Special education teachers seek to understand how having a child with disabilities may influence a family's views of themselves as caregivers and as members of their communities 3.07 Special education teachers share the values and beliefs underlying special education services for individuals with disabilities in the United States, with students, families, and community members and seek to understand ways in which these are compatible or in conflict with those of the family and community. 3.09 Special education teachers actively ask questions, seek information from others, and take actions to guard against inappropriate assessment and identification of students whose cultural, ethnic, gender, and linguistic differences may be confused with manifestations of a disability.

(continued)

TABLE 4.6 (continued)		
Major Chapter Headings	**CEC Knowledge and Skill Core Standard and Associated Subcategories**	**INTASC Core Principle and Associated Special Education Subcategories**
		9.07 Special education teachers reflect on their personal biases and influences of these biases on the instruction they provide to students with disabilities, and on the interactions they have with families, and community
Communication Skills	5: Learning Environments and Social Interactions ICC5K8: Ways to create learning environments that allow individuals to retain and appreciate their own and each others' respective language and cultural heritage. GC5S5: Use skills in problem solving and conflict resolution 8: Assessment ICC8S1: Gather relevant background information 9: Professional and Ethical Practice ICC9S8: Use verbal, nonverbal, and written language effectively 10: Collaboration ICC10S7: Use group problem-solving skills to develop, implement and evaluate collaborative activities 10: Collaboration ICC10S10: Communicate effectively with families of individuals with exceptional learning needs from diverse backgrounds	6.05 All teachers are sensitive to the verbal and non-verbal messages they may convey to students with disabilities through their interactions during instruction. 6.06 All special education teachers know how to assess, design, and implement strategies that foster the language and communication development of students with disabilities, including non-verbal and verbal communication. 9.04 All teachers reflect on the potential interaction between a student's cultural experiences and their disability. 10.05 All special education teachers provide leadership that enables teams to accomplish their purposes.
Collaborative Practices	5: Learning Environments and Social Interactions ICC5S1: Create a safe, equitable, positive and supportive learning environment in which diversities are valued 7: Instructional Planning ICC7K4: Technology for planning and managing the teaching and learning environment ICC7S2: Develop and implement comprehensive, longitudinal individualized programs in	6.07 Special education teachers are familiar with a variety of types of assistive communication devices and know how to access support specialists and services within and outside the school setting. 7.08 Special education teachers provide for the active involvement of students, families, and other professionals in constructing the student's education program. 9.05 All special education teachers reflect on the progress of individual

(continued)

Major Chapter Headings	CEC Knowledge and Skill Core Standard and Associated Subcategories	INTASC Core Principle and Associated Special Education Subcategories
	collaboration with team members ICC7S3: Involve the individual and family in setting instructional goals and monitoring progress GC7S4: Select, design, and use technology, materials, and resources required to educate individuals whose disabilities interfere with communication 8: Assessment ICC8S7: Report assessment results to all stakeholders using effective communication skills. 9: Professional and Ethical Practice ICC9S12: Engage in professional activities that benefit individuals with exceptional learning needs, their families, and one's colleagues 10: Collaboration ICC10S4: Assist individuals with exceptional learning needs and their families in becoming active participants in the educational team ICC10S5: Plan and conduct collaborative conferences with individuals with exceptional learning needs and their families	students with disabilities and work with general education teachers, other professionals, and families to consider ways to build on the students' strengths and meet their needs. 10.04 All teachers accept families as full partners in planning appropriate instruction and services for students with disabilities and provide meaningful opportunities for them to participate as partners in their children's instructional programs and in the life of the school. 10.08 Special education teachers include, promote, and facilitate family members as partners on parent-professional, interdisciplinary, and interagency teams. 10.09 Special education teachers collaborate with families and with school and community personnel to include students with disabilities in a range of instructional environments in the school and community.

Sources: Council for Exceptional Children (2005); Interstate New Teacher Assessment and Support Consortium INTASC Special Education Subcommittee (May 2001).

Web Resources

INTERNET SUPPORT—ORGANIZATIONS

www.pacer.org/—PACER is the Minnesota Parent Training and Information Center.

www.allkindsofminds.org/—All Kinds of Minds translates the latest research on how children learn into a framework that educators can use.

www.beachcenter.org/—The Beach Center is designed to enhance the quality of life of families and individuals affected by disability.

http://www.thearcoftexas.org/—The ARC of Texas provides information, support, and services to persons with intellectual disabilities.

http://www.supportforfamilies.org/internetguide/index.html—Support for Families of Children with Disabilities provides Internet resources for families of children with disabilities.

http://www.familyvoices.org/—Family Voices aims to achieve family-centered care for all children with special health-care needs and/or disabilities.

http://www.netnet.net./mums/—MUMS is a national parent-to-parent organization for parents of a child with any disability.

http://www.fathersnetwork.org/—The Fathers' Network's mission is to celebrate and support fathers and families raising children with special needs and developmental disabilities.

http://www.specialchild.com/—Special Child is an online publication for parents of children with special needs.

http://www.ldonline.org/—LD OnLine is the world's leading Web site on learning disabilities.

http://www.bridges4kids.org/—Bridges 4 Kids provides information and referrals for parents and professionals working with children from birth through transition to adult life.

CHAPTER 5

Overview of Diversity Among Families and Professionals

OBJECTIVES

After reading this chapter you will

1. Understand how the demographics of the U.S. population are changing.
2. Discuss the influences of changing demographics on children receiving special education.
3. Explain the varying views of a "family."
4. Describe various family structures and the influence of culture on those structures.
5. Describe how personal values affect interactions among families and professionals.
6. Explain how having a child with special needs shapes family dynamics.
7. Discuss the impact of poverty on culture and education.

INTRODUCTION

The United States has historically been viewed as a *melting pot,* a place where all persons' cultures are combined and assimilated into a mainstream multiethnic culture (Glazer & Moynihan, 1963; Smith, 2010). In a melting pot society, differences are seen as nonexistent as native languages and cultures are abandoned and fused into a mainstream culture. The melting pot concept moves a society from multiple heterogeneous cultures to a single homogeneous culture (Glazer & Moynihan, 1963). Historically, the concept was used to describe emigration processes in the United States in the 19th and 20th centuries. Although the melting pot concept was seen as a way to merge or blend differences, major concerns with the concept included accusations of racism, discrimination, and prejudice.

Over the decades, as politics in the United States have evolved, the melting pot concept gave way to the *salad bowl* concept. Unlike the melting pot concept, the salad bowl concept does not assume that all cultures are assimilated into a homogeneous society (Glazer & Moynihan, 1963). Instead, in a salad bowl society, various American cultures and cultures of persons who emigrate to the United States are mixed together like salad ingredients, and each culture keeps its own distinct qualities (Glazer & Moynihan, 1963). In essence, the people of the United States form a heterogeneous society. These concepts are important to education systems because they provide glimpses into how the general public typically views issues related to multiculturalism and diversity. As such, although food analogies can provide for colorful visuals, a more contemporary educational term for the salad bowl concept is cultural pluralism.

Cultural pluralism is a concept that supports the idea of racial, ethnic, and cultural diversity among a larger populace. Culture typically refers to patterns of behavior and symbolism that give activities structure and importance (Kalyanpur & Harry, 1999; Super & Harkness, 2002) and has been described, in fact, as "the framework that guides and bounds life practices" (Lynch & Hanson, 2004, p. 4). Although persons from a cultural group may have similar likings or tendencies, not all persons from a particular group will demonstrate the same behaviors. Thus, patterns of behavior are guided by cultural framework, but differences in behavior exist within each culture. Pluralism typically denotes diverse views and supports multiple approaches or methods of understanding (Eck, 2008). Cultural pluralism, then, is the idea that diverse populations comprise American society, including school populations. Public schools, in particular, tend to mimic local societies' racial, ethnic, economic, and religious tendencies, as well as other cultural influences.

School populations are composed of students from local communities. In some small communities, the population tends to be fairly homogeneous, whereas in mid- to large-size communities; the population can be very diverse. The examples in Figure 5.1 are representative of students attending public schools in the United States but are by no means exhaustive.

DEMOGRAPHICS

Changing U.S. demographics have an impact on public school systems and the number of children with and without disabilities who attend public schools. The population of the United States can be broken down by race and ethnic composition. In 2006, according to the American Community Survey (U.S. Census, 2008b):

- Approximately 66% of persons living in the United States identified their primary racial or ethnic group as White (non-Hispanic).

Michelle is from a small town in Wyoming. She attends a public school for 250 children in grades kindergarten through eight, and most of their families are farmers or ranchers. The students' families have lived in the area for generations, with the newest families having moved to the area more than 10 years ago. All but two of the students in the school are White (non-Hispanic), and all speak English as their primary language. Most of the families live a middle-class existence, and the economy is based solely on farming and ranching.

Robby lives in San Diego; he attends an elementary school that has over 1,000 children. There are more than 250 students in his grade level alone. In Robby's class, most of the students speak English as a second language, and some of the students don't speak English at all. Robby's school has a transient population, and many of the students have only lived in the area and attended the school for 6 months to 2 years. Many of the families live a lower socioeconomic existence, and many of the parents work two to three jobs.

Kawika lives in Hawaii; he attends an elementary school that has over 1,500 children. There are about 35 students in his classroom. In Kawika's class, all the students speak English, but they all prefer to speak Pidgin. Most of the students in Kawika's school are "local kids"—Hawaiian, but there are some "haole"—students who are foreign to Hawaii or not from around here. Most of the students have lived in the area their entire lives and consider the adults in the community and some of the teachers to be their aunties and uncles, although they are not related by blood or marriage. Kawika's father is a fisherman, and he is just going to school until he is old enough to join his dad when he goes fishing.

Marielos lives in Houston. She attends an online virtual high school supported by the local school district. Marielos stopped attending her local high school because both her parents work, and she has to stay home and take care of her younger siblings. Marielos doesn't own a computer, so she heads to the local library every evening, when her parents return from work, to complete her assignments online. She doesn't know the other students who attend the virtual high school because she's never met them, but she has been told that there are over 3,000 students from the Houston metropolitan area attending the virtual high school. Marielos hopes to be the first person in her family to attend college and earn a degree.

FIGURE 5.1   Students attending public schools in the United States

- Approximately 15% identified as Hispanic, and about 12% identified as African American.
- Approximately 4% identified as Asian.
- Less than 1% identified as American Indian or Alaska Native. Less than 1% identified as Native Hawaiian or Other Pacific Islander.

Over the past two decades there has been a steady increase in the African American and Hispanic populations and a corresponding decrease in the White (non-Hispanic) population, and the number of American Indian or Alaska Native, and Native Hawaiian or Other Pacific Islander has remained fairly stagnant.

Among children in 2006 (U.S. Census, 2008b), approximately 73½ million were 17 years of age and under living in households in the United States. Among school-age children 5 to 17 years of age, 6.4%, or slightly less than 4 million children, were identified with disabilities. An additional 2.6 million children birth to 5 and 18 to 21 received special education services at the same time. Table 5.1 provides a breakdown of children in the United States by racial and ethnic composition.

The Census Bureau also calculates the size of households in the United States. In 2006 the average household size was 2.61 persons, whereas the average family size was 3.20 persons (U.S. Census, 2008b). Household size was defined as the number of people

TABLE 5.1   Racial and Ethnic Composition of Children Birth to 17 Years of Age

Children by Race and Hispanic Origin	Percentage in 2008
White, non-Hispanic*	57.0
Hispanic**	20.7
African American	15.4
Asian	4.1
All other races***	4.7

Source: ChildStats.gov (2009).
*Excludes persons who are of Hispanic origin.
**Persons of Hispanic origin may be of any race.
*** Includes American Indian, Eskimo and Aleut, Native Hawaiian and Other Pacific Islanders, and all multiple races.

living in a household (U.S. Census, 2008b), and family size was defined as a group of two or more people who reside together and who are related by birth, marriage, or adoption (U.S. Census, 2008b). The key here is that both households and families have children who attend public schools, and typically public school personnel consider both groups to be families. The size and shape of a typical family has changed considerably since the 1970s. In the 1970s the average family size was 4.5 persons and consisted of a father, mother, and 2.5 children. Thus while the population has increased, the size of a household has decreased, and the composition of the household has changed.

Children Receiving Special Education

During 2003, slightly more than 6.6 million children (birth to 21 years of age) received special education services (U.S. Department of Education, 2007). White non-Hispanic children continue to be the largest group receiving special education services. Similarly, there were proportionate numbers of students, based on general U.S. population data, of Hispanic, Asian or Other Pacific Islander, and American Indian or Alaska Native children receiving special education services. Conversely more students from African-American backgrounds are identified for special education services than would be expected based on the percent of U.S. African-American children. In 2003, almost 20% of children receiving special education services were African American, whereas only 15% of all children in the United States were identified as African American.

TABLE 5.2   Percent of Children Birth to 21 Years of Age, by Race, Receiving Special Education Services in 2003

Children by Race and Hispanic Origin	Percentage Receiving Special Education Services in 2003
White, non-Hispanic	60.8%
Hispanic	15.9%
African American	19.9%
Asian or Other Pacific Islander	2.0%
American Indian or Alaska Native	1.5%

Source: U.S. Department of Education (2008).

FAMILIES

A family, and the very definition of what a family is, has changed over time. As you've read in the preceding chapters, family composition is not static. Families come in a variety of shapes and sizes. Formal definitions of family do exist. For example, one dictionary defines family as "a group of individuals living under one roof and usually under one head [of household]" (Merriam–Webster's Online Dictionary, 2008). The U.S. government has created a formal definition to count the number of family households residing in the country. "A family is a group of two people or more (one of whom is the householder) related by birth, marriage, or adoption and residing together; all such people (including related subfamily members) are considered as members of one family" (U.S. Census, 2008c).

It is important to remember that what a family is and how it is defined is determined by who we are, where we grew up, and how we were raised. As educators, we need to be inclusive and recognize various configurations that constitute a family. Look at the examples provided in Figure 5.2. Can you identify a family configuration similar to yours or to a student in your classroom? Think about other families that you know that don't mimic the examples in the figure. How are those family units different?

Every child is a member of a family. Families and the children within them belong to a group of people who share one or more of the following ties: relationship, affection, cultural knowledge, and resources (Allen & Demo, 1995; Stiers, 1999). Although the term *family diversity* is often used to describe racial and ethnic variations, other factors, such as adoption, same-sex partners, presence of a disability, foster care, marriage, divorce, stepparents or siblings, economic status, and lifestyle, also account for differences among families. The amount and quality of nurturing that children receive are not determined solely by these factors. All kinds of families can provide the love and support necessary for healthy educational development and growth (Southern Poverty Law Center, 1993).

Traditions, legends, and stereotypes about the *perfect* family can influence teacher expectations and attitudes regarding the ability of children to learn and behave (Southern

---

- Tim and Lee are married and have two biological daughters.
- Tom and Ann are married and have three daughters, one of whom is adopted.
- Lisa and Rich live together, but are not married, and have two sons and one daughter with Down syndrome.
- Keiko and Sam are divorced but have four children together, two of whom live with Keiko and her parents in Hawaii and two of whom live in San Diego with Sam, his current wife, and their son, who was recently diagnosed with autism.
- Seth is widowed and has two sons, one of whom is in college and one of whom lives in a home for adults with disabilities.
- Yvonne and Helen are unmarried partners and have two children who are adopted, one of whom has been diagnosed with fetal alcohol spectrum disorders.
- Lakeisha is unmarried and has no biological children but is raising her sister's three school-age children.
- Jane is single and has one son who is in the gifted program in his elementary school.
- John and Nancy are retired, have two children who are now adults, and are raising their son's four middle and high school-age children.

FIGURE 5.2   Examples of family membership

Poverty Law Center, 1993). Some homes may be consciously or subconsciously judged to be unsatisfactory or culturally inferior simply on the basis of race, lifestyle, family structure, or socioeconomic status (Super & Harkness, 2002). The prejudices and judging of others associated with these behaviors are deeply rooted in the home culture in which each person was raised (Dewees, 2001; Rank, 2004). By acknowledging, accepting, and celebrating a wide spectrum of families in the curriculum, teachers can discourage prejudgment and reinforce the critical link between home and school (Southern Poverty Law Center, 1993). As you read this chapter, you will learn more about how diversity and differences among family composition and structure vary widely among families and professionals.

Family Structure

As aspects of federal legislation, such as IDEA, have evolved over time, the interest in family involvement in children's education has ebbed and flowed (Sileo, Sileo, & Prater, 1996). Parents and families play essential roles in children's education and development. Parents' levels of education, attitudes toward education, and knowledge and skills of effective parenting contribute to children's growth and development.

Parents and families provide the basic social and caregiving environment essential to the child's acquisition of basic skills; communication patterns; values, roles, and characteristic traits; and all other awareness of the social world (Turnbull, Turnbull, Erwin, & Soodak, 2006). The foundations of children's social and intellectual competencies are built in virtually every realm of human development during the first years of life (Hanson & Lynch, 2003). Parents' influences begin prior to children's birth, especially when prenatal care, the lack of prenatal care, and the overall health of the mother are considered. For example, smoking causes low-birth-weight babies; drug and alcohol use and abuse lead to drug-exposed and/or fetal-alcohol-exposed/syndrome babies; and poverty and a lack of prenatal care are risk factors for developmental delays. All these factors influence children's growth and development.

The attitudinal dispositions of both parents and adult family members affect the well-being, early stimulation, and initial bonding of all children. In addition, the way parents orchestrate children's early experiences and environment are critical to children's academic readiness (i.e., talking to and reading with children as bases for developing receptive and expressive language). As you read the following scenario, think of yourself as Kiernan's and Liesel's kindergarten teacher. Reflect on ways you could involve the parents of the students in your classroom in the education of their children. What activities could you suggest to Liesel's parents to use at home to improve her school readiness skills?

Wendy began reading to Kiernan the day he was born. She reads to him every day. Now, as Kiernan enters kindergarten, he knows what a book is, is aware of sound–symbol relationships, and can read simple words such as cat, dog, me, and book. Liesel's parents have never read to her. There are no books in the home, and although her mother reads magazines, she never thinks to read them aloud to Liesel. As Liesel enters kindergarten, she doesn't really know what a book looks like and cannot identify any letters of the alphabet.

Appropriate parent involvement has a positive impact on children's academic achievement. The challenge to educators, parents, and community members is to establish active and productive working relationships that benefit children (Turnbull et al.,

2006). Parents' investments of interest, concern, time, and effort are likely to be greater when they are active partners in children's education. Interest, intent, and involvement of parents and families in educating children and youth, especially children with disabilities and others who are at risk for school failure, has shifted in concert with dramatic changes in the traditional family structure (Sileo et al., 1996; Sileo & Prater, 1998). For example, in many communities, only 10% of children have *traditional* family structures with a working father, nonworking mother, and one or two children (U.S. Census, 2008a). In reality, about 75% of children in school come from families in which both parents work, or, if the children live with a single parent or with a guardian, that parent works.

Currently, about 51% of America's children live in a traditional nuclear family in which both biological parents are present and all children were born after marriage (U.S. Census, 2008a). The total percentage of children under age 18 in the United States living with two married parents fell from 77% in 1980 to 68% in 2007. In 2007, 23% of children lived with only their mothers, 3% lived with only their fathers, 3% lived with two unmarried parents, and 4% lived with neither of their parents (ChildStats.gov, 2009).

The percentage of children who live with married parents varies greatly by race and ethnicity. Of those who live in traditional nuclear families:

- 86% are Asian American
- 76% are White (non-Hispanic)
- 66% are Hispanic
- 37% are African American (ChildStats.gov, 2009; data for children who were American Indian or Alaska Native, and Native Hawaiian or Other Pacific Islander were not available).

Slightly more than 53% of African-American children live with only one parent, making them by far the largest group of children living with only a single parent. At the opposite end of the spectrum, fewer than 17% of Asian-American children live with only one parent (ChildStats.gov, 2009). Perhaps more important, across all racial and ethnic groups about 4% of all children do not live with a biological or adoptive parent, with the highest group in this category being African-American children (7%; Childstats.gov, 2009). Table 5.3 provides an overview of different family structures found today. Although the list of family structures is comprehensive, it is by no means exhaustive of every possible configuration.

Professionals must be cognizant of changing family structures to help avoid overburdening already stressed families. One approach for professionals to consider is to view parents as consumers with the rights and obligations equivalent to purchasers of high-quality merchandise (Sileo et al., 1996). Professional perspective taking may help to reduce professional egocentrism, may help clarify family needs and priorities, and will help foster a deeper understanding of the challenges that confront families.

Inadvertently, professionals may add stress by having unrealistic expectations for children's school performance and by anticipating a high degree of parent and family involvement. For instance, it may be difficult to hold a parent conference during the school day when parents are at work. It is also difficult for parents to attend evening meetings when they are tired after a full day's work, or they prefer to stay at home with the children. At the same time, it is important to recognize that many teachers are also exhausted at day's end and prefer not to conduct evening conference. Educators need to look at a variety of ways to keep parents informed and involved in their children's education.

Factors that must be addressed in designing parent and family involvement programs acknowledge that (a) families have a variety of strengths and challenges that must

TABLE 5.3 Examples of Family Structure

Type of Family	Family Membership
Natural family	• Same two adults who were married at the time that they conceived the child(ren)
Single-parent families	• Father or mother (separated, divorced, never married, widowed) • Any of the following who assumes the role of parent: oldest sibling, stepparent, grandparent, aunt, uncle, relative, family friend
Blended families (stepparent, stepsibling)	• One natural parent, one stepparent (1 in 5 children is a stepchild) • Blended families (80% of all divorced people remarry; 17.4% of all families with children under 18) • Two stepparents • Mother or dad with (multiple) partner(s)
Extended families	• Living with grandparents or other relatives • Others living in family home
Adoptive families	• Formal (i.e., stranger or family) • Informal (i.e., family or friend)
Foster/substitute care families	• Living with a nonbiological parent or caregiver • Court-appointed guardian or placement
Gay, lesbian, bisexual families	• Two parents of the same gender (male/male or female/female) • Parents may be married (some states) or life partners
Latchkey families (working parents [multiple jobs], kids home alone)	• Living in a household where no adult is present before/after school • Children are dependent on themselves for food, care, supervision
Dysfunctional families	• Alcohol and substance abuse • Violence • Child abuse/spousal abuse • Incarcerated parent/family member
Other families	• Chronically ill parent(s) (physically or mentally) • Teenage parent(s) • Parents with limited parenting skills • Homeless or living below poverty level

be considered and (b) programs must be realistic and manageable within the various family structures. A program that cannot be implemented without disrupting a family's balance may do more harm than good. Therefore, it is important to assess a family's needs and priorities as a foundation for understanding parents' and families' behaviors. An illustration of this may be that a family's physical and physiological needs for food, clothing, and shelter must be addressed prior to considering other needs, such as education and educational supports (see Figure 5.3).

Mr. Rosensteel is concerned that Taha, a student in his class, is doing poorly on classroom assessments. Mr. Rosensteel asks for a meeting with Taha's parents. Taha's parents cancel three meetings before finally coming to school. When he meets with them, Mr. Rosensteel expresses his concerns about Taha's schoolwork. Mr. Rosensteel talks with Taha' parents and asks if Taha has a place at home to study and do his homework.

During the discussion, Mr. Rosensteel learns that Taha's father has lost his job and that the family is in jeopardy of losing their home. Taha's parents explain that Taha is now working every day after school to help support his family and that although education and schooling are important to Taha and his family, right now their needs for income and shelter outweigh their interests in education. Mr. Rosensteel brainstorms ways with Taha and his parents to help support Taha at school and at home. They decide that before school and lunchtime study sessions are the best way to support Taha's school studies. At the same time, the timing of these study sessions frees Taha up after school so that he can help support his family.

FIGURE 5.3 Identifying a family's needs and priorities.

Gay, lesbian, bisexual, and transgendered families (GLBT) are perhaps the newest types of families being discussed in today's educational settings. Research literature with respect to research on gay, lesbian, bisexual, and transgendered families is extremely limited (Allen & Demo, 1995), and the number of children living in GLBT families is difficult to ascertain. Many special education professionals are not adequately prepared to work with GLBT families. The predominant heterosexist belief that everyone is or ought to be heterosexual is most prevalent in the area of child–parent relations (Bohan, 1996).

Estimates of children of GLBT families in the United States range widely from 8 to 14 million (U.S. Census 2008a). GLBT families, like heterosexual families, cross all ethnic, racial, economic, and societal bounds. In addition, there are married, single, divorced, separated, and cohabitating GLBT families. Unlike other household types, such as married, single, and divorced, the U.S. Census Bureau is unable to accurately account for the number GLBT households and the number of children living in those households (Strasser, 1997; U.S. Census, 2008b). In any case, GLBT families are by no means rare.

GLBT families, like heterosexual families have the potential to contribute to all areas of their child's development, including their child's education. However, GLBT families often are silenced by prejudice and discrimination (Bos, 2004). Negative attitudes toward GLBT families are rooted in others' lack of knowledge and understanding, stereotypes, and myths (Garnets & Kimmel, 2003). Public schools are often hostile environments in which persons with same-sex orientation experience discrimination, verbal and physical harassment, and silencing of their sexual identities (Muñoz-Plaza, Quinn, & Rounds, 2002). Consequently, they are forced to isolate themselves socially and emotionally (Stiers, 1999).

The lack of knowledgeable and caring special educators who understand issues of same-sex orientation and gender identity is of primary concern. Professionals must work to understand the unique problems that confront GLBT families and employ strategies that curb harassment and ensure their safety (Garnets & Kimmel, 2003). Heightened awareness leads to increased understanding and acceptance.

GLBT persons and families are at risk of suicide, verbal and physical harassment, substance abuse, sexually transmitted diseases, homelessness and prostitution, and declining academic performance (Muñoz-Plaza et al., 2002). In addition, they identify school campuses as less than empowering settings that inhibit acknowledgment and expression of GLBT perspectives and limit curricular initiatives and research efforts (Muñoz-Plaza et al.,

2002). Consequently, GLBT families respond by concealing their sexual orientation or gender identity from school personnel and sometimes even their children. By educating themselves and others about the unique needs of GLBT families, professionals can lessen intolerance and harassment that exist on many school campuses, especially because the field of special education in general is charged with creating environments that are characterized by inclusion, equal access, mutual respect, and cooperation for all students, faculty, and staff, regardless of cultural differences (Muñoz-Plaza et al., 2002; Rankin, 2003). A list of GLBT resources for educators and families can be found in Table 5.4.

TABLE 5.4 GLBT Resources

Organization	Mission or Goal
GLAAD 5455 Wilshire Blvd, #1500 Los Angeles, CA 90036 Phone: 323/933-2240 Fax: 323/933-2241 E-mail: incident@glaad.org	GLAAD, the Gay & Lesbian Alliance Against Defamation, is dedicated to promoting and ensuring fair, accurate, and inclusive representation of people and events in the media as a means of eliminating homophobia and discrimination based on gender identity and sexual orientation.
GLBT National Help Center 2261 Market Street, PMB #296 San Francisco, CA 94114 National Hotline toll-free phone: 1-888-THE-GLNH (1-888-843-4564) National Youth Talkline toll-free phone: 1-800-246-PRIDE (1-800-246-7743) Phone: 415/355-0003 Fax: 415/552-5498 E-mail: info@GLBTNationalHelpCenter.org	GLBT, the Gay, Lesbian, Bisexual, and Transgender National Help Center is an organization that is dedicated to meeting the needs of the gay, lesbian, bisexual, and transgender community and those questioning their sexual orientation and gender identity.
GLSEN National Headquarters 90 Broad Street, 2nd Floor New York, NY 10004 Phone: 212/727-0135 Fax: 212/727-0254 E-mail: glsen@glsen.org	GLSEN, the Gay, Lesbian and Straight Education Network, is the leading national education organization focused on ensuring safe schools for all students.
COLAGE National Office 1550 Bryant Street Suite 830 San Francisco, CA 94103 Phone: 415/861-5437 Fax: 415/255-8345 E-mail: collage@colage.org	COLAGE, Children of Lesbians and Gays Everywhere, is a national movement of children, youth, and adults with one or more lesbian, gay, bisexual, transgender, and/or queer (LGBTQ) parents, working toward social justice through youth empowerment, leadership development, education, and advocacy.
Family Equality Council PO Box 206 Boston, MA 02133 Phone: 617/502-8700 Fax: 617/502-8701 E-mail: info@familyequality.org	The Family Equality Council works to ensure equality for LGBT families by building community, changing hearts and minds, and advancing social justice for all families.
PFLAG National Office 1726 M Street, NW Suite 400 Washington, D.C. 20036 Phone: (202) 467-8180 Fax: (202) 467-8194 E-mail: info@pflag.org	PFLAG, Parents and Friends of Lesbians and Gays, promotes the health and well-being of gay, lesbian, bisexual, and transgender persons; their families; and their friends

Family and Professional Values

Partnerships among families and professionals necessitate awareness of our values and the values of others as a basis for identifying potential conflict (More-Thomas & Day-Vines, 2008). Attempts to argue or to prove that another person's values are untenable are met with passive or aggressive resistance because values arouse emotional responses in a given society or an individual person (Trumbull, Rothstein-Fisch, & Hernandez, 2003). Values are an internalized set of principles or rules for living that are derived from past experiences during the socialization process. They are ideals, customs, or institutions by which people live that have been analyzed in terms of their morality (Trumbull et al., 2003).

Peoples' values are fairly well established by the age of 10. Values develop and occur through interactions with the people around us, particularly parents, family members, and other caregivers (Weisner, 1998). Religion and church affiliations (threat of God or devil; Gaventa, 2008), superstitions (bogey man, tooth fairy, Santa Claus, Easter Bunny), peers, school, teachers, and the education process, as well as our heroes, all effect the development of values systems. To have a fairly good idea of another person's values, examine their world and environment when they were 10 years old. Because values are learned at an early age, it is important for parents and adult family members to model appropriate behaviors and values for children; even if children's behaviors may not always represent these values, basic values on which the children rely serve as a basis for their behaviors (Super & Harkness, 1997, 2002). Because values are established by an early age, we must be aware of our own value systems. By examining our own value systems, we learn that others have different value systems and that conflict may arise with others with whom we interact.

Educators need to be careful not to place judgments on other people's values or observed behaviors. For example, in the United States, many people eat by sticking forks into food with their left hands, cutting food with their right hands, transferring the fork to their right hands, and putting the food into their mouths. In Europe, Australia, and New Zealand, among other countries, it is more common for people to hold forks in their left hands, cut the food with their right hands, and put the food into their mouths with their left hands.

In other parts of the world, people use their fingers (Morocco), sticks (Asian countries), tortillas (Mexico), matzo (Israel), and other bread forms (Afghanistan) to put food into their mouths. If you were taught how to eat different than someone else, you may judge another's form of eating as not civilized, not educated, or wrong. Value judgments can have negative effects, particularly between educators and family members of their students. Consider the following scenario. Take into account the values and traditions that your family instilled in you. If the teacher in this scenario was your colleague, how would you address his concerns?

Sergio and Cassie are in the same class. They both turn their homework in on time, and they both earn decent grades. Sergio does his homework at his father's desk in his father's office after school each day. Sergio's family eats dinner together every week night at 6:00 p.m. Cassie does her homework in the car between school and gymnastics each day. Cassie eats dinner after gymnastics at about 8:30 p.m. Cassie's teacher believes that the car is not the proper place to complete homework and is concerned that Cassie is not eating with her family. The teacher is making the value judgment that Cassie and her mom do not value homework and family time.

One of the potential destructive forces in parent and professional interactions is that different value systems are often operating during conferences and other communications (Geenen, Powers, & Lopez-Vasquez, 2001). Parents and teachers place value on the behaviors they observe in others. For example, teachers may assume that a child has not been raised correctly because she exhibits inappropriate behavior while at school, and such behavior must have been learned at home. When parents and professionals meet for a conference, professionals may bring to the meeting such preconceived value judgments.

Another common value judgment is made when parent do not keep an appointment for a school conference. The teacher may automatically believe that the parents do not care about their child's education. Similarly, if a parent calls the teacher at home in the evening, the teacher may prejudge that the parent is overanxious. These same behaviors may be valued or interpreted in a different way. For instance, if the parent does not keep an appointment for a conference, it may be interpreted that the parent values being at home with the child rather than coming to school. Or, if the parent calls the teacher at home in the evening, it may be interpreted that the parent is very concerned and interested in the child's progress.

Educators must analyze their own values and determine the interpretation they place on others' behaviors (Trumbull et al., 2003). Teacher and parent conflicts over significant issues can often be resolved through discussion. For example, they may differ when it comes to values. Secondary-level teachers may value socialization and believe that if students get along with peers and other school personnel, those students will be successful in the business world. On the other hand, parents may feel that the student should concentrate on academics. Each adult cares about the student but approaches attainment of a common goal (i.e., preparation for successful living) in a different manner. A quick conference between teacher(s) and parents can help them to understand each other's perspective and potentially resolve their concern.

Family Dynamics

Family dynamics are as diverse as children in any classroom in the country. The previous section focused on how diverse values affect our interactions with families of children and youth with disabilities. Family and professional interactions are also influenced by family dynamics that result from the presence of a child with disabilities in the family.

Families of children with disabilities often express sympathetic feelings for disabilities other than those experienced by their own children. The parents seem to engage in some degree of ranking among the disabilities (Leyser & Kirk, 2005). Professionals need to assess their own attitudes toward the severity of different disabilities. Increased daily contact with a child with a particular disability tends to diminish the severity of the disability in the eyes of both the families and professionals. Parents tend to rank disabilities of children other than their own children as more severe; professionals tend to rank the severity of a disability according to the relative ease with which they manage the disability based on their experience. These internal rankings affect the relationship and interactions of the families and professionals (Leyser & Kirk, 2005).

Most people have not received formal preparation to be parents; thus, they parent their children the way they were parented by their parents. Some of us had parents with inadequate parenting skills and vowed to change the manner in which we interact with our children. Most of the time parents are successful, but sometimes they slip into old patterns. The presence of a child with disabilities in the family constellation complicates the role of parenting.

Parents must make many adjustments and changes in their lives when they learn their child has a disability (Turnbull et al., 2006). Parents must be involved in (a) extensive assessment and consultation with professionals who may overwhelm them with jargon; (b) personal assessment of their abilities to accommodate the adjustments related to parenting a child with a disability; and (c) adjustments and accommodations regarding school-related variables. Many parents report that their children do not receive appropriate education and related services, which create additional stress in their lives. Families of children with disabilities are often subjected to stares, embarrassed silences, rude comments, and disrespectful questions. They must be prepared for negative reactions to their children from strangers, neighbors, friends, and relatives, as well as medical and human services personnel. Quite often, mothers-in-law and fathers-in-law blame the parents for the child's disability and may disagree over diet, caretaking, and parenting styles. The value judgments and negative reactions are major source of stress in their lives and directly affect family dynamics.

Parents and other family members in settings with children with disabilities carry considerable responsibility (Glidden, Billings, & Jobe, 2006); they often display great strength and coping abilities in light of negative social reactions to their children, such as, *how can you bring a child like that out in public?* These reactions are strong reminders to parents that society may never value their child. One of the most damaging aspects for parents is that others hold them responsible for their child's behavior, and parents may hold themselves accountable for the child's behavior even though it is unjustified.

The presence of a child with disabilities may cause people to view the family structure in a negative light and to consider the family constellation as built on a fragile foundation. The positive contributions of a child with disabilities to family dynamics must always be considered. As an educator, remember that families of children with disabilities often demonstrate:

- *Courage*—parents and other family members find strength to forge ahead in light of ongoing adversity.
- *Love*—natural love of parents for their children is deeper because parents realize that the child is special and may need to rely on parents long after other children leave home.
- *Faith*—parents believe that things will improve.
- *Hope*—someone or something will improve the situation (educational, medical, or personal intervention).
- *Positive attitudes*—parents realize that negative attitudes are unhealthy.
- *Adaptation*—parents are able to make accommodations and adjustments to ensure they meet the needs of all family members (Hanson & Lynch, 2003; Turnbull et al., 2006).

Educators often consider these skills as less valuable because they tend to be intangible and immeasurable by educational assessments. Family–professional interactions are influenced by family dynamics. Family dynamics in turn are influenced by external factors such as poverty.

POVERTY. Poverty and the culture of poverty do not discriminate based on ethnicity, race, geographic region, age, or gender. Poverty affects the young, the old, the middle-aged, those who are single or are married, families, and children. The statistics regarding the number of families living in poverty are discouraging. Poverty is a growing problem in the United States and can effect development and cause disabilities (Children's Defense Fund, 2005). Rank (2004) identified some startling statistics regarding poverty in America:

- At age 20, more than 1 in 10 Americans lives in poverty.
- By age 40, more than one in three Americans has lived at least 1 year of their adulthood in poverty.
- Between ages 20 and 65, more than two of three Americans participate in some sort of public assistance program.
- Between ages 20 and 65, two out of five Americans receive some type of public assistance for more than a 5-year period.

Over 37 million people in the United States live in poverty, including more than 13 million children (Children's Defense Fund, 2005). Each of the factors identified in Figure 5.4, in and of itself, is considered to put a child at risk for developmental delays and disabilities. Professionals must be cognizant of the effects of poverty on development and learning when working with children with disabilities and their families.

Education is tightly linked to poverty. Children in poverty and those who live in low-income families are likely to have parents or adult family members who did not finish high school or hold only a high school diploma (Children's Defense Fund, 2006). Professionals working with families need to recognize that educators and school settings may intimidate these adults and negatively affect their involvement in their children's education. Moreover, educators should be aware that adults without a high school diploma or those with only a high school diploma, and their families, are twice as likely to receive Temporary Assistance for Needy Families (TANF; U.S. Department of Health and Human Services, 2008) than whose with some college or a college degree. TANF is a federally funded assistance program, commonly known as welfare, that succeeds Aid to Families with Dependent Children. TANF is designed to (a) assist needy families so that children can be cared for in their own home; (b) reduce the dependency of needy parents by promoting job preparation, work, and marriage; (c) prevent out-of-wedlock pregnancies; and (d) encourage the formation and maintenance of two-parent families.

Many of the children and families who receive TANF also receive assistance with food and housing. Almost 11 million children receive food assistance through either food stamp programs or through school-based free and reduced lunch programs (Children's Defense Fund, 2006). Unfortunately, children are 95% more likely to be hungry and experience poor diets than are adults (Children's Defense Fund, 2005; U.S. Department of

---

In the United States . . .

- every 36 seconds a baby is born into poverty
- every 47 seconds a baby is born with no health insurance
- every minute a baby is born to a teen mother
- every 2 minutes a baby is born with low birth-weight
- 75% of poor children in 2005 lived in a family where an adult family member worked full-time

FIGURE 5.4 Children in Poverty *Source:* Information from Children's Defense Fund, 2005

Health and Human Services, 2008). The effects of a poor diet and hunger can adversely affect a child's health and education performance (Children's Defense Fund, 2006).

Families who receive TANF or food and housing assistance may have priorities that come before the education of their children. Families may struggle to focus on the educational needs of their children if they are unable to feed or provide shelter for them (Children's Defense Fund, 2005; Rank, 2004). Educators often falsely believe that poor families do not care about education when in truth they care very much about education but cannot focus on education because they are consumed by the need to provide food, clothing, and shelter for their children. Educators must be aware of these issues and focus on assisting and supporting the family through the educational experience.

Summary

- The concept of a family has changed over the past 30 to 50 years.
- Society no longer perceives a "family" as a father, a mother, 2.5 children, and a dog.
- Family structure and composition varies greatly and is influenced by ethnicity, race, economic status, gender, geographic regions, and lifestyle.

- More than half of all school-age children live in nonnuclear families.
- Professionals in the field of special education need to be prepared to work not only with children with disabilities, but also with the families of those children.

Linking Standards to Chapter Content

After reading this chapter, you should be able to link basic knowledge and skills described in the CEC Standards and INTASC Principles with information provided in this text. Table 5.5, Linking CEC Standards and INTASC Principles to Major Chapter Topics, gives examples of how they can be applied to each major section of the chapter.

TABLE 5.5 Linking CEC Standards and INTASC Principles to Major Chapter Topics		
Major Chapter Headings	**CEC Knowledge and Skill Core Standard and Associated Subcategories**	**INTASC Core Principle and Associated Special Education Subcategories**
Demographics Families Family structure Family and Professional Values Family Dynamics	1: Foundations ICC1K8 Historical points of view and contribution of culturally diverse groups. ICC1K9 Impact of the dominant culture on shaping schools and the individuals who study and work in them.	3: Diverse Learners 3.03 All teachers understand that a disability can be perceived differently across families, communities, and cultures based on differing values and belief systems. 3.04 All teachers understand and are sensitive to cultural, ethnic, gender, and linguistic differences that may be confused with or

(continued)

TABLE 5.5	(continued)	
Major Chapter Headings	**CEC Knowledge and Skill Core Standard and Associated Subcategories**	**INTASC Core Principle and Associated Special Education Subcategories**
		misinterpreted as manifestations of a disability. 10: Collaboration, Ethics, and Relationships 10.04 All teachers accept families as full partners in planning appropriate instruction and services for students with disabilities, and provide meaningful opportunities for them to participate as partners in their children's instructional programs and in the life of the school. 10.10 Special education teachers understand the impact that having a child with a disability may have on family roles and functioning at different points in the life cycle of a family.

Sources: Council for Exceptional Children (2005); Interstate New Teacher Assessment and Support Consortium INTASC Special Education Subcommittee (May 2001).

Web Resources

INTERNET WEB SITES AND SUPPORT

http://www.childrensdefense.org/—Children's Defense Fund is the foremost national proponent of policies and programs that provide children with the resources they need to succeed.

http://www.childstats.gov/—Childstats.gov—Forum on Child and Family Statistics is a collection of 22 federal government agencies involved in research and activities related to children and families.

http://www.glaad.org/—Gay and Lesbian Alliance Against Defamation is dedicated to promoting and ensuring fair, accurate, and inclusive representation of people and events in the media as a means of eliminating homophobia and discrimination based on gender identity and sexual orientation.

http://www.glsen.org/cgi-bin/iowa/all/home/ index.html—Gay, Lesbian and Straight Education Network (GLSEN) is the leading national education

organization focused on ensuring safe schools for all students.

http://www.cec.sped.org/Content/NavigationMenu/ AboutCEC/Communities/Divisions/Division_for_ Culturally_and_Linguistically_Diverse_Exceptional_ Learners__DDEL_.htm—The Division for Culturally and Linguistically Diverse Exceptional Learners (DDEL), a division of the Council for Exceptional Children (CEC), promotes the advancement and improvement of educational opportunities for culturally and linguistically diverse learners.

http://www.nccrest.org/—The National Center for Culturally Responsive Educational Systems provides technical assistance and professional development to close the achievement gap between students from culturally and linguistically diverse backgrounds and their peers and reduce inappropriate referrals to special education.

CHAPTER 6

Cultural Competence and Working with Families from Diverse Backgrounds

OBJECTIVES

After reading this chapter you will

1. Understand the components needed to effectively practice cultural competence.
2. Discuss multicultural considerations to be examined when working with families.
3. Describe the heterogenic characteristics that occur within diverse populations.
4. Identify how family role patterns influence family dynamics and interactions with the family as well as with professionals.
5. Discuss how language, communication, and culture impact interactions with students and families.
6. Explain how beliefs about health, illness, and disability are subjective, based on cultural heritage.
7. Identify barriers to working with families from diverse backgrounds.
8. Describe strategies for working with diverse students and families.

INTRODUCTION

Diversity is often used to describe differences among racial or ethnic classifications, age, gender, religion, philosophy, physical abilities, socioeconomic background, sexual orientation, gender identity, intelligence, mental health, physical health, genetic attributes, behavior, attractiveness, place of origin, cultural values, or political views, as well as other identifying features (Harry 2002; 2008; Park & Lian, 2001). The ability of families of children with disabilities and education professionals to successfully work together is affected by issues of diversity, customs, and culture (Xu 2007). This chapter offers a discussion on cultural competence and discusses barriers and strategies for working with diverse families and students with disabilities.

CULTURAL COMPETENCE

A child's cultural system is influenced by a variety of factors including socioeconomics, education, primary language, race and ethnicity, religion, lifestyle, and where they live, among others (Cartledge, Kea, & Ida, 2000). When students enter the public school system, they bring with them the culture in which they have been raised. Culture itself is not static and is the framework that guides us as we move through life (Gay, 2000; Lynch & Hanson, 2004). The cultural practices students bring to school influence how they learn, their social interactions, and their interactions with teachers and school personnel. The same can be said for teachers and other school personnel (Dewees, 2001). They too are influenced by the cultural system in which they were raised and the cultural system in which they live.

A person's cultural identity changes over time. A wide range of physical characteristics that people see in themselves and others influences identity, including those we call skin color, facial features, height, and hair texture (Cartledge et al., 2000). Similarly, children acquire ethnic and racial values, customs, language styles, and behavioral codes long before they are able to label and know them as ethnic (Gay, 2000; Lynch & Hanson, 2004). In fact, as with value systems, a child typically has an understanding of the culture in which they live at an early age (Lynch & Hanson, 2004), and the child's understanding of the culture in which they were born and live can cause difficulties when the child enters an unfamiliar culture. The same difficulties often occur for the child's family. The commonly used term for these difficulties is culture shock. Culture shock is the inability to apply concepts learned in one environment effectively in another environment (Lynch & Hanson, 2004). All the experiences discussed in Figure 6.1 can create culture shock for both students and their families. The culture shock and differences in cultural expectations can cause difficulties for students in school and can cause distress among students, adult family members, and professionals. Many people experience culture shock when they travel to another country—the effect of culture shock can be particularly strong when you travel to a country where English is not the primary language.

As they grow and develop, children begin to understand the cultural and political dimensions of race and ethnicity and the significant role these factors play in their lives (Cross, Bazron, Isaacs, & Dennis, 1989). In fact, under stressful situations, a child's behavior is typically affected by deeply rooted values from their first culture. Nevertheless, as the child moves from one culture—the home culture—to a new culture—the school culture—values are adapted and adjusted so that the child can be effective in the new culture (Hanson & Lynch, 2004; Harry, 2002). The same experiences are true for educators as the move from the role of student to the role of teacher and in some cases to the role of administrator.

Many Native Americans who are raised in traditional ways experience culture shock when they attend public schools or boarding schools. Navajo children and youth are raised to speak the Navajo language, to let their hair grow long, to be noncompetitive, and to live in an extended family environment where their skills are gifts to be shared for the benefit of everyone. These children are then sent to public or boarding schools, where they are expected to cut their hair, speak the English language, compete with each other in academics and sports, change their clothes, and wear shoes. The food they eat is also different. Navajos are typically raised to eat meat, potatoes, and bread (e.g., mutton, fry bread). They also eat canned tomatoes as a treat or snack right out of the can. When they are in school, they are served canned tomatoes hot as part of their main meal and are served vegetables and sandwiches.

The circumstances described in this situation lead to culture shock for both Navajo children and their parents. Can you think of a time when you experienced culture shock? Are there instances that may cause families to experience culture shock when their child is referred for special education?

FIGURE 6.1 A closer look at culture shock

MULTICULTURAL CONSIDERATIONS FOR PARENT INVOLVEMENT

Human behavior is complex and rich with diversity. Families and professionals' racial, ethnic, and cultural heritage is the basis for thinking, decision making, and communication (Geenen, Powers, & Lopez-Vasquez, 2001). Professionals must acknowledge the importance of cultural and linguistic traditions as a foundation for serving families and children in today's diverse communities (Haley, 1999). Educators' tendencies to ignore linguistic and cultural differences (a) deny equal educational opportunities to racially, ethnically, and culturally diverse populations; (b) reinforce social class and racial stratification; and (c) perpetuate negative attitudes that result in disenfranchising these students and their families as well as concomitant academic failure (Dewees, 2001). Educators, therefore, must strive for cultural competence because it ensures equal, nondiscriminatory, culturally sensitive, and responsive strategies and services for children, their parents, and other family members (Eberly, Joshi, & Konzal, 2007).

Cultural competence recognizes importance of people's cultures and languages to their outlook on life, encourages individuals' pursuit of culture-specific knowledge, and facilitates nonbiased assessment-intervention strategies in cross-cultural settings (Cartledge et al., 2000; Haley 1999). Cultural competence also includes effective interactions with people of diverse racial, ethnic, cultural, linguistic, political, socioeconomic, religious, and sexual orientations, as well as partnerships with natural, informal, and supportive community networks. These networks include neighborhood centers; religious institutions; day care programs; cultural arts, music, and after-school programs; and extended family (Cartledge et al., 2000; Lynch & Hanson, 2004).

Culturally competent educators acknowledge, respect, and value cultural and linguistic diversity. This is evidenced by their (a) accepting differences; (b) attending to the dynamics of cultural interactions; (c) understanding of the impact of culture and language on relationships with students, parents, and other family members; and (d) demonstrating awareness of cultural knowledge and resources by adapting or incorporating them into service delivery to accommodate the needs of children and families from diverse racial, ethnic, and cultural heritage (Eberly et al., 2007; Gay, 2000; Lynch & Hanson, 2004). Accepting differences in life outlook, communication styles, and the definition of family are critical to successful family–professional partnerships. In addition, teachers, counselors, and other school personnel must assess and understand how personal cultural norms and values shape their day-to-day behaviors. Self-awareness enables them to appreciate the complexities of cross-cultural interactions in helping processes, as well as how their personal biases and prejudices may hamper relationships with others (Harry 2002, 2008).

Cultural competence is the cornerstone for learning about disparate perspectives. It acknowledges, respects, and builds on diverse values, beliefs, traditions, and linguistic dimensions (Cartledge et al., 2000; Lynch & Hanson, 2004). It relies on foundational values, relational skills and attitudes, and knowledge domains, all of which afford professional insight into others' lifestyles, communication, curriculum, and pedagogical needs. Collectively, these understandings, attitudes, beliefs, and behaviors are the keystone for interactions with students and their family members (Hunt, Gooden, & Barkdull 2001). Figure 6.2 provides an overview of foundational values, relational skills and attitudes, and knowledge domains that are essential for cross-cultural competence, as well as skills and activities professionals can engage in to improve cross-cultural competence.

Foundational values necessitate:
- Awareness and understanding of personal worldviews, cultures, values, and belief systems, including biases
- Appreciation of diversity and differences as a source of strength and empowerment
  - Heterogeneity within diverse groups
  - Regional and class variations
- Belief in inherent worth and dignity of all people and rights to self-determination
- Acknowledgment of individual, family, and community expertise to recognize and solve problems
- Commitment to social justice based on racism and marginalization of diverse populations

Therefore—Professionals should develop foundational values that:
- Engage in self-awareness to determine perceptions of themselves, students, and parents and families
  - Recognize and eliminate prejudicial attitudes and the associated damaging effects
  - Acknowledge all individuals' potential to succeed and recognize that differences are not genetic deficiencies
  - Celebrate differences as strengths
  - Encourage diversity rather than homogenizing individuals and identifying departures from the norm as problems thereby reinforcing social, racial, and ethnic discrimination.
  - Capitalize on individual's diverse strengths and interests

Relational skills and attitudes necessitate:
- Demonstrating humility and respect for and willingness to learn from others
- Exhibiting awareness of dynamics of power and privilege in helping relationships
- Developing trust based on positive regard, listening, communication, and conflict-resolution skills
- Affirming trauma, loss, and grief in others' lives
- Validating people's strengths and resiliency
- Acknowledging diverse language structures and communication styles
  - Verbal language (pragmatics, phonology, oral communication, and dialects)
  - Nonverbal language (eye contact, touching, gestures)

FIGURE 6.2 Foundational values, relational skills and attitudes, and knowledge domains
Sources: Eberly et al. (2007); Gay (2000); Hunt et al. (2001); Lum (1999); Lynch & Hanson (2004)

Therefore—Professionals should expand relational skills and attitudes that:

- Increase multicultural competencies and become culturally literate
  - Develop sensitivity to and knowledge of diverse cultures, socioeconomic levels, and inherent lifestyles and apply cultural information when working with colleagues, students, and parents and families
  - Recognize diversity within cultural groups
  - Identify family structures and role responsibilities
  - Identify cultural perceptions of disability, illness, and special learning needs (e.g., etiology and acceptance)
  - Identify cultural perceptions of child-rearing and discipline practices
  - Identify behavioral and developmental expectations for children
- Develop and apply knowledge of diverse language systems to communicate more effectively
  - Acknowledge verbal and nonverbal language characteristics and styles as cultural influences that affect interactions among teachers, students, and parents and families (eye contact, humility, and respect)
  - Identify individual's literacy and basic skill levels in native language as well as potential problems with second language acquisition
  - Determine standard versus nonstandard language dialects

Knowledge domains necessitate:

- Familiarity with local systems and policies that affect educational program planning and implementation
- Collaboration with community leaders, elders, agency personnel to identify program standards
  - Socioeconomic, acculturation, and education levels
  - Religious and spiritual beliefs and cultural values
  - Languages spoken at home and in community
  - Family and community resources

Therefore—Professionals should acquire knowledge domains that:

- Identify levels of acculturation and adaptation to new cultures and environments versus maintaining a separate cultural identity
  - Determine socioeconomic characteristics and their impact on cognitive and learning styles and problem-solving skills
  - Identify physical and mental health status, previous educational experiences, as well as history with discrimination and traumatizing experiences prior to emigration to the United States
- Develop and apply knowledge of cultural characteristics and styles related to
  - Field sensitivity and dependence (i.e., concerns with social environment and relationships with others; difficulty with lectures and competitive, individualized work)
  - Field independence (i.e., concerns with task orientation and independence from external judgment; preference for formal relationships with teachers and to work autonomously for individual recognition)
- Develop and apply knowledge of cultural behavioral styles
  - Personal praise, generosity, concepts of time, respect for nature
  - Separate behaviors based on acculturation from potential emotional overlays (e.g., self-berating remarks, refusal to attempt new tasks, give up easily on assignments may indicate individual's upbringing)

FIGURE 6.2 *(Continued)*

HETEROGENEITY AMONG DIVERSE POPULATIONS

White non-Hispanics are the majority population in the United States and include persons who have lived in America for generations, as well as those who are new to the country. In recent years, there has been an influx of White non-Hispanic persons from the former Soviet Union, as well as a host of other Eastern European countries.

The number of American Indians or Alaska Natives equals about 2.6 million people, or 0.9% of the total population (U.S. Census, 2008b). The American Indian or Alaska Native census category combines people who represent three separate identifiers: American Indians, Eskimos, and Aleuts. In addition to the 565 federally recognized American Indian or Alaska Native Nations, there are 100+ additional tribes acknowledged by states.

African Americans comprise about 37.8 million people, or about 12% of the population of the United States (U.S. Census, 2008b). African Americans reflect people who have lived in the United States for generations as well as recent immigrants from African, Caribbean, and European countries. Data from Census 2000 indicates that 7 to 8 million African Americans were foreign born (U.S. Census, 2008b).

Common language, family, and religious affiliations unite Hispanics. Yet, they are very diverse in terms of race and country of origin. Major Hispanic subgroups include Mexicans, Puerto Ricans, and Cuban Americans, as well as growing numbers of Central and South Americans.

The combined population growth among Asian, Native Hawaiian, or Other Pacific Islander Americans exceeds that of African Americans and Hispanics due to growing numbers of immigrants and refugees who have fled political tyranny and persecution of East and Southeast Asia. Furthermore, changes in refugee policies allowed Vietnamese, especially biracial (Amerasian) youth, to enter the United States as immigrants for family reunification purposes. The Asian, Native Hawaiian, or Other Pacific Islander population is comprised of myriad subgroups. As an example of this heterogeneity, Figure 6.3 provides a closer look at Asian, Native Hawaiian, or Other Pacific Islander Americans.

Population diversity is also evidenced by ever-increasing numbers of people with mixed racial backgrounds. According to Census 2000, about 6.8 million people, or 2.4% of the population, reported more than one racial category, with an estimated 93% reporting two categories (U.S. Census, 2008b). The number of people with multiracial backgrounds illustrates a blurring of racial and ethnic lines in the country.

Population projections indicate that within the next 10 years, the United States will be comprised primarily of American Indians or Alaska Native, African Americans, Hispanics, Asians, Native Hawaiian or Other Pacific Islander Americans, as well as other non-White, non-Hispanic groups from South Asia, Arab countries, and the former communist bloc countries. The U.S. population projections for 2040 (U.S. Census 2008b) further indicate a decrease in the White non-Hispanic population and an increase the non-White population (40.9% non-White), with an increase in African Americans (14.6%), Hispanics (18.0%), and Asians and other non-Whites and non-Hispanics (8.3%).

Changing population demographics are reflected in the nation's children. Current population estimates (ChildStats.gov 2009; U.S. Census, 2008b) indicate about 58 million students are enrolled in elementary and secondary public schools. Growth is particularly acute in southern and western geographic regions of the country as a result of increased births and migration.

- Asian and Native Hawaiian or Other Pacific Islander Americans represent more than 40 distinct groups that differ in nationalities, cultural roots, languages, dialects, religions, customs, immigration, and histories in the United States.
- The majority of Asian Americans are from East Asia, Southeast Asia, and South Asia. Pacific Islanders, on the other hand, are from Polynesia, Melanesia, and Micronesia.
- The Asian or Other Pacific Islander category was divided into two separate racial categories, Asian and Native Hawaiian or Other Pacific Islander, beginning with the 2000 Census (U.S. Census, 2000a).
- In addition to differences among Asian and Native Hawaiian and Other Pacific Islander populations, there is heterogeneity within national groups and among individuals in the same ethnic subgroup.
  - Some people refer to themselves as Asian American or Pacific Islander American; others claim immediate heritage, such as Chinese American or Hawaiian (Hwa-Froelich & Westby, 2003).
- Diversity also exists between foreign-born and American-born Asians, Native Hawaiians, and Other Pacific Islanders in the United States.
  - Recent immigrants, migrants, and refugees may incur difficulty accessing mainstream services due to language and cultural barriers.
  - Customary beliefs, values, thought processes, and behaviors of people who have resided in the United States for three or more generations are modified during acculturation processes in which they adopt characteristics of the mainstream culture.
- The lifestyles of Asian and Native Hawaiian and Other Pacific Islander Americans may be influenced by changes in traditional social structures and family values.

FIGURE 6.3   Heterogeneity among Asian and Native Hawaiian or other Pacific Islander Americans

An estimated 35% of all children and youth are members of racial and ethnic communities. In addition, they are expected to make up 24% of the total school-aged population (ages 5–17) by 2012. A new student majority of Hispanics, African Americans, Asians, Native Hawaiian or Other Pacific Islander Americans, and American Indian or Alaska Natives is emerging rapidly. One in five students (20%) lives in a household headed by immigrant parents (ChildStats.gov 2009; U.S. Census, 2008b).

Although the numbers are relatively small, it is important to also note that a proportion of children and families attending public school are immigrants or foreign born. Educators are likely to encounter students and families from Eastern Europe, Africa, the Middle East, Latin America, and other less-well-known geographical areas. Approximately 12% of the people living in the United States are foreign born. The largest group of foreign-born residents, approximate 53%, comes from Latin American. Relatively few foreign-born people are under age 18—almost 9%—compared with about 30% of those born in the United States. Table 6.1 provides a look at the U.S. foreign-born population.

Professionals need to understand and implement culturally competent strategies when working with families of children with special needs (Flett & Conderman, 2001). They must educate themselves and others to ensure cultural competence and acceptance. Special education professionals, in particular, must recognize that their values and belief systems affect how they view and work with others who are different from themselves (Harry, Rueda, & Kalyanpur, 1999; Kalyanpur, 1998). Moreover, professionals need to overcome any prejudices they may hold and demonstrate cultural competence to focus on the educational needs of the children and families with whom they work (Harry, 2008; Kalyanpur & Harry, 1999).

TABLE 6.1	Foreign-Born Residents in the United States Based on Census Immigration Data	
World Region of Birth	**Percentage in 2003**	
Latin America	53.3%	
Asia	25.0%	
Europe	13.7%	
Other regions	8.0%	
• Africa	4.5%	
• Other	3.5%	

Source: U.S. Census (2009).

WORKING WITH FAMILIES FROM DIVERSE BACKGROUNDS

Culture shapes the way of life shared by members of a population; it is the adaptation or design for living that people have developed throughout the course of their history. Cultures are not static, and cultural attributes are not absolutes, but rather general tendencies that vary greatly and are influenced by a host of factors, such as socioeconomics and geographic factors. Culture is conceptualized best as a continuum of standard expression with different families (and different family members) lying at different points along the continuum (Lynch & Hanson, 2004).

The concept of family is defined by culture. In the mainstream U.S. culture, most individuals tend to isolate into nuclear families (Lynch & Hanson, 2004). However, in African American, American Indian and Alaska Native, Asian, Native Hawaiian and Other Pacific Islander American; and Hispanic families, most individuals tend to identify first and foremost as family members. Teachers, counselors, and other school personnel must attend to a number of characteristics that ensure culturally competent approaches to interacting with families from diverse racial, ethnic, and cultural backgrounds (Bevan-Brown 2001; Hanline & Daley, 1992).

FAMILY ROLE PATTERNS

Teachers' understanding of family role patterns is critically important to facilitating students' academic success as well as positive and productive parent and professional partnerships (Callicott, 2003). Students' learning and behavior characteristics may be traced directly to cultural environments that may limit their educational outcomes. Academic difficulties may result from interactions among social, cultural, educational, and linguistic variables and their participation in educational programs that have little or no relevance to family and community cultures, languages, and values. Many students are at risk for school failure; they may not receive an appropriate, responsive education that enables academic and social success (Murray & Naranjo, 2008). Unfortunately, many students are referred for special education services because teachers are unable to help them and may find their presence disruptive in the classroom.

Many traditional racial and ethnic communities have cultural roots in a *collectivist orientation* that emphasizes individuals' interdependence with their families and society (Chae, 2000). In collectivist families, group concerns outweigh individual goals and aspirations with the focus on cooperative behaviors to attain a common goal and promote group welfare. Perceptions of the family relate strongly to needs of the larger group in contrast to individual needs; family and group members assume social responsibility for others' well-being (Chae, 2000). Youth who are raised in families with collectivist orientations often undertake childcare roles, which in turn, may result in caretaking or authoritarian behaviors in school.

The following discussion more closely examines family role patterns among predominant ethnic and racial groups found in the United States. As you read through the next section, keep in mind that the characteristics discussed are **generalizations** based on results from various research studies and reviews of literature. *Remember that no two people from any cultural group will exhibit the same exact patterns of behavior. When working with families, avoid stereotypes, and treat each family with the respect and dignity they deserve.*

American Indians or Alaska Natives

AMERICAN INDIANS OR ALASKA NATIVES STRESS SPIRITUALITY AND LIVING IN POSITIVE BALANCE AND HARMONY WITH THEIR CREATOR, NATURE, AND HUMANITY; THEY RESPECT AND REVERE THEIR HOMELANDS AND SACRED AREAS.   They also demonstrate ongoing appreciation for life and the inseparable interactions among their physical, mental, emotional, and spiritual well-being. Traditional cultures emphasize giving and altruism in lieu of selfishness; people share personal acquisitions with others, and caring for others is the purpose of life (Hunt et al., 2001; Joe & Miller, 1993).

AMERICAN INDIANS OR ALASKA NATIVES BRING HONOR AND RESPECT TO THEIR FAMILIES.   They maintain a collectivist orientation that embraces family, tribal solidarity, and cohesiveness. Families are the first priority and, customarily, have strong social structures and extended networks of cooperative and supportive relationships among community members (Franklin, Turnbull, Wehmeyer, & Blackmountain, 2003). Women tend to have influential roles in the family as well as the tribal extension. Family and tribal elders, both male and female, receive considerable respect. They have great influence and are revered because age is a mark of honor. Traditionally, grandparents monitor parental behavior and have an official voice in child rearing. They teach children about responsibility, loyalty, and behavioral expectations (Hunt et al., 2001). Children are central to the family; if children are unable to attend a function, then nobody attends (Joe & Miller, 1993).

AMERICAN INDIAN CHILDREN BELONG TO THE COMMUNITY.   Family members and society undertake responsibility for childcare (i.e., *It takes a village to raise a child.*). Child rearing emphasizes autonomy, responsibility for behaviors, self-discipline, and generosity; youth are socialized to make and abide by decisions (Hunt et al., 2001; Joe & Miller, 1993). They identify with and engage in group endeavors and are inspired to develop unique talents, knowledge, and skills that benefit themselves and society. Personal mastery motivates their cognitive, physical, social, and spiritual development; self-improvement is valued over comparison to and competition with others. Adults assume minimal authoritative posture and seldom reprimand children verbally or punish them physically; rather, they respond to inappropriate behaviors with disapproving looks, ridicule, and shaming. People unfamiliar with traditional practices may view traditional child-rearing practices as negligence.

African Americans

AFRICAN AMERICAN FAMILIES EMPHASIZE COLLECTIVE RESPONSIBILITY, STRONG PARENT–CHILD AND SIBLING RELATIONSHIPS, ADAPTABLE FAMILY ROLES WITH EGALITARIAN PATTERNS, AND HIGH ACHIEVEMENT ORIENTATION (LADSON-BILLINGS, 1991). Families' collectivist social identity derives from African origins and the concept of *fictive kinship* in which people reach out to traditional and nontraditional family members, connect to indigenous cultures, and subscribe to group-specific values and communication styles (Ladson-Billings, 1991). Firm parent–child and sibling ties, frequent fosterage of children, and social networks underscore a sense of community and family survival. Extended families provide financial, emotional, educational, and social support, as well as adequate role models for parenting; they also foster wholesome behaviors and curb deviant activities (Hanline & Daley, 1992; Ladson-Billings, 1991).

AFRICAN AMERICAN FAMILIES ARE PRIMARILY MATRIARCHAL IN NATURE. Mothers and grandmothers play essential roles in socializing and equipping children with adaptive strategies that lead to positive self-worth, self-sufficiency, and independence, as well as serving as a source of family assistance (Thompson, 2003). Caregivers encourage children's aspirations, achievement, and goal attainment. Parenting is described as controlling and authoritarian; parents stress obedience, respect for elders, neatness and cleanliness, and avoiding trouble. A strict no-nonsense parenting style represents functional and appropriate discipline. African Americans' social interactions are humanistic with a focus on informality, expressiveness, and a strong connection to historical roots (Thompson, 2003).

Hispanics

HISPANIC FAMILIES ARE ALSO CHARACTERIZED BY COLLECTIVISM AS EVIDENCED BY THE CONCEPT, *FAMILISMO*, WHICH CONCERNS FAMILY CENTEREDNESS AND RELATIONSHIPS. Family members reflect and contribute to the identity of immediate and extended families, which may include nonrelative, or *compadres*. Family integrity is considered within the frameworks of cooperation and defined roles that lend to its emotional and financial support (Lian & Fonanez-Phelan, 2001).

HISPANIC FAMILIES EXHIBIT PATTERNS OF SOCIAL INTERACTION AND BEHAVIORAL STYLE, WHICH RESONATES UNIQUE CULTURAL TRADITIONS AND EXPRESSIONS OF *RESPETO*, A GENERALIZED DEFERENCE FOR INDIVIDUALS, AND RESPECT FOR PARENTS AND ELDERS THAT IS BASED ON SOCIAL RELATIONS (CHAVIRA, LOPEZ, BLACHER, & SHAPIRO, 2000). Families typically are patriarchal in nature, where the father's status is superior to the mother's position. Fathers are disciplinarians and reflect an attitude of full responsibility for family guidance and resources and making major decisions. Mothers are nurturers who oversee and direct children's spiritual development and instruction; they often consult with fathers and grandmothers before making child-related decisions (Chavira et al.,

2000; Lian & Fonanez-Phelan, 2001). Quite often families are intergenerational, and there is an abiding sense of devotion for elders; sibling roles of responsibility and authority depend on their age.

HISPANIC CHILDREN ARE SOCIALIZED TO GENDER-SPECIFIC ROLES AND CHARACTERISTICS (CHAVIRA ET AL., 2000). Traditionally, females are raised in protective environments and educated to assume domestic duties, exhibit spiritual superiority to men, and endure suffering occasioned by men (Chavira et al., 2000). The concept of *marianismo* characterizes female roles related to submissiveness, obedience, dependence, timidity, gentleness, sentimentality, and remaining virginal until marriage. Males, on the other hand, have more freedom and, as they get older, may join groups known as *palo millas,* where they are socialized to typical roles. The concept of *machismo* depicts male roles rooted in physical strength, aggressiveness, masculinity, sexual attractiveness, and ability to consume excessive quantities of alcohol without getting drunk. Machismo men also have an ingrained sense of authority and responsibility for their sisters, and they expect to be the recipients of others' respect.

HISPANIC CHILDREN AND YOUTH ARE SOCIALIZED TO OTHER CULTURAL PATTERNS THAT INCLUDE *FATALISMO*, WHICH REFERS TO A SENSE OF VULNERABILITY AND PERCEPTION THAT PEOPLE CANNOT CONTROL ADVERSITY IN THEIR LIVES. The characteristic *personalismo* concerns people orientation, physical closeness, and contact in personal interactions; *individualismo* considers individual uniqueness and harmony with others. The traits relate closely to the concepts of *dignidad, honor,* and *confianza,* which reflect traditions of respect for and expressions of deference and trust among people.

PARENTING STYLES WITHIN HISPANIC FAMILIES DIFFER DEPENDING ON THE MOTHER'S AGE, RELIGION, AND EDUCATION; LENGTH OF U.S. RESIDENCE AND ACCULTURATION LEVEL; FATHER'S EMPLOYMENT STATUS; CHILD'S GENDER; AND NUMBER OF SIBLINGS (RUEDA, MONZO, SHAPIRO, GOMEZ, & BLACHER, 2005). An authoritative style values democratic decision making, setting guidelines and parameters, communication, problem solving, self-discipline, and responsibility. Authoritative styles are associated with second- and third-generation families and beyond that assume values of competition and individualism. An authoritative style may be seen as antagonistic to communal and cooperative beliefs espoused by traditional Hispanics. An authoritarian style, on the other hand, identifies with new immigrants who adhere to traditional tenets and may reside in lower socioeconomic neighborhoods. These parents attend church regularly and observe the rigors and constraints of their churches. They may establish restrictive family environments, expect youth to follow absolute behavioral rules, incorporate punishment in discipline interactions, and nourish communal and cooperative values.

Asian, Native Hawaiian and Other Pacific Islander Americans

ASIAN, NATIVE HAWAIIAN AND OTHER PACIFIC ISLANDER AMERICAN FAMILIES GENERALLY PLACE GREAT IMPORTANCE ON FAMILY VALUES, SOCIAL UNITY AND COHESIVENESS, AND PARENTAL EXPECTATIONS (BUI & TURNBULL, 2003). For example, traditional Hawaiian, Samoan, and Tongan families uphold a collective family orientation in which individuals' behaviors and actions benefit family and community. Children evidence loyalty and obligation to family members and respect for elders; they are assets and sources of family pride.

FAMILIES OF EAST ASIAN ANCESTRY (I.E., CHINESE, JAPANESE, AND KOREAN) ALSO FOCUS ON SELF-DISCIPLINE AND COLLECTIVIST GOALS THAT VALUE ELDERS AND CONTINUING OBLIGATIONS TO PAST GENERATIONS (BUI & TURNBULL, 2003). Family members have unique responsibility to identify with and represent the family; no one exists without the family (Park, Turnbull, & Park, 2001). Families are patriarchal in nature and guided by *filial piety*, which centers on respecting the father figure, conforming to group standards, fulfilling parental wishes, and establishing harmonious interpersonal relationships as bases for acceptance and approval of behaviors. Men are accorded ultimate authority and maintain a traditional role of leadership, but obedience to elders must be absolute. Sons generally are valued more than daughters; sons are admonished to consult with their fathers prior to undertaking anything important. In many families, the wife is submissive to the husband, younger brothers to older brothers, and sisters to all brothers. Women have authority for daily household affairs; older siblings are responsible for young children. Family members gauge their behaviors in terms of filial piety, which is also the cornerstone for resolving conflicts in a compromising and peaceful manner.

IN MANY TRADITIONAL ASIAN-AMERICAN FAMILIES, PAIN AND HARD WORK ARE CONDITIONS FOR DEVELOPING CHILDREN'S MORAL VALUES, AND PHYSICAL PUNISHMENTS FOR BEHAVIORAL TRANSGRESSIONS ARE EXPRESSIONS OF PARENTAL LOVE AND RESPONSIBILITY (MATTHEWS, 2001). Parents expect children to follow society's ideals and bring honor to the family; children must demonstrate respect for elders and unconditional acceptance of parental and teacher authority. A strong sense of family obligation takes precedence over individual needs; children's identity is based on family membership (Matthews, 2001). Children must fulfill family obligations and maintain traditions; they must be loyal and obedient to family, persevere, work hard, and show emotional restraint. In addition, children, especially boys, are encouraged to attain high educational and occupational aspirations.

SOCIALIZATION IN ASIAN-AMERICAN FAMILIES FOCUSES ON SELF-RESPECT, ENSURING OTHERS' DEFERENCE FOR ONESELF, AND AVOIDING BEHAVIORS THAT PROVOKE DISAPPROVAL (KALYANPUR & GOWRAMMA, 2007). Shame is a principal force in socializing children, who are taught to believe that behaviors reflect the family's dignity. Children are governed by a fear of losing face, external judgments of their behaviors, and failure to fulfill family responsibilities; their successes honor the family, and their failures dishonor and shame the family (Matthews, 2001). The fear of shame, accompanying dishonor, and loss of social status are bases for preventing inappropriate behaviors and ensuring that people comply with laws, cultural norms, and traditions. The sense of shame is also a disciplinary tool, where ridicule may be used to correct children's behaviors. The accompanying derision causes humiliation and loss of self-esteem (i.e., loss of face).

ASIAN-AMERICAN YOUTH AND YOUNG ADULTS' SOCIAL BEHAVIORS ARE MARKED BY DEFERENCE TO OTHERS, SHYNESS, AND ANXIETY, AS WELL AS CONSIDERABLE RESTRAINT AND INDIRECT EXPRESSION OF FEELINGS IN PUBLIC, BASED ON FEAR OF SHAMING THE FAMILY. They also are reluctant to engage in confrontation or elevate themselves beyond the group's status. These internalizing behaviors result from cultural tendencies to maintain family privacy and dignity and to manage problems in a family setting. Collectivism is the norm, whereas individualism and competition are de-emphasized; assertiveness weakens family ties and threatens filial piety.

LANGUAGE, COMMUNICATION, AND CULTURE

Cultures vary in the extent to which they view and interact with their environments, social surroundings, and organizational structures. African Americans; Asian, Native Hawaiian and Other Pacific Islander Americans, Hispanics, and various indigenous populations are *high-context cultural groups* that rely on strong social networks to develop their identities (Chae, 2000). As indicated previously, these groups value interdependence, intragroup interactions, and cohesive, person-oriented relationships that benefit group members. They also evidence (a) harmony with nature, (b) intuitive knowledge based on perceptions and feelings, (c) social integration and stability, and (d) close-knit social structures and conformity to role expectations.

Members of high-context cultures rely more on nonverbal than verbal communication. They communicate with others and ascertain meaning via shared experiences, history, conversational contexts, speaker's status, and implicit messages. For example, parents of African-American heritage often communicate behavioral standards through implicit cues. Children who confront their parents may be given nonverbal cues that indicate the child should *get it together or suffer the consequences*. The approach illustrates respect for parental position. A similar situation exists among Asian or Other Pacific Islander Americans where "a look, a word, or a gesture may convey the equivalent of paragraphs of spoken words" (Lynch & Hanson, 2004, p. 61).

Understanding also evolves from the setting of an encounter, physical cues, and relationships; members of high-context cultures accentuate facial expressions, tensions, movements, speed of interactions, and other subtle nuances. American Indian or Alaska Native cultures consider silence a strength; talking is not always valued, and people tend toward long pauses in conversation (Robinson-Zanartu, & Majel-Dixon, 1996). They also speak in low-keyed monotone voices with a slower-paced discourse style; a few select words express their feelings. They seldom exert dominance over or provide excessive directions to others, nor do they address acquaintances in an overly familiar way. Finally, their conversational language may be allegorical because content of the message is more important than the person's emotional reaction.

Nonverbal Communication

Knowledge of *nonverbal communication styles* that are rooted in cultural heritage is vital to the interactions that occur among teachers and parents. For example, hand gestures should be used with great caution, particularly when communicating with Vietnamese Americans. Yet, the *shaka*, or *hang loose* hand signal is a prominent form of nonverbal communication among Hawaii's local populations that may be used as a greeting or an indication that things are okay.

Pacific Islanders also rely on uplifted nods of their heads or raised eyebrows to acknowledge someone's presence or to agree with a comment or an observation. These nonverbal movements often replace the necessity for any verbal statements. Out of respect and deference to specific groups (e.g., adults, members of the opposite sex, seniors), Asian and Native Hawaiian and Other Pacific Islander Americans may lower their eyes when interacting with them. Teachers must understand that the lack of eye contact does not indicate disinterest or guilty behaviors (Adler, 2004).

A smile is a common form of nonverbal communication in Southeast Asia. People smile when they are happy or sad, when reprimanded, or when they may not understand a lesson or cannot answer a question (Matthews, 2001). Teachers are often shocked by Southeast Asians' smile. The smile does not mean a challenge or disrespectful behavior but conveys a message that students' recognize their fault and do not bear a grudge against the teacher (Adler, 2004).

Professionals should also consider cultural beliefs about touching others. For example, in Cambodian, Laotian, and Hawaiian cultures, touching a person's head may be threatening or offensive because of spiritual beliefs that the head is a sacred part of the body. People's reactions may range from a vague sense of discomfort to resentment, anger, and feelings of physical violation. Other touching, however, is a sign of friendship or affection among Pacific Islanders and occurs with immediate and extended family members and friends. Teachers, counselors, and other school personnel must become knowledgeable of nonverbal cultural behaviors.

Verbal Communication

Knowledge of a family's *primary language and verbal communication styles* are important to identify and understand cultural nuances; language references to disabilities often provide important clues to family attitudes. Language characteristics affect parent–teacher communication, and they are the foundation for perceptions of self-worth and adjustment to new sociocultural environments. Teachers must develop sensitivity to and positive regard for the dynamics of linguistic diversity, including differences in standard and nonstandard language dialects (e.g., Ebonics, Hawaii Creole English), as well as the pragmatics of language (e.g., when to speak, what to discuss, who speaks first, how to initiate and terminate a conversation).

Teachers need knowledge about diverse language systems that operate within families of youngsters in their classrooms. For example, African Americans, Hispanics, and Native Hawaiians engage in a participatory-interactive communication style where speakers and listeners are action-provoking partners in constructing discourse. Speakers in these ethnic groups expect listeners to engage them through vocalized, motion, and movement responses during the conversation. Table 6.2 provides an overview of language characteristics found among various cultural groups. As you review the table, consider the language characteristics and patterns that you may encounter when working with families. How can you adjust your language pattern and communication style to accommodate the families' styles?

HEALTH, ILLNESS, AND DISABILITY BELIEFS

The concept of disability varies across cultures. Many cultures view disabilities as only those that are physically observable or explained (e.g., orthopedic or sensory impairments). In other cases, illnesses and disabilities are *cause–effect events* with varying causes. For example, in many Western cultures, a disability is believed to be the result of a genetic or physical

TABLE 6.2	Language Characteristics of Different Cultural Groups
Cultural Group	**Language Characteristics**
American Indians or Alaska Natives	• Communication is taken seriously and undertaken with great care in American Indian and Alaska Native communities. • Traditional teaching encourages silence among children and emphasizes sensitivity to body language (e.g., pointing with chin). • Continuous, unwavering eye contact is disrespectful and impolite; children avoid looking directly at authority figures out of deference for their position. • Native people often maintain inexpressive faces and seldom expose feelings of joy, surprise, pleasure, or pain (it undesirable to show emotion). • Limited facial expressions, physical touching, and public displays of affection indicate respect in cultures that stress restraint.
African Americans	• Language patterns of many African Americans may not resemble communication within mainstream society. • African-American language patterns often embody a unique framework of grammar, structure, intonation, body language, and communication styles. • Educators must acknowledge that conversations in which speakers do not allow others to complete sentences to *gain the floor* may signify passion for the topic rather than rudeness. • Display of emotions during conflict is perceived as an honest and important step toward resolving discord rather than a sign of emotional instability or inadequate mediation skills. • African Americans who state opinions in a prideful and straightforward manner must not be considered to be challenging authority. Instead, professionals should harness the energy, acknowledge diverse viewpoints, and allow enthusiasm as means to generate collective solutions to problems.
Hispanics	• Communication styles tend to be gentle with emphasis on politeness and tact. • Hispanics view direct disagreement or contradiction as rude and, therefore, something to avoid in an attempt to circumvent misunderstanding. • Interaction in which a translator is used may result in miscommunication. Educators should assume a consultative posture in which they *advise* and *suggest* rather than assume a direct posture.
Asian and Native Hawaiian or Other Pacific Islander Americans	• The concept of harmony is valued in Asian and Native Hawaiian and Other Pacific Islander cultures. • Children and adults are taught to conceal their feelings (except to those closest to them), which may lead to many *apparent agreements* that, in fact, are mere attempts to preserve harmony. • It is preferable to greet members of the opposite sex with a slight bow rather than a handshake. • Lack of direct eye contact is often seen as a sign of respect but can be misconstrued by teachers as a lack of respect.

Sources: Atkin (1991), Franklin et al. (2003), Garcia et al. (2000), Hunt et al. (2001), Ladson-Billings (1991), Lian & Fonanez-Phelan (2001).

anomaly (e.g., *cause*—drinking alcohol while pregnant; *effect*—a child born with fetal alcohol syndrome). However, in other cultures a disability may be seen as the result of a superstitious behavior or psychological event (e.g., *cause*—disrespecting elders and traditional religious behaviors; *effect*—a child born with spina bifida). *As you read the following sections, keep in mind that no two people from the same culture are exactly alike, and the generalizations made in these discussions are based on research and a review of the literature.*

African Americans

African Americas have historically held the belief that they have the power to influence their health and the health of others (Fields, 2002). The mind, body, and spirit are thought to be interconnected, and if you are in good health, it is accepted that you are in harmony with nature (Clarke-Tasker, 1993). Historically, a person who was ill was thought to be in disharmony with nature. Illnesses stem from two sources, namely, natural causes (e.g., germs, cold/heat, impurities in drink or food) or unnatural causes accredited to demons and evil spirits (Campinha-Bacote, 1992).

The treatment goal for any illness is to remove the impurities from the body if the illness was natural or to remove the demons or evil spirits if the illness was unnatural. Women were the traditional healers and were generally called on to cure the person who was ill or exorcise the evil spirits (Belgrave, 1998; Fields, 2002).

Disabilities are typically seen in the similar light as most illnesses or health-related concerns and are attributed to natural or unnatural causes (Atkin, 1991). However, disability is generally seen to exist only if interferes with the ability to be productive (Belgrave, 1998; Fields 2002). Thus, a disability may only be seen or accepted if it interferes with the individual's ability to work. In terms of children, work is equated to schoolwork and success in school (Atkin, 1991; Fields, 2002).

American Indians or Alaska Natives

Health beliefs are related to religion and maintaining balance with the natural world. Most indigenous people attribute illnesses, misfortunes, and disabilities to either supernatural or natural causes (Robinson-Zanartu & Majel-Dixon, 1996). Supernatural causes include witchcraft, spells, spirit loss or intrusion, and various unnatural forces. Natural causes include imbalance and disharmony that result from acculturation, breaching cultural taboos, and/or other accidents (Hunt et al., 2001). For example, Lakota cultural traditions focus on respecting and maintaining balance with the earth and learning from the wind and coyotes. American Indians are likely to accept a person with a disability and facilitate integration into the family and community. They identify the strengths of the family member with a disability and prepare the person for community employment that utilizes their strengths (Robinson-Zanartu & Majel-Dixon, 1996).

Many groups of Hopi Indians equate a disability with impairment only when it renders a person unable to contribute to society. A disabling condition that manifests later in life results from deviating from the traditional *Hopi Way*. Those who deviate open the door to harm and are vulnerable to illness and injury. Indigenous people often turn to tribal healers and shamans to lessen negative effects of a health-related condition and prevent its future occurrence. Traditional rituals and healing ceremonies, which vary from one tribe to the next, are conducted to initiate healing processes and protect people from additional harm.

Many indigenous populations believe that spoken words have great power; therefore, talk of disability and illness is exercised with care. These discussions among traditional Navajos, for example, are taboo because they foreshadow death and disease (e.g., a Navajo student may refuse to role-play an HIV-testing scenario because such activity will cause him to contract HIV; Franklin et al., 2003). Moreover, many Native languages do not have words for specific disabilities or illnesses because the concepts do not lie within their life experiences. Consequently, a description of a disability or an illness may serve as the name for the disability or illness.

Hispanics

Educators must acknowledge the centrality of religion on the beliefs of some Hispanic-American families about the causes and treatment of disability. Health beliefs may be intertwined strongly with religion; disease and/or disability may be perceived as punishment for wrongdoing (Garcia, Mendez-Perez, & Ortiz, 2000). The family will often turn to the church for support; parents' beliefs about special education services may be secondary to their hope of a spiritual healing (*curanderos*) for the child. Therefore, it is important to ensure that professional's actions do not counter the church (Gaventa, 2008).

Asian, Native Hawaiian or Other Pacific Islander Americans

Some Asian-American and Pacific Islander families may consider a child with a disability as their fate and attribute the disability to a previous behavior transgression. For example, in some Asian-American families, children and others with disabilities may cast overwhelming shame on the family; the disability may be viewed as a result of unsatisfactory behavior and lack of self-control and is considered an indictment of a family's inability to comply with cultural norms, social codes, and traditions.

In Cambodian families, the illness (disability) is a cause–effect phenomenon and results from the revenge of the *neak ta*; the spirits of the trees who are offended if one speaks loudly or in a rude manner. In Hmong families, on the other hand, a disability (e.g., epilepsy) may be viewed as a result of losing one's soul (Adler, 2004). Yet, it is considered a blessing and evidence that the person is a member of royalty, has powers of extrasensory perceptions, and may grow up to be a shaman (i.e., *txiv neeb* [tsi neng] = person with a healing spirit). Hmong families' description of a disability serves as the name for the disability (i.e., *Quag dab peg* [kow da pay] = the spirit catches you and you fall down; Fadiman, 1997).

In Hawaiian families, persons with disabilities are accepted and protected within extended family systems, where they function independently, or with the assistance of others, as contributing members of society (Yamauchi, Lau-Smith, & Luning, 2008). Yet, in traditional Samoan families, the birth of a child with a disability is considered to be a censure for the parent's earlier aberrant behaviors. Parents' reactions to a child with a disability initially may be one of nonacceptance. Very often a child is hidden from the public because the disability is an embarrassment and symbolizes the parents' inappropriate behavior. In essence, if the parents engaged in wrongful behavior, the behavior cannot be hidden and will be evidenced in the child. For example, if a rebellious Samoan teenager steals a neighbor's pigs, the teenager's future child may be born with a dark and hairy birthmark as retribution for the behavior.

Asian-American families may also rely on more traditional religious beliefs and medical practices, including herbal medicine, acupuncture, and folk medicine in the treatment of disabilities (Matthew, 2001). Folk medicine treatments, practiced among various Asian populations (e.g., Cambodian, Hmong, Vietnamese), such as the healing practices of *cupping* (i.e., lowering a heated ceramic cup to an infected area of the skin), pinching, scraping, and *coining* (i.e., rubbing a hot coin on an infected area of the skin) often leave marks and abrasions that are mistaken as evidence of child abuse. Cambodians believe that health is a balancing act and that *coining* helps to release *bad winds* from the body as a means of attaining balance.

BARRIERS TO WORKING EFFECTIVELY WITH FAMILIES FROM DIVERSE BACKGROUNDS

Research related to culture, diversity, and family and school relationships indicates issues of diversity and culture influence a person's perception of disability and education (Kalyanpur & Gowramma, 2007). In Chapter 4, you read about barriers that can exist among professionals, students, and families when meeting to discuss students. These barriers or conflicts are influenced by each person's values, culture, and frame of reference (Friend & Cook, 2009). Current research on culturally diverse families and their involvement in the education system suggests multiple barriers preclude them from more thorough involvement in the education process. Chief among these concerns are cultural beliefs and practice, language and communication differences, financial constraints—such as difficulty getting off work or the inability to obtain affordable and secure childcare for other children (DeGangi, Wietlisbach, Poisson, Stein, & Royeen, 1994)—and lack of knowledge or familiarity with the education system, specifically lack of knowledge of parental rights and responsibilities.

As you have read in this chapter, cultural beliefs prevent some families from becoming actively involved their children's education. For example, for some families and among some cultures, having a child with a disability brings shame to the nuclear as well as extended family, and parents may not wish to acknowledge the child by attending a school meeting. A different example also influenced by cultural beliefs is when a father and mother do attend an IEP meeting but do not initiate conversation or question any decisions made by the professionals. Teachers may view this as a lack of caring or involvement, whereas the parents view it as a sign of respect.

Language and the ability or inability to communicate can also hamper family involvement in the education process. For instance, over 134 different languages are identified as the primary language of students who attend school in Clark County School District in Nevada (Clark County School District, 2010). In 2004, in Los Angeles, 92 different languages were spoken by students receiving special education services (Los Angeles Unified School District, 2008). Although IDEA states that materials on family rights, responsibilities, and involvement in the special education process must be provided to each family in their native language, given the number of different languages in many school districts, this does not always happen. To further exacerbate the situation, most teachers speak English as their primary language. Although language interpreters are available in some very large school districts, most districts do not have the capacity to employ language interpreters who speak all the languages spoken in their districts. Thus, families whose primary language is not English are often unfamiliar with the special education process and are at a disadvantage in meetings where English is spoken.

As was mentioned in Chapter 5, families may live in poverty or face financial constraints that prohibit them from attending meetings and school functions. Being from a diverse ethnic or racial group does not mean that a family has poor financial resources. In fact, the largest group of people who live in poverty in the United States is White non-Hispanic (Children's Defense Fund, 2006). Families that live in poverty can have extreme difficulty attending and participating in school meetings. Family members may be prohibited from becoming involved, for example, because they (a) would lose income if they took time off work, (b) do not have transportation to and from the meeting, and (c) cannot secure childcare for other children (DeGangi et al., 1994).

A final barrier that affects culturally and linguistically diverse families' ability to participate in the education process is their lack of understanding or knowledge of the education system. For some families, this may be due to lack of parental education (e.g., did not complete high school); for other families, it may be due to immigrant status (e.g., just moved to the United States), whereas for others, it may be due to a language barrier or the belief that teachers are the professionals and that parents should not interfere in the educational process. These beliefs generally promote the idea that the professional is the *expert* on their child's education and that parents and families should not interfere with the professionals' work. Thus, although parents and families are invited to IEP and IFSP meetings, some families' beliefs lead them to think this is done only as a courtesy. For some families, interacting with professionals and providing an opinion on their child's education would be showing disrespect for the professional.

STRATEGIES FOR WORKING WITH FAMILIES FROM DIVERSE BACKGROUNDS

General approaches to working with families from diverse background include parent and family education programs, parent/family and teacher problem-solving sessions, employment of parents in school settings, and developing curricula that links schools to community and culture (Sileo, Sileo, & Prater, 1996). For example, programs can be designed to (a) help families learn more about the special education process, (b) assist parents to earn a high school or college degree, (c) assist families to learn English, (d) help families to become more comfortable in a school setting, (e) help parents and family members to become paraeducators or language interpreters for the school district, and (f) assist families to set up parent and family assistance centers in schools (Matuszny, Banda, & Coleman, 2007; Sileo et al., 1996). Specific keys to working with families from diverse background include the following:

- ***Show time consideration.*** This includes when and where to meet with parents and families. Time considerations also include approaches to discussions. For example, when holding a meeting with parents and family members, it is customary in Hawaii to *talk story* before any formal discussion takes place. To *talk story* before a formal discussion allows participants to get to know one another or to catch up on things that are happening in each other's lives. *Talking story* is a very important part of any get together, meeting, or discussion.
- ***Develop information sharing and parent preferences for involvement in the process or discussion.*** It may be helpful to send an informal note home prior to the first meeting with a family to ask them to identify some of their concerns about

their child and some of their preferences for involvement in the meeting. For example, designing a brief note or questionnaire that identifies the parents' primary language preference, time and location preferences for the meeting, who will be attending the meeting (both from the family and the school), and concerns or beliefs about their child can lay the foundation for open communication during the meeting.

• **_Understand family structure and lines of authority._** As you read earlier in this chapter, family structure can vary greatly. Although all members of the family are encouraged to become involved in the education process, one parent or another family member may be the primary person involved. Learn what family members will be responsible for attending an IEP meeting and who provides the most educational support to the child at home. In some cases, it may be the grandparents who are both the primary caregivers and the ones to attend the IEP meeting and school functions. As an educator, it is important that you respect the uniqueness of each family. Your ability to accept differences between the family and yourself will go a long way toward establishing a productive relationship.

• **_Be aware of family dynamics._** When meeting with each family, consider how raising a child with a disability has affected them. What are the family's primary concerns? What resources and concerns do the parents bring to the meeting? For example, parents may come to an IEP meeting and be more concerned about afterschool child care (because both parents need to work) than specific IEP goals and objectives. Acknowledge their concerns and brainstorm with the parents to find a solution to the problem.

• **_Develop an exclusive relationship with each family._** Professionals should attempt to get to know the families of the students in their classroom. Awareness of cultural and linguistic differences among families increases a professional's probability of developing successful relationships with those families. Although each relationship you develop will be different, in general, families are more likely to develop an effective collaborative relationship with professionals they accept and trust.

• **_Honor cultural diversity and strive to be culturally competent._** This is the most essential skill and approach to successfully working with families. Professionals must be sensitive to and respectful of the different lifestyles, cultural backgrounds, family needs, and concerns posed by parents and family members (Lawrence-Lightfoot, 2003). Although honesty is always the best policy, professionals should be cognizant of differences in their own belief systems and those of families. View family members as people, and not just the parent or caregiver of the child. Remember that family members bring their beliefs, understandings, and values with them when they come to school. Respect the family members' ideals and work to support the family and child within the construct of the value system.

Summary

• Professionals' knowledge of and ability to reflect on variables in family role patterns and communication and language styles will enable them to respond to parents from diverse backgrounds in a way that conveys positive regard for the dynamics of diversity, establishes trust, and ensures optimal parent and family involvement.

- A child's learning and behavior characteristics are linked directly to home and cultural considerations that may limit educational outcomes.
- Educators must become conversant with child-rearing, disciplinary, and medicinal practices

of the diverse racial, ethnic, and cultural populations with whom they interact as bases for working with families and fulfilling professional responsibilities in a culturally competent manner.

Linking Standards to Chapter Content

After reading this chapter, you should be able to link basic knowledge and skills described in the CEC Standards and INTASC Principles with information provided in this text. Table 6.3, Linking CEC Standards and INTASC Principles to Major Chapter Topics, gives examples of how they can be applied to each major section of the chapter.

TABLE 6.3 Linking CEC Standards and INTASC Principles to Major Chapter Topics

Major Chapter Headings	CEC Knowledge and Skill Core Standard and Associated Subcategories	INTASC Core Principle and Associated Special Education Subcategories
Cultural Competence Multicultural Considerations for Parent Involvement Heterogeneity among Diverse Populations	2: Development and Characteristics of Learners ICC2K3 Characteristics and effects of the cultural and environmental milieu of the individual with exceptional learning needs and the family. 3: Individual Learning Differences ICC3K3 Variations in beliefs, traditions, and values across and within cultures and their effects on relationships among individuals with exceptional learning needs. 4: Family, and schooling. ICC3K4 Cultural perspectives influencing the relationships among families, schools, and communities as related to instruction. 5: Learning Environments and Social Interactions ICC5K9 Ways specific cultures are negatively stereotyped. 6: Communication ICC6K2 Characteristics of one's own culture and use of language and the ways in which these can differ from other cultures and uses of languages.	2: Student Learning 2.07 Special education teachers seek to understand the current and evolving development and learning of individual students from a life-span perspective. . . . listening to family beliefs, priorities and concerns, as a framework for sharing information with families, and as a basis for assessment and planning. 3: Diverse Learners 3.03 All teachers understand that a disability can be perceived differently across families, communities, and cultures based on differing values and belief systems. 3.04 All teachers understand and are sensitive to cultural, ethnic, gender, and linguistic differences that may be confused with or misinterpreted as manifestations of a disability. 8: Assessment 8.09 Special education teachers are aware of and guard against over and under identification of disabilities based on cultural, ethnic, gender, and linguistic diversity.

(continued)

TABLE 6.3 Linking CEC Standards and INTASC Principles to Major Chapter Topics (*continued*)

Major Chapter Headings	CEC Knowledge and Skill Core Standard and Associated Subcategories	INTASC Core Principle and Associated Special Education Subcategories
	ICC6K3 Ways of behaving and communicating among cultures that can lead to misinterpretation and misunderstanding.	9: Professionalism 9.04 All teachers reflect on the potential interaction between a student's cultural experiences and their disability 10: Collaboration, Ethics, and Relationships 10.04 All teachers accept families as full partners in planning appropriate instruction and services for students with disabilities, and demonstrate sensitivity to differences in family structures and social, economic, and cultural backgrounds of students with disabilities. 10.10 Special education teachers understand the impact that having a child with a disability may have on family roles and functioning at different points in the life cycle of a family.

Working with Families from Diverse Backgrounds
Family Role Patterns
  American Indians or Alaska Natives
  African Americans
  Hispanics
  Asian, Native Hawaiian and Other Pacific Islander Americans
Language, Communication, and Culture
  Nonverbal Communication
  Verbal Communication
Health, Illness, and Disability Beliefs
  African Americans
  American Indians or Alaska Natives
  Hispanics
	5: Learning Environments and Social Interactions
	ICC5K8 Ways to create learning environments that allow individuals to retain and appreciate their own and each other's respective language and cultural heritage.
	ICC5K10 Strategies used by diverse populations to cope with a legacy of former and continuing racism
	ICC5S13 Organize, develop, and sustain learning environments that support positive intracultural and intercultural experiences.
	ICC5S14 Mediate controversial intercultural issues among students within the learning environment in ways that enhance any culture, group, or person.
	9: Professional and Ethical Practice
	ICC9K1 Personal cultural biases and differences that affect one's teaching.
		3: Diverse Learners
		3.03 All teachers understand that a disability can be perceived differently across families, communities, and cultures based on differing values and belief systems.
		3.06 Special education teachers use culturally accepted ways of seeking information about the student's cultural background from students, families, and communities in order to understand cultural perceptions of and expectations for individuals with disabilities (e.g., learning family structures, using cultural guides).
		3.07 Special education teachers share the values and beliefs underlying special education services for individuals with disabilities in the United States with students, families, and community members, and seek to understand ways

(*continued*)

TABLE 6.3 (continued)

Major Chapter Headings	CEC Knowledge and Skill Core Standard and Associated Subcategories	INTASC Core Principle and Associated Special Education Subcategories
Asian, Native Hawaiian and Other Pacific Islander Americans Barriers to Working Effectively with Families from Diverse Backgrounds Strategies for Working with Families from Diverse Backgrounds	ICC9S6 Demonstrate sensitivity for the culture, language, religion, gender, disability, socioeconomic status, and sexual orientation of individuals. 10: Collaboration ICC10K4 Culturally responsive factors that promote effective communication and collaboration with individuals with exceptional learning needs, families, school personnel, and community members. ICC10S10 Communicate effectively with families of individuals with exceptional learning needs from diverse backgrounds.	in which these are compatible or in conflict with those of the family and community. 3.08 Special education teachers understand that second language learners can also have language-based disabilities. 3.09 Special education teachers actively ask questions, seek information from others, and take actions to guard against inappropriate assessment and identification of students whose cultural, ethnic, gender, and linguistic differences may be confused with manifestations of a disability. 6: Communication 6.03 All teachers understand that linguistic background has an impact on language acquisition as well as communication content and style. 7: Planning Instruction 7.08 Special education teachers provide for the active involvement of students, families, and other professionals in constructing the student's education program. 9: Professionalism 9.07 Special education teachers reflect on their personal biases and the influences of these biases on the instruction they provide to students with disabilities, and on the interactions they have with other personnel, families, and the community.

Sources: Council for Exceptional Children (2005); Interstate New Teacher Assessment and Support Consortium INTASC Special Education Subcommittee (May 2001).

Web Resources

INTERNET WEB SITES AND SUPPORT

http://www.aynrand.org/site/PageServer?pagename= index—Ayn Rand Center for Individual Rights seeks to spearhead a cultural renaissance that will reverse the antireason, anti-individualism, antifreedom, anticapitalist

http://www.nameorg.org/—National Association for Multicultural Education is envisioned as an organization that would bring together individuals and groups with an interest in multicultural education from all levels of education, different academic disciplines, and diverse educational institutions and occupations.

http://www.nea.org/diversitytoolkit/race.html— National Education Association–Diversity Toolkit: Tools and ideas that provide practical information and resources for educators

http://www.nmci.org/—National Multicultural Institute is proud to be one of the first organizations to have recognized the nation's need for new services, knowledge, and skills in the growing field of multiculturalism and diversity.

http://www.uncf.org/—United Negro College Fund seeks to close the educational attainment gap between African Americans and the majority population.

Understanding the Family Perspective

OBJECTIVES

After reading this chapter you will

1. Describe factors that influence educators' perceptions of IEP processes.
2. Explain ways in which family members respond to disability.
3. Discuss how family dynamics affect parents' responses to their children's condition.
4. Describe barriers to family participation in IEP processes.
5. Describe how educators can support family involvement in special education.

INTRODUCTION

Mr. and Mrs. West have three children. Their oldest children are seven years older than their daughter Olivia. By the time Olivia started school, the Wests were well acquainted with educational systems, and they had a great deal of experience working with teachers. Over the years they developed good relationships with their children's teachers, were involved with parent–teacher associations, and supported education at home. Consequently, their children performed well at school and achieved academic success. When Olivia started school, they expected Olivia's experience at school to be similar to that of their other children. However, Olivia had challenges their other children did not have. She had learning disabilities and qualified for special education services when she was in first grade.

Initially, Mr. and Mrs. West experienced difficulty adjusting to their daughter's diagnosis. They realized that reading was harder for Olivia than it had been for their other children, but assumed that once she learned to read, she would be fine. They did not understand that Olivia's learning disabilities affected her social interactions and her ability to process information in class. Although the Wests expected that Olivia would need support learning to read, they did not comprehend how much support Olivia might need to experience success at school.

In developing an individualized education program (IEP) with Olivia's teachers, Olivia's teachers helped the Wests understand Olivia's instructional needs. Together the teachers and the Wests created an IEP that addressed Olivia's needs for support. As the Wests interacted with Olivia's teachers, they appreciated how informative the teachers were about Olivia's condition, and they were grateful that the teachers were supportive when they were unsure of themselves. For the Wests, collaborating with Olivia's teachers was a beneficial experience that facilitated positive adaptation.

The Individuals with Disabilities Education Act (IDEA) states that parents or guardians must be involved in the IEP (individualized education program) process and in developing IEPs for children who have disabilities. In requiring parent involvement, lawmakers established the expectation that school personnel and families would work together to develop and implement educational programs for students with disabilities. This was to ensure that student advocates served on IEP teams and students' rights were protected.

The provision for parental involvement, however, does not guarantee that integrating parents in educational systems is always successful or an easy endeavor. It takes effort for parents and educators to develop effective working relationships. Parents and teachers typically have different perspectives. Such differences can enhance interactions if these differences are respected and valued. At the same time, different perspectives can become barriers for collaboration if they are pronounced and not handled appropriately. Within this chapter, we discuss the perspectives of both parties and suggest ways to facilitate family involvement in special education processes.

UNDERSTANDING THE PROFESSIONAL PERSPECTIVE

Before a person can become a special educator, extensive course and fieldwork required of university and college-based preparation programs must be completed (Prater & Sileo, 2002). Teacher candidates who complete such programs exit with much knowledge and many skills. Their knowledge and skills then increase and become fine-tuned with experience in the classroom; and over time they become expert teachers. Keeping this in mind, what expertise do special educators have in relationship to the IEP process? Here are just a few things they should know: (a) what the acronym IEP means, (b) the definition of an IEP, (c) steps and proper sequence of the IEP process, (d) required elements of an IEP and why each is important, and (e) who is required to attend IEP meetings and the role each person plays.

Unless parents have experienced the IEP process before (e.g., as a professional or with an older child) they will not know the acronyms, jargon, steps, legal requirements, expected roles and responsibilities, and so forth. Educators must recognize at all times that their own perspective is unique from that of the parent. Teachers have learned through formal preparation and ongoing experience and professional development, and they assume formal roles in IEP processes related to their areas of expertise. Formal roles are a set of expected behaviors on a specific identifiable label (Lytle & Bordin, 2001). For example, special educators have knowledge of curriculum, instructional modifications, and strategies for students with disabilities. They receive specialized training for teaching students with disabilities, and they contribute their knowledge of instructional strategies during IEP meetings. Special education teachers assess students, manage IEP processes, and track student progress toward IEP goals. General educators are experts in grade-level curriculum and standards, and their perspectives reflect understanding of typical academic and social performance in relation to grade-level expectations. General educators assess students' performance, adapt instruction to help students make grade-level progress, refer students to special education, and act as members of IEP teams. Other professionals such as occupational therapists, school psychologists, and administrators also serve as IEP team members. They share their knowledge and experience as they interact with educators and parents.

Although teachers and other professionals act as experts in IEP processes, managing IEPs and participating in meetings can be challenging. Special education teachers often have large caseloads that limit available time for planning and teaching and for monitoring IEPs. It can be difficult for special education teachers to collaborate with general educators and other professionals when their students are in many different classrooms and when students receive services from a number of different providers, such as occupational therapists and speech and language pathologists. Special educators may not have time during the school day to complete paperwork and to collaborate (Johns, Crowley, & Guetzloe, 2002). General education teachers may not feel connected to IEP teams or the IEP development process (Menlove, Hudson, & Suter, 2001). They may (a) be unsure about their contributions to team decisions, (b) not know how to prepare for meetings, (c) lack training for tracking progress, and (d) not perceive the relevance of IEP goals to progress in the general curriculum (Menlove et al., 2001). In addition, teachers and other professionals may be pressured by school district officials to use standard, computer-generated formats for IEPs and to create IEPs that conform to district policy, such as full inclusion (Johns et al., 2002), rather than generate their own IEPs or make educational decisions that reflect individualization of educational services.

Given job pressures, it is not surprising that educators adopt behaviors to streamline IEP processes. To maximize the use of their time, professionals often develop routines for IEP meetings such as using standard agendas. Although routines can be helpful and efficient, they can also create a stale atmosphere. Not unlike the live theater performer who needs to work at making each subsequent performance fresh and alive, school personnel need to enter the IEP process recognizing that for most parents (like the theater attendee), this is a new experience.

Parents often enter IEP processes as novices, and although parental involvement and partnership in their child's educational processes are encouraged, professionals clearly dominate in most school–family relationships. For example, Martin and colleagues (2006) conducted direct observations of middle and high school teacher-directed IEP meetings and discovered that school personnel spoke 75% of the time compared to 15% for family members and 3% for the student (5% were considered multiple conversations and 2% silence). In some ways this is not surprising, given that experienced educators are adept at running IEP meetings and conversing on the topics addressed in such meetings. However, educators should remember that parents have intimate knowledge of their child's medical, developmental, and educational history. They know their child's likes and dislikes, and strengths and weaknesses, and can make significant contributions to IEP decisions.

Parent participation in decision-making processes should be encouraged and supported. When collaborating with parents, educators should recognize that parents and professionals generally view the impact of IEP team decisions from different viewpoints. Parents sometimes only see the needs of their child, whereas professionals may recognize more readily the implications of these decisions on the student, the student's peers, and school personnel. For example, as described in Table 7.1, parents and teachers may have different concerns about student placement in a particular educational setting. Whereas parents may focus on their child's safety and social acceptance, professionals may be concerned about the impact the child will have on the other students and the teacher's workload. Such different perspectives can create conflict.

Another area that affects professional decision making is past experience. For example, general educators who have had positive experiences with inclusion are more willing to accept students with disabilities into their classrooms. On the other hand, those who have had bad experiences are less likely to want to repeat that experience. Many researchers have examined the attitudes of general educators on inclusion (e.g., Avramidis

TABLE 7.1 Parents' and Teachers' Perspectives of Educational Placement

Parent's Perspective	Professional's Perspective
• Their child's physical and emotional safety (protection from bullies) • Opportunities for social development • Social acceptance by peers and educators • Opportunities for academic advancement • Access to general education curriculum • Stigmatization and negative perceptions of their child's abilities • Maneuvering physically without harm in school environments	• The impact the child has on the classroom environment • The impact the child has on classmates • The impact the child has on teacher workload • Social acceptance by the teacher and other students • The feasibility of meeting the child's needs

Source: Information from Taub (2006).

& Norwich, 2002; Salend & Duhaney, 1999). Some view inclusion from the perspective of their own workload, supporting inclusion only if they are required to make minimal accommodations for the student with disabilities. Other general educators are concerned about meeting the needs of the students with disabilities primarily because they believe they have not been adequately prepared to do so (Prater, 2010). These educators feel skeptical about their ability to meet the needs of students with disabilities and will be less likely to see the positive aspects of inclusion for the student, which may be a result the family is promoting.

Inclusion or student placement is only one decision IEP team members make. The team must also agree on related services, goals, amount of time services will be provided, test accommodations, and so forth. In making these decisions, sometimes parents believe the professionals are most knowledgeable about the needs of their child and will acquiesce to them. Other times parents will challenge the decisions professionals consider best, often believing that the needs of the child were not paramount in making that decision. Teams that make the best decisions first recognize that each member comes to the table with different perspectives, experiences, and opinions. Then they must work diligently together through those differences to make appropriate decisions that provide the best education for the individual student. In the next section, we discuss factors that affect parents' capacity to contribute to educational processes. Understanding the parent perspective prepares teachers to collaborate with families.

UNDERSTANDING THE FAMILY PERSPECTIVE

As discussed in previous chapters it is important to remember that just as students with disabilities are unique, no two families are exactly the same. In fact, increasingly, there is significant diversity in the structure and socioeconomic status (SES) of families (Woolfolk, 2010). Students may come from homes that represent traditional nuclear family structures (i.e., father, mother, and siblings), blended families, or nontraditional families (e.g., single parents). In addition, students may live with extended family members such as aunts, uncles, siblings, grandparents; or they may reside in foster or adoptive homes. The SES of each family unit will be different. Disability affects families across all levels of economic status, and families of children with disabilities may be representative of the higher, middle, or lower class, including poverty.

Just as family structure and SES varies from family to family, how families respond to and cope with having a child with a disability varies and is influenced by a number of factors. The type and severity of a child's disability, family circumstances, and parent and caregiver characteristics influence the degree to which families experience stress and whether families adopt positive or negative coping strategies. Educators must recognize that family coping patterns will affect how parents interact with their child and educators.

Coping with Disability

Parents of children with disabilities typically experience more stress than families who do not have children with disabilities (Dowling, 2007; Dyson, 1997; Withers & Bennett, 2003). Family stress can be attributed to different sources, including family conflict related to a child's disability, financial strain, uncertainty surrounding a child's future, lack of formal and informal social support, burdens from care, and inaccurate or limited knowledge of

TABLE 7.2	A Summary of Factors that Influence Family Coping
Factors that Influence Coping	**Description**
Parents' appraisal of the situation	The parents' appraisal is how parents mentally frame the situation; whether parents perceive that having a child with a disability is a positive or negative experience, and whether parents accept their child's condition and have realistic expectations of their and their child's future.
Family cohesiveness	Family cohesiveness refers to stable relationships and family members helping and supporting one another.
Social supports	Support of extended family members and support obtained from formal organization and through informal social interactions.
Child's characteristics	The child's characteristics include the visibility of the disabling condition, the child's behavior and adaptive skills, the severity of the child's disabling condition, and the amount of care the child requires.
Level of education and SES	The parents' or caregivers level of education and SES.

Sources: Roskam et al. (2008); Taanila et al. (2002); Kenny & McGilloway (2007).

the disabling condition (Dowling, 2007; Kenny & McGilloway, 2007). However, even though families experience stress caring for a child with disabilities, not all families have problems coping with their challenges. Many families adopt effective coping mechanisms and lead normal lives (Dowling, 2007; Taanila, Syrjälä, Kokkonen, & Järvelin, 2002; Withers & Bennett, 2003). Coping is defined as "conscious cognitive and behavioral efforts that one interposes between oneself and an event perceived as threatening or uncontrollable in order to master, tolerate, or decrease the event's impact on one's physical and psychological well-being" (Roskam, Zech, Nils, & Nader-Grosbois, 2008, p. 86). Table 7.2 summarizes factors that influence family coping.

APPRAISAL. Some disabling conditions such as Down syndrome and severe developmental disabilities are apparent early in a child's life. Other disabling conditions may not be diagnosed until a child begins to exhibit a developmental delay (usually during preschool years), when a child experiences problems learning in school (during early primary grades), or when a child is involved in an accident and become disabled (Taub, 2006). Depending on a child's condition and when the child was diagnosed, you may be interacting either with families who have known about and dealt with their child's condition for years, or with families who are just learning of and adjusting to the knowledge that their child has a disability.

When parents are initially informed of their child's disabling condition, the information they receive and their acceptance or denial of their child's condition significantly affects family coping. Knowledge helps parents cope with their situations. Therefore, parents need to receive accurate and truthful information about their child's condition (Roskam et al., 2008). Although it may be difficult for professionals to deliver "bad" news to parents, parents need to be informed nonetheless. For example, if a student's evaluation indicates that she has intellectual disabilities, the parents should be told the truth. When professionals do not provide parents with truthful information, parents feel isolated

(Dowling, 2007; Wade, Taylor, Drotar, Stancin, & Yeates, 1996). If parents do not understand a child's condition or if a diagnosis is uncertain, parents may also feel insecure and frustrated, which increases parental stress (Wade et al., 1996).

Understanding a disabling condition is an important aspect of accepting and adjusting to a child's condition. Parents' beliefs about their child may be challenged when they learn that their child has a disability.

> Parents develop wishes, expectations, and dreams for their children, even before the child is born. . . . The discovery that the wished-for child has a disability can be seen as destroying the hopes and dreams held by the parents. Parents need to grieve the loss of these hopes and dreams. (Taub, 2006, p. 54)

If parents are to cope effectively, they need to grieve, as well as readjust dreams and hopes for their child. Accurate information helps them make necessary adjustments. For example, if a parent is informed that his child has autism, the parent who had otherwise expected the child to develop like other children might readjust expectations with the knowledge that individuals with autism have difficulty communicating and interacting with peers and adults.

Having realistic expectations of children with disabilities helps parents cope more effectively, and accurate information helps them develop realistic expectations of their child. For example, Withers and Bennett (2003) studied a family of a child with profound disabilities. The child's disabilities were evident early in her life; however, the parents thought the child had the capacity to form attachments and develop some level of relationship with caregivers. When the child was 5 years old, the parents learned that their 5-year-old daughter had the mental capacity of a 1-month-old infant. Prior to receiving that information, they did not know that their daughter did not recognize them and had not formed social attachments. The assessment information helped the parents develop realistic expectations of their daughter's ability to interact with family members—the daughter would probably never form attachments with family members. Consequently, family relationships improved as the parents realistically dealt with her condition and found ways to integrate the child into the family structure, despite her severe limitations.

Even with accurate information, it can be difficult to accept the reality that a child has a disability. Parents may accept information they receive and adopt strategies for coping with their situation, or they might experience emotional and intellectual disorganization. Parents who accept their child's condition tend to frame the experience in positive terms, which are called *positive framing* (Hasting et al., 2005; Withers, & Bennett, 2003). They focus on how raising a child with disabilities positively affects their experiences in life. Some parents have reported that they became tolerant of others and less judgmental, materialistic, and selfish as a result of caring for children with disabilities. Because they invested time and energy caring for their children, they developed deep bonds with their children and derived satisfaction from helping their children grow and develop (Dowling, 2007; Kenny & McGilloway, 2007).

Positive framing involves developing a positive attitude not only about the child, but also about the family's future. Parents who cope well with their child's condition typically have confidence in their parenting ability and in their child's future. On the other hand, parents who experience difficulty coping tend to doubt their ability to address their child's needs and feel uncertain about their child's future. They might have concerns about independent living (if the child will be self-supporting) or opportunities for employment or education. They may fear that they will lack the resources to adequately care for their child.

Fear and uncertainty are generally alleviated when parents adopt problem-solving strategies. Problem-solving strategies are strategies that enable individuals to change the nature of the problem so that they can cope. Examples of problem-solving strategies include regulating parenting style to match the developmental needs of the child, obtaining social support, seeking information, adjusting expectations, and adopting an optimistic attitude toward the child's and family's future (Gray, 2006; Kenny & McGilloway, 2007; Roskam et al., 2008).

Parents who have difficulty accepting their child's condition tend to adopt emotion-focused strategies to reduce their psychological tension (Roskam et al., 2008). Emotion-focused strategies are avoidance strategies that distract the attention of the individual affected by a stressful situation (Gray, 2006). Self-blame, indecisiveness, disengagement, and denial are avoidance strategies (Hasting et al., 2005). When parents experience difficulty accepting their child's condition, they may unconsciously become ambivalent and simultaneously feel love and hate toward their child (Hasting et al., 2005). Ambivalence can be expressed as indecisiveness concerning the child's placement or schooling. A parent who is not coping well with a child's condition might vacillate between positive and negative emotions regarding the child and the child's placement—seeming to both accept and reject the diagnosis of disability. The parent might agree to special education placement, but then insist on unachievable performance from the child. One parent stated the following about ambivalence:

> When you see our ambivalence . . . maybe you're less likely to be offended by our unintended, and sometimes challenging, dispositions. You may be able to see that our lack of enthusiasm for one more meeting, one more phone call, one more form, one more test, one more transition is less about you and more about our worries and uncertainties. (Fialka, 2001, p. 23)

Another indicator that parents are not coping well with their child's condition is aggression toward the child. Aggression is a form of avoidance. Research indicates, in fact, that children with disabilities are more likely to be maltreated than typically developing children (Sobsey, 2002). Finally, parents might refuse to acknowledge that their child has a disability. To protect themselves from reality, the parents might deny the diagnosis and search for another diagnosis from other professionals. Or, they might refuse to place their child in special education programs and leave their child without educational support.

Even if parents accept a child's diagnosis, parents often go through stages of shock and emotional disorganization as they adjust to the knowledge that their child has a disability. Drotar, Baskiewicz, Irvin, and Klaus (1976) identified a common sequence of reactions that includes shock, denial, sadness, adaptation, and reorganization. Figure 7.1 describes one parent's experience adjusting to her son's diagnosis of autism.

Although most parents progress through adaptation and reorganization, some parents struggle with adapting to their child's condition and experience chronic sorrow as a response to their child's disability. Birthdays, religious celebrations, and developmental milestones can exacerbate grief for these parents as they repeatedly cope with the loss of their "perfect child" (Teel, 1991). The following illustrates how difficult it can be for parents

Ann Boushey's son was diagnosed with autism at the end of his kindergarten year. Although Ann was aware that her son experienced difficulty in social settings and was unusually sensitive to sound, she had not considered the possibility that her child had autism. When his school assessed him for learning problems, she thought they might tell her that he had attention-deficit disorder. She was unprepared for a diagnosis of autism. When she attended her son's first IEP meeting, she was **shocked** when she heard the word *autism*. In fact, she noted on the IEP document that she agreed to the services (she knew her son needed instructional support), but she did not agree with the diagnosis. For months, Ann **denied** that her son had autism. It wasn't until she happened on a book for parents of newly diagnosed children with autism that she realized that the diagnosis was accurate. The book described her son—he had autism.

As Ann accepted the diagnosis she felt **sadness,** guilt, shame, and isolation. She cried just looking at her son. She felt depressed. She wondered if something she had or had not done had caused his autism. As Ann struggled to cope with her son's disability, she panicked, thinking she wasn't doing enough to help him. She attended IEP meetings every 2 weeks to keep on top of her son's education. She read books on autism and **learned** all that she could about the condition. Subconsciously she hoped that she would find something that would make it all go away. But, over time, Ann realized that autism is not a condition that can be cured and that her son would always have autism. She learned to **accept** her son's quirkiness. As she accepted his condition she focused on his strengths—not just his limitations—and tried to help others do the same.

FIGURE 7.1 Illustration of the grief cycle. *Source:* Information summarized from Boushey, A. (2001). The grief cycle—one parent's trip around. *Focus on Autism and Other Developmental Disabilities, 16,* 27–30.

to accept the loss of children they hoped for. Table 7.3 provides suggestions for appropriate responses to parents' reactions to disability.

> We may feel reluctant, ambivalent, and often unwilling [to engage in interactions with professional service providers]. For one thing, if we choose to join you, we have to acknowledge that our child has special needs. We have to acknowledge that we are entering your world—one that is initially unfamiliar and frightening. Entering into our partnership with you demands that we let go of our dreams and begin to build new ones. [For one family], the idea of a wheelchair was introduced. A freshly graduated social worker met this mother at her home eager to take her to select her son's first brand-new wheelchair. The mother hardly shared the social worker's enthusiasm. To the mother, this was another shattering of a dream. She wanted to be selecting a tricycle for her son, not a wheelchair. (Fialka, 2001, p. 22)

FAMILY COHESIVENESS. When a child with a disability joins a family, the cohesiveness of the family changes, and this, in turn, affects the family's coping skills. Family cohesion refers to stable and supportive family relationships and unity. Cohesive families tend to cope better with stressful situations (Roskam et al., 2008; Wade et al., 1996). They cope better because relationships were good before the addition of the child with disabilities. When relationships are good, family members have strong feeling of togetherness, and they talk openly about positive and negative feelings and experiences (Wade et al., 1996). They support one another and share an understanding of family dynamics and circumstances. One means by which spouses or partners show support is by sharing childcare and household tasks. Parents who cope well with their child's condition take turns caring

TABLE 7.3	Family Coping: Suggestions for Professionals
Family coping	**Suggestions for professionals**
Self-blame	Help parents to understand that they did not cause their child's disability. With the exception of abuse and fetal alcohol syndrome, parents are rarely the cause of their child's condition.
Anger	Parents' anger often reflects their anxiety about their child's condition. It is important not to personalize parents' expressions of anxiety or to become defensive.
Bargaining	Parents may feel that they can reverse their child's condition by engaging in redemptive activities. Support parents' involvement in their child's lives. Point out the child's positive characteristics, and remain optimistic without providing guarantees of progress.
Denial	If parents are experiencing denial, be sensitive in responding to them. Do not try to force parents to accept their child's situation. When appropriate, gently point out that their child needs special help. In some cases, diagnoses are not correct or appropriate, so be cautious in assuming that parents who do not accept a professional diagnosis are in denial.
Depression	Mild, temporary depression is normal. Professional counselors can differentiate between normal, temporary depression and clinical depression.
Shame	Provide information about self-help or support groups. Meeting with other families can reduce parents' feelings of isolation.
Acceptance	Recognize that over time it becomes easier for parents to accept their child's condition. Be patient.

Source: Seligman, M., & Darling, R. B. (2007). *Ordinary families, special children.* New York: Guilford Press.

for the child with disabilities and do not place the burden of care on one family member (Taanila et al., 2002). For example, a mother might help a child with learning disabilities with homework, and the father might help the child learn life skills such as washing clothes or driving a car. Working together extends from a common understanding of the family situation. When both parents accept their child's condition and have realistic expectations of the child, their shared understanding enables them to be united in addressing the child's issues (Taanila et al., 2002).

Understandably, new stressful situations exacerbate existing family stress. If family relationships are already strained or if an individual is in a distressed state (e.g., coping with depression, alcoholism, or experiencing financial problems) when a child is born with disabilities or becomes disabled, the child's disabilities increase difficulties in the family (Wade et al., 1996). Family members have more difficulty supporting one another and developing a common understanding related to disabilities when communication is poor and relationships are unstable. In such situations, it is not uncommon for one parent to assume responsibility for caring for the child with disabilities. For example, a mother might do all the housework and take care of the child while the father offers little or no support (Taanila et al., 2002). The burden of caring for the child increases the mother's stress and decreases her emotional resources for effectively coping with the child's situation. If an individual has personal challenges on top of other problems, the responsibility of caring for a child with disabilities might seem overwhelming.

SOCIAL SUPPORT.   Coping with disabilities involves coping intellectually and emotionally. Emotional support from others can reduce parent stress. Support can be informal or formal. Informal support is usually provided by extended family members, friends, or families who have children with similar conditions. Grandparents are often considered a source of instrumental and emotional support for parents, and emotional support offered by grandparents helps parents adjust to their child's condition (Roskam et al., 2008). However, in some cases, extended family members may not be in a position to offer help, or they may not be supportive. Beyond immediate family relationships, families value support from other caregivers. Taanila et al. (2002) and Kenny and McGilloway (2007) reported that families regarded support from other caregivers in similar situations as being particularly helpful.

Formal support can be obtained from organizations and social agencies. Support groups consist of nonprofit organizations, such as the Autism Society of America or the Learning Disabilities Association of America (LDA), as well as government social service agencies. Depending on a child's condition and the specific needs of the family, they may need little to extensive support from external agencies. For example, families with a child who has mild learning disabilities would probably not need social service support although they might benefit from a support network provided by a professional organization, such as LDA. Formal support for the child would most likely be provided at school in the form of special education services. Families with children who have more severe disabilities, on the other hand, may be unable to independently care for their child. Social services might become involved in offering respite care or counseling or in determining appropriate educational placements for children. The availability and accessibility of social service support affects parents' coping ability. Parents who positively cope with their child's condition tend to access social support, whereas families with poor coping mechanisms do not access social support to the same degree as families who cope well with their child's challenges (Taanila et al., 2002). Teachers can help all families by making them aware of support services available in local communities. Table 7.4 summarizes differences in parents' coping.

CHILD'S CONDITION.   The nature, visibility, and severity of the child's disability influences family stress (Dowling, 2007). The parents in Withers and Bennett's (2003) study experienced significant stress caring for their daughter, who had profound disabilities. The parents were on the brink of separation at the outset of the study because the severity of the daughter's condition created marital tension for the parents. In other situations, parents may not experience the same level of stress. A parent of a child with mild reading disabilities will probably not feel the same amount of stress as a parent whose child requires constant care. However, it is important to remember that each family responds to disability in ways that are unique to the family. Teachers should be careful not to make assumptions about families that might experience stress or have difficulty coping.

Interestingly, parents of children with Down syndrome report less stress than parents of children with other disabling conditions (Hodapp, 2007). The phenomenon is referred to as the "Down syndrome advantage." Although researchers do not have a complete understanding of why there is a Down syndrome advantage, the advantage can be explained in part by child and parent characteristics. Generally, children with Down syndrome display sociable, upbeat personalities. Interacting with a happy child may reduce caregiver stress. Another explanation is that mothers who give birth to children with

High-coping families	Items on which the families differed	Low-coping families
All the parents had experienced a novelty shock, but they got over it and accepted the situation quickly. The spouses' onset experiences were similar.	Parents' onset experiences	Most of the parents had experienced a novelty shock. The mothers had accepted the situation quickly, but the fathers had difficulties accepting it.
The parents had an optimistic attitude towards the child's and the family's life and future. They believed that their child would manage in his/her life and that there would be enough supporting systems for him/her to cope later in life.	Personal characteristics	The parents had a very fearful attitude and they were uncertain about their child's future, or they said that they did not think about it at all.
Most parents thought that the family values had changed. "The family became very important." The parents had been able to keep their individual activities or even found some new ones.	Effects on family life	All the parents reported that the family values had not changed. The parents thought that they had to give up their individual activities because of the child.
The spouses did the housework and the child-caring tasks together or took turns.	Acting in everyday life	The mothers did all the housework and the child-caring tasks alone. Only a couple of the fathers helped in the child-caring tasks.
The parents had a very extensive and supportive formal and informal social support network.	Social support	The parents had a very small and mainly formal social support network.

TABLE 7.4 Family Coping

Source: Taanila, A., Syrjälä, L., Kokkonen, J., & Järvelin, M.-R. (2002). Coping of parents with physically and/or intellectually disabled children. *Child: Care, Health & Development, 28*, p. 81. Copyright granted © 2002 Blackwell Science Ltd.

Down syndrome tend to be older on average than mothers of children with other disabling conditions. Because they are older, these mothers have more opportunities to become educated, and their SES may be higher later in life.

With some disabling conditions, children's behavior and skills improve over time, which can reduce family stress. For example, children with mild reading disabilities can be taught to read (Savage & Carless, 2005), and children with emotional and behavioral disorders can learn socially appropriate behaviors (Hudley, Graham, & Taylor, 2007). Gray (2006) studied parents of children with autism and reported that over time, the parents utilized fewer coping strategies then when their children were younger. Gray attributed the decline in coping strategies to reduced family stress. Over time, the children exhibited more appropriate behaviors, which shifted family focus from solving problems to family routines. Also, as the children completed treatment programs, the families relied less on formal social supports than when the children were younger.

EDUCATION AND SOCIOECONOMIC STATUS. Other factors that influence how families address their children's needs are parents' level of education and SES. Parenting children with disabilities involves attending to children's social, physical, and intellectual development. Parents do not approach parenting tasks the same, and individuals' levels of education will affect how parents respond to their child's educational needs. Mothers with a lower level of education reason at a lower level about their child's development than more highly educated mothers (Roskam, 2005). Their reasoning is less complex, and they believe their child's development is influenced by deterministic, intrafamilial, or environmental factors. In contrast, mothers with higher levels of education develop more complex models that integrate interrelated factors to explain their child's development. These mothers are more likely to be active partners in their child's schooling, and they have a greater capacity to absorb educators' assessments, diagnoses, and recommendations than mothers with less education. Mothers with less education tend to make more requests for teachers to address their children's need, rather than becoming actively involved themselves (Roskam et al., 2008).

Along with level of education, SES is a factor in parents' involvement with their children's education. In general, parents of lower SES tend to be less involved in their children's education than parents of higher SES. Although some parents in lower SES households are actively involved in their children's education, many others are not (Ormrod, 2011). In special education, poor, non-White families, headed by single parents are over-represented in groups of parents who do not attend IEP meetings (Lambie, 2000). Economic factors may prevent some parents from attending school meetings and volunteering in classrooms—parents may lack transportation, have difficulty getting off work, or encounter problems finding suitable care for children (Ormrod, 2011). Also, parents of lower SES may have limited education themselves. They may not have the knowledge and skills to become involved with their children's education, or they may have had negative experiences at school themselves and are uncomfortable interacting in educational settings. Substance abuse and mental illness may also be issues for some parents. In such cases, when parents have significant problems themselves, they may lack the resources (social, emotional, and financial) to support their children's development (Ormrod, 2011).

As an educator, you will work with a broad spectrum of families. The structure of each family will be unique, and the family response to disability will vary family to family. You may interact with families who cope well with their child's condition and who are open to and successful with family/professional collaboration. You may also interact with families in states of crises, for whom interacting with school personnel is difficult and threatening. Such families may need professional counseling to help them learn to cope with their circumstances. For all families with whom you interact, it is important for you to be friendly, listen carefully to what families members say, be clear and direct in your communications, treat families with respect, affirm student and family strengths, and honor cultural diversity (Seligman & Darling, 2007). It, therefore, becomes critical that you take time to become acquainted with your students' parents and to understand them as you provide special education support and work with parents.

FAMILY PERCEPTIONS OF SPECIAL EDUCATIONAL SERVICES

Parent involvement in the IEP process is both legally mandated and ethically responsible practice (IDEA, 2004). Parents are responsible for managing their children's lives, and it makes sense to involve them in educational programming. "Parents have to be recognized as special educators, the true experts on their children; and professional people—teachers, pediatricians, psychologists, and others—have to learn to be consultants to parents" (Muscott, 2002, p. 66). Working with parents involves understanding what they can contribute to the IEP process, valuing their contributions, and responding to their concerns.

"What have I learned after weaving my way through the special education maze? Knowledge is power—you must be as informed as possible about your child's disability AND your child's strengths. You must know the law and how to use it. You must have good communication skills. You must believe in yourself. You must believe in your child. You must be creative. You must be patient. You must be part of a team. You will play many roles, not just mother or father but also Cheerleader, Advocate, Tutor, Lawyer, Researcher, Detective, Teacher, Mediator, Psychologist and Student.

Yes, you are the Student and your child is the Teacher. Your child provides the opportunity for growth not just for you as a parent but also for the teachers. Your child provides the opportunity for your school to grow and expand its vision.

Your child says: "Look at me, I am different, I am truly an individual, you must change the way you've been doing things, you must get creative, you must try something new." You will at first cry, you will be frustrated, you will feel overwhelmed, you will feel alone, you will fight. There will be times you feel like giving up, but you won't because you love your child too much. You will make a conscious decision to be part of the solution. You will make a plan (Gloria from New Jersey)."

FIGURE 7.2 Parent perspective—Twenty years later. *Source:* From National Center for Learning Disabilities. (2006). *IDEA parent guide: A comprehensive guide to your rights and responsibilities under the Individuals with Disabilities Education Act (IDEA 2004).* New York: National Center for Learning Disabilities. Copyright granted © 2006 National Center for Learning Disabilities.

Parents make important contributions to their children's education. They interact with their children in more settings than do educators, and they have the perspective of the "whole" person in mind when they participate in educational processes. On IEP teams, they are the only members who remain constant throughout all their children's schooling. Specifically, parents know their child's personality and history. During IEP meetings, they can provide insight into their child's past educational experience as well as help IEP team members understand their child's strengths, needs, and interests (Maryland State Department of Education, 2000).

Educators and parents can benefit when they work together and share information related to a student's educational experience.

The involvement of parents in the IEP process has many benefits, including the following:

1. Increase the teacher's understanding of the child's environment.
2. Add to parents' knowledge of the child's educational setting.
3. Improve communication between parents and the school.
4. Increase the school's understanding of the child.
5. Increase the likelihood that, with improved understanding between home and school, mutually agreed upon educational goals will be attained. (Smith, 2001, p. 2)

In addition to the items listed, when educators and families work together, children do better in school. Research indicates that when parents actively participate in their children's educational programming, the children perform better academically and behaviorally (Muscott, 2002).

BARRIERS TO PARTICIPATING IN SPECIAL EDUCATION PROCESSES

To achieve the benefits of collaboration, educators should understand what facilitates and hinders parent participation in educational endeavors. Many parents who become involved with special education are satisfied with the IEP process in schools. However,

TABLE 7.5	Barriers to Participation
Challenges	**Reasons for Nonparticipation**
Time	Single and working parents may experience difficulty attending meetings and parent–teacher conferences.
Intimidation	Parents may feel intimidated by principals, counselors, and other school professionals. They may have had negative experiences working with educators and may be reluctant to become involved again.
Knowledge	Families may not understand educational systems or their children's conditions.
Cultural difference	A family's culture may clash with school culture.
Relationships with educators	Parents may not feel welcomed by or comfortable around school personnel.
Guilt	Parents may feel guilty about their child's condition. They might be concerned that educators will negatively judge them or their parenting skills.
Anxiety	Parents may feel anxious about their child's education and about their child's future. They may also be worried that they will appear uninformed, indecisive, or confused in front of educators.
Stigma	Some parents might be concerned about the stigma of qualifying for special education. They may fear that teachers, their peers, and their child's peers will have negative perceptions of them and their child.
Resources	Parents may lack financial, educational, and emotional resources to become involved.
Trust	Parents may not trust that educators will be responsive to their concerns or will provide services that their child needs or is legally entitled to.

Sources: Kroth & Edge (1997); Lambie (2000); Stoner et al. (2005).

some parents may be reluctant to participate. Their reluctance to engage in collaborative relationships is often due to issues discussed in the previous section. Table 7.5 lists barriers to family participation in special education procedures.

Facilitating Family Involvement

Understanding the parents' perspective is important for developing effective relationships with parents. Many of the barriers to participation can be eliminated if educators are responsive to parents' concerns and needs. In the following section, we discuss parents' perspective of special education procedures and provide suggestions for increasing parent participation.

INFORMATION. As discussed previously, information is critical when working with parents of children who have disabilities. Parents who do not understand a disabling condition need information about their child's condition (Pruitt, Wandry, & Hollums, 1998), particularly when they are first informed of the child's condition. Accurate and complete information can help them understand the diagnosis so that they can make informed choices about their child's education. Although it can be difficult for educators to be honest with parents, honesty is important for reducing barriers to participation (Turnbull, Turnbull, Erwin, & Soodak, 2006). Parents can feel anxiety about their child's development, and if they lack knowledge

Before my son Jason started school, he was evaluated for learning problems. Test results indicated that his development was significantly delayed in a number of areas (i.e., language development, physical coordination, social skills, and fine motor ability). During preschool years and early elementary grades, Jason received physical, occupational, and speech and language therapy. By the time Jason was in third grade, he began to experience academic difficulty. I talked with his general education teacher and upon his suggestion visited the school's special education resource class. As I observed the class, I was dismayed at the lack of academic instruction. During the hour that I visited the class, the third-grade students wrote two sentences on a piece of paper. Instead of working on academic skills, the teacher used instructional time for listening to music and making figure eights in the air. After visiting the class, I determined that if I could help it, I would not enroll my son in special education. I did not want him to be stigmatized by placement in special education, and I did not want him to be educated in an environment with such low expectations.

Thought Question:

As a teacher candidate, what are your thoughts and feelings about this parent's experience?

FIGURE 7.3 Parent perspective—Special education stigma

about their child's condition, they may depend on team members to identify their child's areas of difficulty and to recommend and implement remedial programs (Lambie, 2000). This is particularly true when parents' level of education is low. Research indicates that poor families with limited education tend to defer more to professionals' opinions than better-educated families. Professionals should help parents understand their child's disability and special education services so that the parents can make informed decisions.

When children qualify for special education services and parents become involved with special education processes, parents also need information about their rights and the IEP process (Fish, 2006; Pruitt et al., 1998; Smith, 2001). Educators need to explain IEP procedures and inform parents of their legal rights in laypersons' terms. Although parents receive copies of their rights at IEP meetings, they may not understand the legal and special education jargon. Depending on a family's familiarity with special education, family members might need training outside IEP meetings to help them understand special education procedures (Spann, Kohler, & Soenksen, 2003; Zhang & Bennett, 2003). Some parents have reported that they felt inadequately informed about the IEP process, and educators can address this issue by helping parents prepare for meetings (Dabkowski, 2004; Spann et al., 2003). Figure 7.4 provides a list of questions parents frequently ask about

Questions Parent Frequently Ask about Special Education Services

1. What is special education?
2. How is eligibility for special education determined?
3. What happens during an evaluation?
4. What happens when my child is eligible for services?
5. What is an individualized education program (IEP)?
6. What information is included in an IEP?
7. Who develops the IEP?
8. What happens if I do not agree with my child's program?

FIGURE 7.4 Frequently asked questions. *Source:* National Information Center for Children and Youth with Disabilities, 1999. National Center for Children and Youth with Disabilities (NICYCH). (1999). Questions often asked by parents about special education services. Briefing Paper, LGI 4th edition.

My name is Alex, and I am the father of twin second graders, Holly and Josh, who attend elementary school in Delaware. Holly and Josh were born 12 weeks premature. Their prematurity resulted in both children having hydrocephalous as well as various learning disabilities. I have participated in IEP meetings for five years starting when Holly and Josh were three years old.

At each IEP meeting I was given a small booklet that described a parent's procedural safeguards under IDEA. To be honest, I never actually read through it. I always trusted school staff and assumed that the teachers and therapists would do all they could to meet my children's specific needs. The district staff never took the time to go over the procedural safeguards document with me and I never realized exactly how important knowing your rights could be.

Then, at my last IEP meeting, I was told that my daughter Holly had only made one month of progress in reading during the previous twelve months time and that she was falling farther and farther behind. During her IEP meeting I asked for some additional intervention from the school reading specialist, but was told the reading specialist was already seeing too many children and did not have any additional time available to spend with my daughter. The school staff told me that Holly would just have to make due with the small group instruction she was getting the special ed. classroom.

I really didn't know what to say. Luckily I talked to other parents and they recommended that I attend a seminar sponsored by our district's special needs PTA. A representative from our state's Parent Information Center was there as well as two attorneys who explained, step by step, all of the parent rights described in that little book that I had previously never read. It was there that I learned the three most important words that a parent of a child with disabilities needs to know: "Prior Written Notice."

At the special needs PTA meeting I learned that Prior Written Notice means that when a school district adds, changes, or denies educational services to your child, they must explain to the parent in writing why the services are being added, changed, or denied. If the school district is denying your services, they most likely will not provide you prior written notice voluntarily—you will have to ask them to do it.

In my situation, the school district took our concerns more seriously when we requested them to give us Prior Written Notice concerning why my request for time with the reading specialist was being denied. The district ended up re-evaluating her reading skills and assigned a reading specialist to coach her teacher on how to better teach to my daughter.

I'm sure my story isn't all that unique but I can't emphasize enough how important it is to know your rights under IDEA—especially those three words: Prior Written Notice. (Alex from Delaware)

Thought Question:

What impact do you think this situation had on the father's relationship with IEP team members? How might the father's trust have been affected?

FIGURE 7.5   Parent Perspective—Those three words: Prior written notice.   *Source:* National Center for Learning Disabilities. (2006). *IDEA parent guide: A comprehensive guide to your rights and responsibilities under the Individuals with Disabilities Education Act (IDEA 2004).* New York: National Center for Learning Disabilities, p. 24. Copyright granted © 2006 National Center for Learning Disabilities.

special education services. Teachers can use these questions as a checklist to ensure that they help parents become knowledgeable about special education procedures.

Just as educators can inform parents about IEP processes, parents can provide teachers with important information about their child. Although children with disabilities share common characteristics (i.e., problems with attention, memory, and social competence), different disabling conditions are characterized by specific behaviors and cognitive limitations, and informed parents can help teachers understand their child's specific condition. For an example, an informed parent can help a teacher understand how her child's anxiety disorder is manifest in social situations. Parents believe that when teachers are better informed about disabling conditions, disagreements can be avoided and mitigated (Fish, 2006). A source of disagreement between parents and teachers is often discipline. If team members do not understand a child's condition, they may not understand why a child behaves in a particular manner. Parents interviewed in Fish's (2006) study believed that teachers misinterpreted their children's behavior because the teachers did not understand autism and interpreted inappropriate behavior as intentional, instead of a manifestation of a disability.

Unfortunately, teachers may not provide opportunities for parents to share information about their children at IEP meetings. Childre and Chambers (2005) reported that during traditional IEP meetings, parents did not have opportunities to share the wealth of information they had regarding their child's needs and functioning. If parents are not provided opportunities to share information with professionals, it may be difficult for them to establish trust with professionals. Trust grows over time. Professionals communicate concern for families when they request information from parents, listen to parents, and address issues and concerns of the parents.

TRUST.   Parents want to trust school professionals. Their trust in professionals increases when they perceive that professionals (a) are competent, (b) consider their children's interest when making educational decisions, and (c) keep their word (Stoner & Angell, 2006). Trust can be violated when parents believe educators are not forthright. Consider the following statements:

> Do I trust them? To an extent. I always feel like they are always answering your question and giving you input, but you never know if they are sharing full knowledge. You know what I mean? I trust them to an extent, but I don't trust them fully. Because I know the bottom line is that they have budgets and they have personnel and they only have so many resources. (Stoner & Angel, 2006, p. 184)

Trust affects relationships and the roles parents assume in the education of their children. The more parents trust the educational system, the more likely they will support the teachers and what they are trying to achieve. Conversely, when parents do not trust school professionals, they (a) increase advocacy efforts, (b) monitor more closely the services provided for their children, and (c) decrease their support for teachers (Stoner & Angell, 2006).

COMMUNICATION.   Effective communication is vital for conveying information and for establishing relationships with parents. The language educators use and how educators communicate can either facilitate understanding and cooperation or create barriers for collaboration. In interactions with educators, parents want to feel that their contributions are valued, and educators must be effective communicators to achieve that end (Pruitt et al., 1998). Effective communication involves sharing information in a way that others can understand, being an active and empathetic listener, and respecting the views and opinions of others. Communication can be formal communication (during meetings) and informal (notes, e-mails, and casual conversations).

During meetings, the language that participants use is important for facilitating understanding. In the normal course of work, educators typically use vocabulary terms and jargon that individuals who do not work in educational systems may not understand.

Terms like *least restrictive environment, curriculum-based assessment,* and *standard scores* might be new and unfamiliar terms for parents, and parents are not always comfortable telling educators that they do not comprehend what is being discussed (Miles-Bonart, 2002; O'Donovan, 2007). Instead, they may restrict their input and become passive during IEP meetings because they do not want to appear stupid (Lambie, 2000). Using jargon can alienate parents and can create communication barriers (Childre & Chambers, 2005; Salembier & Furney, 1998). Educators should either explain jargon or avoid using jargon altogether (Miles-Bonart, 2002; Smith, 2001).

Word choice is also important for facilitating understanding and encouraging participation. Parents feel more involved when educators use words that communicate parity and respect (Dabkowski, 2004). Parents want to feel that their contributions are valued and that they are respected as equal partners in the IEP process (Fish, 2006; Pruitt et al., 1998; Spann et al., 2003). Words used before and during meetings can communicate intent to collaborate. For example, inviting parents to *participate* in a meeting is different than inviting them to *attend* a meeting. Similarly, asking for parents' *input* when decisions are made rather than asking parents to *approve* educators' decisions communicates respect for parents' contributions. Using pronouns like *we* and *us* emphasizes team processes (Lytle & Bordin, 2001). Parents value being treated like equals. They do not appreciate educators dominating meetings (Pruitt et al., 1998).

Using language that encourages participation and communicates respect is one way teachers can develop relationships with parents. Expressing empathy and listening without judging is critical for establishing trust. Parents can feel anxiety and fearful about school interactions (O'Donovan, 2007; Zhang & Bennett, 2003). Families experience enough stress dealing with the challenges of raising children with disabilities that they do not need extra stress from their interactions with teachers. This is especially true when parents are informed about a child's disability or when parents have problems accepting or adjusting to their child's condition. Emotional disorganization can occur at diagnosis or resurface in cycles as parents adjust to their child's developmental progression (Muscott, 2002). At any time, parents may be in shock, experience denial, or express anger at the world (O'Donovan, 2007).

In such cases, parents often need assurance and empathy. They do not want to be blamed for their child's condition or criticized for their or their child's behavior (Fish, 2006). If they feel guilt about their child's condition, they may be sensitive to perceived criticism or blame (Lambie, 2000). Let parents know that you empathize with their situation. Allow them to express their feelings and concerns, and control your own emotional reactions. Avoid engaging in arguments, criticizing the parents, and discounting their feelings. If parents are angry at their situation, do not personalize anger that may be directed at you. Also, respect parents' right to communicate their needs. Parents have reported that they want educators to listen to them and respect their appraisal of what they need. Their appraisal of their needs may differ from educators' opinions. Some families may accept school support, whereas others may benefit more from information and social support (Muscott, 2002).

Parents appreciate frequent communication with teachers. Relationships between parents and educators will not develop if communication occurs only during formal meetings. Parents have stated that they appreciate ongoing, frequent communication with their child's teacher. They want to know how their child is progressing, what their child is learning, and what they can do to become involved in their child's education. Parents view communication with teachers as an ongoing process (Lillie, 1998). Although parents are generally satisfied with communication from their children's teachers, they have reported

---

Involving Parents of Children with Learning and Behavior Problems in the Schools (Darch et al., 2004).

General Guidelines for Involving Parents

- Be proactive. Make contact with parents before behavior problems occur to establish positive interactions.
- Assess families' desire and willingness to participate in school activities.
- Provide parents with information about classroom management plans.

When There Is a Problem Behavior

- Begin a conference with positive examples of the child's academic and/or behavior successes.
- Focus on only one or two problems during the meeting.
- Ask parents for their insights into the problem.
- Make suggestions for interventions and tell the parents why the strategy can be effective.

FIGURE 7.6 Involving parents of children with behavior problems

that teachers infrequently make contact with them, and they are typically the ones who initiate contact (Childre & Chambers, 2005; Spann et al., 2003). Calling parents, sending e-mail updates, and writing progress reports or notes are ways to communicate with parents.

When communicating with families, it is important to communicate both positive information and concerns to parents. In many cases, educators only contact parents when there is a problem (Martin & Hagan-Burke, 2002; Spann et al., 2003). Parents may distance themselves from schools in an attempt to avoid unpleasant interactions when reports from school are mostly negative (Martin & Hagan-Burke, 2002). Considering parent stress, make contact with parents before you experience problems with a student, thereby laying the foundation for open and effective communication (Darch, Miao, & Shippen, 2004).

How you interact with parents and family members will significantly influence their perceptions of special education processes. The climates you create will facilitate parent involvement or present barriers for parent involvement in their child's education. Monitor your behavior, and always maintain an awareness of parents' perspectives so that you interact with parents in ways that invite collaboration.

Summary

- Educators and parents have different perspectives about educating children with disabilities.
- Roles educators adopt in IEP processes reflect their areas of expertise and experience in educational systems.
- Professional pressures affect how educators approach IEP meetings.
- No two families are alike. In collaborating with families, professionals should consider individual family circumstances.
- Responses to disability range from constructive adjustment to limited adjustment. Family mem-

bers may positively frame disability and adapt constructively to having a family member with a disability; and family members may also experience difficulty coping with a child's condition.
- Family members' response to disability is influenced by SES, family cohesion, appraisal of the child's condition, the child's condition, relationships within the family, and access to social support.
- Factors that act as barriers to parent participation in IEP processes are (a) personal factors such as guilt, anxiety, and limited resources;

(b) cultural conflict; (c) negative past experience with schools; and (d) strained or difficult relationships with school personnel.
- Educators can support parent involvement in special education by providing parents with information about disabling conditions and special education processes.
- Communicating effectively with parents and establishing trust enhances relationships and invites parent participation.

Linking Standards to Chapter Content

After reading this chapter you should be able to link basic knowledge and skills described in the CEC Standards and INTASC Principles with information provided in this text. Table 7.6, Linking CEC Standards and INTASC Printiples to Major Chapter Topics, provides examples of how they are addressed in each major section of the chapter.

TABLE 7.6 Linking CEC Standards and INTASC Principles to Major Chapter Topics		
Major Chapter Headings	**CEC Knowledge and Skill Core Standard and Associated Subcategories**	**INTASC Core Principle and Associated Special Education Subcategories**
Understanding the Family Perspective Coping with Disability Family Perceptions of Special Education Services Barriers to Participating in Special Education Processes Facilitating Family Involvement	1: Foundations ICC1K4: Rights and responsibilities of students, parents, teachers, and other professionals, and schools related to exceptional learning needs. ICC1K7: Family systems and role of families in the educational process. ICC1K10: Potential impact of differences in values, languages, and customs that can exist between home and schools. 2: Development and Characteristics of Learners ICC2K4 Family systems and the role of families in supporting development. 10: Collaboration ICC10K3: Concerns of families of individuals with exceptional learning needs, families, school personnel, and community members	3: Diverse Learners 3.03: All teachers understand that a disability can be perceived differently across families, communities, and cultures based on differing values and belief systems. 3.06: Special education teachers seek to understand how having a child with disabilities may influence a family's views of themselves as caregivers and as members of their communities. 10: Collaboration, Ethics, and Relationships 10.10: Special education teachers understand the impact that having a child with a disability may have on family roles and functioning at different points in the life cycle of a family.
Understanding the Professional Perspective	9: Professional and Ethical Practice ICC9S11 Reflect on one's practice to improve instruction and guide professional growth.	9: Reflection and Professional Development 9.07: Special education teachers reflect on their personal biases and the influences of these biases on the instruction they provide to students with disabilities, and on the interactions they have with other personnel, families, and the community.

Sources: Council for Exceptional Children (2005); Interstate New Teacher Assessment and Support Consortium INTASC Special Education Subcommittee (May 2001).

Web Resources

RESOURCES FOR TEACHERS AND PARENTS

www.pacer.org/—Parent Advocacy Coalition for Educational Rights Center (PACER). PACER provides a variety of services, including parent training, publications, and technical assistance on topics such as special education information, early childhood intervention, multicultural services, transition to adult life, and juvenile justice.

http://www.nichcy.org/Pages/Home.aspx—The National Dissemination Center for Children with Disabilities (NICHCY). Parents may benefit from being directed to this Web site. NICHCY provides basic information about special education law and disabling conditions.

http://www.ldonline.org/—Learning Disabilities Online is a leading Web site on learning disabilities and attention-deficit hyperactivity disorder. At this Web site, educators and parents can access information and resources to better understand learning disabilities and ADHD.

http://www.ncld.org/—The National Center for Learning Disabilities (NCLD) provides essential information to parents, professionals, and individuals with learning disabilities. The center promotes research and programs to foster effective learning and advocates for policies to protect and strengthen educational rights and opportunities. Publications about the IEP process are available at the Web site as well as resources for educators.

RESOURCES FOR TEACHING ABOUT DISABILITY

http://www.ldrc.ca/projects/aware/index.php—Learning Disabilities Resource Community, Learning Awareness Series Web site provides a collection of activities used to help learners understand themselves as learners. Although designed for students with learning disabilities, these exercises can be effective for any learner.

Leicester, M. (2007). *Special stories for disability awareness: Stories and activities for teachers, parents and professionals*. Philadelphia: Jessica Kingsley. This book consists of a collection of short stories about children with disabilities written to promote disability awareness and discussion for 4- to 11-year-old students.

Prater, M. A., & Dyches, T. T. (2008). *Teaching about disabilities through children's literature*. Westport, CT: Libraries Unlimited. Over 100 annotated bibliographies of children's literature that include characters with disabilities are provided and categorized by disability. Also included are sample lesson and unit plans, as well as classroom activities and reproducibles teachers can use to teach about disabilities through literature for grades K–12.

http://www.disabilitytraining.com/children.html—Program Development Associates—Disability Awareness for Children provides links to commercially available books, DVDs, and VHS tapes that can be used to teach disabilities awareness. Titles include *KidAbility* and *What Does Normal Mean*, among others.

Ragged Edge Online Community. (2006). *Disability awareness—do it right! Your all-in-one how-to guide*. Louisville, KY: Avocado. This book provides details on planning and implementing disability awareness activities that are not offensive to those with disabilities.

CHAPTER 8

Creating IEPs with Families and Strategies for Involving Students

OBJECTIVES

After reading this chapter you will

1. Describe how to plan and conduct IEP meetings that involve parents.
2. Discuss how to consider parents' perspectives and concerns when making educational decisions for students with disabilities.
3. Discuss strategies for involving students in IEP processes.
4. Describe how to prepare students to participate in their IEP meetings.

INTRODUCTION

Before their son qualified for special education services, the Ortiz family had never heard of IEPs. They knew a little about special education (they knew that their school provided assistance for "special needs children"), but they knew nothing of special education laws or processes. During their first IEP meeting with their son's teachers, they participated as much as they could; yet they did not fully understand what an IEP was (and what it included) or the process by which students with disabilities were served in schools. They wished that someone had provided information about IEPs before they attended their first meeting. They wanted to contribute to the discussions about their son's education, but because the whole process was so unfamiliar, they contributed little to discussions and consequently deferred to teachers to make decisions for their son.

The intent of requiring parent participation in IEP meetings is to have parents participate—not just attend meetings. As discussed in the previous chapter, IDEA mandates parent involvement in IEP processes to ensure that students' interests are represented and to allow parents to have a voice in their children's education. IDEA also specifies that students participate in their IEP development to the extent that they are capable of participating. For parents and students to meaningfully contribute to IEP processes, educators must solicit their opinions and structure meetings to facilitate participation. Students in particular need coaching to prepare for IEP meetings.

In this chapter we discuss how to involve family members and students in creating IEPs. We discuss strategies that promote parent involvement and review issues that should be considered when making decisions about placement, educational goals, assistive technology, assessment, special education services, and transition. The last section of the chapter describes how to prepare students for IEP meetings and provides suggestions for engaging students in IEP processes.

CREATING IEPs WITH FAMILIES

Planning and Conducting IEP Meetings

Developing an IEP involves more than holding an IEP meeting; it also involves developing working relationships with families. "Parent–professional literature suggests that relationships are most effective when based on mutual respect, trust, and honesty; where decision making and planning around mutually agreed-upon goals are shared between parents and professionals" (Keen, 2007, p. 343). It takes planning to accomplish these goals. Not only must arrangements be made for scheduling meetings, but careful attention must be paid to what will be discussed at meetings, who will be involved, and how meetings should be conducted. In this section we discuss how to prepare for and conduct IEP meetings.

The first consideration in planning IEP meetings is the time and location for the meeting. The location where an IEP meeting is held is important to both parents and professionals. According to one study, parents prefer meetings that are held in comfortable, homelike settings. They also prefer to be consulted about the time and location of meeting instead of being told when and where a meeting will take place (Lord Nelson, Summers, & Turnbull, 2004). Teachers should consult with parents prior to scheduling a meeting because the parents may have to change work schedules, arrange for childcare, or obtain transportation to attend a meeting. For some parents it is easier to meet outside professional hours and locations (Lord Nelson et al., 2004). When meetings are held, rooms should be large enough to accommodate team members, and seats should be arranged to facilitate discussion among invited participants (Dabkowski, 2004; Salembier & Furney, 1998). Parents do not like to feel isolated at meetings—with school personnel on one side of the table and the parents on the other. They believe that the physical setting of the meeting should support team collaboration.

Many parents want to feel involved with their child's educational programming. The IEP meeting provides an opportunity for parent participation. And yet, parents do not always fully participate during IEP meetings (Childre & Chambers, 2005; Fish, 2006; Sheehey, 2006). A common practice of writing drafts of IEPs provides some explanation of limited parent participation. Often, special educators create IEP drafts and send them home for parents to review prior to IEP meetings, or they present them for approval at meetings. When educators prepare an IEP without asking for parent input, parents feel uncomfortable sharing their ideas at meetings and feel as though they have to agree with professionals' decisions, rather than participating in the decisions themselves (Childre & Chambers, 2005; Fish, 2006; Salembier & Furney, 1998; Sheehey, 2006). Many parents do not want teams making decisions without them. They want their ideas about curriculum and instructional services to be considered along with the educators' suggestions (Fish, 2006; Pruitt, Wandry, & Hollums, 1998). Contacting parents before developing an IEP and soliciting their input allows them to contribute to the IEP process.

Before the Meeting

- ***Gather information.*** To prepare for the meeting, gather information about the student. Review existing data, and make sure that information necessary for making educational decisions is available and current (American Teacher, 2008).
- ***Contact parents.*** Prior to the meeting, contact the student's parents and ask them their preferences and needs regarding the meeting, including a convenient time and place for meeting. With the parents, decide if the student should be invited to the meeting (Smith, 2001).
- ***Encourage the family to invite an advocate to the IEP meeting.*** An advocate such as a friend, legal advisor, or counselor can assist the parents in asking questions, understanding programming, and identifying family needs and issues (Smith, 2001).
- ***Give notice of the meeting.*** Inform the parents in writing about the purpose of the meeting. The notice of the meeting should include a list of participants and their positions and a meeting agenda.
- ***Confirm attendance.*** Confirm who will attend the meeting. Make certain that those who need to attend the meeting (e.g., the local education agency and school psychologist) are planning to attend.
- ***Develop a draft of the IEP.*** Consult with parents and other teachers before writing a draft of the student's IEP. When you communicate with families, ask families to think about and suggest goals for their child. After obtaining parental input, send copies of the draft to the parents and to the other team members.
- ***Provide training.*** When appropriate, provide training on the IEP process and meetings. If training is not possible, at least orient parents to these procedures so they know what to expect.

During the Meeting

- *Open the meeting.* State the purpose of the meeting, introduce those in attendance, and inform parents of their legal rights. Ask them if they have any questions about the IEP process. If the IEP meeting is an eligibility meeting and the parents have not been involved in special education prior to the meeting, explain basic procedures.
- *Present and review assessment data.* Be certain to explain unfamiliar terms and assessment results. Explain the student's performance in terms the parents can understand. Provide opportunities for parents to ask questions.
- *Affirm a student's strengths and accomplishments.* Parents are usually very aware of their child's limitations. Affirming their child's strengths and successes can help build mutually respectful alliances (Martin & Hagan-Burke, 2002).
- *Solicit input from families.* Provide opportunities for parents to share information about their child, to develop goals, and to make decisions about placement. Avoid excluding parents from conversations or discussions.
- *Be careful not to "talk down" to family members or to "talk above" parents' understanding.* Although some family members may not be as educated as the professionals in the room, they should still be considered equal members of the team. Provide information parents need to understand discussions, but do so in a way that communicates respect and parity.
- *Listen and reflect.* Sometimes disagreements arise during IEP meetings. Families and professionals do not always agree on services and/or goals for the student. When disagreements arise, suspend your reaction and take time to understand the family's position. If the family's perspective is not contrary to the child's best interests, defer to the parents and abide by the family's decisions. Family self-determination will be enhanced by such actions (Van Haren & Fiedler, 2008).
- *Treat parents as key decision makers.* Parents should not have to become assertive to participate in making decisions about their child's education. Invite parents to provide input when decisions are made (Keen, 2007).
- *Understand the family's needs.* Families will vary in their ability to become involved in special education programs. Do not assume that what constitutes "active participation" for one family will be the same for all families. Take time to understand the family and assist them in identifying a level of participation that is realistic, given their time and resources (Coots, 2007; Van Haren & Fiedler, 2008).
- *When making decisions about services, consider family routines and resources.* To the extent possible, services offered to families should fit family routines. Consider the family's ability to transport a student to support services offered before making decisions for related services (Coots, 2007).
- *Provide parents with information necessary to make decisions and understand their child's situation.* Assess the parents' need for information, and provide parents with information about their child's disability, available services, options for interventions, and community resources if such information is requested and relevant to parent concerns (Turnbull, Turnbull, Erwin, & Soodak, 2006).

After the Meeting

- *Plan follow-up.* Before the meeting concludes, identify who will follow up on items discussed during the meeting. Set dates for subsequent meetings or for reporting progress.

- ***Provide all attendees with copies of the IEP.*** Distribute copies of the IEP to all participants in the meeting. Acknowledge parent participation, and invite parents to contact team members if they have any concerns.
- ***Keep current on progress toward IEP goals.*** After goals have been written, track the student's progress and keep parents informed of their child's progress. Do not assume that report cards adequately communicate progress toward IEP goals. Provide parents with specific information about their child's academic and/or behavior progress (American Teacher, 2008).

Attending to the logistics of IEP meetings is critical for conducting productive meetings. During meetings, decisions are made that affect students' education. Parents, educators, and students should collaborate in making decisions for each element of an IEP. Specifically, decisions about placement, goals, assistive technology, related services, assessment procedures, and transition should be reflect the needs and concerns of all parties.

Placement

Legal mandates as well as parent preferences should be considered when teams make placement decisions for students with disabilities. As discussed in Chapter 1, children with disabilities need to be provided a free and appropriate public education (FAPE) in the least restrictive environment (LRE). Placing children in LREs is not always a straightforward choice. A child's academic, social, and physical needs must be considered, and parents and educators may have different concerns about the LRE for a particular child. Such differences are to be expected, given that the parent and the professional come from difference perspectives (see Chapter 7). Differences in priorities should be discussed during IEP meetings. For example, the parents of a child with autism might want their child included in the general education class for the majority of the school day to provide opportunities for the child to interact with nondisabled peers. Teachers, on the other hand, might have concerns about managing the student's behavior, social acceptance by other students, and the feasibility of meeting the child's needs. If the child's level of academic performance is significantly below that of the other students in the class, general education teachers may not have the time or resources to provide specialized instruction to address the child's academic deficits. These parent/educator differences should be discussed during an IEP meeting.

Goals

Before IEP goals can be developed, educators and parents must agree on educational and/or social priorities. Having common goals is a critical aspect of collaboration. However, during traditional IEP meetings, parents often do not have opportunities to express their perspective of the child's needs. This is especially true when educators develop goals independently and present them at IEP meetings. As a result, educational programs typically focus on the school environment and short-term planning. Without family input, educators may fail to consider a child's home or community life or the broader perspective of a child's life outside school (Childre & Chamber, 2005).

Adopting a Student Centered Individualized Education Planning (SCIEP) approach can address this problem. Childre and Chambers (2005) developed forms for families to complete prior to SCIEP meetings. The forms provided opportunities for families to

TABLE 8.1 Examples of Parent Priorities and Team Support	
Parent Priorities	**IEP Team Support**
• For the student to learn how to drive so he can transport himself to school and work. • For the student to pass exit examinations required for obtaining a standard diploma.	• Include a goal for passing the state driver's license exam on the student's IEP. • Enroll the student in cotaught courses (taught by general education and special education teachers) that provide access to the content assessed on exit exams and specialized instruction needed for learning the content. Set goals that support mastery of concepts covered on exit exams. • If the student does not pass an exit exam on the first attempt, write goals that target areas in need of remediation.

consider their goals for their child, family involvement in the community, the child's strengths and preferences, and the child's social relationships. After completing the SCIEP process, families and educators reported that it was beneficial for them to consider the family perspective of the student's future. The family's goals for the future guided the team in developing IEP goals. Prior to IEP meetings, encourage parents to consider the following questions:

1. Where is my son or daughter now in his/her educational performance?
2. Where do I want my son or daughter to be a year from now, or in the future, and how can those expectations be measured?
3. In what ways can the team help her or him to meet those expectations? (Consortium for Appropriate Dispute Resolution in Special Education [CADRE], 2004).

Table 8.1 shows examples of parent goals and how the team can support them.

Assistive Technology

During an IEP meeting, the team makes decisions about a student's need for assistive technology. An assistive technology device is "any item, piece of equipment, or product that is used to increase, maintain, or improve the functional capabilities of children with disabilities" (IDEA, 2004, 20 U.S.C. 1401[25]). Assistive technology services assist individuals with disabilities in the selection, acquisition, or use of an assistive technology device (IDEA, 2004, 20 U.S.C. 1401[25]). Assistive technology items can range from low tech (pencil grips and slant boards) to high tech (hearing aids, computers, and software programs). IEP teams consider a student's needs and make assistive technology decisions that enable students to benefit from special education services. Table 8.2 provides a list of commonly used assistive technology devices.

When considering assistive technology, the IEP team should carefully consider the family perspective before making decisions (Parette & McMahan, 2002). Culture and linguistic background influence family perceptions of assistive technology devices. For example, in some cultures, parents might not want to use assistive technology (e.g., a

TABLE 8.2	Examples of Assistive Technology Tools for Students with Disabilities	
Curriculum	**Functional Challenges**	**Assistive Technology Tools**
Writing	• Writing (forming letters, staying within lines) • Composing written work • Planning writing projects	• Computer software programs that convert speech to written text • Programs that provide support for learning how to compose written compositions • Devices like pencil grips and slant boards that help students correctly hold writing implements • Digital voice recorders
Reading	• Reading grade-level text • Decoding words • Reading small print	• Text-to-speech computer software programs • Computer programs that provide practice/support for improving decoding ability • Enlarged text • Magnifying glass
Math	• Learning basic facts • Solving problems and calculating answers to problems	• Calculators • Software programs that provide practice for learning basic facts • High-interest video problem solving

Source: Information from Prater (2007).

motorized wheelchair) that calls attention to their child's condition. Family goals and expectations should be considered. Specifically, educators should consider the following:

1. What are the family's expectations for child independence?
2. To what extent does the family want the child accepted by others?
3. What are family expectations regarding immediacy of benefits?
4. What are family resource commitments to the implementations of assistive technology? (Parette & McMahan, 2002)

If professionals do not consider the family's perspective, educational resources may be wasted if a family does not adopt and use a selected device. Teams should discuss potential negative outcomes and should determine appropriate team responses when they evaluate assistive technology options.

Related Services

Students with disabilities may or may not need related services such as transportation, counseling, or speech or occupational therapy. In addition to the child's needs, family routines should be taken into account when making decisions about related services. The feasibility of recommendations should be considered along with family routines, beliefs, resources, needs, and abilities (Coots, 2007). For example, one single mother's life became consumed with providing services for her child. The mother had limited financial resources and had to take city buses to transport her child to a recommended speech therapist, whose office was located some distance from her home. Several days a week, she spent hours traveling to and from therapy. Her older child had to accompany her on the trips because she could not afford childcare. On days that her child had therapy, the family returned home close to bedtime. For this mother, it would have been helpful if professionals had worked with her to deliver services that better supported family routines (Coots, 2007).

Assessment

Assessment decisions, including accommodations for assessments, can affect a student's future. Many states require students to pass exit exams to receive high school diplomas, and high-stakes tests (e.g., tests that all students in the school are required to take) are also used to promote students from one grade to the next. Currently, little research exists on the effect of high-stakes assessments on students with disabilities. But it appears as though there are positive and negative consequences. Among the positive consequences are (a) standards for students with disabilities may be rising as educators strive to prepare students for high-stakes tests, (b) educators appear to be aligning IEP goals with assessments, and (c) high-stakes assessments may encourage better communication with parents about student performance. On the negative side, professionals speculate that dropout rates for students with disabilities are increasing because of high-stakes tests although not enough data exists to support such a conclusion. In addition, students retained in lower grades because they did not pass advancement exams may not receive adequate remediation to improve their chances of passing the exams in the future, and students may be retained in a lower grade because of their performance on one exam (Ysseldyke et al., 2004).

Parents should be informed about the issues involved in taking high-stakes exams. They need to be given accurate information about (a) their child's progress and (b) the skills and/or knowledge their child must acquire to pass required exams. Decisions made regarding the appropriateness of participation should be data based, and IEP goals should align with standards, curriculum, and assessments. If students fail on promotion exams, IEP goals should be revised to improve student performance. Retaining a student is ineffective unless instruction significantly changes during the repeated year (Ysseldyke et al., 2004).

Involving parents in assessment processes can improve student performance. Parents and students play vital roles in student achievement. Educators can provide parents with information about assessments, and they can collaborate with parents on supporting learning at home. If parents have the necessary time and skills, as well as the desire to work with their children, they can devote time at home to purposeful learning (Ysseldyke et al., 2004).

Another important consideration in assessment participation is the student's need for accommodations. Parents should be consulted regarding these accommodations, and a team decision should be made on how these accommodations will be addressed in the student's IEP. Most students with disabilities will take the same assessment as their peers. Whether students need testing accommodations depends on students' disabling conditions. Students who have writing disabilities may need more time to complete written sections of assessments, and students who have vision impairments might need tests printed in large print. Examples of testing accommodations include adjusting when the test is administered, altering the format of the test or how it is administered, using format alterations, and providing assistive devices (Carter, Prater, & Dyches, 2008). (See Table 8.3 for examples of specific testing accommodations.)

TABLE 8.3	Examples of Testing Accommodations		
	Testing Accommodations		
Setting	**Scheduling**	**Timing**	**Format**
• Individual • Study carrel • Separate room • Adaptive furniture	• Over several days • Specific day or time • At the best time for the student	• Extended time • Breaks during testing • Multiple sessions	• Large print • Key words highlighted • Increased spacing between lines • Fewer number of items per page

Source: Information from Thurlow, Elliott, & Ysseldyke (2003).

Testing accommodations allow students to demonstrate achievement without being impeded by their disabilities. Accommodation decisions should reflect student need (Ketterlin-Geller, Alonzo, Braun-Monegan, & Tindal, 2007). Students do not benefit from accommodations if the specific accommodation applied is not related to their challenges. For example, deciding to give a student more time on an exam may be appropriate if a student processes information slowly. It may not be appropriate for a student who lacks the ability to read exam questions. Parents should help determine the most appropriate accommodations for their child. They can help monitor whether their child receives testing accommodations and if the accommodations are effective for their child.

Transition

Transition services focus on helping a child transition from school to life as an adult. IDEA mandates that all IEPs include descriptions of transition services for students who are 16 years old and older. When planning transition goals and services for students, it is particularly important to involve parents and students, not only because it is legally mandated, but also because student interests significantly affect decisions made. Before making transition decisions, students should be asked about their interests, type of work they enjoy, work experience, and leisure-time activities. Parents can also provide information about their aspirations for their child's future life, including independence, recreation, employment, and so forth. Teachers who have worked with the student can provide information about the student's academic and affective skills and work behaviors, and they can describe what type of instruction is most effective for the student (Prater, 2007). A person-centered approach to transition planning and assessment considers the student, parent, and professional perspective. The following questions help focus transition discussions:

1. Who is the student?
2. What are the student's dreams?
3. What are the team's greatest concerns for the student?
4. What are the student's strengths, gifts, and abilities?
5. What are the student's greatest challenges?
6. What supports are needed to help the student transition to adult life? (Wehman, 2001)

Planning IEPs for students with disabilities is an individualized process. The educational, social, and/or behavioral needs of the students should drive the process. Decisions

---

IEP checklist

- Did the parents receive written notice of the scheduled IEP meeting at least 10 days in advance?
- Did educators explain procedural safeguards to the family?
- Did parents give their written consent for assessments?
- During the meeting, were parents given an opportunity to describe their goals and expectations for their child?
- Did IEP team members consider the parents' recommendations?
- Did the IEP team discuss participation in statewide assessments?
- Did the IEP team include needed accommodations and/or modifications in the IEP?
- Was transition addressed during the meeting?
- Were the child's social, emotional, and physical needs considered?
- Did team members make decisions about related services?
- Was assistive technology considered?
- Did the team review parents' independent evaluations?
- Did team members consider the parents' need for training?

Student Checklist

- Did the student understand the purpose of the IEP meeting?
- Was the student invited to attend the meeting (when appropriate)?
- Were all the team members introduced to the student?
- Were assessment results explained to the student?
- Did the student have opportunities to ask questions or to provide input?
- Does the student know what comes next?

FIGURE 8.1   IEP Checklist   *Source:* Maryland State Department of Education, Division of Special Education/Early Intervention Services. *Building IEPs with Maryland families: What a great IDEA* (2000), p. 13.

regarding placement, services, goals for learning, transition, assistive technology, and accommodations should reflect the needs of the student. Parents have insight and experience with their child that educators do not have, and their input should be sought and respected as both parties work together to develop IEPs. Figure 8.1 is a checklist educators can use to assess whether they provide opportunities for parents to contribute to the IEP process.

STRATEGIES FOR INVOLVING STUDENTS

The 2004 reauthorization of the Individuals with Disabilities Education Act (IDEA) reinforces the importance of student involvement on the IEP team, particularly in developing postsecondary goals. Such planning requires that these goals be based on the student's needs, strengths, preferences, and interests and cannot be done without student involvement. Other appropriate student involvement is left to the discretion of the team. The implication is, however, that students should participate not only in the IEP meeting, but also in the whole IEP process (Van Dycke, Martin, & Lovett, 2006). In fact, it could be argued that because students are members of families, professionals who fail to include students in their IEP process are inadvertently denying family members the right to be involved. However, given that no additional regulations provide guidance, it is generally inferred that parents should make the decision about student participation. School personnel can share their professional opinion with the parent, but parents should have the discretion to make this decision (Zirkel, 2006).

Given that students are not required to participate in their IEP meetings until post-secondary transition planning is to occur, most students are not involved until then. Van Dycke et al. (2006) compare this to hearing your parents and others plan your birthday party as a young child, but never being invited to attend the party. Then, suddenly when you become an adolescent not only are you invited, but you are also expected to participate. You might feel confused and apprehensive. These authors and others advocate that students participate earlier in their IEP meetings. Early participation provides students opportunities to experience different levels of participation.

Typically, parents will have questions that might include the impact student involvement will have on other team members' participation and the quality of their child's education. Some parents may have concerns specifically about their child's ability to self-advocate. Teachers should explain the rationale for student participation to parents as well as explain exactly what will occur during the meeting. In addition, they should encourage students to talk about their IEPs at home (McGahee, Mason, Wallace, & Jones, 2001).

We discuss strategies for involving students in their IEP process at four levels—namely, (a) pre-IEP planning and preparation, (b) IEP planning and preparation, (c) the IEP meeting, and (d) IEP management.

Pre-IEP Planning and Preparation

Teachers can prepare students to participate in the IEP process first by teaching certain knowledge and skills that will help them participate more fully. By identifying the pre-IEP planning knowledge and skills listed next, we do not suggest that all these need to be implemented and students competent before moving to the IEP planning stage. Rather, we present these strategies as instructional foci that can enhance current and future student IEP involvement. Teachers may teach these skills simultaneous with teaching IEP participation.

- *Teach students about their disabilities.* Before students can become involved fully in the IEP process, they need to understand their disability. Teachers should consider individual students' characteristics as well as seek parental approval and support before determining the depth and breadth of material presented to the students about their disability. Resources are available for teachers to use to teach about disabilities. Some resources focus more on teaching students without disabilities although most could be modified for students with disabilities to better understand themselves. A list of a few resources available to enhance disability awareness may be found in the resource section at the end of the chapter.
- *Teach about special education and the IEP process.* In addition to disability awareness, students need to understand special education and the IEP process (Jones, 2006). They should connect their disability to the need for specialized services as well as understand their legal rights and responsibilities. Depending on the sophistication of the student, she may have questions about why she's been singled out to take individualized tests or attend a different classroom, or why she has more than one teacher. Students' questions should be answered truthfully at a level and in terms they can understand. Older students and those who are higher functioning could be directly taught the key concepts from the Individuals with Disabilities Education Act using student-friendly language (Mason, McGahee-Kovac, & Johnson, 2004).

- *Discuss accommodations.* Teach students what accommodations are and why they are appropriate for students who need them. Provide students a list of accommodations and ask them which ones they have used previously. One way to do this is to ask them to think of their best class and identify what is different in that class (e.g., how tests are designed, the way the teacher instructs; McGahee et al., 2001). Discuss which accommodations they have not used that they think would be helpful or useful. Students can be very astute about their own needs (Kupper, 2002).
- *Teach about confidentiality.* Students need a basic understanding of confidentiality and how it is demonstrated. They should understand who, what, and when they should share information about themselves and their disability (Mason, McGahee-Kovak, & Johnson, 2004).
- *Teach about the IEP document.* Students need a basic understanding of at least the purpose of an IEP, the rationale for an IEP, and the sections of an IEP (McGahee et al., 2001). Students can, perhaps, learn about IEPs best from their own IEP. Konrad (2008) suggests, for example, that students can engage in an IEP scavenger hunt, where they search their own IEPs for certain items, such as the signatures to determine who attended. The complexity of scavenger hunt questions would, of course, be based on students' previous experience with IEPs, as well as their age and skill levels. Kupper (2002) recommends starting small by asking students to find their name and other identifying information. Another suggested activity involves teaching students to evaluate their IEPs according to the sections required by the law. In this case, providing a checklist of required elements and asking them to locate each on their IEP would be helpful (Konrad, 2008). Confidentiality needs to be reinforced when engaged in these activities. It may be best to provide copies of student IEPs to them in large envelopes with clasps (MasonMcGahee-Kovac, & Johnson, 2004).
- *Teach self-advocacy skills.* Students with disabilities need self-advocacy skills to empower them in problem solving and choice making. Persons with cognitive disabilities, in particular, have traditionally engaged very little in self-advocacy (Heward, 2009). Self-advocacy requires self-determination, or knowing what you want and how to get it in appropriate ways. Many authors have written about and researched self-advocacy and self-determination for students with disabilities (e.g., Chambers, Wehmeyer, Saito, Lida, Lee, & Singh, 2007; Fiedler & Danneker, 2007; Mithaug, 2007).

IEP Planning and Preparation

One of the most important facets of student involvement can occur at the IEP planning stage, with the level of participation being determined by student characteristics and parent desires. It is critical that parents be involved in this decision. Younger students or those new to the process may simply attend the meeting. As they mature and understand the process better, their involvement can and should increase. Following we list strategies that can be used to involve students at the IEP planning stage (see Jones, 2006; Kupper, 2002; and Konrad, 2008 for additional information):

- *Teach about assessment.* If appropriate, students can learn about academic assessments and their own performance, which can lead to involvement in setting IEP goals. Parents should be consulted when determining what information to share with students. The role of confidentiality should be reinforced with students when discussing assessment results.

- ***Ask students to write about their strengths and limitations.*** When students write about themselves, it serves several purposes. Students can improve their writing skills, as well as learn to self-reflect. If students write, for example, one paragraph each about their strengths and limitations, these paragraphs, if approved by the IEP team, can be copied and included on the IEP document.
- ***Teach students to create vision statements for themselves.*** Students can be asked to create a vision statement for themselves. For example, they could fill in these blanks prior to an IEP meeting: "After high school, I plan to live ____, learn ____, work ____, and play ____" (Konrad, 2008, p. 237). Jones (2006) describes how a group of teachers found vision planning "particularly motivating for the students to begin thinking about and actually articulating their hopes and dreams for the future. [They] became enthused about the possibilities that lay ahead for them and began taking steps toward realizing their dreams" (p. 14).
- ***Teach students to convert vision statements and use statements of limitations to write goals.*** Students can also be taught to write goals to reflect the areas of limitation they self-identified previously, for example, using "I will" statements (e.g., I will learn to write letters.). Using student-friendly language within goals and objectives helps not only students better understand them, but parents as well.
- ***Ask students to write letters inviting participants to their IEP meeting.*** Through writing letters of invitation to IEP members, students can become more familiar with these individuals and the roles they play (see Figure 8.2). In addition, teachers can use this opportunity to teach letter writing skills. Having students send reminders through e-mail can also be used to enhance their technology skills.
- ***Involve students in making the physical preparations for the meeting.*** Invite students to make name tags or to arrange the chairs for the meeting. Use this as an opportunity to teach about appropriate apparel for such a meeting. Such activities can help students recognize the importance of the meeting and the seriousness with which the team takes the students' education.

Dear Mrs. Ryder:

I am writing to invite you to my IEP meeting on Tuesday, April 23 at 3:00 pm. We will meet in Room 201. Please read the draft IEP before you come. If you have questions or suggestions, let me or Mr. Matsumoto know before the meeting. See you there.

Sincerely,
Isaac

FIGURE 8.2 Sample student-written IEP meeting invitation

> • *Help students create a draft IEP.* Using students' written statements of strengths and limitations, as well as their goal statements, students can draft their IEP documents. Once the drafts are created, students could take them home to share with their parents in preparation for the IEP meeting.

IEP Meeting

In addition to general skills and planning for the IEP meeting, students can be taught to actively participate in the meeting. Research supports that students with disabilities, including students with cognitive disabilities, can learn to conduct their IEP meetings (Snyder, 2002). Student-led IEP meetings have been found to teach students to take ownership for their education and to help them better understanding disabilities, legal rights, and appropriate accommodations while at the same time increasing their self-confidence and self-advocacy. In addition, general education teachers describe students who have these skills as interacting more positively with adults, understanding their legal rights, assuming more responsibility, and being more aware of their limitations and available resources (Mason, McGahee-Kovac, Johnson, & Stillerman, 2002).

> • *Provide a rationale for the importance of student IEP involvement.* When asked, students often state that their IEP meeting is something they would rather avoid. If students are provided a strong, but brief rationale about how their preferences and interests will be used in making decisions, they are more likely to agree they have something to contribute to the meeting (Torgerson, Miner, & Shen, 2004).
> • *Teach students the skills needed to be actively involved in their IEP meeting.* Several levels of student involvement in the IEP are possible. At the lowest level, students may sit in on the meeting as an observer. At the next level students could present or read the proposed goals or make introductions. Even further, students could explain their disability, share their strengths and limitations, and/or explain the accommodations needed. At the highest level, students would lead the IEP meeting discussion (Mason, McGahee-Kovac, & Johnson, 2004).
> • *Teach specific communication skills.* Students may need to learn appropriate communication skills such as maintaining eye contact and appropriate speech volume and speed. Develop cues that you can give the student if they are not maintaining these skills. Practice the cues with the student before the meeting (Kupper, 2002).
> • *Don't assume students are too young for IEP involvement.* As mentioned earlier, parents have the ultimate responsibility for determining when and if their child should be involved prior to transition planning. However, it may be a mistake to assume that children are too young to be involved. Mason, McGahee-Kovac, and Johnson (2004) reported success when involving students as young as 6 years old.
>
> > The vocabulary is different, and the degree of responsibility is different; however, the concept of leadership is maintained through the emphasis that is placed on asking the child about what is important to him or her and using that information in planning goals. (p. 22)
>
> • *Don't assume students are incapable of being involved in their IEP meeting.* Another mistake made is to assume that students with cognitive disabili-

ties or those with limited communication skills cannot be actively involved in their IEP meetings. Picture prompts, communication boards, and other electronic devices can be used for communication purposes. Also, students can be videotaped in advance presenting specific information or they can lead only one section of the meeting (Mason, McGahee-Kovac, & Johnson, 2004). Rather than disallowing them to participate, find ways they can at least be partially involved.

• ***Teach students to lead their IEP meetings.*** Published curricula can be used to teach students the steps involved with conducting an IEP meeting. The *Self-Directed IEP* (Martin, Marshall, Maxson, & Jerman 1997; Snyder, 2002) is one source available. This particular curriculum teaches the following steps to leading the IEP meeting.

  • Begin the meeting by stating the purpose.
  • Introduce everyone.
  • Review past goals and performance.
  • Ask for others' feedback.
  • State your school and transition goals.
  • Ask questions if you don't understand.
  • Deal with differences in opinion.
  • State what support you'll need.
  • Summarize your goals.
  • Close the meeting by thanking everyone.
  • Work on IEP goals all year.

Other commercially available resource materials are listed in the Web Resources section of this chapter.

• ***When starting an instructional program to teach IEP involvement, start small and grow.*** Before starting an instructional program, run a pilot program. Select a few students to participate. Once successful for a few, enthusiasm can spread, making it easier to expand the program. Identify other teachers and school personnel in your building, as well as parents, who will support your pilot program and be your allies (Mason, McGahee-Kovac, & Johnson, 2004).

• ***Show a video of an IEP meeting with active student involvement.*** Incorporate the video into teaching groups of students to lead their IEP meetings. Although commercial videos of IEP meetings are available, it would be most helpful to video-tape a local IEP meeting, particularly with a student conducting his own meeting. As always, written permission would be necessary from all the IEP participants. If necessary, edit the video for length and content. Confidential information should not be included. As students watch the DVD, ask them to identify different elements that they observed.

• ***Invite students who have participated in their IEP meetings to present to other students.*** Once parental permission is obtained, students who have successfully been involved in their own IEP processes could share how they prepared for and conducted the meeting. A panel of students at various levels of involvement would provide a broader perspective and could serve as motivation to students to become even more involved.

Self-Advocacy Strategy—**I PLAN** and **SHARE** (Hammer, 2004)
 Inventory your
  Strengths
  Areas to improve or learn
  Goals
  Choices for learning or accommodations
 Provide your inventory information
 Listen and respond
 Ask questions
 Name your goals
 Sit up straight
 Have a pleasant tone of voice
 Activate your thinking
  Tell yourself to pay attention
  Tell yourself to participate
  Tell yourself to compare ideas
 Relax
  Don't look uptight
  Tell yourself to compare ideas
 Engage in eye contact
Writing IEP Goals and Paragraphs Strategy—**GO 4 IT... NOW!** (Konrad & Test, 2007; Konrad, Trela, & Test, 2006)
 Goal statement (topic sentence)
 Objectives (**4** of them, supporting details)
 Identify a **T**imeline
 Name topic
 Order details
 Wrap it up and restate topic

FIGURE 8.3 Specific strategies for IEP involvement

- *Ask students to interview other students.* In addition to or in lieu of student presentations or panels, students learning about the IEP meeting could interview other students who have been successful participants in their IEP processes. A brief oral or written summary of what they learned could be required. Confidentiality should be reinforced in this process.
- *Provide opportunities for students to practice role-played IEP meetings.* As with any skill being taught, students need opportunities to practice the skill with feedback provided by the teacher. Student IEP meeting involvement has been shown to increase when students are given ample opportunities to verbally rehearse and role-play (with prompting) IEP meetings (Test et al., 2004).
- *Videotape students role-playing conducting the IEP meeting.* Videotaping the students during role-playing is particularly helpful, given that the videotape can be played back for the student to observe. Ways to improve can then be discussed (Mason, McGahee-Kovac, & Johnson, 2004). Skills to be evaluated may include

accuracy and completion of the steps taught as well as specific communication skills such as eye contact, voice quality, and overall demeanor (Torgerson et al., 2004).

- ***Determine how involved the student will be in the IEP meeting.*** Although students who are able should be encouraged to lead or contribute to the meeting, a student who feels uncomfortable should not be forced to do so. Teach students verbal cues they could say to excuse themselves appropriately from the meeting (Jones, 2006).
- ***Prepare other members of the team for student IEP involvement.*** Preparing only the student is not sufficient. All other members of the IEP team also need to be prepared for and comfortable with the students' participation (Jones, 2006). Suggest to the other participants in advance of the meeting that they not interrupt the student, particularly if the student is prepared with a presentation (Kupper, 2002).

IEP Monitoring

Students can do more than just participate in or lead their IEP meeting. They can be taught to manage their IEPs.

- ***Teach self-monitoring skills.*** Using self-monitoring skills, students can assist with monitoring their own progress toward special goal attainment. As described by a high school student, "[Self-monitoring] lets you know what you need to work harder on, so you can be aware and stay more focused on those things you have a tougher time with" (Jones, 2006, p. 15).
- ***Periodically have students review their IEPs and evaluate their progress.*** Periodically reviewing the IEP can help students remember the goals they are working toward accomplishing. Students could highlight or check the goals they believe have been accomplished and discuss them with their teacher. If goals have been accomplished, the teacher and student could discuss and draft future goals.

Although student involvement in the IEP process has been advocated for many years, the field has room for much growth in this area. Student attendance in IEP meetings does appear to be rising. In a recent study 70% of all middle, junior high, and high school students receiving special education services attended their IEP meeting (Martin, Marshall, & Sale, 2004). In this same study the researchers discovered that when students attended, parents, general educators, and related services personnel felt more comfortable saying what they thought, and administrators discussed the student's strengths, needs, and interests to a greater degree. Also, parents indicated they understood the proceedings better, and both parents and general educators knew significantly more of what they needed to do next.

Although student participation is on the rise, active participation of students is often minimal. For example, one study found that only 34% of school personnel were satisfied with the level of student involvement in IEP meetings (Mason, Field, & Sawilowsky, 2004). Martin and colleagues (2004) also found that students understood less the purpose of the meeting and what to do at the meeting, talked less at the meeting, felt less comfortable saying what they thought, understood less what was said, and felt less positive about the meeting than any other IEP meeting participant. Teachers can ensure more student active participation and understanding by teaching them the skills as described in this chapter while soliciting the support of their parents in this process.

Questions professionals and parents can ask themselves these questions to determine how well they are truly involving students in their own IEP processes:

1. How are we encouraging students to become involved in their IEP meetings?
2. At what age are we encouraging involvement?
3. Are we allowing students to help decide who should be invited?
4. Are we giving students opportunities to be responsible for goals on their IEPs?
5. How well do students understand the purpose of the IEP and the IEP meeting? (Van Dycke et al., 2006)

FIGURE 8.4 Questions regarding student involvement

Summary

- When planning and conducting IEP meetings, educators should consider family circumstance and should solicit input from parents.
- Parents and educators may have different perspectives about placement decisions. During IEP meetings, both parties should have opportunity to discuss their perspectives and concerns.
- Adopting a student-centered approach for planning IEP goals facilitations the identification of common goals.
- Parents' preferences, circumstances, routines, and resources should be considered when making assistive technology and related service decisions.
- Assessment decision can affect a student's future. Issues related to high-stakes tests should be discussed with parents before they are expected to make assessment decisions.

- Student-centered transition planning allows for the student, parent, and professional perspectives to be considered.
- Teachers can prepare students to participate in their IEP meetings by educating students about their disabling conditions, teaching about IEP processes and meetings, helping students identify personal strengths and challenges, and encouraging self-advocacy.
- To effectively participate in IEP meetings, students need to learn how to conduct meetings and communicate with adults.
- Showing videos of student-led IEP meetings and engaging students in role-plays are effective strategies for preparing students to conduct their IEP meetings.

Linking Standards to Chapter Content

After reading this chapter you should be able to link basic knowledge and skills described in the CEC Standards and INTASC Principles with information provided in this text. Table 8.4, Linking CEC Standards and INTASC Principles to Major Chapter Topics, provides examples of how they are addressed in each major section of the chapter.

TABLE 8.4 Linking CEC Standards and INTASC Principles to Major Chapter Topics		
Major Chapter Headings	**CEC Knowledge and Skill Core Standard and Associated Subcategories**	**INTASC Core Principle and Associated Special Education Subcategories**
Creating IEPs with Families	6: Language ICC6K4: Augmentative and assistive communication strategies. 7: Instructional Planning ICC7S2: Develop and implement comprehensive, longitudinal individualized programs in collaboration with team members. ICC7S3: Involve individual and family in setting instructional goals and monitoring progress. ICC7S9: Incorporate and implement instructional and assistive technology into the educational program. 9: Professional and Ethical Practice ICC9S4: Conduct professional activities in compliance with applicable laws and policies. 10: Collaboration ICC10K2: Roles of individuals with exceptional learning needs, families, and school and community personnel in planning of an individualized program. ICC10S4: Assist individuals with exceptional learning needs and their families in becoming active participants in the educational team. ICC10S5: Plan and conduct collaborative conferences with individuals with exceptional learning needs and their families.	1: Subject Matter 1.1: Special education teachers have knowledge of the requirements and responsibilities involved in developing, implementing, and evaluating individualized education programs (IEPs), individualized family service plans (IFSPs), and individual accommodation plans (IAPs) for students with disabilities. 4: Instructional Strategies 4.08: All teachers expect and support the use of assistive and instructional technologies to promote learning and independence of students with disabilities. 7: Planning Instruction 7.01: All general and special education teachers contribute their expertise as members of a collaborative team to develop, monitor, and periodically revise individualized educational plans for students with disabilities. 7.08: Special education teachers provide for the active involvement of students, families, and other professionals in constructing the student's education program. 10: Collaboration, Ethics, and Relationships 10.4: All teachers accept families as full partners in planning appropriate instruction and services for students with disabilities, and provide meaningful opportunities for them to participate as partners in their children's instructional programs and in the life of the school.
Strategies for Involving Students	4: Instructional Strategies ICC4S2: Teach individuals to use self-assessment, problem-solving, and other cognitive strategies to meet their needs. ICC4S5: Use procedures to increase the individual's self-awareness, self-management, self-control, self-reliance, and self-esteem.	10.8: Special education teachers include, promote, and facilitate family members as partners on parent–professional, interdisciplinary, and interagency teams. 4: Instructional Strategies 4.07 All teachers use strategies that promote the independence, self-control and self-advocacy of students with disabilities. 5: Learning Environments

(continued)

TABLE 8.4 *(continued)*		
Major Chapter Headings	**CEC Knowledge and Skill Core Standard and Associated Subcategories**	**INTASC Core Principle and Associated Special Education Subcategories**
	ICC4S6: Use strategies that promote successful transitions for individuals with exceptional learning needs. 7: Instructional Planning ICC7S3: Involve individual and family in setting instructional goals and monitoring progress. 10: Collaboration ICC10S4: Assist individuals with exceptional learning needs and their families in becoming active participants in the educational team. ICC10S5: Plan and conduct collaborative conferences with individuals with exceptional learning needs and their families.	5.08: Special education teachers prepare students with disabilities to take an active role in their IEP planning process, when it is appropriate to do so, in order to support their commitment to learning, self-motivation and self-advocacy. 7: Planning Instruction 7.08: Special education teachers provide for the active involvement of students, families, and other professionals in constructing the student's education program.

Sources: Council for Exceptional Children (2005); Interstate New Teacher Assessment and Support Consortium INTASC Special Education Subcommittee (May 2001).

Web Resources

RESOURCES AVAILABLE FOR IEP STUDENT INVOLVEMENT SUPPORT

Helping Students Develop Their IEPs and A Student's Guide to the IEP—(Kupper, 2002) provides guidelines for parents and teacher to help students become involved in developing their IEPs. Lessons and activities are provided as well as suggestions for getting ready for, during, and after the meeting. Appendices are provided with additional suggestions.

http://www.kucrl.org/sim/strategies/advocacy.shtml — The self-advocacy strategy (Hammer, 2004; Test & Neale, 2004; Van Reusen, Bos, Schumaker, & Deshler, 1994) was designed to help students prepare for and participate in any type of conference, including IEP meetings. The strategy includes getting organized before a conference as well as effective communication techniques to use during the conference. Available from Edge Enterprises, Inc., Lawrence, Kansas (see Figure 8.5).

http://web.uccs.edu/education/special/self_determination/cmcr_sdiep.html —The Self-Directed IEP

(Martin et al., 1997; Snyder, 2002) is a multimedia package used to instruct students on how to manage their own IEP meetings. Students are taught 11 steps toward actively participating in or leading their IEP meetings. Students learn to apply the steps to their own lives.

Student-Led IEPs: A Guide for Student Involvement (McGahee et al., 2001) includes activities for assisting secondary-level students develop and participate in the IEP process. The activities are adaptable to meet individual student needs and abilities. Although originally designed to be individualized instruction, adaptations for group or schoolwide implementation are addressed.

http://escholarship.bc.edu/education/tecplus/vol3/iss5/art4 —"Student-Led IEP Meetings: Planning and Implementation Strategies" (Hawbaker, 2007) addresses specific strategies that may be used with students, including activities for teaching about IEPs and an IEP portfolio template that can be used as a script or a prompt at the meeting.

CHAPTER 9

Ethical Considerations When Working with Families

OBJECTIVES

After reading this chapter you will

1. Discuss the ethical considerations impacting educational practices.

2. Know and understand the definition of ethics.

3. Discuss various educational organizations' professional codes of ethics.

4. Describe and apply the concept of "do no harm" to practices in education.

5. Discuss the concept of doing no harm when working with children and youth and parents and families.

6. Describe strategies to ensure ethical practice when working with families.

7. Discuss barriers to ethical and confidential practices when working with families.

CHAPTER OUTLINE

- Objectives
- Introduction
- Ethical Considerations and Educational Practice
- Definition of Ethics
- Codes of Ethics
  - National Education Association
  - National Association for the Education of Young Children
  - Council for Exceptional Children
- The Ethical Concept of Doing No Harm
  - Doing No Harm with Children and Youth
  - Doing No Harm with Parents and Families
- Strategies to Ensure Ethical Practices When Working with Families
- Barriers to Ethical and Confidential Practices When Working with Families
  - Inadequate Communication
  - Educational Jargon
  - Lack of Trust
  - Myriad Points of View
- Summary
- Linking Standards to Chapter Content
- Web Resources

INTRODUCTION

Nathan has a specific learning disability in the area of reading comprehension and has been fully included in the general education setting since second grade. In general, over the past 4 years, Nathan has made incredible progress on his IEP objectives and in his academic perform-ance. Nathan is a good student and is well liked by his teachers and his peers. Recently, how-ever, Nathan's behavior at school has deteriorated. Nathan is no longer on time to school, he rarely brings back his homework, during class he is often clowning around, drawing, or talk-ing back to other students or the teacher, and he seems distracted most of the time.

Mrs. Troutman is concerned about Nathan. She believes his school performance is suf-fering because his dad was recently deployed to the conflict in Iraq, and he is now living with his aunt. Nathan's aunt is not as involved in his education as his father was. Nathan's aunt is a cocktail waitress at a local pub and works nights. Mrs. Troutman does not believe she is a suitable guardian for Nathan. She has tried on numerous occasions to set up a meet-ing with Nathan's aunt, but the aunt never shows up. The aunt has asked Mrs. Troutman to please stop calling her and has told her that she is doing the best she can with Nathan.

In a moment of poor judgment, Mrs. Troutman talked about Nathan's current school problems, including her frustration with his aunt, in the faculty lunchroom with other school personnel. She thought she was just venting, but she divulged confidential informa-tion about Nathan's disability and his family. In a professional development workshop later that week, she learned that she had broken education's code of ethics by sharing informa-tion she should not have shared with others.

Consider this scenario as you read through this chapter. Have you ever been in a posi-tion where you either wittingly or unwittingly divulged confidential information about a student or a student's family?

Parents are considered to have the most knowledge about their children (Fielder, Simpson, & Clark, 2007), and educators must listen to and discuss issues about which parents express concern (Bredekamp & Copple, 1997). Parents' investments of interest, concern, time, and effort are likely to be greater when they perceive themselves as active partners in their chil-dren's education. Educators, accordingly, should acknowledge the expertise and levels of understanding that parents *bring to the table* and that they can learn from each other. This approach to parent–professional communication allows teachers and parents to create and implement beneficial learning experiences for children (Trussell, Hammond, & Ingalls, 2008).

Educators have a legal and ethical responsibility to ensure parent involvement in schools, and they must act in an ethical manner when networking with and exchanging ideas with parents and other family members. Yet, parent participation needs substantial improve-ment, especially in special education, where legal precedents, research, and professional organizations determine ethical standards (Trussell et al., 2008). The purpose of this chapter is to discuss

- Ethical considerations and practice in education
- Concepts of doing no harm in interactions with students and their parents
- The importance of confidentiality in education
- Strategies that ensure ethical practices in parent professional interactions
- Barriers that may interfere with ethical interactions with parents and families of chil-dren and youth with disabilities and others at risk of educational failure

ETHICAL CONSIDERATIONS AND EDUCATIONAL PRACTICE

Ethical practice necessitates that professionals demonstrate essential skills, competencies, and dispositions that "influence their behaviors toward students, families, colleagues, and communities, and affect student learning, motivation, and development, as well as the educator's own professional growth" (National Council for Accreditation of Teacher Education, 2006, p. 53). Therefore, educators must demonstrate fairness, trust, mutual respect, advocacy, and effective communication and collaboration skills (Bredekamp & Copple, 1997; Turnbull, Turnbull, Erwin, & Soodak, 2006).

These behaviors are integral to ethical behavior and must be the foundation for educators' daily interactions. Yet, in comparison to other professions (e.g., medicine, social work, business), little information exists about ethics in education. Historically, ethics in education discussions focused on teaching about character development and behavior, with very little emphasis on teachers' roles in making moral judgments and decisions necessary to provide high-quality education for all students. Thus, educators may overlook the ethical dimensions of professional practice. Educators may ignore moral considerations because (a) they feel overwhelmed with the demands of teaching, (b) their administrators may promote politically and morally neutral school cultures, and (c) ethics were not addressed adequately in their teacher preparation program (Berkeley & Ludlow, 2008; Beyer, 1997). Few teacher education programs address ethical issues and professional standards and practices in a comprehensive manner to ensure teachers' ability to make good moral judgments (Sileo, Sileo, & Pierce, 2008).

DEFINITION OF ETHICS

According to the Oxford American College Dictionary, "ethics are moral principles that govern a person's or group's behavior" (2002, p. 463) and concern acceptable rules of conduct, societal customs, human rights, and democratic principles for living. Ethics requires a critical reflection of people's personal behaviors and obligations.

Professional ethics is a system of moral principles and values that relate to individual behaviors, a class of human actions, or a group of specialists. Educators comprise one such group. Their behaviors are influenced by ethical codes that identify and communicate their responsibilities toward and relationships among colleagues, students and parents, employing institutions, and the general public. Ethical codes help to guide educators' decision-making processes related to predicaments of right and wrong, civil liberties and responsibilities, and human welfare.

CODES OF ETHICS

Several educational professional organizations have ethical codes that emphasize prevention of detrimental practices related to interactions with children and youth, parents and other family members, and colleagues (e.g., Council for Exceptional Children, 2010; National Association for the Education of Young Children [NAYEC], 2005; National Education Association [NEA], 2009). The codes offer frameworks for ethical behavior as well as general support to professionals, within their respective disciplines, when they face ethical dilemmas that test their commitment to maintaining exemplary standards of practice. Table 9.1 provides a brief list of professional organizations, in addition to those discussed in this text, that employ codes of ethics.

TABLE 9.1	Sample List of Professional Organizations with Codes of Ethics

Organization

American Association of University Professors
American Bar Association
American Educational Research Association
American Library Association
American Marketing Association
American Medical Association
American Nurses Association
American Psychological Association
American Veterinary Medical Association

National Education Association

The National Education Association (NEA) code of ethics concerns *commitment to the student* and *commitment to the profession*. The preamble for *commitment to the student*, states:

> The educator strives to help each student realize his or her potential as a worthy and effective member of society. The educator therefore works to stimulate the spirit of inquiry, the acquisition of knowledge and understanding, and the thoughtful formulation of worthy goals. (NEA, 2009, p. 1)

The first two components of student commitment indicate that teachers cannot (a) restrain or deny students' pursuit of learning or varying points of view, nor can they (b) alter content knowledge to inhibit students' progress. The third component addresses teachers' responsibility to protect students from harmful situations related to learning, health, or safety. Components four and five state that teachers cannot intentionally embarrass students, grant advantage to, or discriminate against students based on nationality, race, color, sex, social or cultural background, or sexual orientation. Component six indicates that teachers do not have the right to use "professional relationships with students for private advantage" (NEA, 2009, p. 1). The final component states that unless required by law, teachers must respect and maintain students' confidentiality (see Appendix A for the entire NEA Code of Ethics).

The NEA code of ethics also emphasizes teachers' *commitment to the profession* and their need to participate in *good teaching*, including meeting the diverse needs of children and youth. Special educators demonstrating *good teaching* provide individualized instruction to ensure the success of students with disabilities and others at risk of school failure due to the negative effects of environmental events. Most educators adhere to the NEA ethical code and are committed to working with children in a way that *avoids harming them*.

In addition, teachers' *commitment to the profession* spotlights educators' need to raise professional standards and promote a climate that encourages well-thought-out decisions (NEA, 2009). Specifically, the NEA ethical code requires that educators shall not (a) disclose information about colleagues obtained in the course of professional service, unless disclosure serves a compelling purpose or is required by law; (b) knowingly make

> *Mrs. Ostler is concerned about her daughter Sarah. She asks Sarah's teacher from the previous year, Ms. Isaacson, about her new teacher, Mr. Jung. Ms. Isaacson states that her colleague is a good teacher, but she confirms Mrs. Ostler's fears, that Mr. Jung is very strict. Mrs. Ostler is concerned because Sarah has a tendency to shut down in stressful situations. She does not want her daughter to experience a negative school year. However, she isn't sure about a course of action, so she thanks Ms. Isaacson and walks away.*
>
> *Throughout the course of the evening, Mrs. Ostler thinks a lot about the teacher's comments. She becomes more nervous. Is Mr. Jung as mean as everyone said? What was her daughter's final year in the school going to be like? Did she need to ask the principal to assign Sarah to another class? What should she do? After asking herself these questions, she decides to form her own opinion and allow her daughter to remain in Mr. Jung's class. By the end of the school year she is glad she made this decision because her daughter loves Mr. Jung. She is excited about school and even began to count the hours before she could return to school each day. It was during this year that Sarah decided she wanted to become a teacher!*
>
> In this scenario, the teacher's opinion was potentially harmful to the parent and the child. If the parent listened to the teacher, she may have requested another class assignment and in doing so, perhaps changed the course of her daughter's profession. It is important for educators to think about how their opinions influence others.

FIGURE 9.1 Mrs. Ostler's concerns

false or malicious statements about a colleague; or (c) accept any gratuity, gift, or favor that might impair or appear to influence professional decisions or action.

Ethics encompasses a wide range of behaviors for teachers and other school personnel, and it is equally important for them to act responsibly and ethically with colleagues as it is with students. Therefore, educators should do their best to refrain from making derogatory remarks regarding colleagues, especially in front of students and their parents and other family members.

Parents and teachers need the opportunity to create personal opinions about one another without influence from others. Sometimes, offering an opinion causes more harm than good. Figure 9.1 provides a scenario that examines how personal opinions can influence professional behaviors. After you review the scenario, consider how you might have reacted if you were Mrs. Ostler or how you may have responded to the parent if you were either Ms. Isaacson or Mr. Jung. What have you learned about the NEA Code of Ethics that would inform your response as a teacher?

National Association for the Education of Young Children

The National Association for the Education of Young Children (NAEYC) ethical code, which considers the education of young children birth through 8 years of age, "offers guidelines for responsible behavior and sets forth a common basis for resolving the principal ethical dilemmas encountered in early childhood care and education" (NAEYC, 2005, p. 1). The code includes core values that concern educators' ability to (a) appreciate childhood as a unique and valuable stage of the human life cycle; (b) base their work on knowledge of how children develop and learn; (c) appreciate and support the bond between children and family; (d) recognize that children are understood and supported best within the contexts of family, culture, community, and society; (e) respect the dignity, worth, and uniqueness of each child, family member, and colleague; (f) respect diversity in children, families, and colleagues; and (g) recognize that children and adults achieve their full potential in the context of relationships based on trust and respect. Although not every special educator works with young children, the NAEYC ethical code can be helpful because it provides more depth and breadth than most codes of ethics in the field of education and can be applied across disciplines. The NAEYC core values are broken further into a conceptual framework that concerns educators' professional relationships with children and families, among colleagues, and within the community and society. Specific ideals and principles relate to collaboration, communication, and cooperation (see Appendix B for NAEYC Code of Ethical Conduct and Statement of Commitment).

The first principle of NAEYC's conceptual framework states, "Above all, we shall not harm children. We shall not participate in practices that are emotionally damaging, physically harmful, disrespectful, degrading, dangerous, exploitative, or intimidating to children. This principle has precedence over all others in this Code" (NAEYC, 2005, p. 3).

The second principle of NAEYC's conceptual framework addresses respecting the distinctiveness of children and families. Each individual and family has a unique set of characteristics—racial, ethnic, cultural, socioeconomic, religious, sexual orientation, and age—that contributes to variety in children's upbringing. Educators must respect all children and their families, regardless of their backgrounds and characteristics.

The last principle concerns professionals' need to "acknowledge families' childrearing values and their right to make decisions for their children" (NAEYC, 2005, p. 5). As stated previously, parents are experts regarding their children, and educators, therefore, must acknowledge and learn from their expertise. Teachers also need to appreciate differences in family structures and composition as well as parenting styles.

The NAEYC ethical code and its conceptual framework offer a comprehensive set of standards that guides teachers' behaviors with children and their families. The standards help educators explore moral issues, clarify value conflicts, and make conscientious decisions when faced with ethical dilemmas for which there is more than one possible solution, each with a strong moral justification (Feeney & Freeman, 1999).

Council for Exceptional Children

The Council for Exceptional Children (CEC) is the premier professional organization for educators who work with students who have exceptional abilities. The CEC *Code of Ethics and Standards for Professional Practice* was adopted initially in 1983 and is now in its seventh edition (2010). The principles relate to educators' obligations to establish and maintain high academic and social standards for students with disabilities and other exceptionalities and their families. The eight guiding principles of the CEC Code of Ethics can be viewed in Appendix C.

Individuals with disabilities have long been a part of mainstream society and public school systems, where practices are guided by federal civil rights and education legislation. Consequently, all educators, but most important, special educators, must understand and uphold legislation, regulations, and policies governing their profession. As discussed in Chapter 1, the Individuals with Disabilities Improvement in Education Act of 2004 entitles all children and youth, but especially those with disabilities and other at-risk conditions, with the right to a free appropriate public education in the least restrictive educational environments. Within these settings, teachers establish and maintain high academic and social development standards for students. If teachers set realistic goals, students will rise to the challenge and attain the expectations set for them.

Several components of the CEC code of ethics concern a need for teachers to uphold high standards of practice, which in turn involves acting with integrity. Integrity can be defined as being honest and trustworthy. For most teachers, acting with integrity is relatively easy as they engage in honest and trustworthy relationships with students, parents and other family members, and colleagues.

The CEC *Code of Ethics and Standards for Professional Practice* provides specific guidelines for special education professionals as they strive to develop partnerships with parents based on mutual respect for their roles in achieving benefits for individuals with disabilities. The guidelines identify professional behaviors that include

- Developing effective communication with parents by avoiding professional jargon, and using the primary language of the home and other communication modes, when appropriate
- Utilizing parents' knowledge and expertise in planning, conducting, and evaluating special education and related services for individuals with disabilities
- Maintaining parent professional communications that respect privacy and confidentiality
- Providing opportunities for parent education
- Informing parents of their children's educational rights as well as any proposed or actual practices which violate those rights
- Recognizing and respecting cultural diversity
- Recognizing that the relationship of the home and community environmental conditions affects the behavior and outlook of the individual with disabilities (CEC, 1993; 2010)

Several similarities intersect the NEA, NAEYC, and CEC ethical codes of conduct. First, each code references the concept of *doing no harm*, especially as it concerns interactions with children and youth. Second, the codes include statements about teachers (a) treating children, parents and other family members, and colleagues with respect and dignity; (b) maintaining confidentiality when working with children, families, and colleagues; and (c) participating in professional development activities that increase knowledge. Educational professionals must adhere to these ethical principles when interacting with children, parents, and other family members.

THE ETHICAL CONCEPT OF DOING NO HARM

A primary consideration when discussing education codes of ethics is to acknowledge the ethical principle of *first, do no harm,* which associates most often with the Hippocratic Oath and the medical profession. In education, the principle of doing no harm connotes the idea that no harm should occur when teaching children and youth and when interacting with other constituents served by the profession, including parents. Rude and Whetstone (2008) stated that harm may result from negligence and malpractice and that, "it is unethical to ignore or overlook responsibilities to provide essential professional services . . . and . . . to practice any profession in a manner that brings harm to clients" (p. 12). Preventing harm to others requires educators to balance the moral duty of *doing good* and protecting the interests of individuals with the ethical duty of *doing right* while maintaining the integrity of best practice in education (Courtade & Ludlow, 2008). These responsibilities call for educators to (a) appreciate multiple viewpoints and children's and family members' diverse needs; (b) create and maintain caring, inclusive, and democratic school cultures and communities committed to social justice and change; (c) ensure fairness and equity in interactions with students, families, and colleagues; (d) accept responsibility for students' health and wellness; (e) advance collaboration and partnerships that facilitate students' attainment of a high-quality education; and (f) embrace opportunities for professional development that rely on research and scholarship, promote reflection, and improve instructional and assessment practices (Sileo et al., 2008).

Doing No Harm with Children and Youth

The notion of preventing harm to children is infused throughout the *Safe Schools Manual* (NEA, 2005). The manual provides suggestions for teachers to facilitate cooperative relationships between home and school, and thus deter potential deleterious events to children. The suggestions include (a) modeling positive behaviors and interactions with children and youth, (b) encouraging parental support of children's academic and social endeavors, and (c) developing awareness of parents' roles in educating children. As an educator, you should model appropriate behaviors when working with children and their family members in an effort to prevent harm to children. Figure 9.2 provides examples of appropriate positive behaviors and interactions for working with families and children that are addressed in the first suggestion from the *Safe Schools Manual* (see Figure 9.2).

Parent support of and participation in education is key to children's success in school (Dietel, 2005). Therefore, NEA (2005) further suggests guidelines that promote positive relationships between educators and parents and other family members. Based on the NEA guidelines, educators should (a) communicate regularly with families; (b) establish homework policies, provide tips to help students finish assignments, and create a homework helpline to assist students when they incur difficulty completing assignments; (c) encourage parents to volunteer in classroom settings and attend school functions; and (d) compile a list of local support agencies and provide them to parents and families, when needed.

The third suggestion in the *Safe Schools Manual* addresses the importance of developing awareness of parents' roles in education. Specifically, NEA suggests that school districts provide professional development opportunities for all employees related to (a) identifying children whose behaviors indicate a need for intervention; (b) reporting incidents of potential neglect and violence against children; (c) advocating for children who may have witnessed violence in their homes or communities; and (d) working with families

---

When working with children and families, educators should

- Distribute parenting tips related to nutrition, hygiene, and homework help.
- Model appropriate communication skills, which includes speaking in quiet voices and using positive rather than negative statements with children.
- Teach children to differentiate between feelings and behavior, so they can learn introspection.
- Teach children how to assert themselves appropriately and respectfully.
- Set limits with children and give them choices when their behavior is inappropriate.

FIGURE 9.2 Appropriate educator behaviors for working with children and families
Source: Information from NEA (2005)

to include them in their children's education. Educators' participation in professional development activities helps to increase their awareness of parents' roles in education and to decrease potential harm to children and youth. The principle of doing no harm implies that educators should

- Learn about and remain current in education practices, and legislation that protects children.
- Maintain confidentiality regarding their professional interactions with children and parents.
- Develop trusting and respectful cooperative relationships with peers.
- Provide high-quality education and care programs and services.
- Maintain an open-door policy toward parents and other family members.
- Avoid participation in prejudicial and discriminatory practices. (Feeney & Freeman, 1999)

Doing no harm with children requires that you, as an educator, think about students' potential and attainment of their finest moments. You must recognize the skills that children and youth bring to classroom settings and then set realistic performance goals and expectations, concomitant with the student's stages of physical, cognitive, social, and emotional functioning. Such an approach should occur whether children and youth are learning to crawl or to solve quadratic equations.

The NAEYC code of ethical conduct includes several statements about helping students reach their learning potential. Specifically, the code indicates that teachers must recognize and respect the individuality of all children and recognize their ability to perform at high ability levels. Furthermore, NAEYC points out a need to create and maintain safe environments that foster children's development. Educators' respect for the individuality of children is one of the most important aspects of education. Teachers, therefore, must acknowledge that all children are special and that they have individual characteristics and needs. Once teachers recognize children as individuals, they can plan, organize, and implement lessons that facilitate students' attainment of knowledge.

The CEC code of professional ethics also includes a statement about helping children attain their learning potential. Specifically, the CEC code states that educators within the field of special education are "committed to developing the highest educational and quality of life potential of individuals with exceptionalities" (CEC, 2010, p. 1). This statement illustrates CEC's commitment to helping individuals with disabilities achieve their finest moments. One of the most important changes in special education legislation considers the use of appropriate language when referring to individuals with disabilities. Prior to 1990, special education professionals did not use person-first language. Such language guides teachers and other school personnel to consider the person before the disability. Individualized instruction requires teachers to examine first the students and their potential, and then to select appropriate instructional strategies based on those needs and potential. Teachers should set goals and adapt the curriculum in a manner that enables all children to learn. Such an approach allows teachers to practice the standard of doing no harm to children. Teachers' ability to help children attain their finest moments is perhaps one of the most rewarding components of teaching.

Inclusive educational settings, if appropriate to students' functioning levels, are appropriate to help all children attain their finest moments. The NAEYC conceptual framework and CEC standards consider inclusive education as essential to meeting the needs of children with typical and atypical learning characteristics. The principles of inclusion address all students—typical learners, children with disabilities, gifts and talents, second language learners, and migrant students, among others.

All students, regardless of their learning and behavior characteristics, require support in educational settings to attain success. The assistance, which varies in shape and size, should be unobtrusive and fit within the natural order of the day (McLeskey & Waldron, 2007). For example, students with gifts and talents may need enrichment activities that center around the core curriculum, whereas students with second language learning needs and others with disabilities may need core curriculum modifications to meet their needs. The supports can be provided in myriad ways. For example, additional classroom resources may be provided such as assigning a coteacher or instructional assistant for part of the day to provide support to single students, small groups of students, or the whole class (McLeskey & Waldron; Sileo, 2003; 2005). Changing classroom routines is another way to aid students. For example, rather than sole reliance on direct instruction to teach an entire class, use cooperative learning groups (Jenkins, Antil, Wayne, & Vadasy, 2003) or peer tutoring (Mastropieri, Scruggs, & Berkley, 2007).

You, as a professional, must consider the principle of doing no harm when interacting with children. You can practice this principle by creating and maintaining safe instructional environments that focus on children as individuals. Specifically, you and your colleagues must acknowledge that some children come from violent homes or communities, and attending school provides these children respite from the other part of their lives. Teachers can maintain safe environments by creating structured classrooms in which consequences fit behavioral transgressions. Teachers can also use teachable moments to discuss violence and how it affects all students in a school. Differentiated instruction and inclusive classroom settings are effective strategies to help students attain their academic and social learning promise. These promote all students' individuality, acknowledge students' unique characteristics and needs, and enforce the principle of doing no harm with children.

Doing No Harm with Parents and Families

Previously we discussed ethical codes and the concept of doing no harm from the perspective of teachers' professional interactions with students. Yet, teachers often experience ethical dilemmas and values conflicts in parent–professional interactions that relate to racial, ethnic, and cultural differences; diverse family structures; and disparity in child-rearing practices. The practice of doing no harm also applies to interacting with parents.

The NEA ethical code does not include a specific statement that relates directly to working with parents and other family members. However, the last statement in NEA's *commitment to the student* presupposes the importance of meeting parents' and family members' needs and, therefore, can be viewed as *commitment to the family*. It states that teachers shall not at any time mistreat or do harm to students (or their families) on the basis of race, color, sex, political or religious beliefs, social or cultural background, or sexual orientation (NEA, 2009). Thus, teachers and school districts cannot discriminate against any family members because stereotyping, prejudice, and labeling are undeniably harmful and interfere with people's access to high-quality education programs, as well as their civil rights as U.S. citizens. We can also extend NEA's *commitment to the profession* regarding disclosure of confidential information, making false allegations about colleagues, and accepting gifts that influence ethical decision making to interactions with parents and other family members. Later, our discussion of confidentiality practices in education addresses disclosure of information in more detail.

The NAEYC ethical code is more comprehensive in comparison to the NEA code of ethics and includes a section that concerns working with parents. The majority of ideals and principles in this section focus on collaboration, cooperation, and communication among family members and professionals. However, one principle relates directly to *doing no harm with parents*. It states that educators shall not "use our relationship with a family for private advantage or personal gain, or enter into relationships with family members that might impair our effectiveness working with their children" (NAEYC, 2005, p. 6).

Teachers and parents are more likely to become friends when children are younger rather than older and when children have disabilities. Many parents of younger offspring and those with disabilities often volunteer in their children's classrooms and accompany them to and from school. As a result, teachers and parents have increased opportunities to interact and become friends. Teachers' and parents' involvement in each other's lives heightens the potential for ethical dilemmas (see Figure 9.3).

As we discussed previously, the CEC *Code of Ethics and Standards for Professional Practice* also focuses on collaboration and communication among families and professionals. Given the number of other professionals and parents with whom they interact, effective communication is of primary importance to special educators. Consider using a family communication notebook to communicate with parents and other family members. Send the notebook home daily and include a description of the activities in which the child participated, as well as any milestones the child may have met during the day. Other communication tools you may find useful include voice mail and e-mail. Ongoing effective communication is essential to nurture good relationships with parents; teachers' lack of communication may do harm to parents as illustrated in Figure 9.3.

Parents and families of children with disabilities may experience considerable stress, which accumulates over time, as a result of negative social responses to their children. Such reactions are strong reminders that the general public may never value youngsters with disabilities. Unfortunately, society often views the family structures of these children

---

Jose's teacher, Kate Gehring, becomes friends with his mother, Elena Sanchez, while Elena is going through a divorce. During this time, Jose begins to exhibit inappropriate behaviors such as temper tantrums. Kate recognizes the child's difficulty at home and does her best to manage his classroom behaviors rather than involving her befriended parent or school administrator. During the last week of school, Jose's misbehaviors escalate out of control, and he hits another child. The inappropriate behaviors are reported to the school administrator, who in turn informs Mrs. Sanchez. She is shocked and in disbelief about her son's inappropriate behavior. She learns in a subsequent discussion with Kate that her son has been acting out for some time at school, but she wasn't informed because Kate was protecting her friend from more stress in her life. Elena becomes upset and expresses great displeasure at the teacher's inaction and for not keeping her apprised of her son's behaviors.

Consider whether Kate inadvertently *harmed the parent* by not informing her of the child's inappropriate school behaviors. Did she inadvertently harm the child? Have you ever been in a situation where you, in an effort to "protect" someone who was experiencing difficulty, failed inform the person of an event or incident involving the person's child?

FIGURE 9.3 A teacher's dilemma

in a negative light and does not consider how children with disabilities positively contribute to family dynamics. Other sources of stress relate to unattainable expectations for a child, such as entrance to kindergarten or graduation from high school; excessive financial burden; unsatisfactory personal wherewithal (e.g., cognitive competence, problem solving and planning skills); inadequate family resources (e.g., child and respite care); and lack of social (e.g., self-help groups) and professional support (e.g., care coordination, counseling).

Ethical teachers acknowledge that parents of children with disabilities display a variety of stress-related needs as well as strengths and coping abilities. Parent involvement programs that disrupt family balance may cause more harm than good. Analyze family structures and systems, and avoid placing undue burdens on them. Consider parents' and families' strengths, needs, and priorities as a foundation for designing realistic and manageable parent and family involvement programs. Avoid becoming too zealous about a specific program on behalf of a child with disabilities, and consider its affect on the overall family constellation.

Ethical practice relies on teachers' understanding of how tension and anxiety influence family interactions and concomitant timely intervention to facilitate adaptation to stress. Facilitation involves (a) evaluating existing family resources, (b) documenting parents' or family members' perception of a stressful event, (c) delineating strengths to adapt to demands placed on the family system, and (d) identifying strategies and services to alleviate stress and evaluate progress of the adaptive process. Discussions in Chapters 5 and 6 offer a comprehensive perspective about stress and its affects on parents and other family members of children with disabilities. In addition, each chapter in this text provides a list of resources to support professionals, families, and students.

NAEYC's second guiding principle concerns educators' respect for family characteristics. When you show respect, you demonstrate you have a high opinion or show high regard for the family. Professionals show respect when they honor cultural diversity, treat families and students with dignity, and affirm their strengths (Turnbull et al., 2006). Accordingly, teachers honor diversity when they respect family members' racial, ethnic, and cultural heritage. Furthermore, they dignify families when they demonstrate high regard for parents' opinions and treat family members fairly. Moreover, they affirm families' strengths when they focus on children's and families' assets rather than their deficits. An assets-based approach demonstrates respect for and recognition of children's potential.

STRATEGIES TO ENSURE ETHICAL PRACTICES WHEN WORKING WITH FAMILIES

Unfortunately, the codes of ethics do not provide explicit guidelines for applying them. Fortunately, others provide direction and approaches you can use when confronting ethical dilemmas when interacting with parents and other family members.

Berkeley and Ludlow (2008) identify a number of elements to guide teachers when they consider ethical dilemmas: (a) individual context and feelings about the dilemma and its relationship to others; (b) societal context and interactions among individuals involved in the dilemma; (c) precedence in similar situations, fact gathering, and application regarding the moral dilemma; (d) "line drawing" and taking a specific course of action in lieu of another; (e) self-interest and risk taking that may hinder a stakeholder's

Today was just like any other day, class in the morning, and an IEP meeting in the afternoon. I knew I had Joaquin's transition meeting today, but I didn't have any concerns. It would be a walk in the park. His mother, Maria, and I were on the same page. The morning went smoothly, the children did a wonderful job practicing for kindergarten graduation and were excited to show everyone what they had learned.

I was most enthusiastic about Joaquin's progress. He had advanced so nicely in 9 months. At the beginning of the year, I was a little skeptical. I remember his reeligibility meeting. It was just horrible! Joaquin no longer met the criteria for a developmental disability, and he didn't quite meet requirements for identification as a child with a learning disability. The test results showed that he qualified as a child with mental retardation. It was such a shock! I remember sitting with Maria, who had tears in her eyes, thinking about Joaquin's future. It was at that meeting that we decided we would push him as far as we could and review his progress at the end of the year.

Well, it is now the end of the year. Joaquin made phenomenal progress and is almost ready for first grade. Academically, he knew his letters and numbers and could write his first and last names. Behaviorally, however, he was still one of the most immature children in the class. Despite the behavioral interventions we implemented during the school year, Joaquin continued to display some challenging behaviors. He talked back to the teachers, exhibited off task and out of his seat, and hit and kicked others when he didn't get his way. I couldn't imagine him in a typical first-grade class with a new teacher and 20 other children.

At the IEP meeting, I reviewed Joaquin's goals and discussed the progress he had made throughout the year. The team discussed his present levels of performance and special factors. At this time, I shared my concerns about Joaquin's behavior. I explained that I believed he would out be of his element in a typical first-grade class. We discussed the academic and behavioral requirements of a typical first-grade class and realized that Joaquin wasn't quite ready. The team discussed other placement options and decided that Joaquin needed another year in a self-contained class setting. Maria agreed with the decision. She signed the IEP as it was written, and we went home.

The next day, when Maria brought Joaquin to school, she stated that his father didn't agree with the IEP and that under no circumstances would he allow Joaquin to be in a self-contained program again the following year. He wanted Joaquin in a typical first-grade class. When Maria tried to talk to her husband, he hit her.

What should I do? Maria signed the IEP as it was written, agreeing to place Joaquin in a self-contained class for the following year. Technically, my job was done.

FIGURE 9.4 A teacher's concerns

ability to engage in professional practice; and (f) history and traditions that influence individual and organizational actions and deliberations. The elements facilitate discussions of ethical dilemmas. We discuss the application of each of these six elements in context of the scenario presented in Figure 9.4.

ELEMENT ONE: INDIVIDUAL CONTEXT AND FEELINGS ABOUT THE DILEMMA. The scenario illustrates two dilemmas. The first quandary relates to Joaquin's placement for the following year. In this dilemma, the teacher is confident that she made the best decision. She believes that Joaquin will be more successful in a self-contained class than in an inclusive first-grade classroom. Joaquin made wonderful progress in a self-contained kindergarten program, and the teacher truly believes he needs a more structured program to be successful in school.

The second predicament concerns the family situation and that Joaquin's father hit his wife. In this dilemma, the teacher has concern for Maria's safety. In an effort to help

Maria, the teacher offers to explain to Joaquin's father the basis for the team's decision regarding Joaquin's first-grade placement.

ELEMENT TWO: SOCIETAL CONTEXT AND INTERACTIONS AMONG THOSE INVOLVED IN THE DILEMMA.   Element two relates to the interaction among participants in the dilemma. The teacher and Maria became friendly during the school year. She saw Maria daily at drop-off and pickup time. Maria also attended class functions and volunteered in the class. As a result, the teacher was concerned when Maria approached her and explained the circumstances. She wanted to talk to Maria more specifically and to identify ways she could help, yet she felt strongly that the team's decision was correct. The teacher believes she is caught between a rock and a hard place. Professionally, she knew that she had done her job well, and she was confident that Joaquin needed additional support to be successful in first grade. She also knew that the school district could implement the IEP as written because Maria agreed with the placement. Personally, she was concerned for Maria's safety. Although she knew she wasn't the direct cause of the abuse, she felt that her suggestion to place Joaquin in a self-contained program caused Maria's husband to become upset.

ELEMENT THREE: PRECEDENCE IN SIMILAR SITUATIONS, FACT GATHERING, AND APPLICA-TION REGARDING THE MORAL DILEMMA.   This element relates to precedence setting in other situations, gathering data, and applying the knowledge to the moral dilemma. The teacher would ask herself the following questions with regard to the dilemma: Were there similar situations at other schools? Have other teachers been faced with the same dilemma? What did they do? After asking herself these questions, the teacher would contact colleagues and administrators to determine their approach in a similar predicament. This type of dilemma necessitates that teachers consult with others to determine precedence. If this situation did not occur before, then it would set precedence for other teachers. Therefore, it is critical for the teacher to gather information so she can make an informed decision. Once she answers her questions, she can progress to element four.

ELEMENT FOUR: "LINE DRAWING" AND TAKING A SPECIFIC COURSE OF ACTION IN LIEU OF ANOTHER.   Element four relates to decision making and may be the most difficult element to implement in the process. In this element, the teacher determines a course of action. Prior to choosing a specific action, first, she needs to speak with Joaquin's father to determine his point of view. Perhaps she can explain the team's thinking, and he will change his mind. If she is unsuccessful, she needs to ask herself the following questions. Does she stand her ground and stick with the team's decision to place Joaquin in a self-contained class for first grade? Does she reconvene the team and discuss other options for Joaquin based on previous actions at other schools? The teacher has already spoken with colleagues and the school administration about the situation and, therefore, decides to stand her ground. In her heart of hearts, she knows the team made the correct decision for Joaquin. She also knows that Maria supports the decision. However, she is concerned about Maria's relationship with Joaquin's father. At this point, however, the teacher remembers Maria is an adult and that she can listen to and support Maria's decision.

ELEMENT FIVE: SELF-INTEREST AND RISK TAKING THAT MAY HINDER A STAKEHOLDER'S ABILITY TO ENGAGE IN PROFESSIONAL PRACTICE.   In this element, it is important to review the risks related to making the decision and to weigh all options. Although collaboration often helps solve ethical dilemmas, most often, an individual makes a final decision. In this case, the teacher needs to determine whether her self-interest or risk-taking behaviors will harm others or impede their ability to engage in professional behaviors. The teacher's self-interests relate to her knowledge that as an IEP team member, she helped make the decision to place Joaquin in a self-contained first-grade class. The risk-taking behaviors relate to the teacher and her hopes that to stand her ground doesn't harm Maria.

ELEMENT SIX: HISTORY AND TRADITIONS THAT INFLUENCE INDIVIDUAL AND ORGANIZATIONAL ACTIONS AND DELIBERATIONS.   This last element looks at how personal history and tradition affect the behaviors of those involved in the quandary. In the first dilemma, the teacher believes, based on her history with Joaquin and his progress throughout the school year, that his academic and social learning needs would be met best in a smaller self-contained setting. She also knows that students with needs similar to Joaquin's were more successful in structured learning environments that included appropriate levels of support. In the second dilemma, the teacher had strong convictions about actions that Maria should take about her abusive husband, yet she also knew how difficult it could be for Maria to leave an abusive relationship. So, the teacher decided that her best action was to support Maria. In the end, both Maria and the teacher explained the reasoning behind the self-contained placement decision to Joaquin's father, and he agreed the placement was in Joaquin's best interest.

Brophy-Herb, Kostelnik, and Stein (2001) offer a four-phase model that focuses on ethical literacy, which is the ability to recognize and comprehend ethical issues, succeed in ethical decision making, and engage in ethical practice (Nash, 1996). ***Phase One*** involves developing awareness of and learning about various codes of ethical conduct related to professional education. ***Phase Two*** concerns the ability to differentiate between ethical judgments and other conclusions. It allows an individual the opportunity to determine whether a decision relates to personal morality or professional ethics (Brophy-Herb et al., 2001). Many individuals possess an internal, personal moral compass about right and wrong. Personal morality, however, does not always equate to professional ethics, and there are numerous situations in which a person's moral compass may pose a problem professionally. Consider the following short scenario by applying the first two phases of Brophy-Herb et al.'s model.

During the administration of a standardized test, Ms. Wai, an elementary school teacher, realizes that Raquel is unable to answer the questions. As a consequence, Raquel began to show her frustration. Ms. Wai knew the test was difficult. She began to be concerned about Raquel's welfare. Ms. Wai questioned whether she should help Raquel with the test or allow her to flounder. Morally, she knew that she should assist the child; however, professionally she knew that she must adhere to the test administration procedures.

PHASE THREE of Brophy-Herb et al.'s (2001) model suggests using a systematic process to analyze and solve the ethical dilemma. For example, in addition to reviewing the various codes of ethical conduct and speaking with colleagues, other problem-solving strategies such as those discussed in this chapter would be used in this phase. In the scenario, Ms. Wai would explore, further, her feelings about whether to discontinue the standardized test for Raquel. She would also explore how other teachers dealt with similar situations by asking herself the following questions: Did they allow the student to discontinue the assessment? Did they require the student to continue even though they knew it was difficult? How will she be viewed by the school administration? Did the student complete enough of the test so that the teacher could say she ran out of time? Finally, the teacher could consult with a colleague to determine another viewpoint.

PHASE FOUR allows educators to apply various ethical codes of conduct to problem solution. In the preceding scenario, Ms. Wai would review the codes and determine the right course of action. Specifically, while reviewing the codes, Ms. Wai would read a statement in the NAEYC code related to assessment. The statement indicates that assessment instruments and instructional strategies should have the potential to benefit children (NAEYC, 2005). Ms. Wai decides that although standardized tests are important, in this instance, the stressful testing situation will not benefit the student. As a result, she allows Raquel to do something else while everyone else finishes the standardized assessment.

The final approach to solving professional dilemmas discussed in this chapter is based on a seven-step process for ethical decision making (Sinclair, 1998). The steps, which are similar to those in problem solving, include (a) identifying the ethical issues and practices; (b) developing alternative courses of action; (c) analyzing risks and benefits of each course of action; (d) choosing a course of action after conscientiously applying existing principles, values, and standards; (e) taking action and assuming responsibility for consequences; (f) evaluating results of the action; and (g) assuming responsibility for the consequences, correcting any negative consequences, or reengaging in the decision-making process. An example of the seven-step process is provided in Figure 9.5 followed by discussion.

STEP 1: IDENTIFY THE ETHICAL ISSUE. The first step to solving any dilemma is identification of the problem or ethical issue in this situation. In this scenario, at least two ethical issues arise. The first dilemma relates to a teacher doing the work for a student rather than letting the student do the work for herself. In this instance, although the Mrs. Jones may feel she is helping the child, she, in fact, could be hurting Stacy by not allowing her the opportunity to learn to do things herself. The second dilemma relates to Ms. Walker's decision about whom to contact regarding the first dilemma.

A second question to ask during this stage relates to the attitudes, values, and beliefs of those involved in this issue. In the first dilemma, the question concerns whether Mrs. Jones believes that she is helping Stacy by doing the work for her. Perhaps, Mrs. Jones doesn't realize that she's hindering Stacy's progress toward attainment of her IEP goals. Or, perhaps her teaching style is to help students. A corollary issue relates to Ms. Walker's attitudes and beliefs about how to teach children with disabilities. Perhaps she believes that children should be challenged and then provided the tools to learn by themselves, rather than having someone do the schoolwork for them. In the second dilemma, the answers to these questions could determine how Ms. Walker resolves the problem.

STEP 2: BRAINSTORM SOLUTIONS TO THE ETHICAL DILEMMA. The first step in this stage is to determine where to find guidance to make an ethical choice. Several resources are available to help educators make ethical decisions, including professional standards and

It's Thursday morning and Ms. Walker, the school special education coordinator as well as the kindergarten teacher, is standing in front of the school waiting for her students to arrive. She is chitchatting with other teachers about the upcoming Spring Carnival, when she notices Mrs. Grant walking toward them. Mrs. Grant has two children enrolled in the school. Johnny is in an early childhood special education class for students with developmental disabilities, and Stacy is in first grade. Stacy had been in Ms. Walker's kindergarten class the previous year. Ms. Walker says hello and inquires about Mrs. Grant's well-being. Mrs. Grant says that she's doing fine, but asks for a moment of Ms. Walker's time. As they wander away from the other teachers, Ms. Grant tells Ms. Walker that she is very concerned about Stacy's teacher, Ms. Jones. She explains that Ms. Jones does not challenge Stacy, academically and socially. She expresses concern that Mrs. Jones does everything for Stacy and that she doesn't know how Stacy is going to gain independence if her teacher constantly does everything for her. Mrs. Grant wants Stacy to become independent and therefore requested that an IEP goal be written related to her concerns.

At this point, Ms. Walker recalls a conversation she had with Mrs. Grant in the beginning of the year about this same problem. At that time, Ms. Walker didn't think anything of the issue and assumed it was because it was the beginning of the school year and Mrs. Jones didn't know her students yet. It's now two-thirds of the way through the school year, and Mrs. Grant is concerned that Stacy is not making progress toward her IEP goals related to gaining more independence. Mrs. Grant also expected Stacy to learn new academic skills during the school year, and Mrs. Jones is still teaching colors and shapes. Stacy knew all colors and shapes before beginning the school year. Mrs. Grant spoke with Mrs. Jones about the issue, but she doesn't feel that she's made any progress regarding resolution of her concerns. She asks Ms. Walker for her advice.

The bell rings, and Ms. Walker tells Mrs. Grant that she'll get back to her. Ms. Walker is confronted with a dilemma and unsure of a course of action that she should follow to resolve the situation. Is Mrs. Jones' behavior unethical? If so, does she talk to Mrs. Jones herself? Does she talk with her administrator about the complaint? Does she tell Mrs. Grant to speak with the principal about her concerns?

FIGURE 9.5 A professional predicament

codes of ethical conduct, current research and legislation. Educators can also consult a colleague or other professionals within the field to help them resolve the ethical dilemma. Using these suggestions, Ms. Walker set out to brainstorm solutions to her dilemma.

First, she researched the ethical codes of conduct. During this process, she realized that each code includes a statement about helping children reach their potential to become valuable members of society (CEC, 2010; NAEYC, 2005; NEA, 2009). More specifically, the NEA code states further that educators "shall not restrain students from independent action while in the pursuit of learning" (2009, p. 1). As she read this statement, Ms. Walker realized that Mrs. Jones' behavior was unethical because Mrs. Jones was, in fact, interfering with Stacy's learning by doing everything for her rather than allowing Stacy to work independently. Once Ms. Walker decided that Mrs. Jones' behavior was unethical, she had another ethical decision to make about how to resolve the situation.

Ms. Walker again consulted the codes of ethical conduct and discovered a section in the NAEYC code (2005) related to working with colleagues. While reading this section, she noticed a statement regarding professional behavior, which indicates that when an educator has concerns about a colleague's professional behavior, the educator should discuss the concerns with the colleague in an effort to resolve the issue. Ms. Walker understood that she should speak with Mrs. Jones, but she was unsure about how to approach her. As a result, Ms. Walker asked another colleague for advice about how to handle the situation. The colleague indicated that Ms. Walker should be as diplomatic as possible. And to maintain confidentiality, she should tell Mrs. Jones that a parent approached her to express concerns about a child's academic and social progress.

STEP 3: ANALYZE THE RISKS/BENEFITS OF THE SOLUTIONS AND CHOOSE A COURSE OF ACTION. This step allows for further analysis of the solutions, as well as consultation with a colleague. Oftentimes, it is easier to solve a problem collaboratively rather than individually. In doing so, educators have the opportunity to gain varying perspectives about a given solution. After analyzing the risks and benefits of the solutions, it is important to determine a course of action. At this point, educators can identify plan of action.

Completing this step allows Ms. Walker to discuss the solutions with a colleague and to determine the risks and benefits of each dilemma. In the previous scenario, Ms. Walker determined that Mrs. Jones' behavior was unethical. The risk in making this decision is that Ms. Walker is calling her colleague's ethics into question. Questioning a person's ethics is risky because the potential exists for the situation to escalate into something bigger than intended. On the other hand, the benefit of this decision is that Ms. Walker will affect a child's life in a positive manner. She hopes that Mrs. Jones ultimately will allow Stacy to become more independent in class. In this instance, Ms. Walker believes that the benefits outweigh the risks.

Ms. Walker also recognizes that one of the risks about speaking directly with Mrs. Jones is that she is questioning her colleague's teaching style. In addition to maintaining a collegial relationship, Ms. Walker and Mrs. Jones are also good friends. Ms. Walker does not want to strain her friendship with Mrs. Jones by questioning her teaching abilities. Also, Mrs. Jones may not change her behavior, in which case Ms. Walker would have to speak with the principal. This in turn could further escalate the problem. Ms. Walker knows that one benefit of talking directly to Mrs. Jones is that she is avoiding bringing the administration into the situation. Mrs. Jones has had previous difficulty with the school administration, and Ms. Walker wants to avoid causing her friend additional trouble. Again, in this situation, Ms. Walker feels that the benefits outweigh the risks. After weighing the benefits and risks to her decision, Ms. Walker is ready for the next step.

STEP 4: TAKE ACTION AND ASSUME RESPONSIBILITY FOR THE DECISION. Once the course of action has been chosen, the next step is implementation. In this scenario, Ms. Walker will speak with Mrs. Jones about her concerns. She will approach the situation with diplomacy and explain that a parent expressed concern about a child. Ms. Walker is also going to take responsibility for her decision by explaining that she thought long and hard about how to handle this situation and decided it was best for her to speak with Mrs. Jones rather than speaking with the administration.

STEP 5: EVALUATE THE RESULTS OF THE DECISION-MAKING PROCESS. When implementing step 5, teachers evaluate the whole process. Questions to ask include (a) whether the correct decision was made, (b) what the best outcomes of the decision will be, and (c) if an alternative course of action would have had a better result. In the scenario, Ms. Walker decided to speak with her colleague and friend regarding a parent's concern about an ethical issue. Ms. Walker feels that she made the correct decision. While speaking with

Ms. Walker, Mrs. Jones realized what she had been doing. Although she thought she was helping Stacy, she was actually hurting her by not allowing her to complete tasks independently. She also said that the behavior was unintentional, and until it was brought to her attention, she didn't realize that she was acting in an inappropriate manner with Stacy. Mrs. Jones was grateful that Ms. Walker brought the situation to her attention, rather than to the administration.

STEP 6: EVALUATE RESULTS OF THE ACTION.   Once the action has been implemented the results should be evaluated. Ms. Walker was happy with her decision to approach Mrs. Jones directly rather than speak with the administration and to discuss the efficacy of Mrs. Jones' teaching techniques.

STEP 7: ASSUME RESPONSIBILITY FOR CONSEQUENCES, CORRECT NEGATIVE CONSEQUENCES, OR REFLECT ON THE DECISION-MAKING PROCESS.   The last step involves willingness to take responsibility for the action and to remediate if the consequences are negative. The next day, Ms. Walker told Mrs. Grant that she had spoken with Mrs. Jones and that she would see future progress in the attainment of Stacy's IEP goals. In this instance the outcome is positive. If it were not, Ms. Walker may need to resolve additional issues that could have arisen as a consequence of her action.

There are several strategies to ensure ethical practice when working with parents. The strategies we discussed in this chapter have a number of similarities. Each strategy offers guidelines to (a) identify the dilemma, (b) review and apply various codes of ethical conduct, and (c) choose a solution and take a course of action. Consequently, any strategy may be used to solve ethical dilemmas. One major difference among the strategies is that Sinclair (1998) includes steps to evaluate the results and assume responsibility for potential negative effects. These evaluation steps are crucial to problem-solving processes. Assessing the results of a problem-solving strategy is just as important as assessing the results of instruction.

BARRIERS TO ETHICAL AND CONFIDENTIAL PRACTICES WHEN WORKING WITH FAMILIES

Barriers to initiating and maintaining ethical and confidential practices when working with parents and other family members will always exist (see Chapter 1 for an extensive discussion on confidentiality). These deterrents include (a) lack of effective communication, (b) use of educational jargon, (c) lack of trust, (d) myriad points of view, and (e) scheduling and space issues, among others. The barriers may result from inappropriate actions exhibited by professionals, parents, and family members (Gargiulo & Graves, 1991).

Inadequate Communication

Effective communication is a crucial factor in every personal and professional interaction, and it is especially vital to ensure productive and ethical relationships between parents and teachers and among professionals. Many teachers enter the field because they are passionate about working with children. In fact, many choose teaching as a profession because of their positive personal experiences with a particular teacher when they were children. Furthermore, successful communication between and among teachers and parents also links to an increase in academic achievement for students (Desimone, 1999).

On the other hand, communication with parents can be a source of great angst for teachers. Graue (2005) states, "[H]ome–school interactions are anything but simple, they are sites of struggle full of opportunity but often fraught with frustration" (p. 157). Lack of effective communication is often the largest obstacle to working with families because it causes difficulty for parents and teachers to connect on a personal and professional level. Most parents want to know what is occurring in their children's lives. However, when they ask about school happenings, their children often respond with a noncommittal answer, such as "Nothing," or "I don't know." This answer can be equally frustrating to parents and teachers.

Teachers often assume that students share classroom experiences with their parents (Lord Nelson, Summers, & Turnbull, 2004). Unfortunately, this is not always the case, as illustrated in the following example.

On a recent trip to the grocery store, a mother ran into her son's teacher, Mrs. Coulter. After initial greetings, Mrs. Coulter asked the mother if Randy had shared his excitement about his school experiences, especially as they related to an innovative science project with which he was involved. The mother replied that he hadn't said anything. In fact, she indicated, that whenever she asked Randy about school, he just stated, "It's okay, Mom." Mrs. Coulter was surprised. She clearly thought that because Randy was so engaged in the science project, he surely would have told his mother about it.

This example illustrates parents' reliance on their children to share school events. Unfortunately, when such a lack of communication occurs, parents often feel left out of the loop. They are unsure of what is happening in school and are equally uncertain about how often they should contact their child's teacher to learn about class activities. Although parents and teachers are equally responsible for initiating communication and ensuring continued dialogue, parents often feel that "it is up to the teacher" to keep them informed about school events (Bruneau, Ruttan, & Dunlap 1995; Kosleski et al., 2008).

Homework policies are another area of communication that can be a barrier to maintaining good professional relationships with parents. Many parents are uncertain about their role in helping children with homework. A dilemma ensues when parents are hesitant about whether to solve a learning problem for the child or allow the child make mistakes. On the one hand, most parents want their child to complete the schoolwork on their own; on the other hand, they also want their children to submit correct assignments. Baker (1997) found that elementary school teachers do not want parents doing their children's homework; however, the teachers also realize that some students cannot operate independently. As a result, discuss homework policies with parents and explain that some assignments may be difficult, yet their children should attempt the assignments independently, rather than relying on parents to complete the homework.

Another ethical issue regarding homework concerns students working on assignments collaboratively rather than independently. Study groups are a great way to ensure students' learning and acquisition of new knowledge. They allow students to learn from one another and share educational experiences. Educators know that struggling students often learn best from their schoolmates. In classroom settings, student collaborative learning is called peer tutoring or cooperative learning. In these situations, teachers monitor student progress. In peer study groups, however, the teacher is not present to monitor student progress. For example

---

Suzanne, a student with a learning disability, misses school due to an ear infection. At the end of the day, her friend Michelle drops off the homework assignments. Suzanne asks Michelle about the algebra homework, and Michelle begins to explain it. Suzanne tries to solve the homework assignment while Michelle is still present, but she incurs difficulty. Michelle shows Suzanne how to do the assignment and completes the work for her. Consequently, Suzanne does not learn how to solve the algebra assignment independently.

Therefore, when assigning out-of-class group work, ensure that parents and all study group participants clearly understand the guidelines and expectations. These guidelines may necessitate telling students not to complete assignments for one another, but to help each other solve questions in homework assignments.

Parents and students need to understand which assignments can be completed in a study group setting. For example, math assignments may be better suited for study group assignments because the solution to the problem most often will be the same. However, an essay about the Revolutionary War should not be completed in a study group because there is enough information available for each student's essay to be different from the others. Unless otherwise indicated, teachers prefer that students work on assignments independently (Sileo, 2006; Sileo & Sileo, 2008). Moreover, teachers believe students are cheating when they complete assignments collaboratively rather than independently. Teachers must take responsibility for ensuring that both students and parents understand homework policies. Delineation and clarification of homework policies should avert an ethical dilemma for teachers and parents.

Educational Jargon

Educational jargon often interferes with effective communication between parents and professionals and among professionals in diverse educational fields. Avoid educational jargon when working with parents and family members to ensure their understanding and avoid alienating and excluding them from the conversation (Davern, 2004). Parents appreciate nontechnical information that addresses their questions and concerns, and which is provided by a trustworthy professional. The education profession, especially the field of special education, has many acronyms. However, most parents have limited experiences with this language. Their restricted personal school experiences may be their only educational references. Educators have an ethical responsibility to define educational terms in their discussions with parents. Avoid educational jargon; instead, use everyday language that is understandable to all. Table 9.2 provides some examples of educational jargon used by special educators on a daily basis.

TABLE 9.2	Special Education Jargon
Jargon/Acronym	**Actual terminology**
IEP	Individual Education Program
IFSP	Individualized Family Service Plan
ITP	Individual Transition Plan
IDEA	Individuals with Disabilities Education Act
NCLB	No Child Left Behind
OT	Occupational Therapy (Therapist)
PT	Physical Therapy (Therapist)
SLP	Speech/Language Therapy (Therapist)
LD	Learning Disabilities
ED	Emotional Disturbance or Disorder
BD	Behavior Disturbance/Disorder
MR	Mental Retardation
TBI	Traumatic Brain Injury
DD	Developmental Delay or Developmental Disabilities
IQ	Intelligence Quotient
LRE	Least Restrictive Environment

Lack of Trust

Another barrier to working effectively with families is a lack of trust, which may result from parents' inadequate educational experiences. Parents who have had less-than-high-quality school experiences often distrust teachers. Such distrust may stem from personal negative events along their schooling continuum (Greenwood & Hickman, 1991). This is especially true for parents of children with disabilities and those whose racial and ethnic backgrounds differ from the teacher's heritage.

Many parents of children and youth with disabilities express concern about qualifying their children for special education because they had negative experiences as students in special education settings. The scenario in Figure 9.6 clearly illustrates how a parent's negative experiences may influence a decision to qualify a child for special education services. Think about what influences you to trust one person and not another. As an educator, what are some things you can do to gain a parent's or student's trust? Are there communication strategies you can use to get Mr. Norton to trust your opinions?

Differences in racial, ethnic, and cultural representation also may hinder the quality of parent–professional interactions. Parents and teachers may view the education process from diverse viewpoints. For example, parents' limited experiences with and lack of knowledge regarding the dominant educational system may inhibit active participation in their children's education. They may desire more active roles, yet they adopt the posture that teachers know best about education, and they defer to the authority of school personnel in decision-making processes. Parents' belief that teachers know best when coupled with educators' inadequate awareness of linguistic and cultural diversity complicates the

During a multidisciplinary meeting, Mr. Norton explains to his son's teacher, Mrs. Abrams, that he does-n't know whether or not to qualify Joseph for special education. He realizes that Joseph needs assistance in school settings; however, his own personal negative experiences as a child in special education cloud his thoughts about whether he wants similar experiences for his son. Mr. Norton explains that as a child he felt segregated because he rode the "little yellow school bus" rather than the regular school bus. He was educated in a self-contained class located in a separate building away from his friends. He emphati-cally states that he does not want Joseph segregated from his peers. Often, parents do not realize the advances in special education over the years. Mrs. Abrams tells Mr. Norton that special education has changed and relies on a continuum of service delivery placements as well as a team of professionals who, in concert with the parents, make the most appropriate placement decisions for children.

FIGURE 9.6 A matter of trust

development of productive parent–professional relationships (Sileo, Sileo, & Prater, 1996). Parents may perceive that teachers undervalue their racial, ethnic, and cultural heritage as well as their language differences because they speak a nonstandard form of English. Language and color barriers often separate parents and educational institutions and there-by place children and youth at risk of educational and behavioral difficulties. The mis-match between family values and beliefs and school cultures creates a sense of parental distrust about teachers and the educational systems. Finally, parents may distrust the edu-cational system because they perceive lopsided interactions with school personnel who convey a sense of power, lack sensitivity to cultural diversity, and communicate a feeling of parents' relative unimportance in educational decision making (Sileo et al., 1996).

Myriad Points of View

Varying points of view are another barrier to maintaining productive ethical professional relationships with parents. When working with families, be aware that professionals and parents each have their own points of view. Individual beliefs and perceptions must be understood and respected to attain productive parent–professional partnerships (Bruneau et al., 1995). When individuals' perspectives and/or expertise are ignored or denigrated by others, antagonism may occur between parents and professionals and among profes-sionals themselves.

Educational viewpoints or outlooks are often based on experiential knowledge. Many teachers base their professional positions on knowledge they have gained in spe-cial education coursework, corresponding field experiences, and professional experi-ences in classroom settings. Preservice and in-service teachers spend countless hours learning about assessment and instructional strategies to develop expertise in their field. They participate in practical school-based experiences with children that provide oppor-tunities to put theory into practice and allow them to apply skills they learned in their college courses. Moreover, school-based experiences allow preservice and in-service teachers the opportunity to learn from other colleagues as well as parents. As a result of college courses and school-based experiences, teachers develop their own educational points of view.

Just as you base your educational beliefs on professional experiences, parents base their points of view on personal experiences. As stated previously, parents' positions about education frequently are based on their school experiences as children and youth.

Parents may also base their perceptions on personal parenting experiences or on knowledge of an acquaintance's experiences. These occurrences often guide parents' interactions with teachers. It is vital, therefore, that you recognize and respect parents' knowledge about their children and viewpoints about their children's education (Bruneau et al., 1995). Parents and professionals can work to agree on the best way to meet students' needs, while acknowledging and respecting each others' points of view. According to Baker (1997), teachers and parents must be on the same team rather than opposing teams to ensure students' school success.

Parents' distrust about special education and teachers, lack of understanding of terminology and procedures, as well as the countless perspectives on which they base their beliefs contribute to uncertainty about their roles in meetings to develop children's IEPs. According to Trussell et al. (2008), the relationship between parents and educators is tenuous, and parents' participation in the IEP process lacks parity. Professionals, therefore, must initiate techniques and strategies that ensure parents' full involvement as equal partners in the special education process. They must help parents to become informed decision makers by (a) ensuring their involvement at all levels of their children's educational programs, (b) seeking and valuing parental feedback, and (c) developing their awareness and understanding of legislation as well as their rights and responsibilities as educational partners. You and your special education colleagues have a legal and ethical responsibility to ensure that parents have valuable and meaningful experiences as IEP team members. Consider parents as consumers who have rights and obligations similar to those of purchasers of high-quality merchandise (Sileo et al., 1996). Revisit and reflect on family needs and priorities, and foster a deeper understanding of the challenges that confront parents and family members. The hallmark of your role as a professional educator rests with your abilities to employ best educational practices that promote shared ownership and responsibility for educational decision making.

Several barriers affect educators' interactions with students, parents and other family members, and colleagues, including (a) inadequate communication, (b) use of educational jargon, (c) lack of trust, and (d) myriad points of view. Although teachers and parents share parity in the relationship, it is your responsibility to overcome the barriers.

Summary

- You will interact with parents and families of students throughout your teaching career.
- Parents and other family members often are the most knowledgeable individuals regarding their children.
- Collaboration with families creates a beneficial parent–professional relationship and is more positive than a one-sided relationship in which teachers or parents act as the experts.
- Parent participation is a crucial component to all aspects of children's education because it allows teachers to acquire important information about students and their families that ultimately will have a positive impact on students' development and learning.
- Parents' participation within the field of special education may be especially difficult for some individuals who incur difficulty navigating the system.
- Special educators need to understand the complexities that parents of children with disabilities face and to support them throughout their educational journey.
- The encouragement and assistance that educators provide are crucial to developing and sustaining ethical relationships with parents.

- Professional codes of ethical conduct are good starting places to solve a predicament.
- Although the codes of ethics do not provide specific solutions, they offer guidance about how to resolve the issue.
- One strategy to help unravel an ethical dilemma is to speak with colleagues, who may bring different perspectives to the situation and provide moral support regarding the situation.
- Specific problem-solving strategies, such as those discussed in this chapter, guide educators in resolving ethical dilemmas.

Linking Standards to Chapter Content

After reading this chapter, you should be able to link basic knowledge and skills described in the CEC Standards and INTASC Principles with information provided in this text. Table 9.3, Linking CEC Standards and INTASC Principles to Major Chapter topics, gives examples of how they can be applied to each major section of the chapter.

TABLE 9.3	Linking CEC Standards and INTASC Principles to Major Chapter Topics	
Major Chapter Headings	**CEC Knowledge and Skill Core Standard and Associated Subcategories**	**INTASC Core Principle and Associated Special Education Subcategories**
Introduction	9: Professional and Ethical Practice ICC9S1 Practice within the CEC Code of Ethics and other standards of the profession.	9: Professionalism 9.03 All teachers actively seek out current information and research about how to educate the students with disabilities for whom they are responsible, including information that will help them understand the strengths and needs of students with disabilities as well as ways to effectively promote their learning.
Ethical Considerations and Educational Practice	1: Foundations ICC1K5 Issues in definition and identification of individuals with exceptional learning needs, including those from culturally and linguistically diverse backgrounds. ICC1K7 Family systems and the role of families in the educational process. 9: Professional and Ethical Practice ICC9S2 Uphold high standards of competence and integrity and exercise sound judgment in the practice of the professional.	3: Diverse Learners 3.07 Special education teachers share the values and beliefs underlying special education services for individuals with disabilities in the United States with students, families, and community members, and seek to understand ways in which these are compatible or in conflict with those of the family and community. 9: Professionalism 9.02 All teachers continually challenge their beliefs about how students with disabilities learn and how to teach them effectively.

(continued)

TABLE 9.3 *(continued)*		
Major Chapter Headings	**CEC Knowledge and Skill Core Standard and Associated Subcategories**	**INTASC Core Principle and Associated Special Education Subcategories**
	ICC9S3 Act ethically in advocating for appropriate services. ICC9S5 Demonstrate commitment to developing the highest education and quality-of-life potential of individuals with exceptional learning needs. ICC9S6 Demonstrate sensitivity for the culture, language, religion, gender, disability, socioeconomic status, and sexual orientation of individuals.	9.07 Special education teachers reflect on their personal biases and the influences of these biases on the instruction they provide to students with disabilities, and on the interactions they have with other personnel, families, and the community. 10: Collaboration, Ethics, and Relationships 10.01 All general and special education teachers share instructional responsibility for students with disabilities and work to develop well-functioning collaborative teaching relationships. 10.07 Special education teachers work with related services professionals to design, implement, and evaluate instructional plans for students with disabilities.
Codes of Ethics National Education Association National Association for the Education of Young Children Council for Exceptional Children	1: Foundations ICC1K4 Rights and responsibilities of students, parents, teachers, and other professionals, and schools related to exceptional learning needs. 9: Professional and Ethical Practice ICC9K3 Continuum of lifelong professional development.	1: Subject Matter 1.04 All teachers have knowledge of the major principles and parameters of federal disabilities legislation. 9: Professionalism 9.06 Special education teachers are current in their fields. 10: Collaboration, Ethics, and Relationships 10.05 All special education teachers provide leadership that enables teams to accomplish their purposes. 10.06 Special education teachers take a life span view of students with disabilities and use their broad knowledge of disabilities, legislation, special education services, and instructional strategies to ensure implementation of each student's individual education program.

(continued)

TABLE 9.3 *(continued)*

Major Chapter Headings	CEC Knowledge and Skill Core Standard and Associated Subcategories	INTASC Core Principle and Associated Special Education Subcategories
The Ethical Concept of Doing No Harm	9: Professional and Ethical Practice ICC9S12 Demonstrate sensitivity for the culture, language, religion, gender, disability, socioeconomic status, and sexual orientation of individuals. 10: Collaboration ICC10S8 Model techniques and coach others in the use of instructional methods and accommodations.	10: Collaboration, Ethics, and Relationships 10.07 Special education teachers work with related services professionals to design, implement, and evaluate instructional plans for students with disabilities.
Barriers to Ethical and Confidential Practices When Working with Families Inadequate Communication Educational Jargon Lack of Trust Myriad Points of View	1: Foundations ICC1K10 Potential impact of differences in values, languages, and customs that can exist between the home and school. 2: Development and Characteristics of Learners ICC2K4 Family systems and the role of families in supporting development. 3: Individual Learning Differences ICC3K4 Cultural perspectives influencing the relationships among families, schools and communities as related to instruction. 6: Communication ICC6K3 Ways of behaving and communicating among cultures that can lead to misinterpretation and misunderstanding. 10: Collaboration ICC10S9 Communicate with school personnel about the characteristics and needs of individuals with exceptional learning needs. ICC10S10 Communicate effectively with families of individuals with exceptional learning needs from diverse backgrounds.	2: Student Learning 2.07 Special education teachers seek to understand the current and evolving development and learning of individual students from a life-span perspective. 3: Diverse Learners 3.01 All general and special education teachers build students' awareness, sensitivity, acceptance and appreciation for students with disabilities who are members of their classrooms, schools, and communities. 10: Collaboration, Ethics, and Relationships 10.09 Special education teachers collaborate with families and with school and community personnel to include students with disabilities in a range of instructional environments in the school and community.

(continued)

TABLE 9.3	(continued)	
Major Chapter Headings	**CEC Knowledge and Skill Core Standard and Associated Subcategories**	**INTASC Core Principle and Associated Special Education Subcategories**
Strategies to Ensure Ethical Practices When Working with Families	10: Collaboration ICC10K3 Concerns of families of individuals with exceptional learning needs and strategies to help address these concerns.	3: Diverse Learners 3.06 Special education teachers seek to understand how having a child with disabilities may influence a family's views of themselves as caregivers and as members of their communities. 10: Collaboration, Ethics, and Relationships 10.04 All teachers accept families as full partners in planning appropriate instruction and services for students with disabilities, and provide meaningful opportunities for them to participate as partners in their children's instructional programs and in the life of the school. 10.08 Special education teachers include, promote, and facilitate family members as partners on parent–professional, interdisciplinary, and interagency teams.
	10: Collaboration ICC10S3 Foster respectful and beneficial relationships between families and professionals.	10: Collaboration, Ethics, and Relationships 10.01 All general and special education teachers share instructional responsibility for students with disabilities and work to develop well-functioning collaborative teaching relationships.

Sources: Council for Exceptional Children (2005); Interstate New Teacher Assessment and Support Consortium INTASC Special Education Subcommittee (May 2001).

Web Resources

INTERNET RESOURCES

www.nea.org/—National Education Association (NEA), the nation's largest professional employee organization, is committed to advancing the cause of public education.

http://www.cec.sped.org//AM/Template.cfm?Section=Home—Council for Exceptional Children (CEC) is the largest international professional organization dedicated to improving the educational success of individuals with disabilities and/or gifts and talents.

www.naeyc.org/—National Association for the Education of Young Children (NAEYC) is dedicated to improving the well-being of all young children, with particular focus on the quality of educational and developmental services for all children from birth through age 8.

http://www.dec-sped.org/—Division for Early Childhood (DEC) is one of 17 divisions of CEC and is especially for individuals who work with or on behalf of children with special needs, birth through age 8, and their families.

http://ethics.iit.edu/codes/—Codes of Ethics Online is an extensive collection of professional codes of ethics.

http://www.uvu.edu/ethics/—Center for the Study of Ethics explores the ethical dimensions of a wide variety of disciplines and contemporary moral issues.

http://www.ed.psu.edu/UCEACSLE/VEEA/VEEAFrameset-1. htm—Values and Ethics in Educational Administration (VEEA) is a refereed journal dedicated to promoting and disseminating a broad range of scholarly inquiry relating to the areas of values and ethics, and their relationship to theory and practice in educational administration.

CHAPTER 10

Special Considerations for Families: Birth Through High School

OBJECTIVES

After reading this chapter you will

1. Explain special considerations when working with families of infants, toddlers, and preschoolers with disabilities.
2. Identify IDEA requirements for working with families with infants and toddlers with special needs.
3. Discuss the components of an Individual Family Service Plan.
4. Discuss strategies for working with families of preschool-age children with special needs.
5. Differentiate the needs families of elementary students with special needs compared to families of secondary students with special needs.
6. Identify concerns and strategies for working with families of elementary students with special needs.
7. List the components of Individual Transition Plans.
8. Discuss the ideas for working with families of students in secondary settings.

INTRODUCTION

The challenges that families of young children with disabilities experience differ from those of families of school-age children with disabilities, those who have children who have completed their public school education, and families of children with disabilities who live in residential settings. Throughout this text you have read about issues and concerns that can face all families of children with disabilities. In this chapter, you will read about issues professionals should consider when working with families of children with disabilities at different ages.

WORKING WITH FAMILIES OF INFANTS AND TODDLERS OR PRESCHOOLERS

When Individuals with Disabilities Education Act (IDEA) was first introduced in 1975, services for young children with special needs under the age of 5 or those who were not yet school age were not mandated in the legislation (see Chapter 1 for a more thorough discussion of the evolution of IDEA). In 1986, IDEA was reauthorized, and several amendments were added to the law. These amendments were key to the field of early childhood special education and amended federal legislation to (a) mandate special education services for young children 3 to 5 years of age with developmental delays, and (b) provide for discretionary funds or incentive grants for states interested in providing services to infants and toddlers (birth to 3 years of age) at risk for or experiencing developmental delays and their families. The 1990 reauthorization of the act mandated services for infants and toddlers and their families. Thus, special education services are now mandated by IDEA for infants, toddlers, young children, and students with disabilities from birth to age 21.

The field of early childhood special education continues to transform. Even the terminology used when discussing the field continues to be updated as changes in the field dictate. Early childhood special education is an umbrella term used when talking about family-centered programs and services for young children with special needs from birth through 8 years of age. However, *early intervention* is the term typically used when talking about services for infants and toddlers with special needs (birth through 2 years of age) and their families (Raver, 2009). Regardless of the terms used, the focus of those who work with young children with special needs and their families is on a practical, user-friendly, family-centered approach that promotes the well-being of the child and family.

Families of children with special needs are often first introduced to the field of special education when their children are infants, toddlers, or preschool age. The birth of a child with disabilities or the identification of a child with disabilities during the early years often thrusts parents and families into an emotional crisis or dilemma. Parents and family members experience stages of grief similar to those experienced with the death of a loved one (Kübler-Ross, 1969). The series of stages enable them to accommodate the situation (Cook, Klein, & Tessier, 2007). Figure 10.1 provides an overview of the stages of grief that parents and families may experience. Although most families experience one of more of the stages, not all families progress through the stages in the same order or react in the same manner, nor do they experience every stage. Some parents become fixed at a particular stage and may never reach the final stage of acceptance. Parents can experience one or more stage at the same time and make progress toward acceptance (Cook et al., 2007).

Denial (Shock and Panic) is often the first reaction that parents experience when they learn their child has a disability. Parents often isolate themselves and the child during this stage as a means of dealing with the situation. During this period they may shop around for numerous opinions on the premise that a previous assessment was not fair, complete, or reliable.

Bargaining (Searching) is a stage where parents become involved in support groups and organizations as a means of becoming better informed about the disability and assuring themselves that their child is receiving the best available care. Bargaining is often a period when parents look for magic cures or try to make deals with themselves or God. They rationalize their involvement by hoping to stumble on a solution to their problems.

Anger (Nothingness) often comes from the guilt that parents experience in connection with their responsibility for and to the child. Parents may turn their anger toward themselves, the child, or someone - involved in the care and treatment of the child.

Depression is often experienced when parents reach a stage of confusion. They do not understand completely what is happening to their family or the reason; they often doubt their own abilities to care for the family.

Acceptance (Recovery and Maintenance) is gained once parents have devised a realistic strategy to cope. Coping often results in new perceptions and effective means of seeking assistance as well as new attitudes and behaviors toward the child.

FIGURE 10.1 Stages of grief *Sources:* Cook et al. (2007); Kübler-Ross (1969).

In other instances, they backslide to a less desirable stage. Thus, professionals must work closely with families to meet the specific needs of each family.

Working with Families of Infants and Toddlers

Early intervention services for infants and toddlers at risk for or experiencing developmental delays were initially identified and granted through discretionary funds in 1986. Those services were reauthorized and mandated in 1990 and remained a part of IDEA when it was reauthorized in 2004. Early intervention services for infants and toddlers with special needs differ significantly from special education services for children with disabilities 3 to 21 years of age. Early intervention services fall under Part C of IDEA and include

- Definitions of at-risk/developmental delay
- Multidisciplinary evaluation for services
- Individualized family service plans
- Integration of services in the naturally occurring environment
- Lead agency designated to provide services
- Advisory panels to the lead agency
- Participation of other agencies
- Use of state funds to provide services
- In some cases, minimal costs to parents

Family-centered practices are of primary concern in early intervention and have advanced from the basic concept of parent participation generally associated with IDEA (McWilliam, Tocci, & Harbin, 1998).

Initially, early intervention services were built on a deficit model, as were special education services for older children, and such services did not consider the importance of family input and involvement. Whereas legislation in the 1970s and early 1980s provided for family involvement and secured rights for families of children with disabilities, the focus was still on the child in isolation from the family. Changes in early intervention legislation in the late 1980s and in the 1990s moved the focus from the child to the family as a whole (Howard, Williams, & Lepper, 2010). As a result, early intervention professionals chose to create relationships with families and to empower them (Turnbull, Turnbull, Erwin, & Soodak, 2006).

Family-centered practices orient early intervention services to the entire family and consider the family's needs, as well as those of the child. Family-centered early intervention practices are expected to be delivered in the naturally occurring environment. A naturally occurring environment for infants or toddlers at-risk for or experiencing developmental delays is generally considered to be the place where typically developing infants and toddlers can be found. In most cases, this is the infant's or toddler's home, but in other cases, a naturally occurring environment may be a child development center where typically developing infants and toddlers attend or a playgroup or parent-and-me type class. For early intervention professionals to effectively employ family-centered practices, they must make use of some fundamental components of family-centered practices, including (a) a positive approach, (b) sensitivity to family issues, (c) responsiveness, (d) friendliness, and (e) skills for working with families, children, and communities.

Early intervention professionals must have a positive approach to working with families. A nonjudgmental attitude, a belief in the parents' and children's abilities, and an optimistic and enthusiastic manner to working families are key to a positive approach (McWilliam et al., 1998). Early interventionists need to recognize that parents and families know their children better than anyone else and to consider the best approach to working with each family and child.

Sensitivity to a family's resources, priorities, and concerns is essential. To be successful in their interactions with families, professionals must recognize cultural differences, work through intra- and interpersonal challenges, and recognize parents as experts on their own children. Also recognize parents' hopes and desires for their children and assist them in developing programs that will support these goals (Howard et al., 2010; McWilliam et al., 1998).

The needs and concerns of a family of an infant or toddler with a development delay can change frequently. As an early interventionist, you will need to be responsive to family concerns. Responsiveness to families requires "flexibility, not pushing an agenda, attending to parents' concerns, and taking action when parents express needs" (Howard et al., 2010, p. 449).

Friendliness is another key to the family-centered practices approach. In early intervention, friendliness can be defined as treating families as friends and not just as clients. To do so, you must first build rapport and a relationship with each family, take time to build trust, talk to the family and listen to what the family is saying, offer practical strategies and help, and convey a caring attitude when interacting with both the family and the young child (McWilliam et al., 1998).

Developing and using practical skills when working with young children, families, and communities are also essential to a family-centered approach. These skills may include finding additional social services for the family, a knowledge of local culture and customs, or an appreciation of the families' social and economic status. In some cases, you may assist families of young children with special needs make connections with other families who have similar strengths and challenges.

Family-centered practices continue to be refined and defined. As parents and families take a more active role in early intervention, professionals must acquaint themselves with the skills needed to work with families and their infants and toddlers with special needs. A key component to early intervention is an Individualized Family Service Plan (IFSP).

Individualized Family Service Plan

An IFSP focuses not only on the infant or toddler, but the family as well. In this way it differs from an IEP, which focuses solely on the student. IFSPs are developed once eligibility for services has been established. The IFSP is a legal document like an IEP but differs in that it is reviewed every 6 months or more often, if needed. More frequent review is necessary given the rapid development of infants and toddlers. An IFSP is typically used for children birth through 2 years of age, but recent changes in IDEA 2004 provide for the continued use of an IFSP into the preschool years (3 to 5 years of age) at the discretion of the early intervention agency and the local education agency. An IFSP has eight major components.

STATEMENT OF CHILD'S LEVEL OF DEVELOPMENT. The child's current levels of development across five developmental domains—cognitive, communicative, physical, self-help (also called adaptive), and social/emotional are identified based on a multidisciplinary assessment. As is the case with older students, an infant or toddler may have strengths in some area and difficulties in others. It is vital to document those strengths and difficulties and to discuss the affects on the overall development of the infant or toddler (Howard et al., 2010; Smith, 2010).

STATEMENT OF FAMILY PRIORITIES, RESOURCES, AND CONCERNS. If a family agrees, include a statement of the family's priorities, resources, and concerns as they relate to the development of the infant or toddler (Howard et al., 2010; Smith, 2010). This section of the IFSP really enhances family involvement in early intervention and helps to determine the major outcomes for the child.

MAJOR OUTCOMES. A statement of major outcomes that the child or family is expected to achieve—similar to IEP goals—is included in the IFSP. Each major outcome must have criteria for mastery, a timeline for implementation, an expected date of completion, and a discussion on the procedures for measuring progress (Howard et al., 2010; Smith, 2010). Commonly, one or more of the major outcomes are family, not child, focused. This often occurs when a family concern must be addressed for the family to be able to support the development of their child. Because an IFSP is reviewed every six months, it is possible for the major outcomes to be achieved or revised more rapidly than would be done with IEP goals.

STATEMENT OF EARLY INTERVENTION SERVICES. This section contains a discussion on the types of early intervention services to be provided to the infant or toddler with special needs and the family. Each service that is identified must include the frequency, duration, location, and method of delivery of the service. In some cases, additional services needed by the family are listed here although they are not covered by the major outcomes of the IFSP. For example, a family may need assistance finding access to medical services, or may need assistance working with an insurance agency (Howard et al., 2010; Smith, 2010). These services may not be provided for at public expense but may be included in the IFSP if the team feels they are necessary to the development of their child.

NATURAL ENVIRONMENTS IN WHICH SERVICES WILL BE PROVIDED. Early intervention services must be provided in naturally occurring environments. Therefore, IFSPs must include a statement identifying how and where services will be provided in the natural environment. If for some reason, services are not provided in the natural environment (i.e., in a clinic or hospital setting), the IFSP must include a justification of the extent and reasons services are provided in alternate settings.

PROJECTED DATES FOR INITIATION AND DURATION OF SERVICES. A statement of services and the initiation and duration of those services must be identified in the IFSP (Howard et al., 2010; Smith, 2010). Because the document is reviewed every 6 months, the duration of those services is 6 months or less; however, it is possible, that a major outcome will be identified that will take longer than 6 months. When this occurs, work with the family to establish a timeline for the initiation, delivery, and completion of those services.

SERVICE COORDINATION. Early intervention services, unlike special education services for children 3 to 21, are not necessarily coordinated by a state or local education agency. When IDEA was amended in 1986 to include services for infants and toddler, discretionary incentive grants were made available to states that wanted to participate. In some states the state or local education agency applied for funds, whereas in other states, the state or local department of health or department of social services applied for the funds. Thus, funds were distributed to different agencies within and among the various states. As such, early intervention services, within and among states, may be provided by more than one agency. For example, a school-age child with spina bifida may receive special education services, occupational therapy services, and physical therapy services. All these services are coordinated by the local education agency (i.e., the school district) and are typically provided at the child's home school. In early intervention, an infant or toddler with spina bifida may need the same services—early intervention, occupational therapy, and physical therapy. However, the services are provided by various agencies such as the local department of health and the local department of social services. Multiple agencies providing multiple services can lead to scheduling confusion and can be frustrating for families and professionals. Therefore, IDEA requires that each child with an IFSP have a service coordinator.

A service coordinator generally provides coordination and oversight of an IFSP and works with families to ensure they are receiving the services they need (Smith, 2010) and to cultivate family empowerment (Turnbull et al., 2006). The service coordinator role can be filled by the early interventionist—as is often the case; or by any of the service providers, such as speech pathologist, occupational therapist, physical therapist, or social service provider. Keys to effective service coordination include (a) ensuring evaluations and assessments are completed for the infant or toddler, (b) developing and reviewing IFSPs, (c) identifying available services, (d) notifying families of the services available, (e) coordinating the delivery services, (f) identifying and coordinating the delivery of medical or health services, and (g) when appropriate, developing a transition plan to preschool services (Howard et al., 2010).

TRANSITION PLAN. A transition plan to preschool services must be developed and steps must be taken to ensure the child and family make a smooth transition to those services once the child turns 3 years of age. This transition plan should be in place at least 6 months prior to the child transitioning to early childhood special education preschool services. The transition plan may include visits to the preschool classroom, a visit with the early childhood special education teacher, a multidisciplinary assessment to transition the child from an IFSP to an IEP, an IEP eligibility meeting, and educating the parents and family to the legal and programmatic changes that can be expected (Howard et al., 2010).

IFSPs tend to be viewed as a working document with the emphasis on the foundation and delivery of the interventions. The focus is on the infant or toddler with special needs and the supports necessary to empower the family to assist their child. IFSPs were designed, developed, and continue to have a family-centered focus in which early interventionists work collaboratively with families to meet the needs of the infant or toddler at risk for or experiencing developmental delays.

Working with Families of Preschoolers

Early childhood special education services for young children 3 to 5 years old experiencing developmental delays were first mandated in 1986. These services are generally provided by the local education agency (e.g., the child's neighborhood school). Classrooms for preschool-age children with special needs are typically found on elementary school campuses or at inclusive sites with publically funded programs such as Head Start or privately funded child development centers. Although a family-centered focus remains key in early childhood special education, special education services for preschoolers with developmental delays are more comparable to special education services for school-age children than they are to services for infants and toddlers at risk for or experiencing developmental delays. The focus of early childhood special education services is on the education of the *young child* with special needs. Families who have previously had their preschooler with special needs in an early intervention program often find the transition to an early childhood special education program difficult. Family members may become disenfranchised with the transition process and the system (Turnbull et al., 2006), given that the focus is now on the student, and less on the family (Pruitt, Wandry, & Hollums, 1998). For example, instead of IFSPs, IEPs are developed for preschoolers. (See Chapters 1, 7, and 8 for a thorough discussion on IEPs and parent involvement.) Figure 10.2 provides examples of variations between IFSPs and IEPs.

Parent and family member involvement is key to the success of any early childhood special education program for preschoolers with special needs. Although the focus has shifted to the young child in an education setting, early childhood special educators must continue to involve parents in the development and education of their children. A guiding tenet in early childhood special education is for IEP goals and objectives to be addressed during the course of typical daily activities or routines. Thus, both families and professionals are given the opportunity to provide support and encouragement to the preschooler with special needs (see Figure 10.3 for an example of linking IEP goals to both home and school).

Component	IFSPs	IEPs (for preschoolers with special needs)
Focus of service	Infants and toddlers with special needs (birth through 2 years of age) and their families	Children with special needs (3–5 years of age)
Location of service	Home Childcare facility Naturally occurring environment	Schools
Primary objectives	Provide support and interventions to infants and toddlers with special needs and their families Promote parental confidence and competence in supporting and advocating for their child Encourage family involvement in all aspects of the infant's or toddler's life	Provide support for a child's development Provide supports to build preliteracy skills and social competence Promote the development of skills so the child can become more self-sufficient and independent
Lead agency	Varies among states	State education agency/Local education agency

FIGURE 10.2   Variations among IFSPs and IEPs   *Sources:* Raver (2009); Smith (2010).

One area of focus in early childhood special education is preliteracy and school readiness skills. Kara is learning about letters and sound symbol relationships at school during circle time and while she plays in some centers. To bridge the gap between what is being addressed at school with home, Kara's teachers use a communication journal and e-mail to provide her family an overview of her day. When her parents read the communication journal each night, they learn what Kara has done during the day and can then support Kara by furthering those letter and sound symbol relationship skills at home by reading with her or by playing with letter blocks or magnets. Kara's parents can then write in the communication journal or send an e-mail to her teacher describing how the family supported Kara at home.

FIGURE 10.3   Linking IEPs goals and objectives to both home and school activities

Home visits are another means by which to strengthen family-centered practices with preschool-age children with special needs. As an educator, you can improve the effectiveness of home visits by:

- Building positive relationships with families
- Reinforcing and supporting parent–child relationships as a means to assist the child's development
- Identifying and building on family and child strengths (Bernstein, 2002)
- Modeling interactions with the child
- Providing examples of strategies or methods by which IEP goals can be addressed at home during daily routines
- Perhaps most important, being nonjudgmental of the family's home and belongings (Cook et al., 2007)

Early childhood special educators should also remember that although it is important to involve all family members in the home visit, the focus should be on the young child with special needs.

Summary

Families of young children with developmental delays experience joy, love, and stress associated with raising a child with special needs.

> Because of the unique characteristics, needs, and resources of each child and family, no one curriculum or set of services could be expected to meet the needs of all. An individualized approach to service planning and delivery, therefore, is essential (Bailey & Wolery, 1992, p. 34)

Professionals in the field of early childhood special education need to be aware of the varying needs of families of infants, toddlers, and preschool-age children with special needs. Understanding each family system is crucial to the achievement of the child with special needs and to successful family–professional interactions. Thus, if you work in early childhood special education, it is critical to develop a family-centered approach that is flexible enough to meet the needs of all the children and families with whom you work.

WHEN WORKING WITH FAMILIES OF ELEMENTARY-AGED CHILDREN

The majority of students with disabilities are diagnosed after they enter school. This is due to the large proportion of students being identified with high-incidence disabilities. High-incidence disabilities are generally students with communication disorders, learning disabilities, emotional/behavioral disabilities, and higher functioning intellectual or developmental disabilities.

Eight-year-old Abdul is a delightful child who enjoyed kindergarten, first grade, and the first few months of second grade. Now he says, however, that he doesn't like school. His parents are concerned given that this did not happen to any of their other children. They can't quite figure out why Abdul suddenly doesn't want to go to school. About the same time, Abdul's teacher calls and sets up an appointment to talk to his parents. During this meeting, they learn that Abdul is having difficulty learning to read, and the teacher wants him to receive some more intensive instruction to determine whether or not he has a learning disability. They are very alarmed at this news and at first blame the teacher for not teaching Abdul properly. After all, he hasn't shown any other signs of having difficulties learning in the past. After thinking about it for a few days, Abdul's parents agree that it would be in his best interest to get some additional help, and they agree to these services.

Students may not be identified as having a disability before beginning kindergarten for several reasons. First, students with high-incidence disabilities usually have no physical manifestations of a disability. Second, these students may progress through the developmental stages expected for children their same age. Thus, family members and others who see them on a regular basis (e.g., pediatricians, daycare workers) may not be alerted to a possible disability. Third, the definition of some disabilities is based on academic skill deficits (e.g., learning disabilities) not observable in very young children. It is not until a child is given reading instruction, for example, that the child has difficulty learning to read, and thus the disability becomes apparent. Fourth, some developmental lags will not be manifested until an older age. For example, typical children may not master the articulation of the /r/ sound until 7 or 8 years of age. Children not developing speech articulation skills could qualify for speech services. And fifth, illnesses or accidents may result in a disability, which can occur at any point in a child's life.

Most of what has been discussed in this book relates directly to parents with elementary- and secondary-aged children with disabilities. For example, just as families of children identified while babies, infants, or toddlers, families of children identified during the school years also experience grieving. In fact, such grief can be more difficult than if the child were identified earlier. Parents may, for example, be expecting their child to develop typically because they have so far, and then they are told the child has a disability. Sometimes parents place blame on the school because school personnel are those who call to their attention to the fact that their child is not progressing in a typical manner. In addition, grief isn't an emotion that parents experience once. A parent's sadness related to the disability may be ongoing or occur repeatedly throughout the child's life.

Concerns of Parents of Elementary-Aged Students

Although most of the issues discussed in this book apply to parents across the age span of their children, there are concerns that are paramount in the minds of parents of elementary-aged students with disabilities. All parents who send their child to the first day of kindergarten are concerned about many things, including the safety of their child, how well their child will be received by others, whether their child will make friends, and how well their child will be educated. With good reason, these concerns are exacerbated in the minds of parents with children with disabilities.

SAFETY.   Although all parents are concerned about the safety of their child, children with disabilities may be more vulnerable to accidents and injuries as a result of their disability. A child with a physical disability may not negotiate the staircase or use the playground equipment properly. Parents may worry that school personnel will inadvertently injure the child (such as transferring in and out of a wheelchair). Or parents may fret that their child will more likely be a target of bullying. In addition, parents may worry that their child will not have the skills to report bullying or injury to school personnel or to them (Taub, 2006). Given the recent increase in school violence, even at the elementary school level, parents have reason for concern and worry. Children with disabilities may be even more vulnerable given their inability, for example, to notice that something is not quite right and to let an adult know.

Although parents are understandably concerned about the safety of their child in school, this can lead to overprotectiveness. School personnel can help this situation. First, teachers need to recognize that the parents' concerns about safety are real and serious. Second, they need to do all they can to ensure children's safety while in school and alert officials when safety concerns arise. And third, teachers can encourage parents to help their children become independent by not overprotecting them (Taub, 2006). Educators can also teach safety rules to their students, inviting parents to participate and help.

ATTITUDES OF OTHERS.   Given the increased number of students with disabilities being educated in general education schools and classrooms, another concern of parents can be the attitudes and acceptance of their child in this setting. Parents may be concerned that the other students will not accept their child or that the general education teacher won't have the skills to teach their child or others about their child. For example, they may have concerns about what information is being presented to their child's peers about disabilities. They may have questions such as: Will the information be accurate? Will the presentation violate my child's privacy? Will this information only evoke pity? (Taub, 2006).

Before sharing information to other students, consult the parents about what information they would like to have shared. Whether the student should be present when this takes place should be made on an individual basis and with the parents' and student's feedback. Information could also be shared with a larger audience such as a presentation at back-to-school night. Care should be taken, however, to protect the confidentiality of individual students. Students are protected through both IDEA and the Family Educational Rights and Privacy Act (FERPA). No individual student should be identified, nor information shared about his or her disability diagnosis or Individualized Education Programs (IEPs). You could ask parents and students with disabilities to participate in a class-, grade-, or school-level presentation. Personal stories and experiences can be a very powerful way of educating others. Parents who volunteer to share information have the right to do so. But if students volunteer to present information about their disability, seek parent permission before allowing them to do so.

Again, given the increased number of students with disabilities being educated in the general classroom, parents might also be concerned that the child's disabilities will overshadow his or her abilities in the eyes of the teacher. The teacher may focus on what the child cannot do, not what the child can do. Parents could also be apprehensive about the abilities of the teacher to work with their child.

FRIENDSHIPS.   All parents want their children to have friends. The parents of students with disabilities are particularly concerned about friendship, particularly when students begin kindergarten or change grade levels or schools. Children with mild to moderate disabilities often have difficulty making and keeping friends. This stems from their lack of appropriate social skills and/or inability to express themselves verbally. Paraeducators assigned to students one-on-one can act as a barrier to friendship building. Children in this situation, both the student with and those without disabilities, may be hampered from interacting in a natural and healthy manner. In fact, the child with a disability may develop skills in interacting with adults more readily than with his or her peers. Adaptive equipment used by the student as well as different physical appearances can also result in barriers to making friends. Also, students with physical disabilities may not be able to participate in games and playground activities when typical friendships are often fostered. In addition, students with disabilities may not be readily invited to participate in out-of-school social activities such as their peers' birthday parties.

As described earlier, educating peers and their parents about the students with disabilities can help break down informational and attitudinal barriers, which can, in turn, help foster friendship. In addition, students with and without disabilities can be taught appropriate social skills contributing to making and sustaining friendships. Also, friendship groups that include students with and without disabilities can be created to help those who have difficulty forming them naturally (Taub, 2006).

QUALITY OF THE CHILD'S EDUCATION.   Although all parents want their children to have a quality education, parents of a child with disabilities may be especially concerned about their child's education. Parents may be eager when their child enters kindergarten to see him or her progress academically and socially in a somewhat typical manner. Parents are generally more satisfied with their child's education in the early grades. In fact, one national study discovered that parents of elementary students report higher levels of satisfaction with all aspects of their children's education than do parents of secondary-aged students (Newman, 2006).

When a child is diagnosed with a disability, the parents may feel gratitude for special education services and have unrealistic expectations of how quickly or how much the child will learn. Although high expectations are important to maintain, teachers have an obligation to share with parents the reality of their child's growth as well. One study interviewed 43 parents of students with disabilities who had already entered secondary schools. Many of the parents did not understand why their children were not performing at higher levels. They expressed a collective sense of disappointment in the lack of their children's progres, and, thus, in the services provided in elementary special education (Lovitt & Cushing, 1999).

Working with Families with Elementary-Aged Students

Family members of elementary-aged students are often more involved in volunteering in the schools and assisting with response to intervention implementation than families with secondary-aged students. Within this section we focus on those two topics and touch on IEPs (IEPs are more extensively addressed in Chapters 7 and 8). We also address family member involvement in transition to secondary schools.

VOLUNTEERISM.   Given the formative years of their children, parents who have elementary-aged students are often more involved in their child's education than when the children reach secondary age. Parents often join the Parent Teacher Association (PTA) and willingly participate as volunteers in the school and classroom. This, of course, is not universally true. Factors that affect parent volunteerism include work schedules, childcare needs, transportation difficulties, feeling inadequate, and cultural and language barriers. In addition, some parents are "too stressed or depressed to care" (Kirschenbaum, 1999, p. 20). As addressed in previous chapters, parents and other family members can be made to feel welcome in the schools when special effort is put forward by the administration, teachers, and staff.

Parent volunteers are most frequently used to help with clerical tasks (e.g., organizing or copying materials), making the classroom more inviting (e.g., constructing bulletin boards), chaperoning field trips, or engaging in social activities of the classroom (e.g., parties). One of the most powerful ways parent volunteers can be used in the classrooms, however, is to help students with appropriate learning tasks. For example, parent volunteers could listen to students read, assist students at learning centers, or tutor students on specific subject matter. Teachers need to provide structure to the tutoring sessions and train parents in these procedures, not unlike preparing students to be peer tutors.

For example, a program entitled the Fluency Flyers Club was initiated in which trained parent volunteers pulled students from their elementary general education classroom for about 5 minutes a day to practice fluent reading. On Mondays, the students read a novel passage to the parent volunteer, who assessed their reading fluency. The students then practiced reading the passage two or three times. On Tuesday through Thursday, the parent volunteers taught specific skills, and the students read the passage several times. On Fridays, the students were posttested on the reading passage. After 1 year of intervention, the average reading gain of participating students was greater than 2 years (Conderman & Strobel, 2008).

Parents can also volunteer their services while remaining at home. There are several things they can do that do not require they travel to the school. For example, they could make phone calls to other parents informing them of upcoming events, translate school information into parents' native languages, help with fundraising activities, create flyers or newsletters to disseminate to other parents, host parent meetings, and so forth.

RESPONSE TO INTERVENTION.   When IDEA was reauthorized in 2004, one of the major changes was the inclusion of response to intervention (RTI) as a means of identifying students with learning disabilities (LD). Previously, the severe discrepancy model was prominent in diagnosing LD. That is, students must have exhibited a severe discrepancy between their ability (e.g., intelligence test scores) and their performance (e.g., achievement test scores). Barring no other known disability or difference that could explain their poor performance (e.g., cultural, linguistic), students could be identified with LD. With the most recent IDEA reauthorization, however, states and districts were given more flexibility by eliminating the severe discrepancy requirement and including the option of RTI as part of the evaluation procedures for special education eligibility. Response to intervention is defined as a process that emphasizes how well students respond academically or behaviorally to changes in instruction. When using RTI, students who are having difficulty learning are provided more intensive instruction. If they do not improve satisfactorily, then they may be evaluated for a learning disability.

Parent involvement can be paramount to the implementation of RTI. Core features of the RTI process, including parent involvement, are as follows:

- High quality, research-based instruction and behavioral support in general education
- Universal screening of academics and behavior to identify students needing additional interventions
- Multiple tiers (usually three) of increasingly intensive, scientifically based interventions
- Use of a collaborative approach for developing, implementing, and monitoring
- Objective and continuous monitoring of student progress
- Follow-up measures to ensure the intervention was consistently implemented
- Documentation of parent involvement throughout the process
- Documentation that any evaluation timelines guaranteed through IDEA are followed unless parents and the school agree to an extension (Klotz & Canter, 2007)

Parents can become more informed and involved in the school's RTI process. Professional organizations and centers advise parents to ask the following questions about RTI:

- Does our school use RTI? If not, are they planning to start? Know that the school may call it something different.
- Does our school have written materials for parents explaining the RTI process?
- How can parents get involved in RTI?

- What interventions are being used in RTI, and are they scientifically based?
- How long does an intervention last before the student is seen as having made adequate progress?
- How does the school guarantee the interventions were implemented appropriately?
- How does the school monitor student progress and intervention effectiveness? Do they provide parents with ongoing reports of progress?
- When are parents informed of their due process rights under IDEA during the RTI process, including the right to request an evaluation for special education eligibility? (Klotz & Canter, 2007; National Research Center on Learning Disabilities [NRCLD], 2007)

Prior to the inclusion of RTI, parents' first indication that their child was having difficulty in school was when they were asked for written permission to have their child evaluated for special education. This can be shocking for parents, particularly if they were not aware of any difficulties their child was experiencing before then. Through RTI, students having difficulty are identified as needing more intensive instruction before their difficulties are great enough to qualify for special education services. Parents should be informed when students need more intensive instruction and asked to provide additional assistance at home. The RTI model allows parents to become involved at a much earlier stage.

In schools that do use RTI, parents should expect to receive information about their child's needs, the interventions being applied, who is delivering the instruction, and the academic progress expected for their child. Frequent communication should exist between the school and the parents relaying information such as progress (or lack of progress) and information needed to determine whether their child should be referred for a special education evaluation (NRCLD, 2007).

INDIVIDUALIZED EDUCATION PROGRAMS.   At the elementary level, the child's education program is driven by the IEP. Much has been written in other chapters about the IEP that will not be reiterated here (see Chapters 1, 7, and 8). It must be noted, however, that because the majority of students with disabilities are identified during the early elementary grades, it is during this time that most parents are first exposed to the IEP process. Care should be taken to ensure parents understand their rights and responsibilities and that strong and healthy partnerships develop between the family and the school.

In some ways the IEP for elementary-aged students is less complex than the IFSP or the Individualized Transition Plan (ITP). For example, family needs are not expressed on the IEP nor are the child's postsecondary outcome desires. The importance of quality IEPs and the resulting instruction and services received during these years cannot, however, be overstated. The skills learned during these years provide a foundation for what the child will need in future schooling and postsecondary life.

TRANSITION TO SECONDARY SCHOOLS.   The elementary educational experience for students can be completely different from their secondary experience. Typically, elementary-aged students have one general education teacher in one classroom. Those with disabilities may also have a special education teacher who coteaches in the general classroom or who pulls students out for a portion of the day into a resource room. Sometimes students with disabilities will also receive services in a special education self-contained classroom. Generally speaking, however, the more services the child needs (e.g., physical therapy, speech language therapy), the more "teachers" the child will see in a week.

Nevertheless, the number of teachers and amount of movement the child experiences is usually minimal.

In secondary schools, unless the child is placed in a self-contained special education classroom, he or she will experience multiple teachers in multiple classrooms. This transition can be particularly difficult for students with disabilities. They should be given an opportunity to become familiar with their new school by making visits prior to the first day of school. At that time they should meet their new teachers. These students should also participate in any regular orientation sessions attended by all new students.

Teachers can also alleviate both parental and student concerns about transitioning to secondary schools by discussing what they will be experiencing differently. If necessary, goals to prepare them for transitioning to the secondary school can be written into their IEPs. They can practice the skills needed to move from one class to the next, using a locker, changing in and out of gym clothes, or whatever might be helpful to the individual student.

Summary

A large portion of students are identified with disabilities during their elementary school years, and thus parents are introduced to the IEP process and special education services during these years. Parents of elementary-aged students have concerns of their child's safety, how well their child will be received by peers and general education teachers, whether their child will make friends, and how well they will be educated. They are more likely to volunteer to help in the classroom and should be used, if possible, to improve the academic learning of students. Schools using the response to intervention (RTI) model need to ensure parents are involved in all steps of the process. Transition to secondary schools can also be a concern for parents of older elementary students, which can be addressed through students (with or without parents) visiting the school, meeting their new teachers, and discussing what they will experience differently. IEP goals can also focus on the skills needed to make a smooth transition from an elementary to a secondary school.

WORKING WITH FAMILIES OF SECONDARY STUDENTS

Generally, by the time students enter secondary settings such as middle schools or junior high schools, and certainly high schools, the presence of any disabling condition has already been identified. Although there are exceptions to this premise (e.g., a traumatic brain injury), for the most part, both students with disabilities and family members are familiar with the special education system at the time the child enters a secondary setting. Thus secondary professionals' roles with families vary somewhat from professionals who work in early childhood special education or in elementary settings.

As with elementary-age students, secondary students with disabilities have IEPs that identify each student's abilities, needs, and goals. In addition to providing continued special education services and supports to students with disabilities and their families through the IEP process, the focus for secondary special education personnel is often on transition (Storms, O'Leary, & Williams, 2000). In general, students and families who are new to secondary settings are often concerned with transitions for students from single classroom elementary settings to multiclassroom secondary settings. Fortunately, as discussed earlier, these transitions among classes can be addressed via the IEP and with support from the special education and school staff. In addition, although these transitions may be somewhat more involved for students with disabilities than they are for students in general education setting, both families of students with and without disabilities share this concern. Thus most middle and junior high schools provide support to all new students to assist with the transition from elementary school.

The major change families of students with disabilities generally encounter in secondary settings is the development and implementation of an Individual Transition Plan (ITP). An ITP is a written plan or a component of the IEP that outlines what a student will need to live, succeed in employment or postsecondary education, and engage in recreation as an adult (National Center on Secondary Education and Transition, 2007; Storms et al., 2000). It should be written at least 4 years before a student with disabilities leaves school. This does not necessarily mean, however, 4 years before the 12th grade. Although most students with disabilities complete school or graduate with their classmates without disabilities, there is a provision in IDEA that extends services to some students with disabilities until age 22.

IDEA indicates that the ITP must be developed beginning no later than a child's 16th birthday. ITPs are reviewed annually at the same time as the IEP, but can also be reviewed more frequently if the student's transition needs change. The ITP is written with the help of the student. In fact, IDEA requires that a student with disabilities be invited to all IEP meetings that discuss transition and ITPs. Family members, teacher(s), social workers or service coordinators, and adult service providers are generally also in attendance. The ITP spells out what everyone needs to do to provide the training and services needed for a smooth transition from school. It is a connection between the public education and the IEP and postsecondary adult life. Several changes were made to transition components in IDEA 2004. Specifically IDEA states:

> The term "transition services" means a coordinated set of activities for a child with a disability that: (a) is designed to be within a results-oriented process that is focused on improving the academic and functional achievement of the child with a disability to facilitate the child's movement from school to post-school activities, including postsecondary education, vocational education, integrated employment (including supported employment), continuing and adult education, adult services, independent living, and community participation; (b) is based on the individual child's needs, taking into account the child's strengths, preferences, and interests; and (c) includes instruction, related services, community experiences, the development of employment and other post-school adult living objectives, and, if appropriate, acquisition of daily living skills and functional vocational evaluation. See IDEA 20 U.S.C. 1401(34) and 34 CFR §300.43(a).
>
> Beginning not later than the first IEP to be in effect when the child turns 16, or younger if determined appropriate by the IEP Team, and updated annually thereafter, the IEP must include:
>
> - Appropriate measurable postsecondary goals based upon age-appropriate transition assessments related to training, education, employment and, where appropriate, independent living skills;
> - The transition services (including courses of study) needed to assist the child in reaching those goals; and

- Beginning not later than one year before the child reaches the age of majority under State law, a statement that the child has been informed of the child's rights under Part B, if any, that will transfer to the child on reaching the age of majority. See IDEA §300.520 [see 20 U.S.C. 1415(m)]. [34 CFR 300.320(b) and (c)] [20 U.S.C. 1414 (d)(1)(A)(i)(VIII)].

Individual Transition Plans

Transition from high school to a postsecondary setting does not take place overnight. It takes years to plan, develop, and implement. As an educator, your role in working with families of children with disabilities at IEP meetings now expands to include the "child" as a member of the planning team. The involvement of students and families is important so that students can begin to understand themselves and then identify a team of caring adults who will support their journey. In our culture, a primary rite of passage for into adulthood is graduating from high school (National Center on Secondary Education and Transition 2007; National Transition Network, 1996).

> The beginning of adulthood is celebrated at this time with the idea that students will develop an increasing independence and autonomy and move on to further education, meaningful jobs, finding their own places to live, and their own friends, companions, and life in the community. (National Center on Secondary Education and Transition, 2007, np)

It is important to examine the child's goals for adult life as well as those of the parents. Figure 10.4 provides a transition checklist that you can use when working with students and families. The checklist is designed to assist students and families in identifying transition goals and objectives, as well as goals for life after high school.

Transition Checklist for Families

The following is a checklist of transition activities that you can provide to students and families to consider when preparing transition plans with the IEP team. Each student's skills and interests will determine which items on the checklist are relevant. Suggest to families that they use this checklist to ask themselves whether or not these transition issues should be addressed at IEP transition meetings. The checklist can also help identify who should be part of the IEP transition team. Responsibility for carrying out the specific transition activities should be determined at the IEP transition meetings.

Four to Five Years Before Leaving the School District

- Identify personal learning styles and the necessary accommodations to be a successful learner and worker.
- Identify career interests and skills, complete interest and career inventories, and identify additional education or training requirements.
- Explore options for postsecondary education and admission criteria.
- Identify interests and options for future living arrangements, including supports.
- Learn to communicate effectively your interests, preferences, and needs.

FIGURE 10.4 Transition checklist *Source:* The National Transition Network (1996). *Transition Planning for Success in Adult Life.* Available from: http://ici2.umn.edu/ntn/pub/briefs/tplanning.html. Copyright granted © 1996 National Transition Network, Institute on Community Integration, University of Minnesota.

- Be able to explain your disability and the accommodations you need.
- Learn and practice informed decision-making skills.
- Investigate assistive technology tools that can increase community involvement and employment opportunities.
- Broaden your experiences with community activities and expand your friendships.
- Pursue and use local transportation options outside family.
- Investigate money management and identify necessary skills.
- Acquire identification card and the ability to communicate personal information.
- Identify and begin learning skills necessary for independent living.
- Learn and practice personal health care.

Two to Three Years Before Leaving the School District

- Identify community support services and programs (Vocational Rehabilitation, County Services, Centers for Independent Living, etc.).
- Invite adult service providers, peers, and others to the IEP transition meeting.
- Match career interests and skills with vocational course work and community work experiences.
- Gather more information on postsecondary programs and the support services offered, and make arrangements for accommodations to take college entrance exams.
- Identify health-care providers and become informed about sexuality and family planning issues.
- Determine the need for financial support (Supplemental Security Income, state financial supplemental programs, Medicare).
- Learn and practice appropriate interpersonal, communication, and social skills for different settings (employment, school, recreation, with peers, etc.).
- Explore legal status with regard to decision making prior to age of majority.
- Begin a resume and update it as needed.
- Practice independent living skills (e.g., budgeting, shopping, cooking, and housekeeping).
- Identify needed personal assistant services, and if appropriate, learn to direct and manage these services.

One Year Before Leaving the School District

- Apply for financial support program (Supplemental Security Income, Independent Living Services, Vocational Rehabilitation, and Personal Assistant Services).
- Identify the postsecondary school you plan to attend and arrange for accommodations.
- Practice effective communication by developing interview skills, asking for help, and identifying necessary accommodations at postsecondary and work environments.
- Specify desired job and obtain paid employment with supports as needed.
- Take responsibility for arriving on time to work, appointments, and social activities.
- Assume responsibility for health-care needs (making appointments, filling and taking prescriptions, etc.).
- Register to vote and for selective service (if a male).

FIGURE 10.4 *(Continued)*

As an educator, you can help support families through the transition experience, by having them identify and examine the postsecondary goals and objectives they have for their child. At the same time, it is important that you work with and support the student to develop her/his own goals and objectives. Once the student and family have identified postsecondary goals, you can facilitate a discussion of these goals at the transition meeting.

According to the National Transition Network (1996), the transition checklist and subsequent development of a transition plan will provide the framework for identifying, planning, and carrying out activities that will help a student make a successful transition to adult life. The ITP identifies the type of skills to be learned and the transition services to be provided, when they will be provided, and the party responsible for providing them.

Summary

Families of secondary students with disabilities are generally familiar with the special education system and processes by the time the students enter middle school and beyond. The primary challenge families experience related to their child's disability and special education services is the extension of the IEP to include an ITP. The ITP is designed to provide students with disabilities and their families a road map to follow as the student transitions from high school to a postsecondary setting. For many families, transitioning from a secondary education setting to a postsecondary setting can be difficult for both students and their families. The ITP provides a foundation on which to develop short- and long-term goals for postsecondary placements.

Summary

- Your work with families of children with special needs will be affected by your education, the educational setting in which you work, and the students and families with whom you work.
- There are special considerations that should be addressed when working with families of students with disabilities of varying ages.
- Consider the circumstances the family encountered when they first learned their child was eligible for special education. Ask yourself these questions:
  - Did the child's age dictate the need for early intervention services or early childhood special education?
- Did the child enter the special education system during the elementary years?
- How well prepared was the student to transition from elementary to secondary and then to postsecondary situations?
- When working with families, what experiences has the family had with special education?
- Think about any special circumstances or issues that could be affecting the family currently.
- Understanding the needs of the child and the child's family during the early childhood, elementary, and secondary years is crucial to a successful working relationship with the child's family at any age.

Linking Standards to Chapter Content

After reading this chapter, you should be able to link basic knowledge and skills described in the CEC Standards and INTASC Principles with information provided in this text. Table 10.1, Linking CEC Standards and INTASC Principles to Major Chapter Topics, gives examples of how they can be applied to each major section of the chapter.

TABLE 10.1	Linking CEC Standards and INTASC Principles to Major Chapter Topics	

Major Chapter Headings	CEC Knowledge and Skill Core Standard and Associated Subcategories	INTASC Core Principle and Associated Special Education Subcategories
Working with Families of Infants and Toddlers or Preschoolers Working with Families of Infants and Toddlers IFSP Working with Families of Preschoolers	1: Foundations ICC1K4 Rights and responsibilities of students, parents, teachers, and other professionals, and schools related to exceptional learning needs. GC1K5 Continuum of placement and services available for individuals with disabilities. 8: Assessment GC8K3 Types and importance of information concerning individuals with disabilities available from families and public agencies. 10: Collaboration ICC10S6 Collaborate with school personnel and community members in integrating individuals with exceptional learning needs into various settings.	1: Subject Matter 1.08 Special education teachers have knowledge of when and how to develop, structure, and implement accommodations, modifications, and/or adaptations to provide access to the general curriculum for students with disabilities. They use this knowledge to develop educational programs that meet the needs of individual students. 1.11 Special education teachers have knowledge of the requirements and responsibilities involved in developing, implementing, and evaluating IEPs, IFSPs, and IAPs for students with disabilities. They know what the law requires with regard to documents and procedures and take responsibility for ensuring that both the intent and the requirements of the law are fulfilled. 8: Assessment 8.07 Special education teachers plan and conduct assessments in the school, home, and community in order to make eligibility and placement decisions about individuals students with disabilities. They know the legal requirements related to assessment of students with disabilities and take steps to ensure that these requirements are met. They involve families as partners in the assessment and eligibility placement process, including when planning assessments, gathering information, and making decisions. 10: Collaboration, Ethics, and Relationships 10.09 Special education teachers collaborate with families and with school and community personnel to include students with disabilities in a range of instructional environments in the school and community.

(continued)

TABLE 10.1   (continued)

Major Chapter Headings	CEC Knowledge and Skill Core Standard and Associated Subcategories	INTASC Core Principle and Associated Special Education Subcategories
Working with Families of Elementary-Aged Children Concerns of Parents of Elementary-Aged Students Working with Families with Elementary-Aged Students Working with Families with Secondary Students	5: Learning Environments and Social Interactions LD5S1 Plan instruction for independent functional life skills relevant to the community, personal living, sexuality, and employment. 7: Instructional Planning GC7K2 Model career, vocational, and transition programs for individuals with disabilities. MR7S3 Plan instruction for independent functional life skills relevant to the community, personal living, sexuality, and employment. 10: Collaboration LD10K2 Services, networks, and organizations that provide support across the life span for individuals with learning disabilities.	7: Planning Instruction 7.05 All teachers monitor student progress and incorporate knowledge of student performance across settings into the instructional planning process, using information provided by parents and others in those settings. 7.07 Special education teachers oversee the development of individualized transition plans to guide learners' transitions from preschool to elementary school, middle school to high school, and high school to post-school opportunities. They work within the context of family and community to carry out the education, and sometimes, life goals of students with disabilities. 10: Collaboration, Ethics, and Relationships 10.06 Special education teachers take a life span view of students with disabilities and use their knowledge of disabilities, legislation, special education services, and instructional strategies to ensure implementation of each student's individual education program. In their leadership role, they fill gaps in services for students by advocating for services, consulting with other team members, facilitating team interactions, and finding resources, and collaborating with families.

Sources: Council for Exceptional Children (2005); Interstate New Teacher Assessment and Support Consortium INTASC Special Education Subcommittee (May 2001).

Web Resources

http://www.dec-sped.org/—The Division for Early Childhood (DEC), a division of the Council for Exceptional Children (CEC), is for individuals who work with or on behalf of children with special needs, birth through age 8, and their families.

http://www.cms4schools.com/dcdt/—The Division on Career Development and Transition promotes national and international efforts to improve the quality of and access to career/vocational and transition services, increase the participation of education in career development and transition goals, and influence policies affecting career development and transition services for persons with disabilities.

http://www.naeyc.org/—The National Association for the Education of Young Children is dedicated to improving the well-being of young children birth to 8 years of age.

http://www.ncset.org/topics/ieptransition/default. asp?topic=28—The National Center on Secondary Education and Transition (NCSET) coordinates national resources, offers technical assistance, and disseminates information related to secondary education and transition for youth with disabilities to create opportunities for youth to achieve successful futures.

http://www.nrcld.org/—The National Research Center for Learning Disabilities goal is to help educators, policy makers, and parents understand the complexity and importance of making sound decisions regarding whether a child has a specific learning disability.

http://www.challengingbehavior.org/—The Technical Assistance Center on Social Emotional Intervention for Young Children identifies practices to improve the social–emotional outcomes for young children with, or at risk for, delays or disabilities.

http://www.zerotothree.org/—ZERO TO THREE is a national nonprofit organization that informs, trains, and supports professionals, policy makers, and parents in their efforts to improve the lives of infants and toddlers.

CHAPTER 11

Special Considerations for Families: Postsecondary Students

CHAPTER OUTLINE

OBJECTIVES

After reading this chapter you will

1. Discuss why working with families of postsecondary-aged children often experience new levels of stress as their children age.

2. Identify the benefits and challenges families experience with their adult children with disabilities living at home.

3. List the benefits of community living settings for adults with disabilities.

4. Explain why and how some families experience lack of awareness, lack of adequate preparation, financial barriers, and difficulties with interagency support that affect their family structure and their adult child with disabilities.

5. Describe recommendations, such as problem-solving approaches and futures planning for working with families of postsecondary-aged children.

6. Identify challenges faced by families of children living in residential facilities, such as aging family caregivers, family stress, and the child's desire for change in living placement.

7. Explain recommendations that caregivers and service providers can implement when working with families of children in residential facilities.

INTRODUCTION

Nico is worried. His father has congenital heart failure, and his mother seems to age 10 years every time he sees her. To compound his concern about his parents' health, his adult sister, Adia, has severe multiple disabilities and lives with his aging parents. His father is no longer able to lift Adia out of her wheelchair or bed, and his mother can't do it alone. His parents have secured respite assistance for Adia when she is at home, but it is draining their meager retirement savings.

Nico has to face the very real possibility that his parents will die within the next few years and that his sister will be left without caregivers. He has tried to talk with his parents about planning for Adia's care, but due to their health concerns, he isn't making much progress. Nico is unsure of what to do. On the one hand, he would love for his sister to live with him and his family. On the other hand, he knows that taking care of a family member with severe disabilities can be a full-time job, and he has three school-age children.

Nico needs guidance, resources, and support to assist his parents and Adia while she lives at home. He also needs information and direction on what options, services, and programs are available to him once it is necessary for Adia to move out of his parents' home.

The transition from K–12 education to postsecondary living can create a whirlwind of feelings for families of children with disabilities. On one hand, like parents of children without disabilities, the idea of their child becoming an adult with adult roles is exciting. Going off to college, moving into their first apartment, starting their first job, or building their own families is how most parents imagine life for their children. It is satisfying to watch them apply knowledge they learned from their families and schooling to life outside the family's home. On the other hand, some families view life after high school with apprehension, worry, and in some cases, fear. They no longer have the protections, such as requirements for parent involvement, that existed under Individuals with Disabilities Education Act (IDEA), and they no longer have the same authority. Many experience frustration with the lack of post-secondary resources and supports available for both the family and their child. This often leads family members, particularly mothers, to take on the role of the child's primary caregiver, which can, in turn, lead to higher levels of family stress.

Practitioners working with families of postsecondary children with disabilities must be aware of and understand the unique challenges faced by the family structure and its individual members. Individual factors, such as severity of the disability or family dynamics, should not be used to predict the type of support or services offered to families. Instead, practitioners should use family-centered approaches to identify potential factors that, if not addressed, may lead to increased stress and reduced quality of life for both the family and child.

A variety of interrelated factors predict the successful postsecondary adjustment for individuals with disabilities and their families. How families deal with stress may have the greatest impact on postsecondary adjustment. Those who deal with stress in healthy ways are more likely to have positive adjustment than those families with inadequate copying skills (Sandler & Mistretta, 1998). In addition, families with lower incomes and limited access to community-based support services often struggle more, thus experiencing greater levels of stress and poorer health outcomes for the family members (Caldwell, 2006).

Many would agree that the nature and severity of the disability will inevitably influence the types of challenges faced by families. For example, children with mild learning disabilities will face very different issues than those with intensive medical or behavioral needs even if they both pursue the same postsecondary goals. The effectiveness of school-based transition planning can also have a tremendous impact on the success of the individuals with disabilities and their family's ability to adjust to postschool living. Specifically, families who are informed about the changes in laws, are connected to community supports and agencies, and are equipped with essential skills for postsecondary adjustment may be more likely to experience a seamless transition from school to postsecondary living. Finally, the level of support, from either the family or community, may affect how families and their child deal with difficult and challenges issue. In fact, families who received supports directed at their specific needs experienced decreased caregiver and financial stress, enhanced leisure satisfaction, and increased overall health (Caldwell, 2006).

Decision making about where a transitioning child with disabilities will live is perhaps one of the most difficult issues faced by families. Postsecondary services differ greatly from the entitlement services provided under IDEA. Under IDEA, students with disabilities are entitled to free specialized instruction that is considered necessary for the child to benefit from their education. However, under postsecondary laws, students must be otherwise qualified to participate, and that participation may come at additional costs for the students. The eligibility criteria also change, making some students no longer eligible for the same level of support services they were accustomed to during their K–12 education. To further complicate matters, families of children with disabilities are likely to see an increase in their level of involvement as their child ages, whereas families of young adults without disabilities typically see a reduction. Thus, families may experience less support to meet increasing needs.

Family involvement is a critical component of postschool success for individuals with disabilities. Families help the individual develop positive values, connect them with community and work opportunities, and most important, act as a support system, advocate, and mentor. However, it is important to understand that each family approaches its unique situation differently. Service providers must keep in mind that a one-size-fits-all approach cannot be applied to support families. This chapter provides an overview of special considerations when dealing with families in three common post-secondary situations for individuals with disabilities: coresidency with family, community living, and postsecondary education participation.

SPECIAL CONSIDERATIONS FOR FAMILIES WITH ADULT CHILDREN WITH DISABILITIES LIVING AT HOME

Despite the desire for independent living for individuals with disabilities, Fujiura (1998) found that nearly 60% to 70% of adults with developmental disabilities live with family members. In these cases, parents, and in some cases siblings, often took on the role as the primary caregiver. Supporting families with adult children living at home has changed significantly over the last several decades. In the 1980s and 1990s, Heller (1998) found that most support services were designed to maintain the person in the home. Families were expected to support their child using existing and supplemental income. Respite care and in-home counseling were often provided to help families cope with their new roles although how those services were provided were not at the discretion of the family. Recently, there has been a change in how services are allocated. Supports are now available for individuals to reside in a variety of community-based options, and family members and friends can now be compensated for the caregiving services they provide to their own child. New approaches to supporting families highlight the shift to more family-centered services.

Families choose coresidency for a variety reasons. Some believe the care of their child is a family responsibility (Knox & Bigby, 2007), whereas others may not be aware of alternative living options or available community supports. For example, Chambers, Hughes, and Carter (2004) found that some parents of children with severe disabilities who chose coresidency lacked information about other postschool living options. Families may also select coresidency out of fear for the safety and well-being of their child (Heyman & Huckle, 1993).

Female family members informally and formally provide nearly 80% of long-term care services for family members with disabilities (Doty, Stone, Jackson, & Drabek, 2001). Although some families view managing the care of a child or sibling as part of the "family business" (Knox & Bigby, 2007), many are actually compensated for the work that they do. Doty and Flanagan (2002) identified 139 consumer-directed programs and reported that 80% of them permitted hiring family members to provide care. As individuals with disabilities are living longer, caregiving roles are being transferred to other family members, especially siblings (Jokinen & Brown, 2005). Understanding the perceived benefits and challenges of caring for an adult child at home will better prepare services providers to work with families.

Perceived Benefits

Families often report a range of perceived benefits in caring for an adult child with disabilities in the home. Some found the experience to be particularly rewarding and satisfying (Shearn & Todd, 1997; Taunt & Hastings, 2002). They believed their role in helping their child become an independent adult provided them with a sense of purpose (Rapanaro, Bartu, & Lee, 2008). In addition, parents saw the experience as an opportunity to develop new skills and strengthen relationships with their child and other family members. Although some struggle with how to juggle the demands of parenting, caregiving and other adult responsibilities, the perceived benefits were believed to outweigh the challenges faced by many families (Shearn & Todd, 1997). They believed it helped them grow spirituality and personally, even providing them greater empathy and understanding for families in similar situations.

Although parents reported positive views of their caregiver and parenting relationships with their adult child, Rapanaro and his colleagues (2008) found that service providers are not always sensitive and accepting of family choices. For example, service providers often failed to include family members in decisions about what types of supports the family actually wants and instead made decisions based on a perceived need, not necessarily an actual need. Tennen and Affleck (2002) found that some families interpreted the well-meaning efforts of professionals to encourage families to accept certain supports and services as "an unwelcome attempt to minimize the unique burdens and challenges that need to be overcome" (p. 595). In addition, Todd and Shearn (1996) reported some feel that others do not always value their lives and role as a caregiver.

Perceived Challenges

Despite reporting positive benefits, some families experience a number of challenges or negative feelings related to caring for their adult child at home. Parents have reported feeling a general loss of freedom, sadness and, at times, resentment (Rapanaro et al., 2008). These feelings often result as parents begin reflecting on the differences in their daily and future lives in comparison to their peers, whose adult children have moved away from home. With an adult child who needs constant supervision or care, the ability to be spontaneous and creative with leisure time, considered popular hallmarks of being an "empty nester," is significantly reduced (Shearn & Todd, 1997). Parents cannot devote personal time to other life and career opportunities because of the extent of their parental and caregiving roles.

In addition to feelings of loss, parents may experience increased financial stress and poorer overall health. In fact, Altman, Cooper, and Cunningham (1999) found evidence that caregivers were likely to forgo their own health to continue caring for a family member. Families may also undertake additional financial responsibilities, given the extension of the parental role, resulting in greater costs than families whose children support themselves. Researchers have termed such feelings of loss and constraints related to caregiving as feeling "captive"' in the caregiver role (Todd & Shearn, 1996; Walden, Pistrang, & Joyce, 2000).

Family members serving as the primary caregiver have also reported lower rates of social engagement outside the home, regardless of their age (Seltzer, Krauss, Orsmond, & Vestal, 2000). As a result, families with children with disabilities tend to have smaller networks of supports than families with children without disabilities (Herman & Thompson, 1995). Although some caregivers reported little interest in increasing their social involvement (Todd & Shearn, 1996), others found that this made the caregiver role less satisfying and more stressful. They became less enthusiastic about being involved primarily in the social and recreation life of their child (Shearn & Todd, 1997). Instead, the parents desired to engage in social experiences similar to their peers without children living at home but unfortunately lacked the opportunities to do so.

Some families have reported that the intensity of the child's needs and nature of the disability can predict how families cope and adjust to coresidency with their adult child with a disability. Families with adult children with Down syndrome have generally reported higher levels of life satisfaction and less stress than families with children with other disabling conditions (Hodapp, Ly, Fidler & Ricci, 2001; Hodapp & Urbano, 2007). For example, families with adult children with severe behavior disorders (Shearn & Todd, 1997), autism (Hodapp & Urbano, 2007), and mental illness (Seltzer, Greenberg, Krauss, & Hong, 1997) have reported experiencing higher levels of stress and depression and are more likely to end coresidency sooner. This may attributable to increased attention parents must provide their children, which inevitably reduces personal free time and opportunities to relax and rejuvenate.

Families with Adult Children Living in Community Settings

The independent living movement articulated in the 1970s led to a variety of supports and community living options for individuals with disabilities. It was seen as an alternative to traditional residential living and a way to provide consumers more control over postsecondary living options. This movement was further strengthened by the development and funding of centers for independent living under the Rehabilitation Act of 1973. These support centers continue to provide a variety of consumer-directed services such as personal assistants, transportation, and supported living. Supported living options allow individuals opportunities to lease or own homes or apartments in their own names and then receive support services through separate Medicaid-funding.

The vast majority of individuals with disabilities not cared for in the family home live in some type of supported and nonsupported housing options within the community. Some live in group homes where several people with disabilities reside along with several unrelated caregivers. Other individuals may live in single-family homes with individuals who serve as foster parents. Although the home may include other housemates with disabilities, its purpose is much different than a traditional group home and is often considered a transitional living arrangement. Some communities also offer apartment-like complexes for people with disabilities. Like retirement communities, these complexes provide individuals with disabilities more independent living options, such as individual or shared apartments, while providing the care and support needed for the individual to live independently. With these living arrangements, the agency or family who owns the home or facility typically provides the care.

Although many families continue to select supported living options based on disability labels (e.g., group home for individuals with autism) or access to special services (e.g., availability of 24-hour nurses), individuals with disabilities have increasingly more options for typical residential living. The supported living movement allows individuals with disabilities the opportunity to own their own homes and rent their own apartments while accessing the same level of support. Unlike other community options where the caregiver and home owner are the same, supported living opportunities empower the individual to choose from an array of caregivers and then request that those services be provided in the individuals' personal residence. Despite the significant increases in supported living options over the past several decades (Racino, Walker, O'Connor, & Taylor, 1993), few families are aware of them, and their children with disabilities either remain at home or on waiting lists for other housing options.

Families and adults with disabilities face many challenges in finding community living opportunities. First, it is difficult to obtain affordable housing despite vast networks of state and local housing authorities' development of affordable housing for individuals with low incomes. There are often long waiting lists and even less options for those with less severe disabilities who experience low income due to poor employment outcomes. Second, challenges exist for individuals desiring to build assets and engage in community participation. In the late 1990s and early 2000s several barriers to saving money for home ownership were removed. President Bill Clinton signed into law two pieces of legislation, the Personal Responsibility and Work Opportunities Act of 1996 and the Assets for Independence Act of 1998, which provide dedicated saving accounts for asset building for individuals with low incomes. Although, savings restrictions for Social Security beneficiaries initially prevented many individuals with disabilities from participating in the program, the Social Security Protection Act of 2003 removed many of these barriers. Regardless, these programs continue to remain underutilized unless service providers make efforts to inform families of all the available options.

Families with Adult Children with Disabilities in Postsecondary Education Settings

More and more high school students with disabilities transition into postsecondary education settings, including vocational and career schools, two- and four-year colleges, and universities (Henderson, 2001; Wagner, Cameto, & Newman, 2003). The National Council on Disability (2000) found that as many as 17% of all students attending higher education programs in the United States identify themselves as having a disability—primarily learning disabilities—which is up from less than 3% in the late 1970s (Henderson, 1995). Blackorby and Wagner (1996) reported that within 3 to 5 years following high school graduation, 27% of students with disabilities had attempted postsecondary education. Although this number is significantly higher than attendance rates in the 1970s (Henderson, 1995), the percentage of students with disabilities remains much lower than the 68% of students without disabilities that also attempt postsecondary education.

As access to and participation in postsecondary education increases, families and their children with disabilities face a variety of unique challenges, especially if the child has not been adequately prepared for the transition from school to postschool education settings. As a result, students with disabilities often experience postsecondary outcomes inferior to those of their nondisabled peers (National Council of Disability, 2003). For example although participation rates of students with disabilities are increasing, so is the likelihood they will not finish (Stodden, 2001). Many students struggle with the shift from a relatively passive, structured learning environment to one that requires them to be active in the learning process, divulge information about their disabilities, and self-advocate (Hadley, 2006). Understanding these challenges can prepare service providers to more effectively provide support.

LACK OF AWARENESS.   One of the biggest challenges faced by families and students with disabilities is the misunderstanding between the types of supports and services available. Although most college campuses have offices that support individuals with disabilities, such as the Office of Disability Services or Student Disability Services, these programs expect that students with disabilities are prepared to navigate the system. Unfortunately, parents and students with disabilities are often unaware of the extent to which postsecondary supports differ from supports provided under IDEA. In addition to changes in teacher expectations and class scheduling, parent involvement and roles change significantly. Parents can no longer monitor the progress of their child nor can they work directly with their child's instructors. In addition, families expecting that their child will receive supports in postsecondary education settings may be surprised to learn that although their child was eligible for services under IDEA 2004, they no longer meet the eligibility requirements for Section 504 and ADA in some college and university settings. They may also be surprised to learn that although their child is eligible for accommodations, they are not as extensive as those provided in the K–12 system. Families can experience frustration or become overwhelmed with their inability to navigate through these new requirements.

Service providers can empower families by providing them with sufficient information about their new roles as a parent of a child in postsecondary education settings. Table 11.1 summarizes the differences that families will notice between IDEA 2004 and myriad postsecondary laws that protect individuals with disabilities. Connecting parents

TABLE 11.1	Understanding the major differences in family involvement for individuals with disabilities attending high school and attending postsecondary educations	
	High School	**Postsecondary**
Applicable Laws	IDEA 2004 Section 504 and 508, Rehabilitation Act of 1973.	Americans with Disabilities Act 1990 (ADA), ADA Amendments Act of 2008 (ADAAA) and Section 504 and 508 of the Rehabilitation Act of 1973.
Financial Responsibility	Free public education	Families or students are responsible (e.g., financial aid, scholarships or arranging other types of payment)
Parent Role	Parent or some other adult is considered the student's guardian.	Student is considered his/her own legal guardian, unless parents acquire legal guardianship
Determining Supports and Services	Parents participate with IEP team to determine eligibility, IEP, placement, supports, fundamental accommodations, and services.	No fundamental modifications are required—only accommodations. Students must identify needs and request services. No IEP exists and is not considered sufficient documentation.
Academic Support	Students do homework. Parents support students and encourage them to get their class assignments and homework completed.	Students study. Students are responsible for seeking assistance from the Disability Services Office.
Parent Rights	Access student records, periodic progress reports, and right to request conference at any time.	No access to student records without written consent of their child or progress reports from college staff. Student may sign release forms to allow staff to discuss personal information with whomever he/she chooses.
Advocating	Parents may advocate for their child.	The student must be a self-advocate. Parents are mentors.

to existing agencies within the school and in the community may also help decrease their uncertainty about this new adventure.

LACK OF ADEQUATE PREPARATION.   In addition to lack of knowledge, many families and students are inadequately prepared for involvement in college life. Students often lack advocacy skills, knowledge of how their disability affects their education, efficient strategies for time management and studying, and an understanding of how to negotiate services in postsecondary settings. Although individuals without disabilities may also lack similar skills, individuals with disabilities are more likely to become overwhelmed and drop out of school (Stodden, 2001). Heiman and Precel (2003) found that students with learning disabilities who failed to advocate for themselves had a very difficult time adjusting to college life. Unfortunately, these students may be more likely to become involved in negative aspects of college life, such as drug and alcohol abuse. Students often depend on their families to help them get them back on track. However, when families are ill equipped to support their child, they may experience feelings of helpless and a sense of failure.

FINANCIAL AID BARRIER. Families of students with disabilities often face greater financial costs for secondary education than those without disabilities. They are often responsible for disability-related costs, such as additional academic tutoring or accommodations, not provided through the institution. In addition, students with disabilities often require extended time to complete their degrees, thus increasing the tuition costs. The National Center for Education Statistics (1999) found that only 41% of students had completed their course of study within 5 years. Complicating matters for families is that most are unaware that their financial aid packages can be increased to match their out-of-pocket disability-related expenses, as required by the Higher Education Act.

DIFFICULTIES WITH INTERAGENCY COLLABORATION. Parents and students may also face challenges indirectly related to their postsecondary education experience. For some, the process of navigating the various disability support services can lead to increases in family stress. Unlike their experiences in K–12, the services may be provided by multiple agencies, thus increasing opportunities for fragmented and inconsistent services. In addition, the quality and level of support can vary among postsecondary education settings. Families and students should invest a significant amount of time in learning about the type of services offered and the institution's history in working with outside agencies to support students with disabilities.

Recommendations for Working with Families of Postsecondary Children

Service providers need to acknowledge family choices and use family-focused approaches to identify appropriate ways to support them. As discussed earlier, support services for families are typically designed to alleviate caregiving tasks to give families respite or free time to attend to other adult responsibilities. Although this can be an essential component of support, it does not necessarily help increase the capacity of the family to provide care for their child at home. Service providers should help families address difficult aspects of caregiving by providing them with practical skills and targeted supports. In addition, service providers would benefit families by helping them identify positive aspects or benefits of caregiving as opposed to focusing primarily on challenges or problems. This conceptual shift in how we perceive and respond to parents' needs is necessary if we intend to empower and adequately support them (Herman & Thompson, 1995; Todd & Shearn, 1996). For parents who are satisfied with their caregiving role, it is important that service providers find ways of identifying and sustaining rewards if parental commitment is to be maintained. Several strategies can help services providers work more effectively with families.

PROBLEM-SOLVING APPROACHES. For parents struggling with aspects of coresidency, service providers can use a problem-solving approach to identifying potential problems and assist the caregiver in identifying family-centered solutions to address the issues. The following steps are recommended:

1. Define the problem.
2. Look at potential causes of the problem.
3. Identify potential solutions to the problem.
4. Select the most appropriate solution.

5. Develop an action plan.

6. Monitor the implementation of the action plan.

7. Evaluate the effectiveness.

The first two steps are typically the most difficult part of the process. Service providers and family members can easily misinterpret what the problem and its causes are. Care must be taken to ensure that the actual problem has been identified so that the action plan will result in benefits for the caregiver. Examine the following scenario and think about how the main problem was misinterpreted by the service provider.

In discussions with Sarah, the mother of an adult child with autism, Janie, one of the family's service providers, notices that she is feeling more stressed than usual. Janie has been working with the family for a little over a year and has noticed that Sarah's daughter has become increasingly more aggressive with her parents. She immediately assumes that Sarah is feeling overwhelmed by her inability to control her child's outbursts and that she would benefit from additional in-home support. However, jumping to conclusions, she schedules a meeting with Sarah to work through the problem-solving process. During the meeting, Sarah confirms that she is feeling more stressed than usual. However, she does not necessarily agree with Janie about why. Janie probes Sarah with questions to get at the heart of the problem. Eventually, it becomes clear that Sarah is frustrated with her child's behavior but not for the reasons Janie originally thought. Sarah is more concerned that her daughter's behavior is sign that she is not adequately meeting the needs of her daughter. After further discussion, Sarah concludes that the cause of the problem is likely her limited skills in teaching her daughter new coping skills.

By properly identifying the problem, the two can now determine the best approach to providing Sarah with the skills she needs to assist her daughter.

FUTURES PLANNING.   Futures planning or family-centered planning has a number of features that distinguish it from traditional service planning. First, the focus remains on the individual or family's life, not just the type of services that is needed. Thus, the people involved in the futures planning and the development of the accompanying action plan should be at the discretion of the family. Second, professionals in attendance may act as meeting facilitators or advisors, but they should avoid drawing attention away from the family. Finally, the emphasis of futures planning is on identifying and building on the strengths of the family or individuals. This is a radical shift from traditional service planning, which depends on the identification of individual and family "needs" and "deficits" to select supports and services.

The outcome of futures planning is threefold. First, participants should gain a clear understanding of the family and individual's vision and goals for the future. Second, an action plan should result from the discussion and include information about "who, what, and how" tasks will be completed. Third, the goal is to build the participants' commitment to work together to help move the family and individual closer to their future goals. In some cases, discussions about the types of services and supports needed by the family and individual may occur. Although not required, these discussions may lead to the development of a service plan.

TABLE 11.2	Sample Areas and Guiding Questions for Futures Planning for Adults with Disabilities

Areas	Discussion Topics
Financial Planning	• What are the advantages of transferring financial resources to a trust or directly to the adult child?
	• How will financial resources change in the future?
	• Who will manage the child's resources and assets?
Legal Planning	• Is there a need for guardianship? Are alternatives available?
	• Do family wills reflect current needs of the individual?
	• What will happen in the case of the caregiver's death?
Independent Living	• What are the goals of future living arrangements?
	• What types of supports and services are necessary?
	• How will these change as caregivers become unable to care for the individual?
	• Who will be the primary caregiver?
Transitions	• Who will care for the individual after the death of the primary caregiver?
	• How will the family and the individuals with disabilities prepare for transition in residential placements?

Futures planning general follows four basics steps:

1. Identify family and individual strengths and current situation.
2. Develop a vision for the future—for the both the near and far future.
3. Develop an action plan.
4. Monitor the plan.

Futures planning is seen as an effective way to help families begin thinking about tough topics such as money, death, transitions, and guardianship. Table 11.2 provides a sampling of topic areas along with questions service providers might ask during the futures planning process. Actual topics addressed during the discussions with families will be dependent on the family's current needs and situation. However, service providers should make sure families have at least considered the tough topics listed. The *Family Handbook on Future Planning* (Davis, 2003) is a useful guide for beginning these conversations with families.

CONSUMER DIRECTED SUPPORT. Service providers should not recommend support services before fully understanding the family's view of the situation. Some caregivers reported that many of the stresses they encountered were not directly related to their child but to the difficulties they faced in trying to manage additional parental responsibilities. Caldwell (2006) found that service providers could help caregivers reduce unnecessary stress and improve quality of life by providing consumer-directed supports. He noted that "in its purest and most empowering form, consumer direction provides control of financial resources through cash allowances or individualized budgets" (p. 405). Currently, 22 states provide families with this level of financial assistance to help provide support to family members living at home (Rizzolo, Hemp, & Braddock, 2006). These programs have resulted in fewer out-of-pocket disability expenses, greater access to health care, engagement in more social activities, and greater leisure satisfaction than for caregivers on waiting lists. Service providers should become aware of consumer-directed opportunities in their own state.

EDUCATION AND INFORMATION SHARING.   Probably the most effective thing services providers can do to support families is to equip them with the skills and knowledge needed to advocate for themselves and their family and make informed decisions. For example, providing information on aging to individuals with disabilities and their families can address ongoing concerns about health, health-care access, and future residential transitions (Jokinen & Brown, 2005). In addition, providing families information on all the available community-based options and postsecondary education supports can help families to make decisions appropriate for their situation.

Summary

For parents with children with disabilities in postsecondary education settings, the HEATH Resource Center offers a variety of resources to help ease the transition into college life for individuals with disabilities. The Center provides resources on financial planning and financial aid for individuals with disabilities. In addition, they have designed a variety of educational training modules for families or students on topics ranging from how to work with faculty, legal issues, to living on campus. Service providers may find the *Guidance and Career Counselor's Toolkit* or *Transition Website Directory* to be a useful tool for working with families.

SPECIAL CONSIDERATIONS FOR WORKING WITH FAMILIES WITH CHILDREN WITH DISABILITIES IN RESIDENTIAL SETTINGS

The popularity of residential placements for individuals with disabilities has varied significantly over the last 200 years. Prior to the Civil War, a number of states built residential schools and facilities for individuals who were deaf and blind as well as a handful of special facilities for individuals with mental retardation. These settings were designed to provide specialized education and life skill training. Although the concept of institutions and segregated settings were not widely supported after the Civil War, their numbers increased dramatically until the 1970s (Schopler & Hennike, 1990). By 1969, nearly 190,000 individuals were housed in segregated living facilities, up significantly from the 2,000 in 1900 (Cegelka & Prehm, 1982). Since the 1970s, the number of individuals with disabilities living in segregated residential settings has steadily decreased, particularly in residential settings designed for more than 300 residents (Lakin, Prouty, Polister, & Coucouvanis, 2003). Presently, only 14.3% of all residential service recipients live in settings of 16 or more residents (Prouty, Alba, & Lakin, 2007). Most receive services in settings with six or fewer residents or "community-based" housing options (Lakin et al., 2003). The latter were discussed in more detail in a previous section.

For many, the term *segregated residential setting* conjures up images of large-scale institutions or insane asylums with hundreds of people in white gowns. Despite being portrayed as such in movies and television, it is not an accurate reflection of the types of residential facilities commonly available today. Residential facilities range from apartment-style living where individuals live independently or with roommates while receiving intensive support to hospital-like facilities that provide intensive medical care. These facilities are operated through private, state, or federal funds and can support 16 to over 300 individuals with disabilities. The types of services available often depend on the average age of the residents and the disabilities served. For example, younger students typically receive targeted education and life skill instruction, whereas older residents are more likely to receive support for daily activities and access to adapted leisure activities. The majority of facilities target specific disability types, such as deaf, blind, mental retardation, or psychiatric disabilities.

Medicaid supports two types of residential living options that fall under segregated residential facilities. First, Medicaid provides services in Intermediate Care Facilities for Persons with Mental Retardation (ICFs-MR). ICFs-MR on average house around 15 individuals with mental retardation and other developmental disabilities (Prouty et al., 2007), which is down significantly from the 180+ individuals living in these facilities in the late 1970s. Almost all residents of large state and nonstate residential facilities live in ICFs-MR. In 2007, 90.4% of persons living in large state and nonstate facilities lived in ICF-MR units, and 98.5% of people living in state facilities of 16 or more residents lived in ICF-MR units (Prouty et al., 2007). Second, children and adults who need extensive medical care or who have significant behavioral problems may also end up living in nursing homes or psychiatric hospitals. Although more common in some states versus others (ranges from 5% to 20%), the number of individuals served in nursing homes has decreased steadily (Prouty et al., 2007). Some individuals continue to be served in large institutions (300+ residents); however, more and more participate in smaller state- and non-state-operated facilities as they become available.

Although segregated residential settings are more common for adults with disabilities, some families select residential placements to meet the unique needs, academic or behavioral, for their child with disabilities. Families with children with sensory impairments and severe learning disabilities may consider residential educational placements to ensure that their child receives a free, appropriate education. The deaf and blind have access to nearly 60 state residential school options across 46 states (Deaf Education, 2001). There are also several private residential school options for children with learning disabilities, which may be funded through both private or IDEA funds (Rose & Zirkel, 2007). Although these parents may want their child in specialized residential schools, parents of children with significant behavioral and psychiatric disabilities often choose residential placement as a last resort. Unlike special facilities for individuals with sensory impairments or learning disabilities, the focus is not on improving educational outcomes but on addressing mental health and adaptive skills deficits. Despite the protests of some professionals (e.g., Hammond, 2009), these options are available to families of individuals with disabilities, sometimes at no cost, under the continuum of placements afforded through IDEA. In addition, parents may utilize private insurance, disability benefits, or state programs to provide residential options for children under the age of 18.

Families with Children in Residential Facilities

The movement of a child from home or community living to segregated residential settings is perhaps one of the most difficult times for a family. The family may experience a number of difficult decisions in this process (Alborz, 2003). For example, families may struggle to recognize that a residential setting may be the best option for their child. Aging parents with no other offspring to care for an adult child with disabilities may unintentionally delay planning for long-term care. This may leave the individual in a crisis situation while he or she sits on a waiting list or in temporary care after the death of both parents. In addition, families may also struggle with where their offspring will move. In some cases, available residential facilities may not be located near other family members or available options may not have all the desired supports and services.

In a study conducted by Baker and Blacher (2002), 106 families with a member living in a residential facility reported on three general areas of family functioning: involvement with the child, overall well-being, and their perception of the pros and cons of the placement. Most (90%) concluded that overall the child's placement was beneficial not only for the child, but also for the parents and other family members. Interestingly, involvement and continued levels of family stress varied based on the age of the child. Families with children under age 15 visited more often, but also reported the highest levels of stress and caretaking burden. Shearn and Todd (1997) reported that parents of children in residential facilities were more likely to have service providers call for advice on how to deal with their child's behavior and in some cases actually request the family's help in dealing with a child's outburst. Thus, even though the child was not in the home, many continued to feel the burdens of caregiving (Todd & Shearn, 1996). Families of children in residential settings also experienced lower marital adjustment and saw fewer advantages to the child's placement. On the other hand, families of adult offspring with disabilities who believed out-of-home placement was a normative process of adult living reported adapting well to the placement (Baker & Blacher, 2002).

Families choose residential placement for a variety of reasons. The decision is often made after receiving professional advice, talking with family members, and assessing the needs and desires of the offspring. In retrospect, most families agree that the decision was appropriate for their family and their child. However, making the initial decision to move the child can create tension within a family and cause feelings of guilt and uncertainty, especially among parents. To help families during this challenging time, it is essential that service providers understand what leads many families to consider residential placement for their offspring.

AGING FAMILY CAREGIVERS. Prior to the 1980s, parents typically outlived their child with a disability and thus were able to care for them until their death. However, as access to quality health care improves, individuals with disabilities are living much longer than their parents. The declining health and resources of aging parents often makes it difficult for them to provide the same level of care. As discussed in Chapter 10 and earlier in this chapter, mothers often assume primary caregiver responsibilities. As they become widowed, experience declining health, and experience reduced financial and social support the likelihood of residential placement increases (Lakin et al., 2003; Seltzer et al., 1997). Specifically, Seltzer and his colleagues (2000) found that adults with cognitive disabilities were more likely to be placed in residential settings if their mother was in poor health and older.

In some cases, families fail to plan for their child's residential living situation after their death. They may assume that other family members, such as siblings, will choose to continue caring for the family member with a disability. Unfortunately, this does not always occur. Coresidency between older adults with disabilities and their family member may be unrealistic, especially if other family members have not been prepared for the transition. Unfortunately, these individuals may have no other options except to transition into segregated residential placement.

CHALLENGING BEHAVIORS. Many service providers may assume that individuals with more challenging behaviors are more likely to be placed in residential settings. However, the number of challenging behaviors has not been found to predict an individual's move to a segregated residential setting (Miltiades & Pruchno, 2001). Instead, research suggests that other factors, such as the child injuring a family member or a family's inability to manage the behavior, are more predictive. In other words, families who believed they were able to adequately deal with the behavior were less likely to consider residential placement. However, a family's perception of this may change over time, and service providers should pay careful attention to indicators that this is the case. For example, Alborz (2003) found that the chronic nature of some challenging behaviors can lead families to consider residential placement. In addition, families who believed the challenging behaviors negatively affected their child with a disability (e.g., stressed the child) were more likely to consider out-of-home placement.

Families of children, primarily males, under the age of 18 with severe behavior and psychiatric problems are more likely to consider residential placements at some point in time (Seltzer et al., 2000). These placements, which are usually temporary, often result from a crisis in the home, such as an uncontrollable rage, physical aggression, or destruction of property. During the child's time in the residential placement, service providers typically work with the family and the child to ensure a successful transition back to the community or the home. Unfortunately, families may experience this transition several times before the child and family can adequately maintain appropriate behavior. Alborz (2003) found that parents of children who exhibited high levels of challenging behavior in the home experienced increased levels of family stress, which made it more difficult to cope with daily life. Parents expressed concern about the well-being of both the child with a disability and other family members at home, such as younger siblings. Service providers must provide the family with the skills to adequately support their child as they transition back home. This can sometimes be a challenge soon after the child transitions to the residential setting because families may still be coping with the events that led to the placement.

FAMILY STRESS. Although not as common, some families may consider residential placement when the child's presence in the home causes extreme levels of family stress. As mention previously, challenging behaviors can result in increased stress. However, families may experience stress for other reasons. First, families may feel that they are not equipped to address the specialized needs of their child. They may feel overwhelmed with managing the child's care while also caring for other children in the home and taking care of other adult responsibilities. Second, caring for a child with disabilities at home can lead to family and marital stresses, which result from decreased attention to other family members. Siblings may report the child "hogs" their parent's attention or spouses may feel as though they are second to the needs of the child (Alborz, 2003). Third, some parents have reported feeling completely exhausted and worn out after years of providing constant, intensive care for their child in the home. Some blame limited or reduced services that failed to provide the respite and support the family needed to maintain the child at home (Alborz, 2003). Although they did not want to consider alternative placement, these families felt there were no other options.

Although the decision was difficult, mothers whose child moved out of the home reported a significant reduction in personal and family stress (Krauss, Seltzer, & Jacobson, 2005). With the help of different service providers, they were able to readjust to the new living situation and maintain ongoing, positive contact with their child. Mothers also reported feeling less physical stress and more free time. Despite the positive outcomes, mothers continued to worry about their child's future although the stress was considered manageable (Krauss et al., 2005).

CHILD'S DESIRE FOR CHANGE OF PLACEMENT.   In some cases, the move to a residential facility is the positive choice made by both the individual with disabilities and the family. The move can be considered a sign of increased independence and a way to engage in normal adult living (Alborz, 2003). Parental well-being and satisfaction is often connected to their child leaving home (Seltzer et al., 1997). Parents want their child to lead a more "normal" lifestyle for their age and end dependence on them. Many residential settings now offer intensive levels of care while allowing residents to engage in adult activities, such as leisure, dating, and independent living. Some individuals with disabilities, particularly those with cognitive disabilities, reported living with their family as boring and undesirable (Alborz, 2003). They preferred the semistructured lifestyle offered by the residential setting. For some school-age individuals with visual impairments, residential schools are preferred as they believe the public school and community are ill equipped to meet their specialized needs (Hammond, 2009).

In some cases, aging parents may consult with the child living at home about transitioning to a residential setting. They may agree that moving to a residential setting would result in less stress for the child (Alborz, 2003). Imagine losing your parents and your home on top of dealing with new caregivers simultaneously. The conscious decision to proactively plan for an inevitable transition can help a child adjust to a new living arrangement and reduce worry among family members.

Recommendations for Service Providers

The needs of families who choose residential living for a child with disabilities will vary based on several factors. As mentioned earlier in this section, families who are considering residential placement will have different service and informational needs than families with a child currently living in residential settings. Families who view residential options positively will likely need less support than those who view it as a last resort. In addition, families considering placement for a child will likely have different concerns than a family with an adult with disabilities.

Families who are considering residential placement for their child may need support in assessing their readiness and preparation for the move. They may need information on the types of residential living options available, the pros and cons for each, and how to transition the child into the new living arrangement. Family-centered interviews can assist service providers in understanding the family's choice for residential placement, identifying resource and support needs, and determining next steps. The following questions may help service providers start the conversation with families considering residential placement and begin to gain a better perspective of the family's situation and perspective of the placement.

- What would be an ideal placement for your child?
- How do you and other family members feel about [child's name] placement in a residential facility?
- What are the most important features of a residential placement options for your child?
- What are some of your concerns about this placement?
- How do you feel this move will affect different family members and the individuals with disabilities

Service providers should pay particular attention to the needs of families who are considering residential placement after being the primary caregiver. This transition can upset the family dynamic and cause increased levels of stress, particularly for mothers. The family-centered approach can assist service providers in addressing the needs of members of the family, and not just individual (see Figure 11.1).

Families with a child already receiving support through a residential setting will likely need support based on very different factors. Those families with children in specialized residential schools are more likely to need support in helping their child transition back into the home or community environment. For example, children who have been living in residential placements designed specifically for individuals with visual impairments often struggle with adjusting to more general settings. Oddo and Sitlington (2002) surveyed graduates of a residential school for the blind and found that although employment outcomes had improved, only 20% were prepared for independent living. In fact, nearly half (43%) required supervised living arrangements after graduation. Families may experience increased levels of stress when they learn that their child is struggling to adjust and they are unprepared to assist in the adjustment.

Families with children in temporary residential settings (e.g., 6 months, 1 year) as the result of a crisis may have additional needs. When children with severe behavioral and psychiatric problems are removed from the home, families typically experience a shift in the overall family level of stress and family functioning. Families have reported that one of the most important things service providers can do is to understand the family's circumstances and the incredible struggles that lead up to the placement (de Boer, Cameron, & Frensch, 2007). This understanding can lead to more targeted family-centered supports and services to help them positively adjust to life when the child is out of the home and then eventually life with the child back in the home. Many families also reported that feeling welcomed and included in their child's residential living arrangement helped ease concern and led to positive changes in their relationship with their child (de Boer at al., 2007). Service providers' biggest challenge, though, may be assisting families with the transition of the child from a residential living setting back to the family home. Unlike many families with children transitioning from educational residential placements, families may experience increased levels of apprehension and concern over the child's move. They may remember the struggles prior to the placement and believe that things will continue once the child moves back home. Service providers can assist by maintaining regular contact with family members and ensuring that they have additional respite and support during the transition as needed (de Boer et al., 2007).

The Walkers have been carrying for Jake, their 47-year-old offspring with significant cognitive disabilities, in the home since birth. Although Jake does not engage in any negative behaviors, he needs extensive support for all his daily living activities and requires intensive medical support. His parents are also approaching their 80s and are finding it more and more difficult to care for Jake, even with the support provided by numerous state and local programs. Jake appears to be getting restless with his current living situation. His parents are unable to drive him around, and his home is not served by any community transportation options.

The Walkers are beginning to worry about the future of their child. They contacted one of their service providers for information on other living options. The service provider used a person-centered approach to identify the long-term vision of the Walker family. Once their vision for Jake's future was clear, she conducted a thorough assessment of Jake's daily care and medical needs as well as his current level of independent functioning. The service provider provides the family with information on a variety of living options, and the family discusses each with Jake and other family members.

After making several visits to potential residential and community-based living options and talking with staff, Jake and his family decide on Greystone, an assisted-living facility for individuals with disabilities. Jake seems happy with the daily leisure activities available and the idea of living with other peers, instead of his parents. Although the Walkers would prefer that Jake remain at home, they understand that Jake wants a change of placement and that they are not able to meet all his needs. Greystone appears to be a great option for Jake. Not only does he like the facility, but Greystone is also equipped to meet Jake's extensive medical and daily living needs while providing him with a more normative adult experience. The facility is also close to the Walkers and other family members who will maintain regular contact with Jake after his parents pass.

The service provider understands that the transition will not be easy for the family. The Walkers' daily life has centered around Jake and his care for nearly a half century. In addition, Jake has been with his family nearly every day of his life and may not adjust well to new caretakers. The service provider and staff at the residential facility work with the family to develop and implement a transition plan. The goal is for Jake to begin living full time in the facility in 4 to 6 weeks. The team decides that each week Jake will spend more and more time at the facility until he is comfortable in his new residence. The service provider is worried that even with the transition plan, Mrs. Walker may have a difficult time with the move. On several occasions, Mrs. Walker has expressed that she is disappointed that she cannot care for Jake and is concerned that her friends might see not see her as a good mother. The service provider and staff at Greystone work with Mrs. Walker to identify potential support services for her. Greystone staff connect Mrs. Walker with several families of other residents at the facility. The service provider also agrees to meet regularly with the family throughout the transition process to make sure their needs are also being addressed.

FIGURE 11.1 Jake's Transition to a Care Facility

Families with adult children with disabilities living permanently in residential settings will likely need less informational support. However, they may continue to need emotional and family support, particularly those who once served as the primary caregiver. Many older families may remember the negative stereotypes associated with institutional- and disability-based residential living. In the 1950s and 1960s, families were often considered the cause of a child's behavioral and psychiatric problems and were demoralized as a result (Schopler & Hennike, 1990). Children were often moved to specialized residential settings, and parents were rarely involved in their child's care or daily life. Some family caregivers may feel that their failure to adequately care for their child is reflected by the child's need for residential placement. These feeling can be exasperated by service providers who do not adequately support a family's decisions to choose these types of residential placements. Although service providers may choose to provide families with information about alternative living arrangements, they must support the family and child's choice.

Summary

Professionals' view of the parent role in residential placement has changed. Once viewed as the cause of the child's problem, parents are now seen as collaborators in the care process. Service providers can improve the effectiveness of this collaboration by engaging families in family-centered planning regarding selecting the appropriate living arrangement for their child, appropriate resources and supports, and future planning. Families should be encouraged to maintain regular contact while the child is living in residential settings. Although contact is more frequent for those with younger children, families generally maintain regular contact with their offspring. Seltzer and his colleagues (2000) reported that nearly 94% of families of individuals with cognitive disabilities and 87% of families of individuals with psychiatric disabilities called or visited as least once a week. When families are actively involved, their offspring often experiences fewer behavior problems and increased quality of life, and the family experiences greater satisfaction with the placement (de Boer et al., 2007).

Summary

- Working with families of students with special needs in postsecondary settings, including those in residential settings, can be challenging.
- Practitioners working with families of postsecondary children with disabilities must be aware of and understand the unique challenges faced by the families.
- Families will face a new set of challenges as their children transition to postsecondary settings; practitioners will needs the skills and tools to assist families.
- Planning for the future is often difficult for parents and guardians, but is an effective way to help families begin thinking about tough topics such as money, death, transitions, and guardianship.

Linking Standards to Chapter Content

After reading this chapter, you should be able to link basic knowledge and skills described in the CEC Standards and INTASC Principles with information provided in this text. Table 11.3, Linking CEC Standards and INTASC Principles to Major Chapter Topics gives examples of how they can be applied to each major section of the chapter.

TABLE 11.3	Linking CEC Standards and INTASC Principles to Major Chapter Topics	
Major Chapter Headings	**CEC Knowledge and Skill Core Standard and Associated Subcategories**	**INTASC Core Principle and Associated Special Education Subcategories**
Special Considerations for Families with Adult Children with Disabilities Living at Home Perceived Benefits Perceived Challenges Families with Adult Children Living in Community Settings Families with Adult Children with Disabilities in Postsecondary education settings Recommendations for Working with Families of Postsecondary-Aged Children Special Consideration for Working with Families with Children with Disabilities in Residential Settings Recommendations for Service Providers Summary	10: Collaboration BD10K2 Parent education programs and behavior management guides that address severe behavioral problems and facilitate communication for individuals with emotional/behavioral disorders. DH10S2 Provide families with knowledge, skills, and support to make choices regarding communication modes/philosophies and educational options across the lifespan. VI10S1 Help families and other team members understand the impact of a visual impairment on learning and experience.	10: Collaboration, Ethics, and Relationships 10.04 All teachers accept families as full partners in planning appropriate instruction and services for students with disabilities and provide meaningful opportunities for them to participate as partners in their children's instructional programs in the life of the school. They demonstrate sensitivity to differences in family structures and social economic, and cultural backgrounds of students with disabilities. They communicate with families in ways that honor families' beliefs and practices and seek to promote thee family's confidence and competencies furthering their child's development and learning. In addition, teachers understand the functions of agencies and organization within the larger community and work with other professionals to help families access resourses that facilitate their participation in their child's education. 10.09 Special education teachers collaborate with families and with school and community personnel to include students with disabilities in a range of instructional environments in the school and community. 10.10 Special education teachers understand the impact that having a child with a disability may have on family roles and functioning at different points in the life cycle of a family. They understand the implications of a variety of different approaches to family involvement and parent–professional partnerships and use this knowledge to facilitate families' participation and involvement in the instructional program.

Sources: Council for Exceptional Children (2005); Interstate New Teacher Assessment and Support Consortium INTASC Special Education Subcommittee (May 2001).

Web Resources

http://www.childrensdefense.org/—The Children's Defense Fund is the leading national proponent of policies and programs that provide children with the resources they need to succeed.

www.DisabilityInfo.gov/—The Disability Info Web site provides quick and easy access to comprehensive information about disability programs, services, laws, and benefits.

http://www.ncd.gov/newsroom/publications/2003/ education.htm—National Council on Disability is a federal agency designed to support individuals with disabilities, regardless of the nature or severity of the disability and to empower individuals with disabilities to achieve economic self-sufficiency, independent living, and inclusion and integration into all aspects of society.

http://www.ncset.org/topics/ieptransition/default. asp?topic=28—The National Center on Secondary Education and Transition (NCSET) coordinates national resources, offers technical assistance, and disseminates information related to secondary education and transition for youth with disabilities to create opportunities for youth to achieve successful futures.

http://ici2.umn.edu/ntn/pub/briefs/tplanning.html—The National Transition Network is designed to provide technical information and support to individuals with disabilities and their families on transition.

CHAPTER 12

Family Voices

OBJECTIVES

After reading this chapter you will

1. Understand parents' and sibling's perspectives about having a child with a disability in the family

2. Discuss how parents must advocate for their children's right to an education.

3. Identify ways that cultural and religious beliefs influence parents' decisions about their children.

4. Explain how language barriers can negatively affect a child's (and family's) right to appropriate special education services.

5. Describe ways that parents can change and improve the special education process and system for their children and others.

INTRODUCTION

This chapter is designed to provide you a perspective of what it's like to live with a child with a disability. Each section has been written or contributed by a person who has a family member with a disability. One "family voice" was cowritten by a person with a disability and his mother. An applications and considerations section follows each "family voice" and is designed to link what you've learned throughout the textbook to an actual family.

A FAMILY'S VOICE BY KAROLYN KING-PEERY MS

Today has been the saddest day of my life. Today we learned that Matthew is retarded. We know very little at this time. I feel numb. Our future is so changed. It is hard to know what to express. All I do know is that I love and adore my Mattie! I am so glad he is part of my life!—Journal entry 11/21/1987.

If it takes a village to raise a child, what does it take to raise a child with disabilities? It takes a mother, a father, siblings, extended family, friends, a town, a school district, a children's hospital, and a nation with laws against discrimination that provide legal rights to those with disabilities.

My family moved to a rural community when I was 12 years old. I graduated from the one community high school with high honors and attended a private local university. I was internally driven to complete my degree as quickly as possible, graduating before I turned 21. I began teaching second grade in my home district.

My husband's family had lived for generations in the same small town. They knew everyone in town. We attended the same high school. He was the quarterback of the football team, involved in student government, and graduated with high honors. He attended the same private university. We didn't date until years later but fell in love quickly and married within a year. People would often stop us and comment that there was something special about us. Perhaps they could feel the love we had for each other simply by looking at us. We bought our first home up the street from Bart's parents and just a few blocks from a small elementary school. Bart taught at the same high school we graduated from and coached football.

While expecting our second son, I remember sitting in the kitchen talking to Mom while she was loading the dishwasher. Something didn't seem right. I told her that I felt like something was wrong with my baby. She told me that all mothers are worried about their babies. I told her this was different. I had worried about my first child but not like this. Somehow I knew things were different.

It was a Saturday morning when we walked into the doctor's office. The nurse took my husband, Matthew (our new baby), and me to the doctor's office. We sat there and waited for the doctor to come in. The doctor finally came. He hung up his coat and sat by me. He began to talk. He told us that Matthew had the 5p–syndrome, or cri-du-chat syndrome, a severe form of mental retardation. We got in the car and started to drive home. I kept turning and looking at Matthew to see if in some small visible way he might have changed. Matthew was still my beautiful little boy with thick white blond hair and fine features. Matthew still looked the same but our whole world looked different. Bart and I cried as we drove home.

We decided that when we got home we would immediately tell our parents and siblings what we had learned. We were still proud to be Matthew's parents. But we also knew that we wanted and needed their support. Each family member reacted differently. Matthew was born on my younger brother's birthday. Soon my brother was standing at the door with a bundle of yellow balloons for Matthew. Matthew loved balloons, and my brother loved Matthew.

I knew Matthew would need support services as soon as I could find them. I opened the phone book and began calling agencies. Our doctor had told us about a program his son with Down syndrome had participated in. Soon Matthew began preschool. I flew to Philadelphia to meet with a geneticist that studied the 5p–syndrome, trying to learn everything I could to best help Matthew.

Matthew had speech therapy, occupational therapy, preschool, horseback therapy, and swimming. Each specialist, teacher, and therapist helped Matthew learn new skills, each making a difference in his life.

Soon Matthew was 5. Our district provided two special education options, a special education kindergarten 20 minutes away, or a special education school that would require Matthew to be on a bus for two hours a day. Our neighborhood school had an excellent kindergarten teacher, I had taught with her before I stayed at home with my young boys. Under the law, I knew that Matthew had the right to participate in the least restrictive educational environment. I wanted Matthew at our neighborhood school with a great teacher. My last principal and Bart's fifth-grade teacher was now the school district's new special education supervisor. With his help, Matthew began kindergarten at our neighborhood school.

Matthew now had the chance to include nondisabled peers in his life. A group of children, starting as peer tutors, became his friends. Matthew learned from them, and they learned from him. In fifth grade one girl asked Matthew to run as co-school president, putting his name and picture on her poster. Children came to our house to play. Still others invited him to their homes to play. He went to birthday parties and played community soccer, basketball, and T-ball on teams with these friends.

There were times when some teachers, therapists, and children did not accept Matthew, or see him as a child rather than disability. Fortunately, others would open their hearts and take their places. I learned that some people needed to be shown and taught how to work with Matthew and others with disabilities, that this skill didn't always come naturally. I learned that if I came to meetings with the attitude of collaboration rather than animosity, Matthew received the services he needed. It also helped that Matthew had his mom, dad, grandma, aunts, uncles, and close friends of the family that taught at each of the schools he attended.

Matthew walked across the stage to his father, now an assistant principal, with his cousin by his side, and with his graduating class. He still attends sport events at the high school with his dad, has crushes on the cheerleaders, and gets specialty team jerseys with his favorite star senior's number for each season. People in town know him, accept him, see his many strengths, and know what interests they have in common. Matthew is more than just a disability, he is someone that has worked hard and has learned from those that have worked hard to teach him.

It has now been nearly 21 years since that sad Saturday. We feel so grateful for all those that helped us raise Matthew and have made his life meaningful and sweet. I love and adore my Matthew! I am so glad he is part of my life!

Applications and Considerations

1. Karolyn gives an overview of her background and education before discussing her son Matthew. How do you think these influenced her ability to secure appropriate services and placements for Matthew?

2. How did Karolyn and Matthew's extended family play a role in his education? What types of support did they provide?

3. At the time Matthew was born, IDEA did not encompass young children with special needs, but Karolyn had a background in education and knew immediately that her son would need early intervention type supports. Reflect on what you read in Chapter 10. What resources are available to families who have infants with disabilities? What supports are in place to ensure families learn about and have access to these services?

4. Karolyn states: "I learned that if I came to meetings with the attitude of collaboration rather than animosity, Matthew received the services he needed." This would also apply to teachers and other school personnel. Think about what you read in Chapter 4; as a new teacher, what strategies would you use to ensure all members of the IEP team supported collaboration?

5. Do you think living in a small town made a difference in the education that Matthew received? Would Karolyn have been so successful in her advocacy for Matthew if they lived in a large town with a large school district?

6. Do a Google search on cri-du-chat syndrome. In Chapter 11, you read about some postsecondary options. What types of postsecondary options do you think are available to Matthew and Karolyn?

A FAMILY'S VOICE BY CLAIRE LYNOUGH TREDWELL, PhD—OUR JOURNEY TOGETHER

Claire has a PhD in special education and is director of a fully inclusive early childhood center. She has been in the field of education for most of her adult life. Claire and her husband, Glenn, are powerful advocates for families of children with disabilities and have been instrumental in changing special education practice and policy in their community and state.

Stephanie Lauren is a remarkable young woman. She is caring, friendly, passionate about country music, and a college graduate with an A.S. degree in Medical Office Administration. Her struggle to find full-time employment and live independently is similar to many young adults in the United States today. Her incredible strong will has supported her survival through more than two dozen surgeries associated with her disability, spina bifida. It has taught our family the virtue of patience, the art of perseverance, and the sustenance of hope.

Hearing that our precious new baby would have a limited life span, possible brain damage, and severe physical impairment sent my husband, Glenn, and myself into a whirlwind of emotions and worry about our ability as parents to care for a child with critical special needs. In the 1980s, available multidisciplinary services and resources were limited and inadequate. Lengthy and numerous out-of-state visits for medical care became a way of life. Our financial resources were depleted quickly in the first few years, and we recognized the overwhelming fact that our lives would have to change in order for us to make informed decisions.

We turned to the Spina Bifida Association of America and researchers in the field for accurate information to begin networking with others. Consequently, we founded the Spina Bifida Association of Nevada and the Spinal Defects Clinic. Additional families and professionals joined our journey, and together we ventured through myriad medical, legal, and educational issues that faced our children in the 1980s and 1990s. "Inclusion" was our motto during a time when families were pioneering for their children's rights in general education classrooms. Stephanie deserved to be educated in her neighborhood school with her friends, not segregated into a special class or school for children with physical disabilities. Through hard work, we were able to achieve this goal. I was an early childhood educator for more than 10 years at that time, and our family expanded with the birth of our son, Jonathan, who was born very healthy.

Families who had children with disabilities began contacting us for support and guidance through initial medical and educational plans. "Collaboration" was announced by professionals in the medical and educational arena, but all too often, ended in powerful submission of the family to a preconceived plan with little value placed on the family's wants and needs. Achieving a quality of life for Stephanie and others born with disabilities took constant deliberation mixed with patience and strong direction. Building public awareness, training and collaborating with professionals, and positively supporting the family unit evolved into a way of life for our entire family. The important message we continue to send to families is to have a mission and to have each member acknowledged for one small moment of success on their journey together. "Never doubt that a small group of thoughtful, committed citizens can change the world; indeed, it is the only thing that ever has" (Margaret Mead, American anthropologist).

Applications and Considerations

1. Consider how Claire advocated for her daughter's rights and for persons with disabilities in general. What can you infer from her story about the types of services and programs that were available for Stephanie when she entered school?
2. Chapters 2 and 3 of this text address the roles of families. What are some of the roles that Claire and her husband assumed to ensure an appropriate education for their daughter?
3. How do you think the addition of a brother affected Stephanie's and her parents' lives? Consider the sibling discussion in Chapters 2 and 3 and think about how Stephanie's disability and needs may have affected her brother, Jonathan.
4. Claire mentions collaboration in her discussion. Do you think collaborative practices have changed, or do you think families still submit to the will of professionals?
5. Chapter 4 focuses on collaboration and communication. Think about some of the barriers you read about and consider how you can apply strategies to help families similar to Claire's who are in need of services.
6. As a (future) teacher, what resources may be available to you that you could share with families whose financial resources are affected by having a child with a disability?

A FAMILY'S VOICE BY RAMON

Ramon is a successful restaurant manager who speaks with intelligible but broken English. His ex-wife is a homemaker who speaks almost no English. Their son, Jonathan, the youngest of three, has a language disability and speaks only English. Ramon shared his experiences and frustrations about Jonathan's special education program and teachers.

Jonathan was diagnosed with aphasia in second grade. We didn't know what aphasia was. Nobody explained it to us. Even if they explained it, in our short English, it was not comprehended. When Jonathan was put in special education; we went through endless meetings of what to do, what not to do, and how to help him. But at the end of the day, nothing was getting done, and Jonathan's learning and life were suffering.

The problem with the Latino community is that we are misinformed. We come to this country to better ourselves, and we find out that yes, we work hard and there are better roofs and food, but the system is still hard to navigate. It's like trying to cover the sun with your thumb. It's not effective. We need someone to be with us and help us understand. It is so horrible to see how the school district tried to deny us information. They need to know it's not about saving one person; it's a matter of saving the next 10. If Jonathan gets an education, it means his kids will get an education.

What normal people like us need is not a big presentation, we need people to come with us on a more personal basis to show the district that we have someone on our side who knows what they are talking about. Just because school personnel are in a higher position, they think they are entitled. Guess what? I worked hard to become an American citizen, and I have earned certain rights. Why should I allow someone with that feeling of entitlement to take certain things away from my son and cripple the education of Jonathan? If you want something, you need to keep talking about what you want. I kept talking about what we wanted for Jonathan, but the district wasn't listening. Finally, a neighbor, who was a special education professor, was able to listen to our family's needs and help the district understand what we wanted for him.

In the beginning the district offered Jonathan nothing, all through school and even into high school he could not read. Our neighbor was an English speaker, and she went to mediation with us and helped us understand what they were saying and what they were offering. We were lucky that we had all his records to share at mediation. Most Latino families wouldn't save things like that because of a lack of communication and lack of awareness. We come from countries where we respect the word of the teacher. We trust people that are making decisions.

We ultimately got more assistance, and 1 year later, we have the scores that show that with the intensive help, Jonathan's reading finally improved. Without our friend who knew the system, we would not have gotten this help and may not have known to go through mediation or known what to do at all. The district did not want to deal with the problem, but our neighbor showed us that that was not the last door to be opened, that there were other doors to open to get what we needed for Jonathan.

What can teachers do to help parents? The solution to this is to teach the parents. Teach us like 2-year olds if you have to. Make sure we understand. Be there for us.

Applications and Considerations

1. As you read Ramon's and Jonathan's story what were some of the cultural and linguistic concerns that arose? Think back to Chapters 5 and 6 and reflect on the barriers that Ramon faced and the strategies that you could use to help Ramon overcome those barriers.

2. How did Ramon's and his wife's limited use of spoken English affect the special education services that their son received?

3. Do you think that parents and families whose primary language is not English are at a disadvantage when it comes to learning about and understanding special education services that are available in the United Stated?

4. Think about what you read in Chapters 1, 7, and 8. What are some of the strategies that you can employ to ensure that all families understand the special education system and their rights? What could you do to ensure that Jonathan (and his family) received appropriate special education services?

5. Think about this statement made by Ramon: "What normal people like us need is not a big presentation, we need people to come with us on a more personal basis to show the district that we have someone on our side who knows what they are talking about." Brainstorm with classmates and describe three different ways that information/materials could be presented to families with a more personal touch.

6. Consider what you read in Chapters 5 and 6. How can you apply what you've learned about cultural differences and cultural competence when working with families with limited English?

A FAMILY'S VOICE BY ANGELA QUIDILEG, MEd—LIFE EXPERIENCE AND MY CULTURE

Angela recently earned her MEd in special education with an emphasis in early intervention and early childhood special education. Her family is second-generation American, and she often feels like she is caught between two cultures. She and her husband have two children.

Family Roles

I recently read in a textbook that I was using for a course in my master's degree program that the survival rate of low-birth-weight infants has increased to more than 90%. To this date more and more infants with low birth weight are given an optimal chance of survival due to technology. Experiencing this situation myself was a very traumatic experience. My twins were born prematurely and weighed very little at birth. They were immediately placed in the neonatal intensive care unit. This occurred with a lot of mixed feelings along especially for a first-time mom. Our family was faced with a choice to continue intensive care intervention or to discontinue intensive care intervention.

Many thoughts ran through my mind that day. First, I was not in a position to make this decision for my husband and myself. Second, I was asked, but did not have the ability or the knowledge to make this decision for the family. Third, I attempted to foresee the quality of life for my child's life. My background was in education, so I knew my children might have disabilities if I continued the intervention. Fourth, it was difficult to watch my children go through the pain and suffering just to survive and breathe on their own. This was a complex decision to make in one day. I chose not to continue intensive care intervention. It was not the best decision of my life.

Fortunately, my husband had the ability to step in, talk with me, and make the decision in the best interest of our family. It was made clear by my husband that we would continue intensive care intervention to the fullest capacity. I was so very glad that he was able to make the decision. I once read that parents are the legitimate surrogate decision makers for their children, and they should be granted broad discretion in decisions about the health care of their children, including declining, continuing, limiting, and discontinuing treatment, whether life sustaining or not. I'm fortunate that the doctors took time to talk not only with me, but also with my husband several times. They understood that we wanted our babies to live, but that we had been unprepared to be the ones to make that decision.

Culture

My family is of Philippine descent. Within our culture we rely on family support and religious beliefs. While I was growing up, and even as an adult, my family preferred not to discuss family medical issues and kept them hidden from outsiders and other family members. It was considered taboo to discuss family issues outside the immediate family and home. It seemed like illnesses, dysfunctions, disabilities, and diseases were rarely talked about, and never outside the immediate family. We were, however, grounded in the belief that we would and could accept whatever illness, disability, or incident came our way.

We are religious people by nature. *Bahala na* involves accepting whatever comes and having faith in the higher power. It also includes a belief in the supernatural and spirits. Prayer was very crucial during the time my babies were in the intensive care unit. At one point, I felt that the Gods were punishing our family. Prayer had given us hope, understanding, and a time of meditation but had also let me down and allowed my babies to be born too soon. My children are now in preschool and will soon begin kindergarten. Both my daughter and my son have disabilities. I couldn't love them more. I believe the strength of my religious and spiritual beliefs, our strongly rooted family, and the compromise to rely on modern medicine gave us the strength to get past the initial hurdles and upheaval that surrounded my children's birth.

Applications and Considerations

1. Angela discusses the difficult decision of whether to continue life support for her premature twins or whether to stop the intervention. In Chapter 9 you read about ethical practices in education. What ethical dilemma was Angela given by the doctors?
2. How did Angela's family values and culture affect her decisions about her twins' care? What were some of the conflicts that arose for Angela?
3. Think about some of the strategies you read about relating to culture and ethics in Chapters 5, 6, and 9. How would you apply them to Angela's situation?
4. Angela discusses her family's strong religious beliefs as well as their belief in the supernatural and spirits. How would you work to integrate her beliefs in the power of prayer with practical services for her children?

5. In Chapter 10 you read about special considerations for working with very young children with disabilities. What are some of the strategies that you learned about that could be used to ensure that Angela could make informed choices about special education services for her children?

6. Angela discussed "Bahala na"—the acceptance of whatever comes and faith in the higher power. How might this affect her decisions about special education services for her twins?

A FAMILY'S VOICE BY ELIZABETH AND MICHAEL FERRO

Michael is an 18-year-old young man with cerebral palsy. He is in his senior year of high school and is looking forward to attending college. Elizabeth, his grandmother, has had custody of Michael since he was an infant.

I still remember that day so many years ago. It was my first IEP meeting. Michael was entering kindergarten, and the school district agreed to allow Michael to attend his home school. I was so excited. I remember thinking that "this was going to be easy." I walked out of the meeting and my friend, Mrs. Wurst, said, it's not going to happen. I remember thinking, yes it is, they agreed to send Michael to Beatty Elementary School.

Boy was I wrong. About two weeks before school started I received a letter in the mail from the school district. It said that they, the school district, held a meeting and adjusted Michael's IEP. The letter included an ADA paragraph about accessibility and that all schools did not have to be accessible, and Michael could attend a school within a reasonable distance. As a result, he was going to attend Edwards Elementary School instead of Beatty. I couldn't believe it. Attendance at Edwards meant that Michael, a kindergartener, must spend two hours on the bus in order to get to school and two hours on the bus to come home. Mind you, kindergarten was only a half-day program in those days. He only went to school for two and one-half hours a day. I called the superintendent's office to find out what was going on, but I never heard from them. I knew Michael needed to attend school, so I sent him to Edwards. Luckily, my mother lived down the street from Edwards, and I didn't have to be at work until 9:00 a.m. So, I was able to take Michael to school in the morning; he went to my mother's house after school.

Michael attended Edwards for first and second grade. It took two years to convince the school district that the best thing for Michael would be attendance at his home school. The principal at Beatty attended all IEP meetings and explained that she was concerned about Michael's safety. Her reasons included statements, such as the floors are slippery in winter, there are steps Michael needs to use to get to the gym, and the upper elementary classrooms in the school are located upstairs. I understood her concerns about the slippery floors, but the floors were just as slippery at Edwards. I talked with Michael's physical therapist, who said that climbing stairs would be good for Michael and that he should use the stairs as a form of therapy. Again, I thanked the principal for her concerns, told her that I didn't agree, and that I was only looking out for

Michael's best interests. I wanted him to attend school with his neighborhood friends. I even asked the physical therapist to write a letter stating that Michael would use the stairs during physical therapy. I tried everything but with no avail. Finally, I requested a due process hearing. I spoke with a lawyer, who explained the process to me. The superintendent called the day before the hearing and told me Michael could attend his home school.

Michael fit right in, and he didn't have any problems a typical kid wouldn't have. As a matter of fact, when Michael was in the upper elementary grades, the new principal asked for teachers to volunteer to move downstairs to accommodate Michael's needs. A fourth-grade and a fifth-grade teacher volunteered to move downstairs. It was that simple! As a matter of fact, one teacher had arthritis, and it was easier for her to teach downstairs than to teach upstairs.

Thinking back, I can't imagine what would have happened if I didn't have someone to help me navigate the special education system. I'm very grateful to my friend, Mrs. Wurst. In some cases, she would actually tell me when to call the school or the school district and exactly what to say.

Michael graduated in 2009 and is entering a New Vision's program to learn about a career in law. He has been an honor roll student since sixth grade. School has not always been easy for him, but he puts time and effort into his education. We recently took a trip to London. One of Michael's friends went with them. He is a friend Michael has known his entire life. Their friendship developed as most friendships develop because they went to the same school.

Applications and Considerations

1. Elizabeth talks about the first IEP meeting she ever attended for Michael and her belief that he would go to his home school. If you were an advocate for Michael, how would you apply what you learned in Chapter 1 about IDEA, FERPA, and ADA to ensure that Michael received a free appropriate public education in his home school?

2. What role did Mrs. Wurst play in Elizabeth's mission to ensure Michael had the best education possible? How can you as a teacher support families in a similar way?

3. What are some of the teacher tips and parent perspectives that you learned about in Chapters 7 and 8 that could have been used to assist Elizabeth in her quest to get Michael placed in his home school?

4. Elizabeth was a strong advocate for Michael. Contemplate the student-driven IEP meetings that you learned about in Chapters 7 and 8. Discuss how Michael may have contributed at his IEP meetings and become an advocate himself.

5. Elizabeth's story ends with Michael completing high school. Think back to what you read in Chapters 10 and 11 about transitions to postsecondary placements. Describe three supports you would put in place while Michael was in high school to ensure a smooth transition.

6. What supports would need to be in place for Michael to be successful pursuing a career in law. Consider what you learned about ADA and transition in Chapters 1, 10, and 11, and extend your discussion from item 3 to include supports that Michael may need in a college setting.

A FAMILY'S VOICE BY SARAH HANSON, LEE HANEY, AND JENNIFER HANSON

Sarah and her husband raised three daughters: Lee, Pam, and Jennifer. Lee is the oldest, Pam is the middle daughter, and Jennifer is the youngest. All the daughters are now adults. Pam is an adult child with a disability and lives at home with her parents. Sarah, Lee, and Jennifer shared their thoughts about life with Pam.

Sarah's Perspective

Raising a child/adult with disabilities requires both emotional and physical strengths. My daughter Pam is 27 years old, weighs 75 pounds, and is approximately 5 feet tall. She has cerebral palsy in all four extremities and is legally blind. She is in a wheelchair, cannot walk or sit without assistance, and must have help feeding, going to the bathroom, bathing, and all other daily living requirements.

Pam was born prematurely at a little over 2 pounds and has had disabilities since birth. As you raise a special child, you adapt to what you need to do and things you need to change in your home to make caring for her easier on everyone. Gone are the independence you once knew and the light at the end of the tunnel (when your children leave home). Things most people take for granted, like hopping in the car to run to the corner store to pick up something needed for dinner, are a major undertaking. It's a very big deal to load Pam up and drive to the store, unload her and then reload her for the return trip. It has been very trying and has affected our family and our marriage greatly.

Pam must always have someone with her because she requires so much assistance with her daily living needs. She loves a one-on-one relationship and dislikes television, going to the movies, or any place where she has to be quiet (except church). Pam talks all the time because it's the only way she has to interact with people. Therefore, if you're working on something that requires quiet and concentration, she makes it impossible for you to think. If you try to ignore her, she begins to have a little tantrum, screaming or moaning. Sometimes she wets her pants or tries to make herself throw up. She's very good at manipulating the situation to her advantage.

Pam goes to an adult care facility Monday through Friday for 5 hours each day, but the balance of the time she is in our care, including all weekend. My other grown children and my grandchildren live out of town, and having Pam makes it difficult for me to travel. When I go to visit them, my husband is left with the total care of Pam without help. If we want to go out without Pam, on an adult date, we have to hire a sitter to come and stay with her. We are fortunate to have a lady in our life who can lift Pam and takes wonderful care of her. Of course, this is at a charge of $10+ per hour and $100 per day when we are out of town and she is required to stay overnight.

We are lucky to have a caring family and network of understanding friends. The reach of having a child with disabilities is beyond what most could fathom. Holidays or regular get-togethers are often at our house because we have modified our home to fit Pam's needs. It's nearly impossible to take Pam to a family gathering at a house not equipped for a handicapped/disabled person, from getting up the porch stairs with her wheelchair, to taking her to the bathroom becomes a major feat.

My husband and I are not "footloose and fancy free" like our friends. When we go out we take Pam with us; it's just easier than getting a sitter for a few hours. Pam gets jealous and angry if we have her caregiver stay late, and we go out on a date together. Sometimes we come to the conclusion that it's not worth the hassle or repercussions and just stay home. My husband and I are now in our 60s, and it makes us wonder at what point will we have an opportunity to enjoy life? We would not change the way we have handled the experience of having Pam in our lives. She has taught us patience and compassion from a different standpoint. We love her and will always provide for her. We feel that she is our "gift," but it still makes our lives difficult.

Lee and Jennifer's Perspective

Having a sibling with disabilities can be both demanding and stressful. There are times when selfishly you want to be first and foremost in your parents' minds, yet you know it is impossible. Pam requires so much care and attention that our parents didn't always have enough time and energy to go around when we were younger. As Pam's sisters, this sometimes made us feel like our wants and needs had to take a back seat to her needs. As adults, we've talked about these situations as a family and all realize that it's no one's fault. The fact is, Pam was born into our family with severe disabilities, and it changed our family dynamics.

Growing up and living in a home with a person with disabilities can make you feel bitter and resentful at times. There have been many occasions when we've been out in public, and Pam has gotten frustrated and had an outburst. It is often impossible to figure out what has set her off, and there is no way to reason with her and calm her down. As an adult it is bad enough when this happens, but as a child, this was very traumatic. To the point that we sometimes wanted to disassociate ourselves from the family because of the embarrassment it caused.

At times when we feel sorry for ourselves, we try to help each other take a step back and think of what it must be like for Pam. We consider what her life is like and what she must endure on a daily basis, through no fault of her own. None of us would trade places with her, but one thing is for sure, we are all better people because Pam is part of our lives.

Applications and Considerations

1. Sarah and Lee and Jennifer are very frank in their discussion about having an adult child [sibling] with severe disabilities. Yet it is clear that they love Pam very much. What are some of the struggles associated with raising child with disabilities that have affected Sarah, Lee, and Jennifer's lives?
2. Have you ever thought about what it would be like to have a child with severe disabilities? Sarah provides an example of how just running to the store can be a major undertaking. Think about Sarah's life and describe likely obstacles she and Pam would face when traveling long distances. What other impediments might Sarah face on a daily basis?
3. In Chapters 2 and 3, we talked about family roles and family structures. Consider the sibling perspective in this family voice. Identify at least four ways having a sibling with severe disabilities affected Lee and Jennifer's lives.

4. Sarah mentions an adult care facility that Pam attends on weekdays. Do a Google search and identify other programs, facilities, and respite-type care that may be available to Pam, her family, and other adults with disabilities.

5. In Chapter 11 we focused on families with adult children with disabilities. Discuss and give examples of at least three programs or supports that are available to Pam's parents and siblings.

6. Sarah states: "My husband and I are now in our 60s and it makes us wonder at what point will we have an opportunity to enjoy life?" Think back to what you read in Chapter 11 about futures planning for adult children with disabilities. If you were working with Sarah and her family, what types of assistance, guidance, and strategies could you provide?

Summary

- All families experience the special education process and system differently.
- Professionals should look to parents and families for guidance when making educational decisions for their children.
- Through advocacy, parents not only advocate for a better education for their child, but also for a better education for all children.
- Families may change their mind about decisions they've made once they have had time to consider all options and to fully understand the impact of the decision they are making.
- Cultural and linguistic differences can both positively and negatively affect a family's experience with their child's education.
- When making decisions about special education services for a child, it is important to not only listen, but to also hear what the family is saying.

APPENDIX A

NEA Code of Ethics

PREAMBLE

The National Education Association believes that the education profession consists of one education workforce serving the needs of all students and that the term 'educator' includes education support professionals. The educator, believing in the worth and dignity of each human being, recognizes the supreme importance of the pursuit of truth, devotion to excellence, and the nurture of the democratic principles. Essential to these goals is the protection of freedom to learn and to teach and the guarantee of equal educational opportunity for all. The educator accepts the responsibility to adhere to the highest ethical standards.

The educator recognizes the magnitude of the responsibility inherent in the teaching process. The desire for the respect and confidence of one's colleagues, of students, of parents, and of the members of the community provides the incentive to attain and maintain the highest possible degree of ethical conduct. The Code of Ethics of the Education Profession indicates the aspiration of all educators and provides standards by which to judge conduct.

The remedies specified by the NEA and/or its affiliates for the violation of any provision of this Code shall be exclusive and no such provision shall be enforceable in any form other than the one specifically designated by the NEA or its affiliates.

PRINCIPLE I

Commitment to the Student

The educator strives to help each student realize his or her potential as a worthy and effective member of society. The educator, therefore, works to stimulate the spirit of inquiry, the acquisition of knowledge and understanding, and the thoughtful formulation of worthy goals.

In fulfillment of the obligation to the student, the educator—

1. Shall not unreasonably restrain the student from independent action in the pursuit of learning.
2. Shall not unreasonably deny the student's access to varying points of view.
3. Shall not deliberately suppress or distort subject matter relevant to the student's progress.
4. Shall make reasonable effort to protect the student from conditions harmful to learning or to health and safety.
5. Shall not intentionally expose the student to embarrassment or disparagement.
6. Shall not on the basis of race, color, creed, sex, national origin, marital status, political or religious beliefs, family, social or cultural background, or sexual orientation, unfairly—
   a. Exclude any student from participation in any program
   b. Deny benefits to any student
   c. Grant any advantage to any student

7. Shall not use professional relationships with students for private advantage.
8. Shall not disclose information about students obtained in the course of professional service unless disclosure serves a compelling professional purpose or is required by law.

PRINCIPLE II

Commitment to the Profession

The education profession is vested by the public with a trust and responsibility requiring the highest ideals of professional service.

In the belief that the quality of the services of the education profession directly influences the nation and its citizens, the educator shall exert every effort to raise professional standards, to promote a climate that encourages the exercise of professional judgment, to achieve conditions that attract persons worthy of the trust to careers in education, and to assist in preventing the practice of the profession by unqualified persons.

In fulfillment of the obligation to the profession, the educator—

1. Shall not in an application for a professional position deliberately make a false statement or fail to disclose a material fact related to competency and qualifications.
2. Shall not misrepresent his/her professional qualifications.
3. Shall not assist any entry into the profession of a person known to be unqualified in respect to character, education, or other relevant attribute.
4. Shall not knowingly make a false statement concerning the qualifications of a candidate for a professional position.
5. Shall not assist a noneducator in the unauthorized practice of teaching.
6. Shall not disclose information about colleagues obtained in the course of professional service unless disclosure serves a compelling professional purpose or is required by law.
7. Shall not knowingly make false or malicious statements about a colleague.
8. Shall not accept any gratuity, gift, or favor that might impair or appear to influence professional decisions or action.

Note: Adopted by the NEA 1975 Representative Assembly.

Source: National Education Association (1975/2009). *Code of Ethics.* Available at: http://www.nea.org/home/30442.htm).

APPENDIX B

NAEYC Code of Ethical Conduct and Statement of Commitment

PREAMBLE

NAEYC recognizes that those who work with young children face many daily decisions that have moral and ethical implications. The NAEYC Code of Ethical Conduct offers guidelines for responsible behavior and sets forth a common basis for resolving the principal ethical dilemmas encountered in early childhood care and education. The Statement of Commitment is not part of the Code but is a personal acknowledgement of an individual's willingness to embrace the distinctive values and moral obligations of the field of early childhood care and education. The primary focus of the Code is on daily practice with children and their families in programs for children from birth through 8 years of age, such as infant/toddler programs, preschool and prekindergarten programs, child care centers, hospital and child life settings, family child care homes, kindergartens, and primary classrooms. When the issues involve young children, then these provisions also apply to specialists who do not work directly with children, including program administrators, parent educators, early childhood adult educators, and officials with responsibility for program monitoring and licensing.

Core Values

Standards of ethical behavior in early childhood care and education are based on commitment to the following core values that are deeply rooted in the history of the field of early childhood care and education. We have made a commitment to

- Appreciate childhood as a unique and valuable stage of the human life cycle
- Base our work on knowledge of how children develop and learn
- Appreciate and support the bond between the child and family
- Recognize that children are best understood and supported in the context of family, culture, community, and society
- Respect the dignity, worth, and uniqueness of each individual (child, family member, and colleague)
- Respect diversity in children, families, and colleagues
- Recognize that children and adults achieve their full potential in the context of relationships that are based on trust and respect

Conceptual Framework

The Code sets forth a framework of professional responsibilities in four sections. Each section addresses an area of professional relationships: (1) with children, (2) with families, (3) among colleagues, and (4) with the community and society. Each section includes an introduction to the primary responsibilities of the early childhood practitioner in that context. The introduction is followed by a set of ideals (I) that reflect exemplary professional practice and a set of principles (P) describing practices that are required, prohibited, or permitted.

The ideals reflect the aspirations of practitioners. The principles guide conduct and assist practitioners in resolving ethical dilemmas. Both ideals and principles are intended to direct practitioners to those questions, which, when responsibly answered, can provide the basis for conscientious decision making. While the Code provides specific direction for addressing some ethical dilemmas, many others will require the practitioner to combine the guidance of the Code with professional judgment.

The ideals and principles in this Code present a shared framework of professional responsibility that affirms our commitment to the core values of our field. The Code publicly acknowledges the responsibilities that we in the field have assumed and in so doing supports ethical behavior in our work. Practitioners who face situations with ethical dimensions are urged to seek guidance in the applicable parts of this Code and in the spirit that informs the whole.

Often, "the right answer"—the best ethical course of action to take—is not obvious. There may be no readily apparent, positive way to handle a situation. When one important value contradicts another, we face an ethical dilemma. When we face a dilemma, it is our professional responsibility to consult the Code and all relevant parties to find the most ethical resolution.

SECTION I:

Ethical Responsibilities to Children

Childhood is a unique and valuable stage in the human life cycle. Our paramount responsibility is to provide care and education in settings that are safe, healthy, nurturing, and responsive for each child. We are committed to supporting children's development and learning; respecting individual differences; and helping children learn to live, play, and work cooperatively. We are also committed to promoting children's self-awareness, competence, self-worth, resiliency, and physical well-being.

IDEALS

I-1.1 To be familiar with the knowledge base of early childhood care and education and to stay informed through continuing education and training.

I-1.2 To base program practices upon current knowledge and research in the field of early childhood education, child development, and related disciplines, as well as on particular knowledge of each child.

I-1.3 To recognize and respect the unique qualities, abilities, and potential of each child.

I-1.4 To appreciate the vulnerability of children and their dependence on adults.

I-1.5 To create and maintain safe and healthy settings that foster children's social, emotional, cognitive, and physical development and that respect their dignity and their contributions.

I-1.6 To use assessment instruments and strategies that are appropriate for the children to be assessed, that are used only for the purposes for which they were designed, and that have the potential to benefit children.

I-1.7 To use assessment information to understand and support children's development and learning, to support instruction, and to identify children who may need additional services.

I-1.8 To support the right of each child to play and learn in an inclusive environment that meets the needs of children with and without disabilities.

I-1.9 To advocate for and ensure that all children, including those with special needs, have access to the support services needed to be successful.

I-1.10 To ensure that each child's culture, language, ethnicity, and family structure are recognized and valued in the program.

I-1.11 To provide all children with experiences in a language that they know, as well as support children in maintaining the use of their home language and in learning English.

I-1.12 To work with families to provide a safe and smooth transition as children and families move from one program to the next.

PRINCIPLES

P-1.1 *Above all, we shall not harm children. We shall not participate in practices that are emotionally damaging, physically harmful, disrespectful, degrading, dangerous, exploitative, or intimidating to children. This principle has precedence over all others in this Code* [emphasis added].

P-1.2 We shall care for and educate children in positive emotional and social environments that are cognitively stimulating and that support each child's culture, language, ethnicity, and family structure.

P-1.3 We shall not participate in practices that discriminate against children by denying benefits, giving special advantages, or excluding them from programs or activities on the basis of their sex, race, national origin, religious beliefs, medical condition, disability, or the marital status/family structure, sexual orientation, or religious beliefs or other affiliations of their families. (Aspects of this principle do not apply in programs that have a lawful mandate to provide services to a particular population of children.)

P-1.4 We shall involve all those with relevant knowledge (including families and staff) in decisions concerning a child, as appropriate, ensuring confidentiality of sensitive information.

P-1.5 We shall use appropriate assessment systems, which include multiple sources of information, to provide information on children's learning and development.

P-1.6 We shall strive to ensure that decisions such as those related to enrollment, retention, or assignment to special education services, will be based on multiple sources of information and will never be based on a single assessment, such as a test score or a single observation.

P-1.7 We shall strive to build individual relationships with each child; make individualized adaptations in teaching strategies, learning environments, and curricula; and consult with the family so that each child benefits from the program. If after such efforts have been exhausted, the current placement does not meet a child's needs, or the child is seriously jeopardizing the ability of other children to benefit from the program, we shall collaborate with the child's family and appropriate specialists to determine the additional services needed and/or the placement option(s) most likely to ensure the child's success. (Aspects of this principle may not apply in programs that have a lawful mandate to provide services to a particular population of children.)

P-1.8   We shall be familiar with the risk factors for and symptoms of child abuse and neglect, including physical, sexual, verbal, and emotional abuse and physical, emotional, educational, and medical neglect. We shall know and follow state laws and community procedures that protect children against abuse and neglect.

P-1.9   When we have reasonable cause to suspect child abuse or neglect, we shall report it to the appropriate community agency and follow up to ensure that appropriate action has been taken. When appropriate, parents or guardians will be informed that the referral will be or has been made.

P-1.10 When another person tells us of his or her suspicion that a child is being abused or neglected, we shall assist that person in taking appropriate action in order to protect the child.

P-1.11 When we become aware of a practice or situation that endangers the health, safety, or well-being of children, we have an ethical responsibility to protect children or inform parents and/or others who can.

SECTION II

Ethical Responsibilities to Families

Families are of primary importance in children's development. Because the family and the early childhood practitioner have a common interest in the child's well-being, we acknowledge a primary responsibility to bring about communication, cooperation, and collaboration between the home and early childhood program in ways that enhance the child's development.

IDEALS

I-2.1   To be familiar with the knowledge base related to working effectively with families and to stay informed through continuing education and training.

I-2.2   To develop relationships of mutual trust and create partnerships with the families we serve.

I-2.3   To welcome all family members and encourage them to participate in the program.

I-2.4   To listen to families, acknowledge and build upon their strengths and competencies, and learn from families as we support them in their task of nurturing children.

I-2.5   To respect the dignity and preferences of each family and to make an effort to learn about its structure, culture, language, customs, and beliefs.

I-2.6   To acknowledge families' childrearing values and their right to make decisions for their children.

I-2.7   To share information about each child's education and development with families and to help them understand and appreciate the current knowledge base of the early childhood profession.

I-2.8   To help family members enhance their understanding of their children and support the continuing development of their skills as parents.

I-2.9   To participate in building support networks for families by providing them with opportunities to interact with program staff, other families, community resources, and professional services.

PRINCIPLES

P-2.1   We shall not deny family members access to their child's classroom or program setting unless access is denied by court order or other legal restriction.

P-2.2   We shall inform families of program philosophy, policies, curriculum, assessment system, and personnel qualifications, and explain why we teach as we do—which should be in accordance with our ethical responsibilities to children (see Section I).

P-2.3   We shall inform families of and, when appropriate, involve them in policy decisions.

P-2.4   We shall involve the family in significant decisions affecting their child.

P-2.5   We shall make every effort to communicate effectively with all families in a language that they understand. We shall use community resources for translation and interpretation when we do not have sufficient resources in our own programs.

P-2.6   As families share information with us about their children and families, we shall consider this information to plan and implement the program.

P-2-7   We shall inform families about the nature and purpose of the program's child assessments and how data about their child will be used.

P-2.8   We shall treat child assessment information confidentially and share this information only when there is a legitimate need for it.

P-2.9   We shall inform the family of injuries and incidents involving their child, of risks such as exposures to communicable diseases that might result in infection, and of occurrences that might result in emotional stress.

P-2.10   Families shall be fully informed of any proposed research projects involving their children and shall have the opportunity to give or withhold consent without penalty. We shall not permit or participate in research that could in any way hinder the education, development, or well-being of children.

P-2.11   We shall not engage in or support exploitation of families. We shall not use our relationship with a family for private advantage or personal gain, or enter into relationships with family members that might impair our effectiveness working with their children.

P-2.12   We shall develop written policies for the protection of confidentiality and the disclosure of children's records. These policy documents shall be made available to all program personnel and families. Disclosure of children's records beyond family members, program personnel, and consultants having an obligation of confidentiality shall require familial consent (except in cases of abuse or neglect).

P-2.13   We shall maintain confidentiality and shall respect the family's right to privacy, refraining from disclosure of confidential information and intrusion into family life. However, when we have reason to believe that a child's welfare is at risk, it is permissible to share confidential information with agencies, as well as with individuals who have legal responsibility for intervening in the child's interest.

P-2.14   In cases where family members are in conflict with one another, we shall work openly, sharing our observations of the child, to help all parties involved make informed decisions. We shall refrain from becoming an advocate for one party.

P-2.15   We shall be familiar with and appropriately refer families to community resources and professional support services. After a referral has been made, we shall follow up to ensure that services have been appropriately provided.

Statement of Commitment

As an individual who works with young children, I commit myself to furthering the values of early childhood education as they are reflected in the ideals and principles of the NAEYC Code of Ethical Conduct. To the best of my ability I will

- Never harm children
- Ensure that programs for young children are based on current knowledge and research of child development and early childhood education.
- Respect and support families in their task of nurturing children.
- Respect colleagues in early childhood care and education and support them in maintaining the NAEYC Code of Ethical Conduct.
- Serve as an advocate for children, their families, and their teachers in community and society.
- Stay informed of and maintain high standards of professional conduct.
- Engage in an ongoing process of self-reflection, realizing that personal characteristics, biases, and beliefs have an impact on children and families.
- Be open to new ideas and be willing to learn from the suggestions of others.
- Continue to learn, grow, and contribute as a professional.
- Honor the ideals and principles of the NAEYC Code of Ethical Conduct

Note: A position statement of the National Association for the Education of Young Children. Revised April 2005

Source: National Association for the Education of Young Children (2005). Code of Ethical Conduct and Statement of Commitment. Available from: http://www.naeyc.org/about/positions/PSETH05.asp).

APPENDIX C

CEC Code of Ethics for Educators of Persons with Exceptionalities

CEC ETHICAL PRINCIPLES FOR SPECIAL EDUCATION PROFESSIONALS

Professional special educators are guided by the CEC professional ethical principles and practice standards in ways that respect the diverse characteristics and needs of individuals with exceptionalities and their families. They are committed to upholding and advancing the following principles:

A. Maintaining challenging expectations for individuals with exceptionalities to develop the highest possible learning outcomes and quality of life potential in ways that respect their dignity, culture, language, and background.

B. Maintaining a high level of professional competence and integrity and exercising professional judgment to benefit individuals with exceptionalities and their families.

C. Promoting meaningful and inclusive participation of individuals with exceptionalities in their schools and communities.

D. Practicing collegially with others who are providing services to individuals with exceptionalities.

E. Developing relationships with families based on mutual respect and actively involving families and individuals with exceptionalities in educational decision making.

F. Using evidence, instructional data, research and professional knowledge to inform practice.

G. Protecting and supporting the physical and psychological safety of individuals with exceptionalities.

H. Neither engaging in nor tolerating any practice that harms individuals with exceptionalities.

I. Practicing within the professional ethics, standards, and policies of CEC; upholding laws, regulations, and policies that influence professional practice; and advocating improvements in laws, regulations, and policies.

J. Advocating for professional conditions and resources that will improve learning outcomes of individuals with exceptionalities.

K. Engaging in the improvement of the profession through active participation in professional organizations.

L. Participating in the growth and dissemination of professional knowledge and skills.

Source: Council for Exceptional Children (2010). CEC Code of Ethics for Educators of Persons with Exceptionalities. Available from: http://www.cec.sped.org/Content/NavigationMenu/Professional Development/ProfessionalStandards/RedBook6thEditionWebVersion.pdf.) *Adopted by the CEC Board of Directors, January 2010.*

REFERENCES

Adams, K. S., & Christenson, S. L. (2000). Trust and the family–school relationship examination of parent– teacher differences in elementary and secondary grades *Journal of School Psychology, 38,* 477–497.

Adler, R. B., Rosenfeld, L. B., & Proctor, R. F. (2009) *Interplay: The process of interpersonal communication* (11th ed.). New York: Oxford University Press.

Adler, S. M. (2004). Home–school relations and the construction of racial and ethnic identity of Hmong elementary students. *School Community Journal, 14*(2), 57–75.

Albin, R. W., Dunlap, G., & Lucyshyn, J. M. (2002). Collaborative research with families on positive behavior support. In J. Lucyshyn, G. Dunlap, & Albin, R.W. (Eds.), *Families and positive behavior support: Addressing problem behaviors in family contexts* (pp. 373–389). Baltimore: Brookes.

Alborz, A. (2003). Transitions: Placing a son or daughter with intellectual disability and challenging behaviour in alternative residential provision. *Journal of Applied Research in Intellectual Disabilities, 16,* 75–88.

Aldrich, R. (n.d.). John Locke. *UNESCO: International Bureau of Education.* Retrieved from http://www.ibe.unesco.org/fileadmin/user_upload/archive/publications/ThinkersPdf/lockee.PDF

Allen, K. R., & Demo, D. H. (1995). The families of lesbians and gay men: A new frontier in family research. *Journal of Marriage and the Family, 57,* 111–127.

All Kinds of Minds. (2006). Parent toolkit helpful tips: Homework help. *All Kinds of Minds.* Retrieved from http://www.allkindsofminds.org/resources

Alper, S., Schloss, P. J., & Schloss, C. N. (1995). Families of children with disabilities in elementary and middle school: Advocacy models and strategies. *Exceptional Children, 62,* 261–270.

Altman, B. M., Cooper, P. F., & Cunningham, P. J. (1999). The case of disability in the family: Impact on health care utilization and expenditures for nondisabled members. *Milbank Quarterly, 77,* 39–74.

American Teacher. (2008). Advance work for special education meetings pays off. *Education Digest, 73,* 45–46.

Anafara, V. A. (2008). Varieties of parent involvement in schooling. *Middle School Journal, 39,* 58–64.

Apgar, V. (1953). A proposal for a new method of evaluation of the newborn infant. *Current Researches in Anesthesia & Analgesia, 32*(4), 260–267.

Ashbaker B. Y., & Minney, R. B. (2007). *Planning your paraprofessionals' path: An administrator's legal compliance and training guide.* Horsham, PA: LRP.

Atkin, K. (1991). Health, illness, disability, and Black minorities: A speculative critique of present day discourse. *Disability, Handicap and Society, 6,* 37–47.

Avramidis, E., & Norwich, B. (2002). Teachers' attitudes toward integration/inclusion: A review of the literature. *European Journal of Special Needs Education, 17,* 129–147.

Bailey, D. J., & Wolery, M. (1992). *Teaching infants and preschoolers with disabilities* (2nd ed.). Upper Saddle River, NJ: Merrill/Pearson.

Baker, A. J. L. (1997). Improving parent involvement programs and practice: A qualitative study of teacher perceptions. *The School Community Journal, 7*(2), 27–55.

Baker, B. L., & Blacher, J. (2002). For better or worse? Impact of residential placement on families. *Mental Retardation, 40,* 1–13.

Belgrave, F. (1998). *Psychosocial aspects of chronic illness and disability among African Americans.* Westport, CT: Auburn House.

Benderix, Y., Nordström, B., & Sivberg, B. (2007). Parents' experience of having a child with autism and learning disabilities living in a group home. *The National Autistic Society, 10,* 629–641.

Berger, E. H. (1991). Parent involvement: Yesterday and today. *Elementary School Journal, 91,* 209–219.

Berkeley, T. R., & Ludlow, B. L. (2008). Ethical dilemmas in rural special education: A call for a conversation about the ethics of practice. *Rural Special Education Quarterly, 27*(1/2), 3–9.

Bernstein, V. J. (2002, Summer). Supporting the parent–child relationship through home visiting. *IDA News, 29*(2), 1–8.

Bevan-Brown, J. (2001). Evaluating special education services for learners from ethnically diverse groups: Getting it right. *The Journal of The Association for Persons with Severe Handicaps, 26,* 138–147.

Beyer, L. E. (1997). The moral contours of teacher education. *Journal of Teacher Education, 48,* 245–254.

Blackorby, J., & Wagner, M. (1996). Longitudinal post-school outcomes of youth with disabilities: Findings from the National Longitudinal Transition Study. *Exceptional Children, 62,* 399–413.

Bloomfield, D. C., & Cooper, B. S. (2003). NCLB: A new role for the federal government, *T.H.E. Journal, 30*(1), 6–9.

Blue-Banning, M., Summers, J. A., Frankland, H. C., Nelson, L. L., & Beegle, G. (2004). Dimensions of family and professional partnerships: Constructive guidelines for collaboration. *Exceptional Children, 70,* 167–184.

Bohan, J. S. (1996). *Psychology and sexual orientation: Coming to terms.* New York: Routledge.

Bos, H. M. W. (2004). *Parenting in planned lesbian families.* Amsterdam, The Netherlands: Amsterdam University Press.

Bredekamp, S., & Copple, C. (1997). *Developmentally appropriate practice in early childhood programs* (rev. ed.). Washington, DC: National Association for the Education of Young Children.

Brodkin, A. (2006). "That's Not Fair!" Helping the child with a sibling who has special needs. *Journal of Early Childhood Today, 20*(4) 18–19.

Bronfenbrenner, U. (1979). *The ecology of human development.* Cambridge, MA: Harvard University Press.

Brophy-Herb, H. E., Kostelnik, M. J., & Stein, L.C. (2001). A developmental approach to teaching about ethics using the NAEYC code of ethical conduct. *Young Children, 56*(1), 80–84.

Bruneau, B., Ruttan, D., & Dunlap, S. K. (1995). Communication between teachers and parents: Developing partnerships. *Reading and Writing Quarterly, 11,* 257–266.

Bui, Y. N., & Turnbull, A. (2003). East meets west: Analysis of person-centered planning in the context of Asian American values. *Education and Training in Developmental Disabilities, 38*(1), 18–31.

Caldwell, J. (2006). Consumer-directed supports: Economic, health, and social outcomes for families. *Mental Retardation, 44,* 405–417.

Callicott, K. J. (2003). Culturally sensitive collaboration within person-centered planning. *Focus on Autism and Other Developmental Disabilities, 18,* 60–68.

Campinha-Bacote, J. (1992). Voodoo illness. *Perspectives in Psychiatric Nursing, 28*(1), 11–19.

Canella, G. S. (1998). Early childhood education: A call for the construction of revolutionary images. In W. E. Pinar (Ed.), *Curriculum: Toward new identities.* New York: Garland.

Carter, N., Prater, M. A., & Dyches, T. T. (2008). *Making accommodations and adaptations for students with mild to moderate disabilities.* Upper Saddle River, NJ: Pearson.

Carter, S., & Consortium for Appropriate Dispute Resolution in Special Education. (2003). *Educating our children together: A sourcebook for effective family–school–community partnerships.* Eugene, OR: Consortium for Appropriate Dispute Resolution in Special Education.

Cartledge, G., Kea, C. D., & Ida, D. J. (2000). Anticipating differences—celebrating strengths: Providing culturally competent services for students with serious emotional disturbance. *TEACHING Exceptional Children, 32*(3), 30–37.

Cegelka, P. T., & Prehm, H. J. (1982). *Mental retardation.* Columbus, OH: Merrill.

Chae, M. H. (2000). *Gender and ethnic identity development among college students from four ethnic groups.* Retrieved from ERIC database. (ED454469)

Chambers, C. R., Hughes, C., & Carter, E. W. (2004). Parent and sibling perspectives on the transition to adulthood. *Education and Training in Developmental Disabilities, 39,* 79–94.

Chambers, C. R., Wehmeyer, M. L., Saito, Y., Lida, K. M., Lee, Y., & Singh, V. (2007). Self-determination: What do we know? Where do we go? *Exceptionality, 15,* 3–15.

Chavira, V., Lopez, S. R., Blacher, J., & Shapiro, J. (2000). Latina mothers' attributions, emotions, and reactions to the problem behaviors of their children with developmental disabilities. *Journal of Child Psychology and Psychiatry and Allied Disciplines, 41,* 245–252.

Childre, A., & Chambers, C. R. (2005). Family perceptions of student centered planning and IEP meetings. *Education and Training in Developmental Disabilities, 40,* 217–233.

Children's Defense Fund. (2004). *Yearbook 2004: The state of America's children.* Washington, DC: Author.

Children's Defense Fund. (2005). *The state of America's children.* Washington, DC: Author.

Children's Defense Fund. (2006). *The 2006 annual report.* Washington, DC: Author.

ChildStats.gov. (2009). *America's children in brief: Key national indicators of well-being, 2008.* Retrieved from http://childstats.gov/americas children/index.asp

Clark County School District. (2008). *CCSD: Total languages represented.* Retrieved from http://ccsd.net/ellp/Statistics/region_monthly_stats/ELL_Fast_Facts.pdf

Clarke-Tasker, V. (1993). Cancer prevention and detection in African-Americans. In M. Frank-Stromburg & S. J. Olsen (Eds.), *Cancer prevention in minority populations: Cultural implications for health care professionals* (pp. 139–186). St. Louis, MO: Mosby.

Clausen, J. M., Landsverk, J., Ganger, W., Chadwick, D., & Litrownik, A. (1998). Mental health problems of children in foster care. *Journal of Child and Family Studies, 7,* 283–296.

Conderman, G., & Strobel, D. (2008). Fluency flyers club: An oral reading fluency intervention program. *Preventing School Failure, 53*(1), 15–20.

Consortium for Appropriate Dispute Resolution in Special Education (CADRE). (2004). *Facilitated IEP meetings: An emerging practice.* Eugene, OR: The Alliance.

Cook, R. E., Klein, M. D., & Tessier, A. (2007). *Adapting early childhood curricula for children with special needs* (7th ed.). Upper Saddle River, NJ: Merrill/Pearson.

Cooper, H. M., & Gersten, R. M. (2002). A teacher's guide to homework tips for parents: Talking points for presenters to use with transparencies. Washington, DC: Department of Education. (ERIC Document Reproduction Service No. ED468048).

Coots, J. J. (2007). Building bridges with families: Honoring the mandates of IDEIA. *Issues in Teacher Education, 16,* 33–40.

Cornille, T. A., Pestle, R. E., & Vanwy, R. W. (1999). Teachers' conflict management styles with peers and students' parents. *International Journal of Conflict Management, 10,* 69–79.

Correa, V. I., Jones, H. A., Thomas, C. C., & Morsink, C. V. (2005). *Interactive teaming: Enhancing programs for students with special needs* (4th ed.). Upper Saddle River, NJ: Merrill/Pearson.

Council for Exceptional Children. (1993). *CEC policy manual, Section three, part 2* (p. 4). Reston, VA: Author. Retrieved from http://www.cec.sped.org/AM/Template.cfm?Section=Other_ Policy_ Resources&Template=/CM/ContentDisplay.cfm&ContentID=1458

Council for Exceptional Children. (2005). *CEC knowledge and skill based for all beginning special education teachers: Common core cross-listed with INTASC special education (Common core-2001).* Received via e-mail attachment from: S. Morris at CEC April 2005.

Council for Exceptional Children. (2010). *Code of ethics and standards for professional practice.* Arlington, VA: Author.

Courtade, G. R., & Ludlow, B. L. (2008). Ethical issues and severe disabilities: Programming for students and preparation for teachers. *Rural Special Education Quarterly, 27*(1/2), 36–42.

Crain, W. (2011). *Theories of development: Concepts and applications* (6th ed.). Upper Saddle River, NJ: Prentice Hall.

Cross, T. L., Bazron, B. J., Isaacs, M. R., & Dennis, K. W. (1989). *Towards a culturally competent system of care: A monograph on effective services for minority children who are severely emotionally disturbed.* Washington DC: Georgetown University Center for Child Health and Mental Health Policy, CASSP Technical Assistance Center.

Dabkowski, D. M. (2004). Encouraging active parent participation in IEP team meetings. *TEACHING Exceptional Children, 36*(3), 34–39.

Darch, C., Miao, Y., & Shippen, P. (2004). A model for involving parents of children with learning and behavior problems in the schools. *Preventing School Failure, 48*(3), 24–34.

Davern, L. (2004). School-to-home notebooks. *TEACHING Exceptional Children, 36*(5), 22–27.

Davidson, J., & Wood, C. (2004). A conflict resolution model. *Theory into Practice, 43,* 6–13.

Davis, S. (2003). *A family handbook on futures planning.* Washington, DC: The Arc and the

Rehabilitation Research and Training Center (RRTC) on Aging with Developmental Disabilities.

Deaf Education. (2001). *U.S. State residential schools for the Deaf.* Retrieved from http://www.deafed.net/PageText.asp?hdnPageId=105

Deaux, K., Reid, A., Mizrahi, K., & Ethier, A. (1995). Parameters of social identity. *Journal of Personality and Social Psychology, 68,* 120–132.

DeBoer, A. (1995). *Working together: The art of consulting and communicating.* Longmont, CO: Sopris West.

de Boer, C., Cameron, G., & Frensch, K. (2007). Siege and response: Reception and benefits of residential children's mental health services for parents and siblings. *Child & Youth Care Forum, 36,* 11–24.

DeGangi, G. A., Wietlisbach, S., Poisson, S., Stein, E., & Royeen, C. (1994). The impact of culture and socioeconomic status on family–professional collaboration: Challenges and solutions. *Topics in Early Childhood Special Education, 14,* 503–520.

DeLaTorre, W., Rubalcava, L. A., & Cabello, B. (Eds.). (2004). *Urban education in America: A critical perspective.* Dubuque, IA: Kendall/Hunt.

Desimone, L. (1999). Linking parental involvement with student achievement: Do race and income matter? *Journal of Educational Research, 93,* 11–30.

Dettmer, P., Thurston, L. P, & Dyck, N. (1999). *Collaboration, consultation, and teamwork for students with special needs.* Boston: Allyn & Bacon.

Dettmer, P., Thurston, L. P., Knackendoffel, A., & Dyck, N. (2009). *Collaboration, consultation and teamwork for students with special needs* (6th ed.). Upper Saddle River, NJ: Merrill/Pearson.

Dewees, M. (2001). Building cultural competence for work with diverse families: Strategies from the privileged side. *Journal of Ethnic & Cultural Diversity in Social Work, 9,* 33–51.

Dietel, R. (2005). Achievement gaps in our schools. *Our Children, 30*(6), 4–5.

Divorky, D. (1973). Cumulative records: Assault on privacy, *Learning Magazine, 2*(1), 18–23.

Doty, P., & Flanagan, S. (2002). *Highlights: Inventory of consumer-directed support programs.* Washington, DC: Office of Disability, Aging and Long-Term Care Policy, U.S. Department of Health and Human Services.

Doty, P. J., Stone, R. I., Jackson, M. E., & Drabek, J. L. (2001). Informal care giving. In C. J. Evashwick (Ed.), *The continuum of long term care: An integrated systems approach* (2nd ed., pp. 132–151). Albany, NY: Delmar Thomson Learning.

Dowling, F. A. (2007). Supporting parents caring for a child with a learning disability. *Nursing Standard, 22,* 14–16.

Downing, J. E. (2008). *Including students with severe and multiple disabilities in typical classrooms* (3rd ed.). Baltimore: Brookes.

Drotar, D., Baskiewicz, A., Irvin, N., & Klaus, M. (1976). The adaptation of parents to the birth of an infant with a congenital malformation: A hypothetical model. *Pediatrics, 56,* 710–717.

Dunst, C., Trivette, C., & Deal, A. (1988). *Enabling and empowering families: Principles and guidelines for practice.* Cambridge, MA: Brookline.

Dunst, C. J. (2002). Family-centered practices: Birth through high school. *The Journal of Special Education, 36,* 139–147.

Dyson, L. L. (1997). Fathers and mothers of school-age children with developmental disabilities: parental stress, family functioning, and social support. *American Journal on Mental Retardation, 102,* 267–279.

Eberly, J. L., Joshi, A., & Konzal, J. (2007). Communicating with families across cultures: An investigation of teacher perceptions and practices. *The School Community Journal, 17*(2), 7–26.

Eck, D. (2008). *What is pluralism?* Retrieved from Harvard University http://www.pluralism.org/pluralism/what_is_pluralism.php

Epstein, J. L. (1995). School/family/ community partnerships: Caring for the children we share. *Phi Delta Kappan, 76,* 701–712.

Fadiman, A. (1997). *The spirit catches you and you fall down.* New York: Noonday.

Family Educational Rights and Privacy Act (FERPA). (1974). Retrieved from U.S. Department of Education http://www.ed.gov/policy/gen/guid/fpco/ferpa/index.html

Feeney, S., & Freeman, N. (1999). *Ethics and the early childhood educator: Using the NAEYC code.* Washington, DC: National Association for the Education of Young Children.

Feinburg, E., Beyer, J., & Moses, P. (2002). *Beyond mediation: Strategies for appropriate early dispute resolution in special education.* Eugene, OR: Consortium for Appropriate Dispute Resolution in Special Education.

Fialka, J. (2001). The dance of partnership: Why do my feet hurt? *Young Exceptional Children, 4*(2), 21–27.

Fiedler, C. R., & Danneker, J. E. (2007). Self-advocacy instruction: Bridging the research-to-practice gap. *Focus on Exceptional Children, 39*(8), 1–20.

Fiedler, C. R., Simpson, R. L., & Clark, D. M. (2007). *Parents and families of children with disabilities: Effective school based support services.* Upper Saddle River, NJ: Pearson.

Fields, S. D. (2002). Health belief system of African-Americans: Essential information for today's practicing nurses, *The Journal of Multicultural Nursing & Health.* Retrieved from http://findarticles.com/p/articles/mi_qa3919/is_200101/ai_n8931688

Fish, W. W. (2006). Perceptions of parents of students with autism towards the IEP meeting: A case study of one family support group chapter. *Education, 127,* 56–68.

Flett, A., & Conderman, G. (2001). 20 ways to enhance the involvement of parents from culturally and linguistically diverse backgrounds. *Intervention in School and Clinic, 20,* 53–55.

Franklin, H. C., Turnbull, A. P., Wehmeyer, M. L., & Blackmountain, L. (2003). An exploration of the self-determination construct and disability as it relates to the Dine (Navajo) culture. *Education and Training in Developmental Disabilities, 39,* 191–20.

Friend, M., & Cook, L. (2009). *Interactions: Collaboration skills for school professionals* (6th ed.). Boston: Allyn & Bacon.

Fujiura, G. T. (1998). Demography of family households. *American Journal on Mental Retardation, 103,* 225–235.

Gamble, T. K., & Gamble, M. (2009). *Communication works* (10th ed.). New York: McGraw-Hill.

Garcia, S. B., Mendez-Perez, A., & Ortiz, A. A. (2000). Mexican American mothers' beliefs about disabilities: Implications for early childhood intervention. *Remedial and Special Education, 21,* 90–100.

Gargiulo, R. M., & Graves, S. B. (1991). Parental feelings: The forgotten component when working with parents of handicapped preschool children. *Childhood Education, 67,* 176–178.

Garnets, L., & Kimmel, D. C. (2003). *Psychological perspectives on lesbian, gay, and bisexual experiences.* New York: Columbia University Press.

Gaventa, B. (2008). Spiritual and religious supports: What difference do they make? *Exceptional Parent Magazine, 38*(3), 66–68.

Gay, G. (2000). *Culturally responsive teaching: Theory, research, and practice.* New York: Teachers College Press.

Geenen, S., Powers, L. E., & Lopez-Vasquez, A. (2001). Multicultural aspects of parent involvement in transition planning. *Exceptional Children, 67,* 265–282.

Gestwicki, C. (1987). *Home, school, and community relations: A guide to working with parents.* Albany, NY: Delmar.

Gibb, G. S., & Dyches, T. T. (2007). *Guide to writing quality individualized education programs* (2nd ed.). Needham Heights, MA: Allyn & Bacon.

Gibb, J. R. (1961). Defensive communication. *Journal of Communication, 11,* 141–148.

Glazer, N., & Moynihan, D. P. (1963). *Beyond the melting pot.* Cambridge, MA: MIT Press/Harvard University Press.

Glidden, L. M., Billings, F. J., & Jobe, B. M. (2006). Personality, coping style and well-being of parents rearing children with developmental disabilities. *Journal of Intellectual Disability Research, 50,* 949–962.

Gordon, I. J. (1977). Parent education and parent involvement: Retrospect and prospect. *Childhood Education, 54,* 71–78.

Graue, E. (2005). Theorizing and describing preservice teachers' images of families and schooling. *Teachers College Record, 107,* 157–185.

Gray, D. E. (2006). Coping over time: The parents of children with autism. *Journal of Intellectual Disability Research, 50,* 970–976.

Green, S. E. (2001). Grandma's hands: Parental perspectives of the importance of grandparents as secondary caregivers in families of children with disabilities. *International Journal of Aging and Human Development, 53,* 11–33.

Greenspan, S. L., & Wieder, S. (2003). *The child with special needs* (2nd ed.). Cambridge, MA: Da Capo.

Greenwood, G. E., & Hickman, C. W. (1991). Research and practice in parent involvement: Implications for teacher education. *Elementary School Journal, 91,* 279–289.

Hadley, W. M. (2006) L.D. students' access to higher education: Self-advocacy and support. *Journal of Developmental Education, 30*(2), 10–12, 14–16.

Haley, J. (1999). Beyond the tip of the iceberg: Five stages toward cultural competence. *Reaching Today's Youth Journal, 3*(2), 9–12.

Hammer, M. R. (2004). Using the self-advocacy strategy to increase student participation in IEP conferences. *Intervention in School and Clinic, 39,* 295–300.

Hammond, B. (2009, April 9). *State could close Oregon School for the Blind this summer.* Retrieved from http://www.oregonlive.com/education/index.ssf/2009/04/oregon_school_for_the_blind.html

Hanline, M. F., & Daley, S. E. (1992). Family coping strategies and strengths in Hispanic, African-American, and Caucasian families of young children. *Topics in Early Childhood Special Education, 12,* 351–366.

Hanson, M. J., & Lynch, E. W. (2003). *Understanding families approaches to diversity, disability, and risk.* Baltimore: Brookes.

Harry, B. (2002). Trends and issues in serving culturally diverse families of children with disabilities. *The Journal of Special Education, 36,* 131–138.

Harry, B. (2006). "These families, those families": The impact of researcher identities on the research act. *Exceptional Children, 62,* 292–300.

Harry, B. (2008). Collaboration with culturally and linguistically diverse families: Ideal versus reality. *Exceptional Children, 74,* 372–388.

Harry, B., Rueda, R., & Kalyanpur, M. (1999). Cultural reciprocity in sociocultural perspective: Adapting the normalization principle for family collaboration. *Exceptional Children, 66,* 123–136.

Harvard Family Research Project. (2007). *Family involvement makes a difference: Evidence that family involvement promotes school success for every child of every age* (No 3). Boston: Harvard Family Research Project, Author.

Hasting, R. P., Kovshoff, H., Brown, T., Ward, N. J., Espinosa, F. D., & Remington, B. (2005). Coping strategies in mothers and fathers of preschool and school-age children with autism. *The National Autistic Society, 9,* 377–389.

Hawbaker, B. W. (2007). Student-led IEP meetings: Planning and implementation strategies.

TEACHING Exceptional Children Plus, 3(5), Article 4. Retrieved from http://escholarship.bc.edu/education/tecplus/vol3/iss5/art4

Heiman, T., & Precel, K. (2003). Students with learning disabilities in higher education: Academic strategies profile. *Journal of Learning Disabilities, 36,* 248–258.

Heller, T. (1998). Aging with intellectual disabilities and later-life family care giving. In C. A. Edelstein (Ed.), *Comprehensive clinical psychology: Vol. 7. Clinical geropsychology.* Oxford: Pergamon/Elsevier.

Heller, T., Hsieh, K., & Rowitz, L. (2000). Grandparents as supports to mothers of persons with intellectual disability. *Journal of Gerontological Social Work, 33,* 23–34.

Henderson, C. (1995). *College freshman with disabilities: A triennial statistical profile.* Washington, DC: American Council on Education/HEATH Resource Center.

Henderson, C. (2001). *College freshman with disabilities: A biennial statistical profile.* Washington, DC: Heath Resource Center of the American Council on Education.

Herman, S. E., & Thompson, L. (1995). Families' perceptions of their resources for caring for children with developmental disabilities. *Mental Retardation, 33,* 73–83.

Hess, R. S., Molina, A. M., & Kozleski, E. B. (2006). Until somebody hears me: Parent voice and advocacy in special education decision making. *British Journal of Special Education, 33,* 148–158.

Heward, W. L. (2009). *Exceptional children: An introduction to special education* (9th ed.). Upper Saddle River, NJ: Merrill/Pearson.

Heyman B., & Huckle S. (1993) Not worth the risk? Attitudes of adults with learning difficulties and their formal and informal careers to the hazards of everyday life. *Social Science and Medicine, 12,* 1557–1564.

Hodapp, R. M. (2007). Families of persons with Down syndrome: New perspectives, findings, and research and service needs. *Mental Retardation and Developmental Disabilities, 13,* 279–287.

Hodapp, R. M., Ly, T. M., Fidler, D. J., & Ricci, L. A. (2001) Less stress, more rewarding: Parenting children with Down syndrome. *Parenting: Science and Practice, 1,* 317–37.

Hodapp, R. M., & Urbano, R. C. (2007). Adult siblings of individuals with Down syndrome versus with autism: Findings from a large-scale U.S. survey. *Journal of Intellectual Disability Research, 51,* 1018–1029.

Hoover-Dempsey, K. V., & Sandler, H. M. (1995). Parental involvement in children's education: Why does it make a difference? *Teachers College Record, 97,* 311–331.

Howard, V. F., Williams, B. F., & Lepper, C. (2010). *Very young children with special needs: A foundation for educators, families, and service providers.* Upper Saddle River, NJ: Merrill/Pearson.

Hudley, C., Graham, S., & Taylor, A. (2007). Reducing aggressive behavior and increasing motivation in school: The evolution of an intervention to strengthen school adjustment. *Educational Psychologist, 42,* 251–260.

Hughes-Lynch, C. E. (2010). *A parent's travel guide to autism: Mapping a puzzling world.* Austin, TX: Prufrock.

Hunt, D. E., Gooden, M., & Barkdull, C. (2001). Walking in moccasins: Indian child welfare in the 21st century. In A. L. Sallee, H. A. Lawson, & K. Briar-Lawson (Eds.), *Innovative practices with vulnerable children and families* (pp. 165–187). Dubuque, IA: Bowers.

Hwa-Froelich, D. A., & Westby, C. E. (2003). Frameworks of education: Perspectives of Southeast Asian parents and head start staff. *Language, Speech, and Hearing Services in Schools, 34,* 299–319.

Individuals with Disabilities Education Act (IDEA). (2004). L 108-446, 20 USC 1400 et seq.

Interstate New Teacher Assessment and Support Consortium (INTASC) Special Education Subcommittee. (2001, May). *Model standards for licensing general and special education teachers of students with disabilities: A resource for state dialogue.* Retrieved from http://serge.ccsso.org/pdf/standards.pdf

Jackson, C. W., & Turnbull, A. P. (2004). Impact of deafness on family life: A review of the literature. *The Journal of Early Childhood Special Education, 2,* 167–184.

Jenkins, J., Antil, L., Wayne, S., & Vadasy, P. (2003). How cooperative learning works for special education and remedial students. *Exceptional Children, 69,* 279–292.

Joe, J., & Miller, D. (1993). *American Indian cultural perspectives on disability.* Tucson, AZ: The University of Arizona.

Johns, B. H., Crowley, E. P., & Guetzloe, E. (2002). Planning the IEP for students with emotional and behavioral disorders. *Focus on Exceptional Children, 34*(9), 2–12.

Jokinen, N., & Brown, R. (2005). Family quality of life and older parents. *Journal of Intellectual Disability Research, 49,* 789–793.

Jones, M. (2006). Teaching self-determination: Empowered teachers, empowered students. *TEACHING Exceptional Children, 39*(1), 12–17.

Kalyanpur, M. (1998). The challenge of cultural blindness: Implications for family-focused service delivery. *Journal of Child and Family Studies, 7,* 317–332.

Kalyanpur, M., & Gowramma, I. P. (2007). Cultural barriers to South Indian families' access to services and educational goals for their children with disabilities. *The Journal of the International Association of Special Education, 8,* 69–82.

Kalyanpur, M., & Harry, B. (1999). *Culture in special education: Building reciprocal family-professional relationships.* Baltimore: Brookes.

Keen, D. (2007). Parents, families, and partnerships: Issues and considerations. *International Journal of Disability, Development and Education, 54,* 339–349.

Kenny, K., & McGilloway, S. (2007). Caring for children with learning disabilities: An exploratory study of parental strain and coping. *British Journal of Learning Disabilities, 35,* 221–228.

Ketterlin-Geller, L. R., Alonzo, J., Braun-Monegan, J., & Tindal, G. (2007). Recommendations for accommodations: Implications for (in)consistency. *Remedial and Special Education, 28,* 194–206.

Kirschenbaum, H. (1999). Night and day: Succeeding with parents at school. *Principal, 78*(3), 20–23.

Klotz, M. B., & Canter, A. (2007). *Response to intervention (RTI): A primer for parents.* Retrieved from the National Association of School Psychologists http://www.nasponline.org/resources/handouts/revisedPDFs/rtiprimer.pdf

Knackendoffel, E. A. (2005). Collaborative teaming in secondary schools. *Focus on Exceptional Children, 37,* 1–16.

Knox, M., & Bigby, C. (2007). Moving towards midlife care as negotiated family business: Accounts of people with intellectual disabilities and their families "Just getting along with their lives together." *International Journal of Disability, Development and Education, 54,* 287–304.

Konrad, M. (2008). Involve students in the IEP process. *Intervention in School and Clinic, 43,* 236–239.

Konrad, M., & Test, D. W. (2007). Effects of GO 4 IT . . . NOW! Strategy instruction on the written IEP goal articulation and paragraph-writing skills of middle school students with disabilities. *Remedial and Special Education, 28,* 277–291.

Konrad, M., Trela, K., & Test, D. W. (2006). Using IEP goals and objectives to teach paragraph writing to high school students with physical and cognitive disabilities. *Education and Training in Developmental Disabilities, 41,* 111–124.

Kornhaber, A. (2002). *The grandparent guide.* Chicago: Contemporary Books.

Kozleski, E. B., Engelbrecht, P., Hess, R., Swart, E., Eloff, I., Oswald, M, et al. (2008). Where differences matter: A cross-cultural analysis of family voice in special education. *The Journal of Special Education, 42,* 26–35.

Krauss, M. W., Seltzer, M. M., & Jacobson, H. T. (2005). Adults with autism living at home or in non-family settings: Positive and negative aspects of residential status. *Journal of Intellectual Disability Research, 49,* 111–124.

Kübler-Ross, E. (1969). *On death and dying.* New York: Scribner.

Kupper, L. (2002). *Helping students develop their IEPs and a student's guide to the IEP* Retrieved from ERIC database. (ED309427)

Ladson-Billings, G. (1991). *The dreamkeepers: Successful teachers of African American children.* San Francisco: Jossey-Bass.

Lake, J. F., & Billingsley, B. S. (2000). An analysis of factors that contribute to parent-school conflict in special education. *Remedial and Special Education, 21,* 240–251.

Lakin, K. C., Prouty, R., Polister, B., & Coucouvanis, K. (2003). Change in residential placements for persons with intellectual and developmental disabilities in the USA in the last two decades. *Journal of Intellectual and Developmental Disability, 28,* 205–210.

Lambie, R. (2000). Working with families of at-risk and special needs students: A systems change model. *Focus on Exceptional Children, 32*(6), 1–23.

Lamme, L. L., & Lamme, L. A. (2003). *Welcoming children from sexual-minority families into our schools.* Bloomington, IN: Phi Delta Kappa Educational Foundation.

Lawrence-Lightfoot, S. (2003). *The essential conversation: What parents and teachers can learn from each other.* New York: Random House.

Leyser, Y., & Kirk, R. (2005). Evaluating inclusion: An examination of parent views and factors influencing their perspectives. *International Journal of Disability Development and Education, 51,* 271–285.

Lian, M. G., J., & Fonanez-Phelan, S. M. (2001). Perceptions of Latino parents regarding cultural and linguistic issues and advocacy for children with disabilities. *The Journal of The Association for Persons with Severe Handicaps, 26,* 189–194.

Lillie, T. (1993). A harder thing than triumph: Roles of fathers of children with disabilities. *Mental Retardation, 31,* 438–443.

Lillie, T. (1998). *What research says about communicating with parents of children with disabilities and what teachers should know.* Retrieved from ERIC database. (ED426547)

Lord Nelson, L. G., Summers, J. A., & Turnbull, A. P. (2004). Boundaries in family–professional relationships: Implications for special education. *Remedial and Special Education, 25,* 153–165.

Los Angeles Unified School District. (2004). *LAUSD: Back to school news release.* Retrieved from http://notebook.lausd.net/portal/page?_pageid= 33,205014,33_892781&_dad=ptl&_schema=PTL_EP

Lovitt, T. C., & Cushing, S. (1999). Parents of youth with disabilities: Their perceptions of school programs. *Remedial and Special Education, 20,* 134–142.

Lum, D. (1999). *Culturally competent practice: A framework for growth and action.* Belmont, CA: Brooks/Cole.

Lynch, E. W., & Hanson, M. J., (2004). *Developing cross-cultural competence: A guide to working with children and their families* (3rd ed.). Baltimore: Brookes.

Lytle, R. K., & Bordin, J. (2001). Enhancing the IEP team: Strategies for parents and professionals. *TEACHING Exceptional Children, 33*(5), 40–44.

Martin, E. J., & Hagan-Burke, S. (2002). Establishing a home-school connection: Strengthening the partnership between families and schools. *Preventing School Failure, 46*(2), 62–65.

Martin, J. E., Marshall, L. H., Maxson, L., & Jerman , P. (1997). *Self-directed IEP kit*. Frederick, CO: Sopris West.

Martin, J. E., Marshall, L. H., & Sale, P. (2004). A 3-year study of middle, junior high, and high school IEP meetings. *Exceptional Children, 70,* 285–297.

Martin, J. E., Van Dycke, J. L., Greene, B. A., Gardner, J. E., Christensen, W. R., Woods, L. L. et al. (2006). Direct observation of teacher-directed IEP meetings: Establishing the need for student IEP meeting instruction, *Exceptional Children, 72,* 187–200.

Maryland State Department of Education. (2000). *Building IEPs with Maryland families: What a great IDEA*. Baltimore: Author.

Mason, C. Y., Field, S., & Sawilowsky, S. (2004). Implementation of self-determination activities and student participation in IEPs. *Exceptional Children, 70,* 441–451.

Mason, C. Y., McGahee-Kovac, M., & Johnson, L. (2004). How to help students lead their IEP meetings. *TEACHING Exceptional Children, 36*(3), 18–25.

Mason, C. Y., McGahee-Kovac, M., Johnson, L., & Stillerman, S. (2002). Implementing student-led IEPs: Student participation and student and teacher reactions. *Career Development of Exceptional Individuals, 25,* 171–192.

Mastropieri, M. A., Scruggs, T. E., & Berkeley, S. L. (2007). Peers helping peers. *Educational Leadership, 64*(5), 54–58.

Matthews, R. (2001). Cultural patterns of South Asian and Southeast Asian Americans. *Intervention in School and Clinic, 36,* 101–104.

Matuszny, R. M., Banda, D. R., & Coleman, T. J. (2007). A progressive plan for building collaborative relationships with parents from diverse backgrounds. *TEACHING Exceptional Children, 39*(4), 24–31.

McGahee, M., Mason, C., Wallace, T., & Jones, B. (2001). *Student-led IEPs: A guide for student involvement*. Retrieved from ERIC database. (ED455623)

McLeskey, J., & Waldron, N. L. (2007). Making differences ordinary in inclusive classrooms. *Intervention in School and Clinic, 42,* 162–168.

McWilliam, R. A., Tocci, L., & Harbin, G. L. (1998). Family centered services: Service providers' discourse and behavior. *Topics in Early Childhood Special Education, 18,* 206–232.

Menlove, R. R., Hudson, P. J., & Suter, D. (2001). A field of IEP dreams: Increasing general education teacher participation in the IEP development process. *TEACHING Exceptional Children, 33*(5), 28–33.

Merriam-Webster (2008). *Merriam-Webster online dictionary: Family*. Retrieved from http://www.merriam-webster.com/dictionary/family

Miles-Bonart, S. (2002). *A look at variables affecting parent satisfaction with IEP meetings*. Paper presented at the Annual National Conference of the American Council on Rural Special Education, Reno, NV.

Miltiades H. B., & Pruchno R. (2001). Mothers of adults with developmental disability: Change over time. *American Journal on Mental Retardation, 106,* 548–561.

Minnesota Parent Center. (2000a). *Communication with schools can help Hmong parents cope with discipline issues*. Retrieved from http://www.pacer.org/mpc/pdf/mpc-31.pdf

Minnesota Parent Center. (2000b). Family–teacher partnerships. Retrieved from http://www.pacer.org/MPC/pdf/MPC45.pdf

Mithaug, D. E. (2007). *Self-instruction pedagogy: How to teach self-determined learning*. Springfield, IL: Thomas.

More-Thomas, C., & Day-Vines, N. L. (2008). Culturally competent counseling for religious and spiritual African American adolescents. *Journal of Professional School Counseling, 11,* 159–165.

Morse, P. S., & Ivey, A. E. (1996). *Face to face: Communication and conflict resolution in the schools*. Thousand Oaks, CA: Corwin.

Muñoz-Plaza, C., Quinn, S. C., & Rounds, K. A. (2002). Lesbian, gay, bisexual, and transgender students: Perceived social support in the high school environment. *High School Journal, 85*(4), 52–63.

Murawski, W.W., & Spencer, S. A. (in press). *Taking collaboration out of the abstract: How to play nicely with other adults*. Thousand Oaks, CA: Corwin.

Murdick, N. L., Cartin, B., & Crabtree, T. (2007). *Special education law* (2nd ed.). Upper Saddle River, NJ: Merrill/Pearson.

Murray, C., & Naranjo, J. (2008). Poor, Black, learning disabled, and graduating: An investigation of factors and processes associated with school completion among high-risk urban youth. *Remedial and Special Education, 29,* 145–160.

Muscott, H. S. (2002). Exceptional partnerships: Listening to the voices of families. *Preventing School Failure, 46*(2), 66–69.

Nash, R. J. (1996). *"Real world" ethics: Frameworks for educators and human service professionals.* New York: Teachers College.

Nashshen, J. (2000). Advocacy, stress, and quality of life in parents of children with developmental disabilities. *Developmental Disabilities Bulletin, 28,* 39–55.

National Association for the Education of Young Children (NAEYC). (2005). *Code of ethical conduct and statement of commitment.* Retrieved from http://www.naeyc.org/files/naeyc/file/positions/PSETH05.pdf

National Center for Education Statistics. (n.d.) *Summary of key Federal Laws U.S.* Retrieved from Department of Education Institute of Education Services. Retrieved from http://nces.ed.gov/pubs97/p97527/Sec2_txt.asp

National Center for Education Statistics. (1999). *An institutional perspective on students with disabilities in postsecondary education.* Washington, DC: U.S. Department of Education, Office of Educational Research and Improvement.

National Center on Secondary Education and Transition. (2007). *IEP and transition planning.* Retrieved from http://www.ncset.org/topics/ieptransition/default.asp?topic=28

National Council for Accreditation of Teacher Education. (2006). *Professional standards for the accreditation of schools, colleges, and departments of education.* Washington, DC: Author.

National Council on Disability. (2000). *National disability policy: A progress report November1999–November 2000.* Washington DC: Author.

National Council on Disability. (2003). *People with disabilities and postsecondary education.* Retrieved from http://www.ncd.gov/newsroom/publications/2003/education.htm

National Education Association (NEA). (2005). *Safe schools manual.* Washington, DC: Author.

National Education Association (NEA). (2009). *Code of ethics for the education profession.* Retrieved from http://www.nea.org/aboutnea/code.html

National Research Center on Learning Disabilities (NRCLD). (2007). *Parent involvement.* Retrieved from http://www.nrcld.org/rti_practices/parent.html

National Transition Network (1996). *Transition planning for success in adult life.* Retrieved from http://ici2.umn.edu/ntn/pub/briefs/tplanning.html

Nelson, L. G. L., Summers, J. A., & Turnbull, A. P. (2004). Boundaries in family-professional relationships: Implications for special education. *Remedial and Special Education, 25,* 153–165.

Newman, L. (2006). *Parents' satisfaction with their children's schooling.* Retrieved from ERIC database. (ED497545)

Oddo, N. S., & Sitlington, P. L. (2002). What does the future hold? A follow-up study of graduates of a residential school program. *Journals of Visual Impairments & Blindness, 12,* 842–852.

O'Donovan, E. (2007). Making individualized education programs manageable for parents: Reaching out is the right thing to do. *District Administration.* Retrieved from http://www.districtadministration.com/ViewArticle.aspx?articleid=1224

Office of Special Education Programs. (2001). *Homework practices that support students with disabilities* (No. 8). Washington, DC: Author.

O'Neill, R. E., Horner, R. H., Albin, R. W., Storey, K., & Sprague, J. R. (1997). *Functional analysis of problem behavior: A practical assessment guide* (2nd ed.). Pacific Grove, CA: Brookes/Cole.

Ormrod, J. E. (2011). *Educational psychology: Developing learners* (7th ed.). Upper Saddle River, NJ: Merrill/Pearson.

Osher, T. W., & Osher, D. M. (2002). The paradigm shift to true collaboration with families. *Journal of Child and Family Studies, 11,* 47–60.

Oxford American College Dictionary. (2002). Ethics. New York: Putnam.

Parette, P., & McMahan, G. A. (2002). What should we expect of assistive technology? Being sensitive to family goals. *TEACHING Exceptional Children, 23*(1), 56–61.

Park, H. S., & Lian, M. G. J., (2001). Introduction to special series on culturally and linguistically diverse learners with severe disabilities. *The Journal of the Association for Persons with Severe Handicaps, 26*(3), 135–137.

Park, J., & Turnbull, A. (2001). Cross-cultural competency and special education: Perceptions and experiences of Korean parents of children with special needs. *Education and Training in Mental Retardation and Developmental Disabilities, 36,* 133–147.

Park, J., Turnbull, A. P., & Park, H. S. (2001). Quality of partnerships in service provision for Korean American parents of children with disabilities: A qualitative inquiry. *The Journal of the Association for Persons with Severe Handicaps, 26,* 158–170.

Park, J., Turnbull, A. P., & Turnbull, H. R. (2002). Impacts of poverty on quality of life in families of children with disabilities. *Exceptional Children, 68,* 151–170.

Patterson, K., Grenny, J., McMillan, R., & Switzler, A. (2002). *Crucial conversations: Tools for talking when stakes are high.* New York: McGraw-Hill.

Pelchat, D., Lefebvre, H., & Perreault, M. (2003). Differences and similarities between mothers' and fathers' experiences of parenting a child with a disability. *Journal of Child Health Care, 7,* 231–247.

Poston, D. J., Turnbull, A., Park, J., Mannan, H., Marquis, J., & Wang, M. (2003). Family quality of life: A qualitative inquiry. *Mental Retardation, 41,* 313–328.

Prater, M. A. (2007). *Teaching strategies for students with mild to moderate disabilities.* Boston: Allyn & Bacon.

Prater, M. A. (2010). Inclusion of students with special needs in general classrooms. In E. Baker, P. Peterson, & B. McGaw (Eds.), *International encyclopedia of education* (3rd ed., pp. 721–726). Oxford: Elsevier.

Prater, M. A., & Dyches, T. T. (2008). *Teaching about disabilities through children's literature.* Santa Barbara, CA: Libraries Unlimited, an imprint of ABC-CLIO.

Prater, M. A., & Sileo, T. W. (2002). School-university partnerships in special education field experience: A national descriptive study. *Remedial and Special Education, 23,* 325–335.

President's Panel on Mental Retardation. (1962). *A proposed program for national action to combat mental retardation.* Washington, DC: Superintendent of Documents.

Prouty, R. W., Alba, K., & Lakin, K. C. (2007). *Residential services for persons with developmental disabilities: Status and trends through 2007.* Minneapolis, MN: Research and Training Center on Community Living and Institute on Community Integration/UCEDD.

Pruitt, P., Wandry, D., & Hollums, D. (1998). Listen to us! Parents speak out about their interactions with special educators. *Preventing School Failure, 42*(4), 161–166.

Pugach, M. C., & Johnson, L. J. (2002). *Collaborative practitioners, collaborative schools* (2nd ed.). Denver, CO: Love.

Racino, J., Walker, P., O'Connor, S., & Taylor, S. (1993). *Housing, support, and community: Choices and strategies for adults with disabilities.* Baltimore: Brookes.

Ragin, N. W., et al. (2000). *Strategies for resolving conflicts.* Retrieved from ERIC database. (ED453458)

Rank, M. R. (2004). *One nation, underprivileged.* New York: Oxford University Press.

Rankin, S. R. (2003). *Campus climate for gay, lesbian, bisexual, and transgender people: A national perspective.* New York: The National Gay and Lesbian Task Force Policy Institute.

Rapanaro, C., Bartu, A., & Lee, A. H. (2008). Perceived benefits and negative impact of challenges encountered in caring for young adults with intellectual disabilities in the transition to adulthood. *Journal of Applied Research in Intellectual Disabilities 21,* 34–47.

Raver, S. A. (2009). *Early childhood special education—0 to 8 years: Strategies for positive outcomes.* Upper Saddle River, NJ: Merrill/Pearson.

Rizzolo, M., Hemp, R., & Braddock, D. (2006). Family support services in the United States. *Policy Research Brief, 17*(1), 1–11.

Robinson-Zanartu, C., & Majel-Dixon, J. (1996). Parent voices: American Indian relationships with schools. *Journal of American Indian Education, 36,* 33–54.

Rose, T., & Zirkel, P. (2007). Orton-Gillingham methodology for students with reading disabilities: 25 years of case law. *Journal of Special Education, 41,* 171–185.

Roskam, I. (2005). A comparative study of mothers' beliefs and child-rearing behavior: The effect of the child's disability and the mother's educational level. *European Journal of Psychology of Education, 20,* 139–153.

Roskam, I., Zech, E., Nils, F., & Nader-Grosbois, N. (2008). School reorientation of children with disabilities: A stressful life event challenging parental cognitive and behavioral adjustment. *Journal of Counseling & Development, 86,* 132–142.

Rudawsky, D. J., & Lundgren, D. C. (1999). Competitive responses to negative feedback. *International Journal of Conflict Management, 10,* 172–190.

Rude, H. A., & Whetstone, P. J. (2008). Ethical considerations for special educators in rural America. *Rural Special Education Quarterly, 27*(1/2), 10–18.

Rueda, R., Monzo, L., Shapiro, J., Gomez, J., & Blacher, J. (2005). Cultural models of transition: Latina mothers of young adults with developmental disabilities. *Exceptional Children, 71,* 401–414.

Ryan, S., & Runswick-Cole, K. (2008). Repositioning mothers: mothers, disabled children and disability studies. *Disability & Society, 23,* 199–210.

Salembier, G. B., & Furney, K. S. (1998). Speaking up for your child's future. *The Exceptional Parent, 28,* 62–65.

Salend, S. J., & Duhaney, L. M. G. (1999). The impact of inclusion on students with and without disabilities and their educators. *Remedial and Special Education, 20,* 114–126.

Sandler, A. G., & Mistretta, L. A. (1998). Positive adaptation in parents of adults with disabilities. *Education and Training in Mental Retardation and Developmental Disabilities, 33,* 123–130.

Savage, R., & Carless, S. (2005). Learning support assistants can deliver effective reading interventions for "at-risk" children. *Educational Research, 47,* 45–61.

Schmuck, R. A., & Runkel, P. J. (1994). *The handbook of organization development in schools and colleges* (4th ed.). Prospect Heights, IL. Waveland.

Schopler, E., & Hennike, J. (1990). Past and present trends in residential treatment. *Journal of Autism and Developmental Disorders, 20,* 291–298.

Seligman, M., & Darling, R. B. (2007). *Ordinary families, special children: A systems approach to childhood disability.* New York: Guilford.

Seltzer, M. M., Greenberg, J. S., Krauss, M. W., & Hong, J. (1997). Predictors and outcomes of the end of co-resident care giving in aging families of adults with mental retardation and mental illness. *Family Relations, 46,* 13–22.

Seltzer, M. M., Krauss, M. W., Orsmond, G. I., & Vestal, C. (2000). Families of adolescents and adults with autism: Uncharted territory. *International Review of Research on Mental Retardation, 23,* 267–294.

Shearn, J., & Todd, S. (1997). Parental work: an account of the day-to-day activities of parents of adults with learning disabilities. *Journal of Intellectual Disability Research, 41,* 285–301.

Sheehey, P. H. (2006). Parent involvement in educational decision-making: A Hawaiian perspective. *Rural Special Education Quarterly, 25*(4), 3–15.

Siegel, B., & Silverstein, S. (2001). *What about me? Growing up with a developmentally disabled sibling.* New York: Percus.

Sileo, J. M. (2003). Co-teaching: Rationale for best practices. *Journal of Asia-Pacific Special Education 3*(1), 17–26.

Sileo, J. M. (2005). *Co-teaching: Best practices for all.* Retrieved from Inclusive and Support Special Education Congress http://www.isec2005.org/isec/abstracts/papers_s/sileo_j.shtml

Sileo, J. M. (2006). *Investigating the perceptions of academic dishonesty among special educators* (Doctoral Dissertation). Retrieved from Dissertations and Theses (ProQuest). (ATT324407)

Sileo, J. M., & Sileo, T. W. (2008). Academic dishonesty and online classes: A rural education perspective, *Rural Special Education Quarterly, 27*(1/2), 55–60.

Sileo, N. M., Sileo, T. W., & Pierce, T. B. (2008). Ethical issues in general and special education teacher preparation: An interface with rural education, *Rural Special Education Quarterly, 27*(1/2), 43–54.

Sileo, T. W., & Prater, M. A. (1998). Preparing professionals for partnerships with parents of students with disabilities: Textbook considerations regarding cultural diversity. *Exceptional Children, 64,* 513–528.

Sileo, T. W., Sileo, A. P., & Prater, M. A. (1996). Parent and professional partnerships in special education: Multicultural considerations. *Intervention in School and Clinic, 31,* 145–153.

Sinclair, C. (1998). Nine unique features of the Canadian code of ethics for psychologists. *Canadian Psychology/Psychologie Canadienne, 39,* 167–176.

Smith, D. D. (2010). *Introduction to special education: Making a difference* (7th ed.). Boston: Allyn & Bacon.

Smith, S. W. (2001). *Involving parents in the IEP process.* Retrieved from ERIC database. (ED455658)

Snell, M. E., & Janney, R. (2000). *Collaborative teaming.* Baltimore: Brookes.

Snell, M. E., & Janney, R. (2005). *Collaborative teaming* (2nd ed.). Baltimore: Brookes.

Snyder, E. P. (2002). Teaching students with combined behavioral disorders and mental retardation to lead their own IEP meetings. *Behavioral Disorders, 27,* 340–357.

Sobsey, D. (2002). Exceptionality, education, and maltreatment. *Exceptionality, 10,* 29–40.

Song, J., & Murawski, W. W. (2005). Korean-American parents' perspectives on teacher–parent collaboration. *Journal of International Special Needs Education, 8,* 32–38.

Southern Poverty Law Center. (1993). *Small differences.* Montgomery, AL: Author.

Spann, S. J., Kohler, F. W., & Soenksen, D. (2003). Examining parents' involvement in and perceptions of special education services: An interview with families in a parent support group. *Focus on Autism and Other Developmental Disabilities, 18,* 228–237.

Stiers, G. A. (1999). *From this day forward—commitment, marriage, and family in lesbian and gay relationships.* New York: St. Martin's Press.

Stodden, R. A. (2001). Postsecondary education supports for students with disabilities: A review and response. *Journal for Vocational Special Needs Education, 23*(2), 4–11.

Stone, M. (1975). Off the record: The emerging right to control one's school files. *5 N.Y.U. Rev. L. & Soc. Change, 39,* 42.

Stoner, J. B., & Angell, M. E. (2006). Parent perspective on role engagement: An investigation of parents of children with ASD and their self-reported roles with education professionals. *Focus on Autism and Other Developmental Disabilities, 21,* 177–189.

Stoner, J. B., Bock, S. J., Thompson, J. R., Angell, M. E., Heyl, B. S., & Crowley, E. P. (2005). Welcome to our world: Parent perceptions of interactions between parents of young children with ASD and education professionals. *Focus on Autism and Other Developmental Disabilities, 20,* 39–51.

Storms, J., O'Leary, E., & Williams, J. (2000, May). *The IDEA of 1997: Transition requirements: A guide for states, districts, schools, universities, and families.* Minneapolis: University of Minnesota, Institute on Community Integration.

Strasser, M. (1997). *Legally wed—same-sex marriage and the constitution.* Ithaca, NY: Cornell University Press.

Super, C. M., & Harkness, S. (1997). The cultural structuring of child development. In J. Berry, P. Dasen, & T. Saraswathi (Eds.), *Handbook of cross-cultural psychology: Basic processes and human development* (pp. 1–39). Needham, MA: Allyn & Bacon.

Super, C. M., & Harkness, S. (2002). Culture structures the environment for development. *Human Development, 45,* 270–274.

Taanila, A., Syrjälä, L., Kokkonen, J., & Järvelin, M. R. (2002). Coping of parents with physically and/or intellectually disabled children. *Child: Care, Health & Development, 28,* 73–86.

Tannen, D. (1990). *You just don't understand: Men and women in conversation.* New York: Morrow.

Taub, D. J. (2006). Understanding the concerns of parents of students with disabilities: Challenges and roles for school counselors. *Professional School Counseling, 10,* 52–57.

Taunt, H. M., & Hastings, R. P. (2002). Positive impact of children with developmental disabilities on their families: A preliminary study. *Education and Training in Mental Retardation and Developmental Disabilities, 37,* 410–420.

Teel, C. S. (1991). Chronic sorrow: Analysis of the concept. *Journal of Advanced Nursing, 16,* 1311–1319.

Tennen, H., & Affleck G. (2002). Benefit finding and benefit reminding. In C. R. Snyder & S. J. Lopez (Eds.), *Handbook of positive psychology* (pp. 584–597). New York: Oxford University Press.

Test, D. W., Mason, C., Hughes, C., Konrad, M., Neale, M., & Wood, W. M. (2004). Student involvement in individualized education program meetings. *Exceptional Children, 70,* 391–412.

Test, D. W., & Neale, M. (2004). Using the self-advocacy strategy to increase middle graders' IEP participation. *Journal of Behavioral Education, 13,* 135–145.

Thomas, K. W., & Kilmann, R. H. (1974). *Thomas-Kilmann conflict mode instrument.* Tuxedo, NY: Xicom.

The Association for Retarded Citizens (The ARC). (2008). The first 50 years of The Arc. Retrieved from https://www.thearc.org/sslpage.aspx?pid=186&bm=-1083459099

Thompson, G. L. (2003). *What African American parents want educators to know.* Westport, CT: Praeger/Greenwood.

Thurlow, M. L., Elliott, J. L., & Ysseldyke, J. E. (2003). *Testing students with disabilities: Practical strategies for complying with district and state requirements* (2nd ed.). Thousand Oaks, CA: Corwin.

Todd, S., & Shearn J. (1996). Time and the person: The impact of support services on the lives of parents of adults with intellectual disabilities. *Journal of Applied Research in Intellectual Disabilities, 9,* 40–60.

Torgerson, C. W., Miner, C. A., & Shen, H. (2004). Developing student competence in self-directed IEPs. *Intervention in School and Clinic, 39,* 162–167.

Trumbull, E., Rothstein-Fisch, C., & Hernandez, E. (2003). Parent involvement in schools: According to whose values? *The School Community Journal, 13*(2), 45–72.

Trussell, R. P., Hammond, H., & Ingalls, L. (2008). Ethical practices and parental participation in rural special education, *Rural Special Education Quarterly, 27*(1/2), 19–23.

Turnbull, A. P., Turbiville, V., & Turnbull, H. R. (2000). Evolution of family–professional partnerships: Collective empowerment as the model for the early twenty-first century. In S. J. Meisels & J. P. Shonkoff (Eds.), *Handbook of early intervention* (pp. 630–650). New York: Cambridge University Press.

Turnbull, A., Turnbull, R., Erwin, E., & Soodak, L. (2006). *Families, professionals, and exceptionality* (5th ed.). Upper Saddle River, NJ: Merrill/Pearson.

Turnbull, R., & Cilley, M. (1999). *Explanations and implications of the 1997 amendments to IDEA.* Upper Saddle River, NJ: Merrill/Pearson.

United Nations. (1994). United Nations Proclamation of the International Year of the Family. *United Nations/Division for Social Policy and Development.*

U.S. Census Bureau, Housing and Household Economic Statistics Division. *1960 to 2007 Annual Social and Economic Supplements.* Retrieved from http://www.census.gov/hhes/www/poverty/poverty06/graphs06.html

U.S. Census. (2008a). *Census 2000: American fact finder.* Retrieved from http://factfinder.census.gov/servlet/DTGeoSearchByListServlet?ds_name=DEC_2000_SF1_U&_lang=en&_ts=238427213803

U.S. Census. (2008b). *American community survey 2006.* Retrieved from http://factfinder.census.gov/servlet/ACSSAFFFacts?_event=&geo_id=01000US&_geoContext=01000US&_street=&_county=&_cityTown=&_state=&_zip=&_lang=en&_sse=on&ActiveGeoDiv=&_useEV=&pctxt=fph&pgsl=010&_submenuId=factsheet_1&ds_name=null&_ci_nbr=null&qr_name=nul

U.S. Census. (2008c). *Current population survey (CPS)—definitions and explanations.* Retrieved from http://www.census.gov/population/www/cps/cpsdef.html

U.S. Census. (2009). *Current population survey, annual social and economic supplement (2003).* Retrieved from http://www.census.gov/population/www/socdemo/foreign/slides.html

U.S. Department of Education. (2007). *27th annual report to congress on the implementation of the individuals with disabilities education act, 2005 Vol. 2.* Retrieved from http://www.ed.gov/about/reports/annual/osep/2005/parts-b-c/index.html

U.S. Department of Education. (2008). *Office of Special Education Programs, Data Analysis System (DANS), OMB #1820-0043: "Children with Disabilities Receiving Special Education Individuals with Disabilities Education Act," 2003.* Retrieved from http://www.ed.gov/about/reports/annual/osep/2005/parts-b-c/index.html

U.S. Department of Education. (n.d.). *History: Twenty-five years of progress in educating children with disabilities through IDEA.* Retrieved from http://www.ed.gov/policy/speced/leg/idea/history.html

U.S. Department of Education Assistance to States for the Education of Children with Disabilities and Preschool Grants for Children with Disabilities; Final Rule, 34 CFR Part §300 and §301. (2006).

U.S. Department of Education, Office of Special Education and Rehabilitative Services. *Annual Report to Congress on the Implementation of the Individuals with Disabilities Education Act,*

1995–2004, table 2-5, data from Individuals with Disabilities Education Act (IDEA) database. Retrieved from http://www2.ed.gov/about/reports/annual/osep/index.html

U.S. Department of Health and Human Services. (2008). *Temporary assistance to needy families: TANF.* Retrieved from http://www.acf.hhs.gov/programs/ofa/tanf/about.html

Van Dycke, J. L., Martin, J. E., & Lovett, D. L. (2006). Why is this cake on fire? Inviting students into the IEP progress. *TEACHING Exceptional Children, 38*(3), 42–47.

Van Haren, B., & Fiedler, C. R. (2008). Support and empower families of children with disabilities. *Intervention in School and Clinic, 43,* 231–235.

Van Reusen, A. K., Bos, C. S., Schumaker, J. B., & Deshler, D. D. (1994). *The self-advocacy strategy.* Lawrence, KS: Edge Enterprises.

Wade, S. L., Taylor, H. G., Drotar, D., Stancin, T., & Yeates, K. O. (1996). Childhood traumatic brain injury: Initial impact on the family. *Journal of Learning Disabilities, 29,* 652–661.

Wagner, M., Cameto, R., & Newman, L. (2003). *Youth with disabilities: A changing population: A report of findings from the National Longitudinal Transition Study (NLTS) and the National Longitudinal Transition Study–2 (NLTS2).* Menlo Park, CA: SRI International.

Walden. S., Pistrang, N., & Joyce, T. (2000). Parents of adults with intellectual disabilities: quality of life and experiences of caring. *Journal of Applied Research in Intellectual Disabilities 13,* 62–76.

Walker, J. M. T., Wilkins, A. S., Dallaire, J. R., Sandler, H. M., & Hoover-Dempsey, K. V. (2005). Parental involvement: Model revision through scale development. *The Elementary School Journal, 106,* 85–104.

Walther-Thomas, C., Korinek, L., McLaughlin, V. L., & Williams, B. T. (2000). *Collaboration for inclusive education: Developing successful programs.* Boston: Allyn & Bacon.

Wang, M., Mannan, H., Poston, D., Turnbull, A. P., & Summers, J. A. (2004). Parents' perceptions of advocacy activities and their impact on family quality of life. *Research & Practice for Persons with Severe Disabilities, 29,* 144–155.

Wehman, P. (2001). *Life beyond the classroom: Transition strategies for young people with disabilities* (2nd ed.). Baltimore: Brookes.

Weisner, T. S. (1998). Human development, child well-being, and the cultural project of development. *New Directions for Child Development, 81,* 69–147.

Withers, P., & Bennett, L. (2003). Myths and marital discord in a family with a child with profound physical and intellectual disabilities. *British Journal of Learning Disabilities, 31,* 91–95.

Woodgate, R. L., Ateah, C., & Secco, L. (2008). Living in a world of our own: The experience of parents who have a child with autism. *Qualitative Health Research, 18,* 1075–1083.

Woolfolk, A. (2010). *Educational psychology: Active learning edition* (11th ed.). Boston: Pearson Education.

Woolfson, L. (2004). Family well-being and disabled children: A psychosocial model of disability-related child behaviour problems. *British Journal of Health Psychology, 9,* 1–13.

Xu, Y. (2007). Empowering culturally diverse families of young children with disabilities: The double ABCX model. *Early Childhood Education Journal, 34,* 431–437.

Yamauchi, L. A., Lau-Smith, J. A., & Luning, R. J. I. (2008). Family involvement in a Hawaiian language immersion program. *The School Community Journal, 18*(1), 39–60.

Ysseldyke, J., Nelson, J. R., Christenson, S., Johnson, D. R., Dennison, A., Triezenberg, H., et al. (2004). What we know and need to know about the consequences of high-stakes testing for students with disabilities. *Exceptional Children, 71,* 75–94.

Zhang, C., & Bennett, T. (2003). Facilitating the meaningful participation of culturally and linguistically diverse families in the IFSP and IEP process. *Focus on Autism and Other Developmental Disabilities, 18,* 51–59.

Zionts, L. T., Zionts, P., Harrison, S., & Bellinger, O. (2003). Urban African American families' perceptions of cultural sensitivity within the special education system. *Focus on Autism and Other Developmental Disabilities, 18*(1), 41–50.

Zirkel, P. A. (2006). What does the law say? *TEACHING Exceptional Children, 39*(1), 65–66.

NAME INDEX

A

Adler, R. B., 62, 65, 66, 74, 77, 80, 81, 84
Adler, S. M., 120, 123
Affleck G., 227
Alba, K., 235, 236
Albin, R. W., 74
Alborz, A., 237, 238, 239
Aldrich, R., 25
Allen, K. R., 95, 99
Alonzo, J., 161
Alper, S., 41, 42
Altman, B. M., 228
Anafara, V. A., 27, 28, 31
Angell, M. E., 145, 148
Antil, L., 182
Apgar, V., 24
Ashbaker B. Y., 17
Ateah, C., 48, 49
Atkin, K., 121, 122
Avramidis, E., 134–135

B

Bailey, D. J., 210
Baker, A. J. L., 192, 196
Baker, B. L., 237
Banda, D. R., 125
Barkdull, C., 110, 115, 121, 122
Bartu, A., 227, 228
Baskiewicz, A., 138
Bazron, B. J., 108
Beegle, G., 64, 81
Belgrave, F., 122
Bellinger, O., 64
Benderix, Y., 49
Bennett, L., 135, 136, 137, 141
Bennett, T., 146, 149
Berger, E. H., 30
Berkeley, S. L., 182
Berkeley, T. R., 175, 184
Bernstein, V. J., 209
Bevan-Brown, J., 114
Beyer, J., 84
Beyer, L. E., 175
Bigby, C., 227
Billings, F. J., 103
Billingsley, B. S., 49
Blacher, J., 116, 117, 237

Blackmountain, L., 115, 121, 123
Blackorby, J., 230
Bloomfield, D. C., 15
Blue-Banning, M., 64, 81
Bock, S. J., 145
Bohan, J. S., 99
Bordin, J., 133, 149
Bos, C. S., 172
Bos, H. M. W., 99
Braddock, D., 235
Braun-Monegan, J., 161
Bredekamp, S., 174, 175
Brodkin, A., 54
Brophy-Herb, H. E., 187
Brown, R., 227, 235
Brown, T., 137, 138
Bruneau, B., 192, 195, 196

C

Cabello, B., 66
Caldwell, J., 225, 226, 234
Callicott, K. J., 114
Cameto, R., 230
Campinha-Bacote, J., 122
Canter, A., 214, 215
Carless, S., 142
Carter, E. W., 227
Carter, N., 160
Carter, S., 29, 31, 34, 50
Cartin, B., 26
Cartledge, G., 108, 109, 110
Cegelka, P. T., 235
Chadwick, D., 52
Chae, M. H., 115, 119
Chambers, C. R., 148, 149, 150, 155, 157, 164, 227
Chavira, V., 116, 117
Childre, A., 148, 149, 150, 155, 157
Christensen, W. R., 134
Christenson, S., 160
Cilley, M., 5
Clark, D. M., 174
Clarke-Tasker, V., 122
Clausen, J. M., 52
Coleman, T. J., 125
Conderman, G., 214
Cook, R. E., 203, 204, 209
Cooper, B. S., 15

Woods, L. L., 134
Woolfolk, A., 135
Woolfson, L., 49

X
Xu, Y., 108

Y
Yamauchi, L. A., 123
Yeates, K. O., 137, 139, 140

Ysseldyke, J., 160
Ysseldyke, J. E., 161

Z
Zech, E., 136, 138, 139, 141, 143
Zhang, C., 146, 149
Zionts, L. T., 64
Zionts, P., 64
Zirkel, P., 163, 236

SUBJECT INDEX

Note: Page numbers followed by "*f*" and "*t*" indicate figures and tables respectively.